College Reading

with the

Active Critical Thinking Method

BOOK 2

Sixth Edition

JANET MAKER

Los Angeles Trade-Technical College

MINNETTE LENIER

Los Angeles Pierce College

Wadsworth
Thomson Learning™

Australia • Canada • Denmark • Japan • Mexico • New Zealand • Philippines • Puerto Rico
Singapore • South Africa • Spain • United Kingdom • United States

Executive Manager: Elana Dolberg
Senior Development Editor: Kimberly Johnson
Editorial Assistant: Sally Cobau
Marketing Assistant: Jessica McFadden
Project Editor: Christal Niederer
Print Buyer: Barbara Britton
Permissions Editor: Joohee Lee
Production Service: Thompson Steele, Inc.
Text Designer: Thompson Steele, Inc.
Art Editor: Thompson Steele, Inc.

Photo Researcher: Thompson Steele, Inc.
Copy Editor: Thompson Steele, Inc.
Compositor: Thompson Steele, Inc.
Cover Designer: Thompson Steele, Inc.
Cover Image: Maurice de Vlaminck, "Olives."
    © 2000 Artists Rights Society (ARS),
    New York/ADAGP, Paris.
Cover Printer: Phoenix Color Corp.
Printer/Binder: RR Donnelley & Sons,
    Crawfordsville

Library of Congress Cataloging-in-Publication Data
College reading with the active critical thinking method.
Book 2 / [compiled by] Janet Maker, Minnette Lenier.
—6th ed.   p.   cm.
    ISBN 0-534-51851-6 (alk. paper)
    1. College readers. 2. Critical thinking—Problems, exercises, etc. I. Maker, Janet. II. Lenier, Minnette.
PE1122.C572   2000
428.6—dc21   00–25013

Annotated Instructor's Edition
    ISBN 0-534-51852-4

For more information, contact
Wadsworth/Thomson Learning
10 Davis Drive
Belmont, CA 94002-3098
USA
www.wadsworth.com

International Headquarters
Thomson Learning
290 Harbor Drive, 2nd Floor
Stamford, CT 06902-7477
USA

UK/Europe/Middle East
Thomson Learning
Berkshire House
168-173 High Holborn
London WC1V 7AA
United Kingdom

Asia
Thomson Learning
60 Albert Street #15-01
Albert Complex
Singapore 189969

Canada
Nelson/Thomson Learning
1120 Birchmount Road
Scarborough, Ontario M1K 5G4
Canada

Wadsworth Developmental English

New for 2000

Writing

Rogers/Rogers, *Patterns and Themes: A Basic English Reader*, 4th Ed.
Robinson/Tucker, *Texts and Contexts: A Contemporary Approach to College Writing*, 4th Ed.
Tyner, *College Writing Basics: A Student-Writing Approach*, 5th Ed.
McDonald/Salomone, *The Writer's Response: A Reading-Based Approach to College Writing*, 2nd Ed.
McDonald/Salomone, *In Brief: A Handbook for Writers*

Reading

Maker/Lenier, *College Reading with the Active Critical Thinking Method, Book 1*, 5th Ed.
Sotiriou/Phillips, *Steps to Reading Proficiency*, 5th Ed.

Study Skills

Van Blerkom, *College Study Skills: Becoming a Strategic Learner,* 3rd Ed.

Other Developmental English Titles

Writing

Richard-Amato, *World Views: Multicultural Literature for Critical Writers, Readers, and Thinkers* (1998)
Salomone/McDonald, *Inside Writing: A Writer's Workbook, Form A*, 4th Ed. (1999)
Wingersky/Boerner/Holguin-Balogh, *Writing Paragraphs and Essays: Integrating Reading, Writing, and Grammar Skills*, 3rd Ed. (1999)

Reading

Atkinson/Longman, *Reading Enhancement and Development*, 6th Ed. (1999)
Maker/Lenier, *Academic Reading with Active Critical Thinking* (1996)

Study Skills

Longman/Atkinson, *College Learning and Study Skills*, 5th Ed. (1999)
Longman/Atkinson, *Study Methods and Reading Techniques*, 2nd Ed. (1999)
Sotiriou, *Integrating College Study Skills: Reasoning in Reading, Listening, and Writing*, 5th Ed. (1999)
Smith/Knudsvig/Walter, *Critical Thinking: Building the Basics* (1998)

College Success

Gardner/Jewler, *Your College Experience: Strategies for Success,* 4th Ed. (2000)
Gardner/Jewler, *Your College Experience: Strategies for Success,* Concise 3rd Ed. (1998)
Holkeboer/Walker, *Right from the Start: Taking Charge of Your College Success,* 3rd Ed. (1999)
Petrie/Denson, *A Student Athlete's Guide to College Success: Peak Performance in Class and Life* (1999)
Santrock/Halonen, *Your Guide to College Success: Strategies for Achieving Your Goals* (1999)
Wahlstrom/Williams, *Learning Success: Three Paths to Being Your Best at College and Life*, 2nd Ed. (1999)

Contents

UNIT I

Reading Fundamentals   1

UNIT II

Introduction to the Active Critical Thinking (ACT) Method   23

Reading Selections

UNIT III

Textbook Learning with the ACT Method   135

Creating a Study System Using the ACT Method   136

Textbook Reading Selections

UNIT IV

Critical Reading with the ACT Method　243

Critical Thinking Using the ACT Method　245

Critical Reading Selections

Additional Resources

Tests: Comprehension and Vocabulary Checks 337

Contents by Skills

Study Reading

Critical Reading

Reading Efficiency

Preface

The College Reading Series

College Reading with the Active Critical Thinking Method, Book 2, 6th Edition is the second book in a three-part reading series by Maker/Lenier, for students reading at a developmental level. The books in this series include:

1. ***College Reading with the Active Critical Thinking Method, Book 1.*** Written at the 6th to 9th grade reading level, this book is intended for lower-level developmental reading courses. *Book 1* focuses on reading fundamentals such as vocabulary building, subject, main idea, theses, arguments, and supporting details. Students apply the ACT method with different types of readings (general interest and study).

2. ***College Reading with the Active Critical Thinking Method, Book 2.*** Written at the 9th to 12th grade reading level, this book is intended for intermediate developmental reading courses. After a review of reading fundamentals, *Book 2* stresses study reading *and* critical reading. The study reading section contains challenging textbook selections from a variety of subjects. The critical reading section presents pairs of reading selections with opposing viewpoints on controversial subjects. Both sections utilize the six-step ACT Method.

3. ***Academic Reading with the Active Critical Thinking Method.*** Written at the 10th to 13th (college) grade reading level, this book is intended for higher-level developmental reading courses. This book provides advanced practice with the ACT Method, helping students sharpen their critical reading and study skills together in real academic contexts.

The Maker/Lenier series teaches fundamental, study, and critical reading skills in the context of high-interest readings. As students become more confident in their newly acquired reading skills, they are expected to work more independently. The central component of their highly effective approach is the Active Critical Thinking Method.

The Active Critical Thinking Method

The Active Critical Thinking Method is an innovative six-step method that provides a unified approach to reading. Students can easily master this method and apply it to *any* reading, whether it's for pleasure, information, study, or analysis.

1. **Preread.** The first task for general and study reading, the prereading step consists of skimming for subject and main idea, activating background knowledge, and generating questions. Readings are taken from actual college textbooks in a wide variety of content areas.

   For critical reading of persuasive material, students skim to ascertain the subject and the author's thesis. They then compare their own points of view with the author's, consider what they know and don't know about the subject, and generate questions. For most critical reading, we use pairs of articles taking opposing viewpoints on controversial subjects that are frequently debated by college students.

2. **Read.** As in SQ3R, students are asked to read without marking their texts; they concentrate on comprehension, and memory is a separate step. After reading, they mark any parts they didn't understand and make a plan to gain understanding (e.g., ask in class, read another source, etc.).

3. **Analyze What You Read.** Most of the teaching time is spent on this third step; students use practice activities that are highly structured at first, moving toward increasing independence. For study reading, students prepare for both objective and subjective evaluation. They go back to the section they have read and predict what will be on the test. They underline only what they believe will be on the test and only what they don't think they will remember. They make marginal notes as in SQ3R to test themselves on what they have underlined. They practice marking the text differently for objective vs. essay questions. They then create at least one graphic organizer for the article, such as a study map, chart, time line, or outline.

   For critical reading, students identify the thesis (author's point of view), the arguments supporting the thesis and the support given for each argument, and finally they evaluate the support. They identify the type of support (facts, testimony, examples, reasons) and they evaluate the support by means of practice activities for whichever skills are relevant (e.g., fact vs. opinion, provable vs. unprovable data, valid vs. invalid inferences, logical reasoning, credibility of sources, recognizing bias, and using criteria for evaluating research). They then create at least one graphic organizer for the article.

4. **Remember What's Important.** Students memorize by self-testing, using their underlining, marginal notes, and graphic organizers, all of which may be transferred to flash cards. Mnemonic devices are used as appropriate.

5. **Make Use of What You Read.** This step refers to output, such as class discussions, written assignments, oral reports, or tests. We give our students a test for each reading selection, including objective, short answer, and essay questions.

6. **Evaluate Your Active Critical Thinking Skills.** Students analyze feedback from the previous step using an evaluation checklist. For example, they decide whether wrong answers were caused by predicting the wrong questions; by not making sufficient use of the marginal notes, flash cards, and graphic organizers for memorization; and/or by poor test-taking skills, such as poor use of time or poor organization of the essay. They then make a plan for improvement, and evaluate their progress using a Progress Chart.

Key Features

Besides the innovative ACT Method, *College Reading, Book 2* offers the following benefits:

- All the skills instruction is based on 30 high-interest reading selections that appear after the skills review in the introductory unit.

- A strong emphasis on vocabulary development, with vocabulary skills instruction in Unit I, review of the skills in Unit II, and vocabulary previews and checks for each reading, builds vocabulary skills in context, step-by-step.

- Two tables of contents: In addition to the regular table of contents, a skills-based table of contents allows instructors to assign activities that reinforce particular skills.

- The level of difficulty increases as students progress through the text.

New to the Sixth Edition

- 30% new **high-interest reading selections.** Readings have been replaced or updated with particular regard to student interest, such as *Safer Sex* and *How Almost Anyone Can Become a Millionaire.*

- **Expanded testing materials** to help instructors and students prepare for tests.
  - A new test section at the end of the book includes 30 Comprehension Checks and Vocabulary Checks.
  - A Progress Chart has been added so students can measure their progress and use the results to analyze their strengths and weaknesses.

- The Instructor's Manual's testing section has also been expanded to include testing of cognitive understanding of the skills in each unit as well as testing for application of the skills.

■ **Improved clarity and design** of the ACT Method so that the steps are even easier for students to follow. The two-color design improves pedagogy and readability. The sixth edition has an easier-to-read font, and the pages are perforated so assignments can be torn out and submitted. The Annotated Instructor's Edition has answers in a contrasting color.

■ **Expanded coverage of key prerequisite and vocabulary skills.**

- Unit I now provides more vocabulary and critical reading skills practice.

- Expanded Vocabulary Skill Review activities now follow the reading selections in Unit II.

■ **Removable bookmark** attached to the cover helps students easily reference the ACT Method while reading this book or any others.

■ **Three alternate tables in the Instructor's Manual** correlate the text's activities to the skills required for the Texas, Florida, and Georgia state reading tests (TASP, CLAST, Regents).

Teaching and Learning Aids

Supplements for *College Reading, Book 2*

■ **Instructor's Manual and Test Bank** (0-534-51853-2). Fully updated and revised to reflect key revisions in the main text, this 8½ x 11 resource now includes the following and more: tests, teaching philosophy, instructional suggestions, additional help for adjuncts, and reading efficiency perception exercises. Unit I tests cover vocabulary and comprehension. Units II, III, and IV feature cognitive, applications, and vocabulary tests.

■ **Web Site.** Visit Wadsworth's Developmental English web site at **http://devenglish.wadsworth.com.** Here you will find many online teaching and learning aids.

Other Supplementary Materials Available from Wadsworth

Please contact your Wadsworth sales representative for additional information regarding policy, pricing, and availability for any of these products or services. You may locate your representative via the Internet on our Wadsworth home page: **http://www.wadsworth.com.**

- **Wadsworth Developmental English Internet-at-a-Glance Trifold**
  (0-534-54744-3). This handy guide shows your students where to find
  online reading and writing resources. Package this trifold card with any
  Wadsworth Developmental English text. (Please contact your Thomson
  Learning representative for pricing information.)

- **Newbury House Dictionary** (0-8384-5613-8). Make this developmental-
  level dictionary available to your students at a reduced cost by bundling
  it with this text. Contact your sales representative for information on
  this option.

- **InfoTrac® College Edition.** This fully searchable, online database with
  access to full-text articles from over 900 periodicals provides a great
  resource for additional readings and/or research. Now available **free**
  with this text, InfoTrac College Edition offers authoritative sources,
  updated daily and going back as far as four years. Both you and your
  students can receive unlimited online use for one academic term. (Please
  contact your Thomson Learning representative for policy, pricing, and
  availability; international and school distribution is restricted.)

- **Custom Publishing.** You can combine your choice of chapters from
  specific Wadsworth titles with your own materials in a custom-bound
  book. To place your order, call the Thomson Learning Custom Order
  Center at 1-800-355-9983.

- **Videos.** Wadsworth has many videos available to qualifying adopters
  on topics such as improving your grades, notetaking practice, diversity,
  and many more. Contact your local Wadsworth representative for more
  information.

Acknowledgments

Thanks to my children, Thomas and Jane Maker, for sharing the computer
with their mom. Thanks to Kim Johnson, super editor, and to the entire
Wadsworth Editorial and Production teams, especially Karen Allanson,
Godwin Chu, and Christal Niederer for their hard work on this sixth edition.
I am also grateful to the reviewers for all their helpful suggestions.

Reviewers of the Sixth Edition

Patricia Farabee, *Southern Illinois University, Edwardsville*
Mary Jane Farley, *Dyersberg State Community College*
Nadine Gandia, *Miami Dade Community College, Inter-America Campus*
Carol Helton, *Tennessee State University*
Alice K. Perrey, *St. Charles County Community College*
Lynda Wolverton, *Polk County College*

Reviewers of the Previous Edition

Sandra Finstuen, *Long Beach City College*
Carol Hunt, *Nassau Community College*
Leslie King, *SUNY College at Oswego*
William E. Loflin, *Catonsville Community College*
Thomas A. Smith, *Urbana University*
Anne Willekens, *Antelope Valley College*
Ruby Wossum, *State Technical Institute at Memphis*

To the Student

As a college student, you will probably spend about a fourth of your waking hours reading textbooks. The purpose of this book is to help you do that as efficiently as possible—to get the most out of your reading in the least amount of time and to succeed in your classes.

In this book you will improve your reading and study skills by practicing them on reading selections. Because reading should be enjoyable, we tried to make the reading selections as interesting as possible, by choosing subjects such as *How Almost Anyone Can Become a Millionaire* and *Safer Sex.*

The book is divided into four units:

- **Unit I,** *Reading Fundamentals,* reviews the basic skills in vocabulary and comprehension that you will need for the other three units.

- **Unit II,** *Introduction to the Active Critical Thinking Method (ACT),* begins with an introduction to the six-step ACT method. Then you will read ten selections of general interest and analyze them using the six steps.

- **Unit III,** *Textbook Learning with the ACT Method,* begins by explaining how to use the six steps for study reading of college textbooks. Then you will read ten selections from college textbooks on a variety of subjects and prepare study guides using the six steps.

- **Unit IV,** *Critical Reading with the ACT Method,* begins with an explanation of how to use the six steps to read persuasive writing. Then you will read five pairs of articles, each pair taking opposing viewpoints on a controversial subject, such as affirmative action or mercy killing.

Each of the 30 reading selections in the book comes with two tests: one for comprehension and study skills, and one for vocabulary. You will use the tests to evaluate your strengths and weaknesses and measure your progress.

Using this book will help you understand and remember what you read. You will learn what to study and how to study to get the grades you want.

UNIT I

Reading Fundamentals

If you are an average full-time college student, you read between eight and ten textbooks per year, or 5000 pages—not counting any other reading you do for work or for pleasure. Your challenge is to handle this load efficiently and get high grades.

The six-step ACT (Active Critical Thinking) method can help you improve your reading efficiency and your grades. Unit I reviews the basics of vocabulary and comprehension skills. In Unit II you will begin using the ACT method on readings taken from a variety of sources. In Unit III you will use ACT for study reading of textbook material, and in Unit IV you will use ACT for critical reading of persuasive writing. Each reading you do will be followed by a comprehension check and vocabulary check. You will be evaluating your test performance to correct any weaknesses. By the time you have finished this book, you will have the skills to succeed in nearly any college course.

Improving Vocabulary

One of the biggest reasons for poor reading speed and comprehension is having a poor vocabulary. If you don't know the words, you will have trouble understanding the ideas.

Beginning in elementary school, many students are told, "If you don't know a word, look it up in the dictionary." We disagree. Going often to the dictionary interrupts your reading and can interfere with comprehension. Instead, we recommend that every time you see an unfamiliar word, you do the following:

1. Try to figure the word out from the context of the sentence.

2. See if you can use the prefix and/or root as a clue to meaning.

3. Only if the first two steps fail, and if the word is important to understanding what you are reading, should you look it up in the dictionary.

Context Clues

The way babies learn to talk is by hearing words over and over until they figure out from the context what the words mean. When you learn to read, unfamiliar words are presented in the context of sentences. By thinking about the sentence you can usually figure out what the unfamiliar word means. People who read a lot have bigger vocabularies than those who don't because they have seen many more words in context.

   In the four sentences that follow, you can figure out the meanings of the difficult words by using four types of context clues: definition clues, contrast clues, example clues, and experience clues. Circle the letter of the definition that comes closest to the meaning of the underlined word. Do not use a dictionary.

1. It's usually hard to differentiate, or tell the difference between, identical twins.

   a. confuse

   b. distinguish

   c. talk to

   d. ignore

   The answer is b. The context clue used in this sentence is a **definition clue.** The phrase *or tell the difference* defines the word *differentiate.*

2. Anything from limited to extensive damage can be caused by a hurricane.

   a. major

   b. minor

   c. unusual

   d. new

   The answer is a. The context clue used in this case is a **contrast clue.** Extensive damage is contrasted with limited damage.

3. Examples of holidays unique to the heritage of the United States are the Fourth of July and Thanksgiving.

   a. tradition

   b. future

   c. problems

   d. economics

   The answer is a. The context clue used is an **example clue.** The sentence gives examples of holidays unique to the heritage of the United States.

4. Most students are elated when final exams are over.

   a. depressed

   b. anxious

   c. angry

   d. joyous

The answer is d. The context clue used is an **experience clue.** Anyone who has ever taken final exams knows that students are happy when they are over.

Word Parts

A second important skill in figuring out unfamiliar words is to use word parts. Most of the difficult words in English come from Latin or Greco-Latin. Latin is very closely related to Spanish, French, Portuguese, Italian, and Romanian. If you know any of these languages, you have a huge advantage in figuring out difficult words in English. However, even if the only language you know is English, you still know many of the important Latin word parts. For example, guess the meanings of the following word parts (the first one is done for you as an example; the answers appear upside down at the bottom of the page).

Word part	Example	Meaning of word part
1. bi	bicycle	two
2. ex	exit	_____
3. psyche	psychology	_____
4. homo	homosexual	_____

There are three types of word parts: prefixes, roots, and suffixes. A **prefix** is a syllable added at the beginning of a word to change its meaning. For example, the word *mispronounce* means "pronounce wrong," because the meaning of *mis* is "wrong." A **root** forms the basis of a word. *Dict,* meaning "speech or word," is a root used with different prefixes to form many words, such as predict, contradict, and indict. A **suffix** is a syllable added at the end of a word to change its meaning or its part of speech. An example of a suffix that changes a word's meaning is the suffix *less,* which means "without." *Useless* means "without use." An example of a suffix that changes a word's part of speech is the suffix *ize.* Adding the suffix *ize* to the noun *ideal* changes it to the verb *idealize.* Page 466 at the back of the book contains 60 common prefixes and 150 common roots. Most of them you probably know already, and learning them all will make a huge difference in your vocabulary. We include suggestions about the best ways to learn these word parts. Whenever you have time, we recommend that you work with them.

For practice, write the correct word part from the following list in each blank of the numbered exercises. Make sure that the words match their definitions. Use the underlined words as clues. (The answers appear upside down at the bottom of the page.)

Prefixes	Roots	Suffixes
con = together	fus = pour, melt	or = someone who
pro = forth, forward	tract = draw, pull	or something that
re = back	mit = send	ion = state of
de = away	vok = call, speak	
sub = under		

Word

1. pro __ __ __ ion
2. re __ __ __ e
3. con __ __ __ __ __
4. detract __ __
5. __ __ __ voke
6. con __ __ __ ion
7. re __ __ __
8. __ __ voke
9. sub __ __ __ __ __
10. __ __ __ mit

Definition

1. state of pouring forth
2. to call back
3. to shrink or draw together
4. someone who belittles or draws from you
5. to call forth
6. state of disorder (melting together)
7. to send (back)
8. to cancel or call back
9. to take away (pull from under)
10. yield (send under)

Dictionary

Sometimes the context does not provide a clue to meaning, or sometimes you cannot understand the ideas being presented without finding out what a word means. In such cases, you will have to use a dictionary. Most people know how to look words up, but very few know how to make the most out of the information that a good dictionary provides.

A dictionary entry has five major parts:

1. main entry
2. pronunciation
3. part or parts of speech

4. etymology (word history)

5. definitions

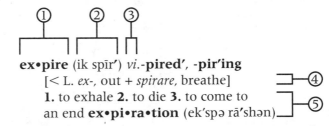

ex•pire (ik spīr′) *vi.*-**pired′**, -**pir′ing**
[< L. *ex-*, out + *spirare*, breathe]
1. to exhale **2.** to die **3.** to come to
an end **ex•pi•ra•tion** (ek′spə rā′shən)

When you look up a word in the dictionary, the first thing you see is the **main entry.** The main entry word is divided into syllables, and the syllables are separated by dots.

The **pronunciation** appears in parentheses after the main entry. You can figure out how to pronounce words by using the brief pronunciation guide, which is usually located at the bottom of every other page. A full explanation of pronunciation is usually found at the beginning of a dictionary. Here is a brief pronunciation guide.

cat, āte, fäther; pen, ēvil; if, kīte; nō, ôr, fo͞od, book; boil, house; up, tʉrn; chief, shell; thick, *the*; zh, treasure; ŋ, sing; ə for *a* in *about*; ′ as in *able* (ā′b′l)

It is sometimes necessary to use the pronunciation guide because you can't always tell how to pronounce a word from its spelling. There are twenty-six letters in English representing about forty-four sounds, depending on one's dialect. For example, the letter *a* is pronounced differently in the words *cat* (kat), *father* (fä′ther), *ago* (ə gō′), *all* (ôl), and *late* (lāt).

One sound that is common in English is the **schwa sound.** It is written ə and is pronounced "uh." It occurs in unstressed syllables. A stressed syllable is pronounced in a louder voice than an unstressed syllable. For example, in the word *ago* (ə gō′), the stress is on the second syllable. The schwa sound can be spelled with any vowel letter, but it is always pronounced the same way.

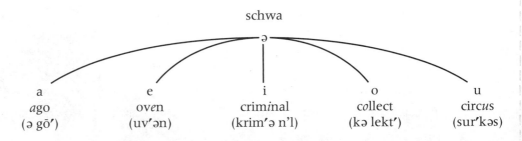

schwa

a	e	i	o	u
ago	*oven*	crim*i*nal	c*o*llect	circ*u*s
(ə gō′)	(uv′ən)	(krim′ə n′l)	(kə lekt′)	(sur′kəs)

When you look up a word in the dictionary, you should always take the time to figure out its pronunciation. If you can pronounce a word to yourself, you are more likely to remember it. For example, let's go back to the word *expire*. The pronunciation is presented in the dictionary as ik spīr'.

| First syllable (ik): | i | appears in the guide as the vowel sound in *it* |
| | k | does not appear in the guide, because it can be pronounced only one way |

The syllable *ik* rhymes with *sick*.

Second syllable (spīr):	s	does not appear in the guide because it has only one pronunciation
	p	does not appear in the guide because it has only one pronunciation
	ī	appears in the guide as the vowel sound in *kite*
	r	does not appear in the guide because it has only one pronunciation

The syllable *spīr* rhymes with *fire*.

The accent mark on the second syllable (spīr') means that the second syllable is stressed.

For practice in using the dictionary pronunciation guide, translate the following movie titles into English spelling. (The answers to these three questions appear upside down at the bottom of the page.)

cat, āte, fäther; pen, ēvil; if, kīte; nō, ôr, fōōd, book; boil, house; up, turn; chief, shell; thick, *the*; zh, treasure; ŋ, sing; ə for *a* in *about*; ' as in *able* (ā'b'l)

1. joo ras'ik pärk

2. stär' wôrz

3. tī tan'ik

The **part of speech** appears after the pronunciation in a dictionary entry. Here are a few of the abbreviations you will see in dictionary entries:

| *n.* = noun: | a word that names a person, a place, or a thing |
| *v.* = verb: | a word that shows an action or a state of being |

vt. or *tr. v.* = transitive verb:	an action word that affects a person or thing: "Jim *dropped* the pencil." A transitive verb requires a direct object to complete its meaning.
vi. = intransitive verb:	an action word that does not affect a person or thing: "The apple *fell* to the ground."
adj. = adjective:	a word that modifies a noun
adv. = adverb:	a word that modifies a verb, an adjective, or another adverb

If you know parts of speech, you can use words correctly in a sentence. For practice, circle the letter before the correct part of speech of the underlined words in the following sentences. Use the dictionary if you need help. (The answers appear upside down at the bottom of the page.)

1. The man was a work <u>addict</u> who often spent twelve hours a day at the office.
   a. *v.*, ə dikt′
   b. *n.*, ad′ikt

2. People living under a cruel dictator will often try to <u>rebel</u>.
   a. *n.*, reb′′l
   b. *v.*, ri bel′

3. Going to school at night to get a degree can be a difficult <u>project</u>.
   a. *n.*, präj′ekt
   b. *v.*, prə jekt′

   For practice on parts of speech, complete the table on the next page. The first item is done for you as an example. If you don't know the part of speech, you will have to use the dictionary. Begin with the word on the left. If you find it, look up its part of speech. Then look around for a similar word in the new part of speech, and check its meaning. Be aware that not all parts of speech have their own entries in the dictionary. They are sometimes listed at the bottom of another entry. For example, in some dictionaries the word *bashful* (adjective) has its own entry, but *bashfully* (adverb) and *bashfulness* (noun) do not. Instead, they are listed at the bottom of the entry for *bashful*. Another possibility is that the word may change its spelling in another part of speech. For example *acquire* is a verb, but the noun form is *acquisition*. You may need to look around in the dictionary to find the word you want. The answers appear upside down at the bottom of page 9.

Pronunciation: 1. b   2. b   3. a
ANSWERS

Word	Part of speech	New part of speech	New word
1. happy	adjective	noun	happiness
2. jealousy		adjective	
3. weigh		noun	
4. building		verb	
5. slow		adverb	

The **etymology,** or origin of the word, appears in brackets after the part of speech.

    ex•pire (ik spīr´) *vi.* **-pired´, -pir´ing** [< L. *ex-*, out + *spirare*, breathe]
       1. to exhale **2.** to die **3.** to come to an end

The etymology for *expire* says that the word comes from the Latin word parts *ex* (meaning "out") and *spirare* (meaning "to breathe"). The symbol < (meaning "comes from") and the letter L. (the abbreviation for *Latin*) are defined in the front of the dictionary, along with other symbols and abbreviations.

    Taking the time to read the etymology is important in vocabulary building. For example, if you know that *spir* means "to breathe," you will have an important clue to an entire word family:

Word	Meaning
expire	end, die (breathe out)
conspiracy	plot (breathe together)
respiration	act of breathing (breathe again)
aspire	to be ambitious (breathe to)
spirit	soul (breath)
inspire	motivate (breathe in)
esprit de corps	group spirit (breath of body)
perspire	sweat (breathe through)
transpire	happen (breathe across)
sprightly	lively (full of breath)
spire	tapering point (breath)

    Definitions form the next part of a dictionary entry. Many words have more than one definition. You must choose the one that best fits the context in which the word is used. For example, the following entry shows that the word *expire* has three definitions:

> **ex•pire** (ik spīr′) *vi.* **-pired′, -pir′ing** [< L. *ex-*, out + *spirare*, breathe] **1.** to exhale **2.** to die **3.** to come to an end

In the sentence "He confessed to the crime before he expired," definition 2 is the one that is meant.

The following words also have more than one meaning. Read each sentence, and identify the dictionary meaning that best describes how the underlined word is used. Write the number of the definition in the space provided. Be sure to choose the definition that matches the part of speech written under the blank. (The answers appear upside down at the bottom of the page.)

_____   1. You can <u>express</u> shades of meaning that aren't even possible in
vt.   other languages.

> **ex•press** (ik spres′) *vt.* [< L. *ex*, out + *primere*, to press] **1.** to squeeze out (juice, etc.) **2.** to put into words, state **3.** to reveal, show **4.** to signify or symbolize **5.** to send by express —*adj.* **1.** expressed, stated, explicit **2.** exact **3.** specific **4.** fast and direct [an *express* bus, highway, etc.] **5.** related to express —*adv.* by express —*n.* **1.** an express train, bus, etc. **2.** *a)* service for transporting things rapidly *b)* the things sent by express

_____   2. John is in the sophomore <u>class</u>.
n.

> **class** (klas) *n.* [< L. *classis*, class or division] **1.** a number of people or things grouped together because of likeness; kind; sort **2.** social or economic rank [the working *class*] **3.** *a)* a group of students taught together *b)* a group graduating together **4.** grade or quality **5.** [Slang] excellence, as of style —*vt.* to classify —*vi.* to be classified

_____   3. I'll have to hurry to <u>catch</u> the train.
vt.

> **catch** (kach) *vt.* **caught, catch′ing** [< L. *capere*, take] **1.** to seize and hold, capture **2.** to take by a trap **3.** to deceive **4.** to surprise **5.** to get to in time [to *catch* a bus] **6.** to lay hold of; grab [*catch* a ball] **7.** to become affected with [he *caught* a cold] **8.** to understand **9.** to get entangled **10.** [Colloq.] to see, hear, etc. —*vi.* **1.** to become held, fastened, etc. **2.** to take hold, as fire **3.** to keep hold, as a lock —*n.* **1.** a catching **2.** a thing that catches **3.** something caught **4.** one worth catching as a spouse **5.** a snatch or fragment **6.** a break in the voice **7.** [Colloq.] a tricky qualification, to catch at, to seize desperately

Whenever you read a definition in the dictionary, you should do two things to make sure you really understand it. First, put the definition into your own words. Second, make up a sentence using the word. Practice by defining the word *expire* and using it in a sentence. (Sample answers appear upside down at the bottom of the page.)

Definition:_____

Sentence: _____

Before each reading selection in this book, there is a preview of difficult words that appear in the reading. Use the pronunciation guide at the bottom of each Vocabulary Preview to figure out how to pronounce the words. Read the definitions before you read each selection. Then you will be more likely to know what the words mean when you see them.

Word Memory

You will learn hundreds of new words in your college classes, but you may have a problem remembering them all. Pronouncing the word, checking the etymology, putting the definition in your own words, and using the word in a sentence are all aids to memory. In addition, there are two more ways to remember words: using word association and using flash cards.

Word association means linking the new word with one you already know. For example, to remember that *striations* refers to thin lines or grooves, you could associate it with the word *stripes*. Or to remember that *inexplicable* means "not able to be explained," you could remember the phrase *not explainable*.

For practice with word association, make up a word or phrase that you could use to remember each of the following words. (Some possible word associations appear upside down at the bottom of the next page.)

1. commentary (käm′ən ter′ē): series of explanatory remarks

_____

2. transfixed (trans fikst′): motionless

_____

3. aghast (ə gast′): feeling great horror or dismay

_____

ANSWERS
Definition: to come to an end
Sentence: I had to move because my lease expired.

4. ad lib (ad'lib'): to make up and perform without any preparation

_____

5. insight (in'sīt): clear understanding of the nature of things

_____

Another way to memorize a word is to put it on a **flash card.** Write the word and its pronunciation on one side of the card, and write the definition and a sentence using the word on the other side. Your cards should look like the sample card below.

Front	Back
non sequitur (nän' sek'wi tər)	an inference that does not follow from the premises His speech was full of non sequiturs.

You can test yourself by looking at the front of the card and trying to give the definition. When you are sure you can remember a word, you can retire the card. Carry ten to twenty cards with you so that you can use spare moments (such as when you are standing in line or eating lunch by yourself) to memorize vocabulary. That way you won't have so much work to do the night before an exam.

Paragraph Comprehension

Literal Comprehension

The most important skills in literal comprehension of paragraphs are understanding the subject, the main idea, and supporting details.

Subject

A good paragraph is a group of sentences that explain one central idea, called the subject, or topic, of the paragraph. You can find the subject of a paragraph by asking yourself who or what the whole paragraph is about. Read the following paragraph, and then circle the letter that identifies its subject.

> Newfoundland is Canada's newest province and its oldest. It is the newest because it was the last to join the Dominion, in 1949. But it is also the oldest in that it was the first to be discovered. Scientists have found the remains of a Viking camp almost 1,000 years old on the province's northern shore. Even modern Europeans discovered Newfoundland before they discovered the rest of Canada. John Cabot discovered the southern portion of the province only 5 years after Columbus landed in the West Indies and discovered America. Sir Humphrey Gilbert claimed Newfoundland for England in 1583.

The subject of the paragraph is

a. Newfoundland's age.

b. Newfoundland.

c. Vikings in Newfoundland.

d. provinces of Canada.

The answer is a. Choices b and d are too broad. They both cover more than what's in the paragraph. Choice c is too narrow; it covers only part of what's in the paragraph.

Now read the following paragraph, and circle the letter that identifies its subject.

> Most people with disabilities want to work, but many cannot find employment. The main reason more disabled people are not working is that employers don't understand that people with disabilities can perform many jobs.

The subject of the paragraph is

a. disabilities.

b. employment of the disabled.

c. employers' attitudes.

d. the need for legal protection.

The answer is b. Answers a and c are too broad; they go beyond what's in the paragraph. Answer d is off the subject; it's not mentioned in the paragraph.

Main Idea

Every paragraph should have a main idea, or a central point. The main idea of a paragraph is usually a complete sentence. To find the main idea, ask yourself what the subject is and what the author is saying about the subject.

Now look again at the paragraph about Newfoundland. Circle the letter that identifies its main idea.

a. Newfoundland is a province in Canada.

b. Newfoundland is the newest and oldest province in Canada.

c. Newfoundland was discovered by Vikings.

d. Newfoundland was discovered before other Canadian provinces.

The answer is b. Choice a is too broad, and choices c and d are too narrow.

Look again at the paragraph about employment of the disabled. Which of the following is its main idea?

a. Disabled people are underpaid.

b. Employers have prejudices.

c. Many disabled people cannot find work.

d. Disabled people can do volunteer work.

The answer is c. Choices a and d are not discussed or implied in the paragraph. Choice b is implied, but it is not the main point the author is making.

Supporting Details

A good paragraph has details that support the main idea. The supporting details explain, clarify, or justify the main idea. Supporting details can be reasons, facts, examples, or testimony.

In the paragraph about Newfoundland, the main idea is supported by **facts**—things that have actually happened or that are true. Facts can include numbers, scientific laws, historical information, and so forth. The paragraph about Newfoundland is supported by historical facts.

In the paragraph about employment of the disabled, the main idea is supported by **reasons.** The author explains why many disabled people cannot find employment.

Sometimes an author uses one or more **examples** to support the main idea. Read the paragraph and fill in the blanks.

Yellowstone National Park has unusual natural attractions. It has a massive cliff of black volcanic glass. It also has geysers that release 15,000 gallons of hot water into the air hour after hour. Finally, it has bubbling mudpots and boiling springs that sometimes reach 150°F.

Subject _____

Main idea _____

Example 1 _____

Example 2 _____

Example 3 _____

The subject is the natural attractions in Yellowstone National Park. The main idea is that Yellowstone National Park has unusual natural attractions. The examples are (1) cliff of black volcanic glass, (2) geysers, and (3) mudpots and boiling springs.

To give **testimony** as support for the main idea means to give opinions or findings of people other than the author. Read the paragraph and fill in the blanks.

> According to the *Guinness Book of World Records,* people with the highest IQs are often ordinary. They do not generally have remarkable intuition or freedom from prejudice. They often have rather ordinary jobs, and they do not necessarily excel in the academic world.

Subject _____

Main idea _____

Testimony by _____

The subject is people with the highest IQs. The main idea is that they are often ordinary. The testimony is by the *Guinness Book of World Records.*

Finding Main Ideas

In each of the paragraphs above, the main idea is located in the first sentence. Main ideas are usually, but not always, found in the first sentences of paragraphs. One way to locate the main idea is to look for such **signal words** as *therefore, thus, in other words,* and *most important.*

See if you can locate the main idea and signal words in the following paragraph.

> The main idea can fall in several places within the paragraph. For example, it can, and usually does, begin the paragraph. The author clearly states her most important idea and then spends the rest of the paragraph clarifying, expanding, proving, or explaining it.

The main idea is in the first sentence, and *for example* signals a supporting detail.

Now locate the main idea and signal words in this next paragraph.

> An author could also begin a paragraph by giving examples of an idea. Or she might choose to describe a scene or a historical event. At other times, the writer might begin by using a quotation from another person. In this case, the author begins with supporting details and then moves

to a general conclusion. In other words, she puts the main idea at the end of the paragraph.

The main idea is in the last sentence, signaled by *in other words*. Signal words indicating supporting details in this paragraph are *also, or, at other times,* and *in this case.*

Locate the main idea and signal words in the next paragraph.

The author who chooses to begin a paragraph with examples might not always place the main idea at the end. The main idea could be found toward the middle of the paragraph. In this case, the author follows the main idea with more supporting details. How much support precedes or follows the main idea depends on the author's purpose.

In this example, the main idea is in the second sentence. *In this case* signals a detail.

Now use what you have learned to locate the main idea and signal words in the next paragraph.

The Amazon River is the widest river in the world, with one-fifth of all the fresh water on earth moving through its mouth. In length it is second only to the Nile, and if stretched across the United States, it would reach from New York to Los Angeles. In addition, the Amazon covers the largest area of any river. Therefore, it can be argued that the Amazon is the mightiest river on Earth.

The main idea is in the last sentence, signaled by *therefore.* The other sentences are supporting details. One of them is preceded by the signal words *in addition.*

Inferential Comprehension

Implied Main Idea

In each of the preceding paragraphs the main idea is stated somewhere in the paragraph. In some paragraphs, however, the main idea is implied rather than stated. You have to read between the lines to infer (reason out) the main idea. To do this, look at the supporting details and try to think of a statement that they all point to. This statement is the implied main idea. Read the following paragraph, and fill in the blanks.

Osiris, Egyptian god of the underworld, was often portrayed in mummy wrappings. Isis, frequently represented with a cow's head or horns, was the nature goddess. Ra was the sun god, whose symbol was the pyramid. Amon was often represented as a ram or with a ram's head.

Subject _____

Supporting detail 1 _____

Supporting detail 2 _____

Supporting detail 3 _____

Supporting detail 4 _____

Type of supporting details _____

Implied main idea _____

    The subject is ancient Egyptian gods. The supporting details are (1) Osiris, (2) Isis, (3) Ra, and (4) Amon. They are examples. The implied main idea is that there were several Egyptian gods.

Valid and Invalid Inferences

Implied main idea is one type of inferential comprehension. Another type is judging whether an inference is valid or invalid. A valid inference is supported by what the author has implied; an invalid inference is not. Use the paragraph about Egyptian gods to complete the following exercise. Mark each inference V if it is valid or I if it is invalid.

_____ 1. Osiris was more important than Ra.

_____ 2. Egyptian gods always represent the spirits of animals.

_____ 3. Egyptians believed in an underworld.

_____ 4. Egyptians had one principal god and several minor ones.

_____ 5. The cow was sacred to the Egyptians.

    The only valid inference is 3; you can infer this because Osiris was the god of the underworld. The other statements are not implied in the paragraph.

Read the next paragraph and fill in the blanks.

Thomas Alva Edison invented or improved on the telegraph, phonograph, stock ticker, microphone, telephone, light bulb, battery, motion picture projector, and many other things. He held more than 1,300 U.S. and foreign patents and was the first American director of a research laboratory for inventors. His various companies later combined to become General Electric.

Subject _____

Supporting detail 1 _____

  Minor detail a _____

  Minor detail b _____

Minor detail c _____

Minor detail d _____

Minor detail e _____

Minor detail f_____

Minor detail g _____

Minor detail h _____

Supporting detail 2 _____

Supporting detail 3 _____

Supporting detail 4 _____

Type of supporting details _____

Implied main idea _____

The subject is Thomas Alva Edison. The supporting details are that
(1) he invented or improved on many things having to do with electricity
(telegraph, phonograph, stock ticker, microphone, telephone, light bulb,
battery, and motion picture projector), (2) he held more than 1300 U.S. and
foreign patents, (3) he was the first director of a research laboratory for
inventors, and (4) his various companies later combined to become General
Electric. The supporting details are historical facts. The implied main idea is
that Edison was an important figure in American technology.

Mark each statement V if it is a valid inference. Mark I if it is invalid.

_____ 1. Edison was a great American inventor.

_____ 2. Edison was as intelligent as Einstein.

_____ 3. Edison was a good businessman.

_____ 4. Edison was more interested in science than in money.

_____ 5. Edison set up a school to train young scientists.

Statement 1 is implied by the fact that Edison invented so many things.
Statement 3 is implied by the fact that he obtained patents, directed a
research laboratory, and founded General Electric. The other statements are
not implied in the paragraph.

Read the next paragraph and fill in the blanks.

The first horselike creature lived 700 million years ago and was only
about 11 inches high. It had four toes on each forefoot and three on
each hind foot. By 45 million years ago the creature had doubled in
size and had three toes on all four feet. By 10 million years ago it had

doubled in size again, and its feet had a single toe forming a hoof. The true horse, *Equus,* appeared in North America about a million years ago. It migrated to Asia and later became extinct in America. It was finally reintroduced by European settlers.

Subject _____

Supporting detail 1 _____

Supporting detail 2 _____

Supporting detail 3 _____

Supporting detail 4 _____

Type of supporting details _____

Implied main idea _____

The subject is the evolution of the horse. The supporting details are how the horse looked (1) 700 million years ago, (2) 45 million years ago, (3) 10 million years ago, and (4) a million years ago. The supporting details are facts. The implied main idea is that the horse evolved over 700 million years.

Mark V if the statement is a valid inference. Mark I if it is invalid.

_____ 1. There was a land bridge to Asia about a million years ago.

_____ 2. Europeans were the first to domesticate wild horses.

_____ 3. Prehistoric horses were larger than modern horses.

_____ 4. The modern horse has been around for 70 million years.

_____ 5. Horse toes evolved into hooves.

Statement 1 can be inferred from the fact that the horses migrated from North America to Asia. Statement 5 can be inferred from the number of toes on prehistoric horses. The other statements are not implied in the paragraph.

Critical Comprehension

Thesis, Argument, and Support

Authors usually have one of three purposes for writing: to inform, to entertain, or to persuade. An author who is trying to persuade us of something has an idea, or thesis, in mind. The thesis in a persuasive paragraph is like the main idea in an informative paragraph: it is the main point the author is trying to make. It can be either stated or implied. The thesis is supported by arguments, which are like the major supporting details. Minor details consist of support for the arguments.

Read the paragraph and fill in the blanks.

Antioch College in Ohio instituted a brilliant policy to stop sexual abuse on campus. If any student wants to touch another student (usually on a date), he or she must ask first. For example, "May I kiss you?" If things heat up, the student must ask before he or she proceeds to each new level of intimacy. This puts a complete stop to sexual aggression and the familiar claim that when she said "no" she really meant "yes."

Subject _____

Thesis _____

Argument _____

Type of support (facts, examples, testimony, reasons)_____

The subject is the Antioch policy. The thesis is that the policy is brilliant. The argument is that it stops sexual aggression and the problems of misinterpretation. The supporting details are reasons.

Read the paragraph and fill in the blanks.

The Antioch policy is ridiculous. Having to discuss such things is so embarrassing that it would take all the fun out of dating.

Subject _____

Thesis _____

Argument _____

Type of support _____

The subject is the Antioch policy. The thesis is that the policy is ridiculous. The argument is that it would take all the fun out of dating. The type of support is reasons.

Read the paragraph and fill in the blanks.

Immigration into the United States should be reduced in order to protect the people who already live here. Because they work for low wages and no benefits, immigrants take jobs away from the native born. They pollute our environment and use up our natural resources. They place a huge burden on public services like schools and health clinics that native-born Americans have to pay for.

Subject _____

Thesis _____

Argument _____

Supporting detail 1 _____

Supporting detail 2 _____

Supporting detail 3 _____

Type of support _____

The subject is immigration. The thesis is that immigration should be reduced. The argument supporting the thesis is that immigration is not good for native-born Americans. The details supporting the argument are (1) immigrants take jobs away, (2) immigrants pollute our environment and use up our natural resources, and (3) immigrants place an expensive burden on public services. The type of support is reasons.

Read the paragraph and fill in the blanks. (Be careful with this one; the thesis and argument are in different places.)

The United States needs immigrants. Our birth rate is now below the replacement rate, and without immigrants there wouldn't be enough young people to support our aging population and keep Social Security from collapsing. Because most immigrants are young and healthy, and because the illegals want to keep a low profile, they tend to pay more in taxes than they use in services. Immigrants also create new jobs, both because they buy American products and because many start their own businesses. Immigration should not be reduced.

Subject _____

Thesis _____

Argument _____

Supporting detail 1 _____

Supporting detail 2 _____

Supporting detail 3 _____

Type of support _____

The subject is immigration. The thesis is that immigration should not be reduced. The argument supporting the thesis is that we need immigrants. The details supporting the argument are (1) immigrants will help support our aging population, (2) they pay more in taxes than they use in services, and (3) they create jobs. The type of support is reasons.

UNIT II

Introduction to the Active Critical Thinking (ACT) Method

ACT: A Six-Step Process

In Unit II you will start to use the six-step ACT (Active Critical Thinking) method.

Preread

Before you read each selection in Unit II, you will preview it in three ways:

1. You will go over the difficult words in advance so that they do not interfere with your comprehension when you read the selection.

2. You will preview the content to understand the subject and main idea before reading. This will increase your comprehension and speed. Psychologists have found that the mind works something like a library. A library stores information by filing it under certain categories. You retrieve information in a library by looking it up under the same categories. In order for your mind to store (learn) and retrieve (remember) information, it also needs to file it in categories. Prereading the selection gives you the categories in advance.

3. You will think about what you already know about the subject. In psychology, this is called "activating your schema." The idea is that you already know something about most subjects. When you read, you should use your experience—what you already know—to help you put what you are learning from the page in the right category in your mind. Using your experience will help you realize that A is like B, that C is a result of D, and that E and F cannot both be true, for instance. The more experience you can bring to your reading, the deeper your comprehension will be. You will also be asked to think about what you don't know about the subject, and you will think of some questions that might be answered by reading the selection. This will activate your curiosity, which will also deepen your comprehension.

Read

In this book you will always read just to comprehend, without underlining or highlighting. This is because your underlining will be much better if you go back after reading and do it as a separate step. In this book, you will practice underlining or highlighting in Units III and IV.

Analyze What You Read

This is where study techniques come in. Underlining is one such technique. The study technique we practice in Unit II is called making graphic organizers. A graphic organizer is a type of picture. It can be an outline, a chart, an idea map, or any other type of drawing. Because of the way the brain works, we cannot remember large blocks of words, but we can remember pictures.

Remember What's Important

The reason you memorize information is so that you can recall it when you need it. If you will not be needing it, you don't have to memorize. But in college, you usually have to do something, whether it's write a paper or pass a test, with the information you read. The best way to memorize is not to reread your textbook or listen to taped lectures. The most effective way is to test yourself on what you are trying to remember until you reach the level of memory you need. In Unit II, you will put everything you are trying to remember into the format of your graphic organizer. Then you will memorize the graphic organizer.

Make Use of What You Read

This step refers to your output. In college courses, you will be expected to take tests, participate in class discussions, write papers, and possibly give oral reports. In this book, there is a Comprehension Check for each reading. There is also a Vocabulary Check in which you use the words from the Vocabulary Preview. Both of these activities can be used as tests.

Evaluate Your Active Critical Thinking Skills

After you take a test or other evaluation for Step 5, you will find out how well you did. If you are not satisfied with your performance, you should review the six steps of ACT. Did you read the material actively and understand it? Did you make a graphic organizer? Did you test yourself on your graphic organizer enough to remember it? With ACT, a poor grade should not be a reason to become discouraged. It should be seen as a chance to figure out how to improve, so you will do better next time. In this book we have provided an Evaluation Checklist on p. 457.

1   How to Improve Your Vocabulary

Vocabulary Preview

addict (ad′ikt): one unable to give up a habit, such as using drugs

differentiate (dif ə ren′shē āt′): to make unlike; to show the difference between

context (kän′tekst): parts just before and after a word or passage that influence its meaning

extensive (ik sten′siv): having a great or far-reaching area or scope

heritage (her′ə tij′): a tradition handed down from one's ancestors or the past

origin (ôr′ə jin): beginning; source; root

emancipate (i man′sə pāt′): to free from confinement

corroborate (kə räb′ə rāt′): to support or confirm

literal (lit′ər əl): following the exact words of the original

elated (i lāt′id, ē lāt′id): raised the spirits of; made very proud or happy

cat, āte, fäther; pen, ēvil; if, kīte; nō, ôr, fōōd, book; boil, house; up, turn; chief, shell; thick, *the*; zh, treasure; ŋ, sing; ə for *a* in *about*; ′ as in *able* (ā′b′l)

Preread

STEP 1

Preview the following selection (pp. 27–30) by reading the title, the author's name (he is a famous actor), and the numbered headings. Answer the following questions without looking back at the selection.

1. What is the subject?

   _____

2. What is the main idea (the main thing the author is saying about the subject)?

   _____

3. Take a moment to think about how to improve your vocabulary. Think about what you know, what you don't know, and what you might find out from reading the selection. Make up three questions that might be answered by reading it.

   a. _____

   b. _____

   c. _____

Read

Read the selection without underlining.

Write your starting time here: _____

◆ *How to Improve Your Vocabulary*

Tony Randall

Words can make us laugh, cry, go to war, fall in love. Rudyard Kipling called words the most powerful drug of mankind. If they are, I'm a hopeless addict—and I hope to get you hooked, too!

Whether you're still in school or you head up a corporation, the better command you have of words, the better chance you have of saying exactly what you mean, of understanding what others mean—and of getting what you want in the world.

English is the richest language—with the largest vocabulary on earth. Over 1,000,000 words!

You can express shades of meaning that aren't even *possible* in other languages. (For example, you can differentiate between "sky" and "heaven." The French, Italians and Spanish cannot.)

Yet, the average adult has a vocabulary of only 30,000 to 60,000 words. Imagine what we're missing!

Here are five pointers that help me learn—and remember—whole *families* of words at a time.

They may not *look* easy—and won't be at first. But if you stick with them you'll find they *work*!

What's the first thing to do when you see a word you don't know?

1. Try to Guess the Meaning of the Word from the Way It's Used

You can often get at least *part* of a word's meaning—just from how it's used in a sentence.

That's why it's so important to read as much as you can—different *kinds* of things: magazines, books, newspapers you don't normally read. The more you *expose* yourself to new words, the more words you'll pick up *just by seeing how they're used.*

For instance, say you run across the word "manacle":

"The manacles had been on John's wrists for 30 years. Only one person had a key—his wife."

You have a good *idea* of what "manacles" are—just from the context of the sentence.

But let's find out *exactly* what the word means and where it comes from. The only way to do this, and to build an extensive vocabulary *fast,* is to go to the dictionary. (How lucky, you *can*—Shakespeare *couldn't.* There wasn't an English dictionary in his day!)

So you go to the dictionary. (NOTE: Don't let dictionary abbreviations put you off. The front tells you what they mean, and even has a guide to pronunciation.)

2. Look It Up

Here's the definition for "manacle" in *The American Heritage Dictionary of the English Language.*

> **man-a-cle** (man′ə kəl) *n.* Usually plural. **1.** A device for confining the hands, usually consisting of two metal rings that are fastened about the wrists and joined by a metal chain; a handcuff. **2.** Anything that confines or restrains. – *tr. v.* **manacled, -cling, -cles. 1.** To restrain with manacles. **2.** To confine or restrain as if with manacles; shackle; fetter. [Middle English *manicle,* from Old French, from Latin *manicula,* little hand, handle, diminutive of *manus,* hand.]

The first definition fits here: A device for confining the hands, usually consisting of two metal rings that are fastened about the wrists and joined by a metal chain; a handcuff.

Well, that's what you *thought* it meant. But what's the idea *behind* the word? What are its *roots*? To really understand a word, you need to know.

Here's where the detective work—and the *fun*—begins.

3. Dig the Meaning Out by the Roots

The root is the basic part of the word—its heritage, its origin. (Most of our roots come from Latin and Greek words at least 2,000 years old—which come from even earlier Indo-European tongues!)

Learning the roots: (1) Helps us *remember* words. (2) Gives us a deeper understanding of the words we *already* know. And (3) allows us to pick up whole families of *new* words at a time. That's why learning the root is the *most important part of going to the dictionary.*

Notice the root of "manacle" is *manus* (Latin) meaning "hand."

Well, that makes sense. Now, other words with this root, <u>man</u>, start to make sense, too.

Take <u>man</u>ual—something done "by hand" (<u>man</u>ual labor) or a "handbook." And <u>man</u>age—to "handle" something (as a <u>man</u>ager). When you e<u>man</u>cipate someone, you're taking him "from the hands of" someone else.

When you <u>man</u>ufacture something, you "make it by hand" (in its original meaning).

And when you finish your first novel, your publisher will see your—originally "handwritten"—<u>man</u>uscript.

Imagine! A whole new world of words opens up—just from one simple root!

The root gives the *basic* clue to the meaning of a word. But there's another important clue that runs a close second—the *prefix*.

4. Get the Powerful Prefixes Under Your Belt

A prefix is the part that's sometimes attached to the front of a word. Like—well, *prefix*! There aren't many—fewer than 100 major prefixes—and you'll learn them in no time at all just by becoming more aware of the meanings of words you already know. Here are a few. (Some of the "How-to" vocabulary-building books will give you the others.)

prefix				
Latin	**Greek**	**meaning**	**examples**	**literal sense**
com, con, co, col, cor	sym, syn, syl	with, very, together	conform sympathy	"form with" "feeling with"
in, im, il, ir	a, an	not, without	innocent amorphous	"not wicked" "without form"
contra, counter	anti, ant	against, opposite	contravene antidote	"come against" "give against"

Now, see how the *prefix* (along with the context) helps you get the meaning of the italicized words:

- "If you're going to be my witness, your story must <u>*corroborate*</u> my story." (The literal meaning of *corroborate* is "strength together.")

- "You told me one thing—now you tell me another. Don't <u>*contradict*</u> yourself." (The literal meaning of *contradict* is "say against.")

- "Oh, that snake's not poisonous. It's a completely <u>*innocuous*</u> little garden snake." (The literal meaning of *innocuous* is "not harmful.")

Now, you've got some new words. What are you going to do with them?

5. Put Your New Words to Work at Once

Use them several times the first day you learn them. Say them out loud! Write them in sentences.

Should you "use" them on *friends*? Careful—you don't want them to think you're a stuffed shirt. (It depends on the situation. You *know* when a word sounds natural—and when it sounds stuffy.)

How about your *enemies*? You have my blessing. Ask one of them if he's read that article on pneumonoultramicroscopicsilicovolcanoconiosis. (You really can find it in the dictionary.) Now, you're one up on him.

So what do you do to improve your vocabulary?

Remember: (1) Try to guess the meaning of the word from the way it's used. (2) Look it up. (3) Dig the meaning out by the roots. (4) Get the powerful prefixes under your belt. (5) Put your new words to work at once.

That's all there is to it—you're off on your treasure hunt.

Now, do you see why I love words so much?

Aristophanes said, "By words, the mind is excited and the spirit elated." It's as true today as it was when he said it in Athens—*2,400 years ago!*

I hope you're now like me—hooked on words forever.

1000 words

Write your ending time here:_____

Subtract your starting time: _____

Total time: _____

Check the Rate Chart on p. 462 to find out how many words per minute you have read, and then record your score on the Reading Efficiency Progress Chart on p. 463.

Analyze What You Read

Make Graphic Organizers

It is often easier to understand and remember what we read when we put it into some kind of picture. Following is an outline of the selection you just read.

How to Improve Your Vocabulary

    I. Try to guess the meaning of the word from the way it's used.

   II. Look it up.

  III. Dig the meaning out by the roots.

IV. Get the powerful prefixes under your belt.

V. Put your new words to work at once.

An outline is a type of picture, but a concept or idea map is easier to remember because it is even more visual. Following is a blank concept map. Write the title in the circle, and write the Roman numeral headings in the rectangles.

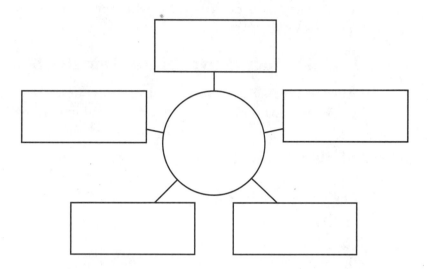

Remember What's Important

1. To prepare for a Comprehension Check, memorize the concept map. Test yourself or have someone test you on the ways to improve vocabulary. Keep testing until you think you can remember everything you need to know.

2. To prepare for a Vocabulary Check, make flash cards as described on p. 12 for each of the words in the Vocabulary Preview that you do not know. Test yourself or have someone test you until you think you can remember them.

How to Answer an Essay Question: Each of the Comprehension Checks in this book contains an essay question. Writing an essay is easy when you use a graphic organizer, but difficult when you don't. Before you write the essay, draw the graphic organizer that you memorized from your study guide. In this chapter the graphic organizer is a concept map for the five ways to improve vocabulary. Sometimes the question requires you to use the whole graphic organizer, and sometimes you will need only part of the graphic organizer to answer the question. For example, the essay in this chapter might ask you about all five ways to improve vocabulary, or it might ask about only some of them. Write the essay from your graphic organizer and use signal words such as *first, most important,* and *finally* so that your essay is organized and easy to read.

Make Use of What You Read

When you are ready, complete the Comprehension Check on p. 339 and the Vocabulary Check on p. 341. Do them from memory, without looking back at the book or your notes.

Evaluate Your Active Critical Thinking Skills

After your tests have been graded, record your scores on the Progress Chart, p. 456, and answer the questions on the Evaluation Checklist on p. 457.

Vocabulary Skills Review

For explanation see pp. 9–11

Dictionary Definitions

Here are the dictionary entries for five words used in the reading. Above each entry is the sentence in which the word was used. In the blank before the sentence, put the number of the definition that fits the way the word is used. The abbreviation under each blank tells you which part of speech the word is, so you can more easily find the proper definition.

_____ 1. "Here are five <u>pointers</u> that help me learn—and remember—
n.   whole *families* of words at a time."

    point•er *n.* **1.** a long, tapered rod for pointing to things **2.** an indicator on a meter, etc. **3.** a large, lean hunting dog with a smooth coat **4.** [Colloq.] a helpful hint or suggestion

_____ 2. "The more you <u>expose</u> yourself to new words, the more words
v.   you'll pick up *just by seeing how they're used.*"

    ex•pose (ik spōz′) *vt.* **-posed′, -pos′-ing** [see EXPOUND] **1.** to lay open **2.** to reveal; exhibit; make known **3.** *Photography* to subject (a sensitized film or plate) to actinic rays

_____ 3. "A <u>device</u> for confining the hands, usually consisting of two
n.   metal rings that are fastened about the wrists and joined by a metal chain; a handcuff."

    de•vice (di vīs′) *n.* [see DEVISE] **1.** a thing devised; plan, scheme, or trick **2.** a mechanical contrivance **3.** an ornamental design, esp. on a coat of arms—**leave to one's own devices** to allow to do as one wishes

      adj.   4. "Take manual—something done 'by hand' (<u>manual</u> labor) . . ."

    man•u•al (man′yo͞o wəl) *adj.* [<L. *manus,* a hand] **1.** made or worked by hand [*manual* typewriter] **2.** involving skill or hard work with the hands –*n.* **1.** a handy book for use as a guide, reference, etc. **2.** prescribed drill in the handling of a weapon

      n.   5. ". . . the better <u>command</u> you have of words, the better chance you have of saying exactly what you mean, or understanding what others mean—and of getting what you want in the world."

    com•mand (kə mand′) *vt.* [<L. *com-,* intens. + *mandare,* entrust] **1.** to give an order to; direct **2.** to have authority over; control **3.** to have for use [to *command* a fortune] **4.** to deserve and get [to *command* respect] **5.** to control (a position); overlook –*vi.* to have authority –*n.* **1.** order; direction **2.** controlling power or position **3.** mastery **4.** a military or naval force, or district, under a specified authority

Pronunciation Practice

For explanation see pp. 6–7

For practice with the pronunciation guide, do the exercises below.

cat, āte, fäther; pen, ēvil; if, kīte; nō, ôr, fo͞od, book; boil, house; up, turn; chief, shell; thick, *the*; zh, treasure; ŋ, sing; ə for *a* in *about*; ′ as in *able* (ā′b'l)

1. Translate these famous book titles into English spelling.

    a. bē luv′id—Toni Morrison

    _____

    b. ə tāl uv to͞o sit′ēz—Charles Dickens

    _____

    c. prīd and prej′ə dis—Jane Austen

    _____

    d. *th*ə good urth—Pearl Buck

    _____

    e. *th*ə tīm mə shēn′—H. G. Wells

    _____

2. Say each word below out loud and listen for the sounds. Then circle the words that contain the sound of schwa (ə).

    differentiate   context   origin   literal   elate

3. Say each word below out loud and listen for the sounds. Then circle the words that contain long vowel sounds (ā, ē, ī, ō, ū).

addict   extensive   heritage   emancipate   corroborate

For explanation see pp. 7–9

Parts of Speech

For each word below, write its part of speech. Then change it to the new part of speech. Write a sentence using the new word. Use a dictionary if you need help.

Word	Part of speech	New part of speech	New word
1. differentiate		adjective	
Sentence:			
2. extensive		verb	
Sentence:			
3. origin		verb	
Sentence:			
4. emancipate		noun	
Sentence:			
5. corroborate		noun	
Sentence:			
6. literal		adverb	
Sentence:			
7. elated		noun	
Sentence:			

2 ▪ How Almost Anyone Can Become a Millionaire: Simple Rules for Attaining Future Wealth

Vocabulary Preview

attaining (ə tān'iŋ): gaining through effort; accomplishing; achieving

substantial (səb stan'shəl): considerable; ample; large

virtually (vʉr'chōō ə lē): in effect, although not in fact; for all practical purposes [*virtually identical*]

subsistence (səb sis'təns): means of support or livelihood; often, specif., the barest means in terms of food, clothing, and shelter needed to sustain life

fritter (frit'ər): to waste (money, time, etc.) bit by bit on petty things; usually with *away*

compound interest (käm'pound in'trist): interest paid on both the principal and the accumulated unpaid interest

forgo (fôr gō'): to do without; abstain from; give up

frivolous (friv'ə ləs): of little value or importance; trifling; trivial

availing (ə vāl'iŋ): taking advantage of (an opportunity, etc.); utilizing

frugal (frōō'gəl): not wasteful; not spending freely or unnecessarily; thrifty; economical

incentive (in sent'iv): something that stimulates one to take action, work harder, etc.; stimulus; encouragement

diligence (dil'ə jəns): the quality of being hardworking, conscientious; careful; persevering

cited (sīt'id): referred to or mentioned by way of example, proof, or precedent

amass (ə mas'): to accumulate (esp. wealth)

derisive (di rī'siv, -ziv): ridiculing

perseverance (pʉr'sə vir'əns): continued, patient effort

plethora (pleth'ə rə): overabundance; excess

retorts (ri tôrts'): replies or responses

validated (val'ə dāt'id): proven to be valid; confirmed the validity of; verified

rationally (rash'ən əl ē): reasonably; not foolishly; sensibly

cat, āte, fäther; pen, ēvil; if, kīte; nō, ôr, fōōd, book; boil, house; up, tʉrn; chief, shell; thick, *the*; zh, treasure; ŋ, sing; ə for *a* in *about*; ' as in *able* (ā'b'l)

Preread

Preview the following selection (pp. 36–42) by reading the title and the headings. Answer the following questions without looking back at the selection.

1. What is the subject?

   _____

2. What is the main idea (the main thing the author is saying about the subject)?

   _____

   _____

3. Take a moment to think about building wealth. Think about what you know, what you don't know, and what you might find out from reading the selection. Make up three questions that might be answered by reading it.

   a. _____

   b. _____

   c. _____

Read

Read the selection without underlining.

Write your starting time here: _____

◆ *How Almost Anyone Can Become a Millionaire: Simple Rules for Attaining Future Wealth*

Richard B. McKenzie and Dwight R. Lee

Too many people in America believe that the rich got their wealth in ways that are not open to most people. The rich inherited most of their wealth, or they were born with special talents—such as singing, acting, or playing sports—or they just happened to be lucky.

Inheriting money, being a star in the National Basketball Association, and winning the lottery are ways of getting rich. But these are not the ways most people get rich in America, and it is a costly mistake to believe they are. Most rich people in America got rich because they chose to do so, and they pursued a path to wealth that is wide open to most of the rest of us. Becoming rich is not particularly difficult.

The rules for acquiring substantial wealth are few, simple, and proven. For most Americans, becoming rich (defined, let's say, by having a net worth of $1 million) is in fact largely a matter of choice.

Starting Out

The first rule for becoming rich is to have a reasonable income base. Few people who have only subsistence-level income can expect to ever be rich because they must devote themselves entirely to survival, which means they can't save and their wealth can't grow. But most Americans have reasonable income virtually by the fact of their birth. By world standards, most Americans start with a reasonable income base from which they can save, invest, and build their net worth. Even poor Americans have more than the subsistence-income levels of people in Ethiopia and many other countries.

How can an ordinary American with a modest annual income become rich? One surefire method is to live modestly—if not close to poverty—and save a substantial portion of one's earned income. This is precisely the route most rich people have taken to their good fortunes. For most Americans of modest or above-modest means, the savings will eventually make for a substantial net worth—and an income level that will be the envy of those who have chosen to fritter away their incomes on compact discs, cigarettes, and new cars. Indeed, a modest and continuous saving plan started early in life can ensure wealth at retirement.

As a simple illustration, suppose that a newly minted 22-year-old college graduate, with a starting salary of $30,000 a year, salts away a mere $2,000 the first year (and only the first year) on his or her first job (for a saving rate of 6.6%).

If this person could only achieve a 10% compounded rate of return (which is approximately equal to the appreciation of the stock market over the last half century), then his or her one-time $2,000 investment would reach $194,000 at 70—not bad compared with what most retirees have. With a compounded return of only 6% the investment would reach just under $33,000 at age 70. The investor would not then be rich at age 70, but neither would he or she have sacrificed much in consumer goods along the way, since the calculations are based on a one-time saving of only $2,000. Indeed, the person's sacrifice would have been zero during every year of his or her career other than that very first year.

The Power of Compound Interest

The second rule for becoming rich is to take the power of compound interest seriously and do so very early in life. An obvious reason many Americans are not rich is that they save little or wait until late in life to take saving seriously, and then they are not able to achieve a big return on their investments. They end up their careers with modest means because they resisted the opportunities to live modestly along the way.

If someone resisted the temptation to consume away all earnings and saved more aggressively but still modestly—for example, $2,000 a year from age 22 until retirement—the investment would mount more rapidly. If the investor were able to get 10% annual return, the nest egg would exceed $2.1 million at 70. If the return were only 6%, the retirement fund would still be well over a half million dollars upon retirement at 70—many times the net worth of the typical retired American today.

Reasonable raises in one's pay and regular saving of 10% would run the wealth to extraordinary levels at retirement. Suppose that a college graduate's first job paid $30,000 a year and that over the course of the student's career he or she gets raises that average 2% a year (after adjusting for inflation). The person's annual income would be about $77,600 at age 70. The person would not be "rich" based on salary alone, but he or she could be very rich, assuming the person saved 10% of each year's salary. Even at a rate of return of 6% on investments, the person's wealth would be $1.1 million at age 70. At a 10% compounded rate of return, it would be $3.9 million; at 15%, $21.7 million. This person would be "rich" by any standard.

Save Consistently

The third rule for being rich is to save a lot and do it consistently and, again, from an early age. Many Americans have simply been unwilling to forgo the good life along the way. They were unwilling to resist expensive cars and cigarettes.

Bad habits add up in terms of lost wealth: A retired person who smoked two packs of cigarettes a day since college graduation may have spent $547 a year on cigarettes. If the money that literally went up in smoke had been invested, the person's retirement fund would obviously have been much greater. At age 70, the smoker's retirement fund would have been almost $150,000 greater with a rate of return of 6% and an eye-popping $3.4 million greater at 15%.

Spend Carefully

The fourth rule for being rich is to avoid "irresistible" (meaning frivolous) temptations. We are not saying that all people must lead a pure and joyless life. We mean only to point out that the great majority of those 4% of Americans who have $1 million in net worth achieved it in part by controlling their pleasures—for example, by buying less-expensive cars so they could build up their savings.

Education Builds Wealth

The first auxiliary rule for becoming rich is to stay in school or, if out of school, go back to school. Of course, this presumes that students will do more than "tread water" while in school; it presumes they will learn something worth the time and effort.

Contrary to all the talk about the rising costs of education, it has never been easier for Americans to get an education. Public schools are free for the taking. College costs have been rising steadily in real terms and relative to family income levels for more than a decade, but the rate of return on a college education has also been rising, making the investment a good deal. (This explains why more and more Americans are availing themselves of higher education opportunities and remain willing to pay higher prices.) Furthermore, the cost of self-education has surely fallen with the decreases in the prices of books and a multitude of sources of knowledge and information available on CD-ROMs and the Internet.

Select a Career for Wealth

The second auxiliary rule for becoming rich is to pick your education carefully. Teachers can expect to earn half as much over their careers as engineers, so teachers will find getting rich tougher than engineers. History and music professors can expect to earn less than accounting professors. For that matter, history and music professors can expect to earn a lot less than their students who major in business. That means that to become rich some people with lots of degrees will have to be more frugal than those people with few degrees.

Invest in Marriage

The third auxiliary rule is to marry someone with an equal or higher education, and then stay married. By itself, marriage seems to provide a stable institutional setting that promotes greater earnings, which affords greater savings. Married couples not only earn more than single people, they also economize on the costs of running their households, which allows them to save and invest at higher rates. Moreover, the binding legal contract at the foundation of marriage, which reflects the couple's personal commitments to each other, gives them an added economic incentive to invest in the joint assets of the union.

Two people simple living together without a binding contract between them must worry if they agree to invest in assets for their mutual benefit (a house, farm, business, car, or other durable goods). If one person walks away, the other person has limited claims on that partner's income stream to cover the debt on the assets. Breaking up is simply harder to do for married couples, a fact that gives each partner additional claims on the other. Hence, married couples should be expected, as a rule, to build up more assets than two single people or couples simply living together, and this is precisely what researchers have found and survey data show.

Since people with better educations tend to earn more money, it stands to reason that most educated Americans can assure they achieve the ranks of the rich by marrying someone who is similarly educated, thus guaranteeing a family income level that will allow for substantial annual savings. Of course, staying married ensures that past savings will not be used to finance the legal costs of divorce or to support two households. Divorce is a gateway to poverty for many Americans, especially women with children.

Rewards of Hard Work

The fourth auxiliary rule for becoming rich is simple: Be willing and able to work for a living. Diligence still pays, obviously, given that household incomes rise markedly with the number of workers in them.

Households with one breadwinner take home on average nearly 70% more than households with none, and households with two earners have incomes that are 80% higher than households with one earner (and three times the incomes of households with no earners). And more of the added income from hard work can be saved with greater ease and with the power of compound interest in mind. Of course, one of the most fundamental justifications for hard work is that it reduces the need for frugality and denial in the wealth-accumulation process.

Wealth-Building Takes Time

The fifth auxiliary rule for becoming rich is to be able to work with some diligence and to work and save for a long time.

People must not expect to become rich early in life. It's understandable why most people are in their 50s before they become rich: It takes time for savings to accumulate and for the power of compound interest to work.

Give Value to Others

The sixth auxiliary rule for becoming rich is to do something of value for a large number of people. The late Wal-Mart founder Sam Walton and Microsoft founder and chairman Bill Gates are often cited for having amassed vast fortunes, sometimes with a derisive tone, as if they took their wealth from others. What should be noted is that Walton and Gates achieved their fortunes in a well-worn way, by providing their customers with value for the dollars collected. They accumulated a lot of wealth by adding to the well-being of large numbers of other Americans. Very likely, the collective increase in the wealth of Wal-Mart and Microsoft customers has, over the years, been far greater than the increase in Walton's and Gates's personal wealth.

Take Some Risks

The final auxiliary rule for becoming rich is to take some risks. Investments can go sour, but for young people, the risk of an investment is moderated by the long period over which the investment will be in place. Young people can ride out the temporary and expected ups and downs in the stock market. The fact that people are now living longer has reduced the risk of investment. Moreover, there has never been a time in which the problems of risk could be more minimized. This is because there has never been a time when people could more easily build a portfolio of varied assets that neutralize the problems of not knowing exactly which investments will pay off.

Not too many decades ago, Americans could invest only in a few important assets: their own human capital, their houses, and a few stocks and bonds. Now, however, in addition to the old investment outlets, they can invest in a wide range of stocks and bonds through mutual funds. Indeed, they can buy the entire stock market by way of index mutual funds (which buy shares of all companies in the Standard & Poor's stock index, for example). They can also diversify their portfolios by buying shares in a host of different mutual funds (close to 8,000 at last count), many of which are focused on foreign investments.

It It Really So Simple To Become Rich?

The process of becoming rich is far more complex than our rules suggest. Becoming rich normally takes decades and a lot of hard work. Above all, for most Americans it takes sacrifice, dedication, and perseverance. Some likely objections to our rules include:

Most people don't have the incomes to save what is required to become rich.

Our estimates of wealth growth are much too unrealistic.

The world is filled with too many temptations carefully cultivated by a plethora of mean-spirited multinational corporations.

A lot of people are unlucky, with lives full of problems that range from business failures to expensive spells of poor health to unemployment.

The list of retorts could easily be extended, and they may help explain why more people aren't rich. But these reasons for not becoming rich are beside our central point, which is that devising a strategy for becoming rich is not as complicated or unattainable as many Americans seem to believe.

From our perspective, becoming rich (or richer) is really a matter of choice. Opportunities to do so abound. Our point is validated by the hundreds of thousands or millions of people who have achieved wealth starting with only modest means. At the same time, they have eased the lives of others because they have invested and contributed to the wealth of the country while they have done well for themselves.

Recognizing that you can choose to become rich does not mean that you should do so. Choosing to become rich requires sacrifices that many people have quite rationally chosen not to make. One can lead a life rich in satisfaction and accomplishment without becoming rich financially, and nothing we write here is meant to suggest otherwise. The distinction we wish to stress is more fundamental: It is one thing to make a conscious choice not to pursue great wealth and another not to know the choice exists. Even if you decide that becoming rich is not the right choice for you, understanding how to become rich can help you determine, and realize, the best financial goal for you.

2500 words

Write your ending time here:_____

Subtract your starting time: _____

Total time: _____

Check the Rate Chart on p. 462 to find out how many words per minute you have read, and then record your score on the Reading Efficiency Progress Chart on p. 463.

Analyze What You Read

Make Graphic Organizers

Fill in the following outline.

I. Rules for attaining future wealth

   A. _____

   B. _____

   C. _____

   D. _____

II. Auxiliary rules for becoming rich

   A. _____

   B. _____

   C. _____

   D. _____

   E. _____

   F. _____

   G. _____

Remember What's Important

1. To prepare for a Comprehension Check, memorize the outline. Test yourself or have someone test you on the rules for attaining wealth. Keep testing until you think you can remember everything you need to know. If necessary, review *How to Answer an Essay Question* on pp. 31–32.

2. To prepare for a Vocabulary Check, make flash cards as described on p. 12 for each of the words in the Vocabulary Preview that you do not know. Test yourself or have someone test you until you think you can remember them.

Make Use of What You Read

When you are ready, complete the Comprehension Check on p. 343 and the Vocabulary Check on p. 345. Do them from memory, without looking back at the book or your notes.

Evaluate Your Active Critical Thinking Skills

After your tests have been graded, record your scores on the Progress Chart, p. 456, and answer the questions on the Evaluation Checklist on p. 457.

Vocabulary Skills Review

For explanation
see pp. 9–11

Dictionary: Confused Words

Here are dictionary entries for three pairs of words that are commonly confused. Fill in the blanks with the correct word from the pair that precedes each group of sentences.

cite (sīt) *vt.* **cit'ed, cit'ing** [ME *citen* < OFr *citer,* to summon < L *citare,* to arouse, summon < *ciere,* to put into motion, rouse < IE base **kei-* > Gr *kinein,* to move, OE *hatan,* to command] **1.** to summon to appear before a court of law **2.** to quote (a passage, book, speech, writer, etc.) **3.** to refer to or mention as by way of example, proof, or precedent ☆**4.** to mention in a CITATION (sense 5) **5.** [Archaic] to stir to action; arouse *–n* [Colloq.] CITATION (sense 3) **–cit'able** or **cite'able** *adj.*

site (sīt) *n.* [ME < L *situs,* position, situation < pp. of *sinere,* to put down, permit, allow < IE base **sei-,* to cast out, let fall: see SIDE] **1.** a piece of land considered from the standpoint of its use for some specified purpose [a good *site* for a town] **2.** the place where something is, was, or is to be; location or scene [the *site* of a battle] *–vt.* **sit'ed, sit'ing** to locate or position on a site

1. If you break a traffic law, the police may _____ you.

2. The usual _____ for a fortified castle was at the top of a hill.

af•fect[1] (ə fekt'; *for* n. 2, af'ekt') *vt.* [ME *affecten* < L *affectare,* to strive after < *affectus,* pp. of *afficere,* to influence, attack < *ad-,* to + *facere,* DO[1]] **1.** to have an effect on; influence; produce a change in [bright light *affects* the eyes] **2.** to move or stir the emotions of [his death *affected* us deeply] *–n.* **1.** [Obs.] a disposition or tendency **2.** [Ger *affekt* < L *affectus,* state of mind or body: see the *v.*] *Psychol. a)* an emotion or feeling attached to an idea, object, etc. *b)* in general, emotion or emotional response **–af•fect'able** *adj.*

ef•fect (e fekt', i-; *often* ē-, ə-) *n.* [ME < OFr (& L) < L *effectus,* orig., pp. of *efficere,* to bring to pass, accomplish < *ex-,* out + *facere,* DO[1]] **1.** anything brought about by a cause or agent; result **2.** the power or ability to bring about results; efficacy [a law of little *effect*] **3.** influence or action on something [the drug had a cathartic *effect*] **4.** general meaning; purport [he spoke to this *effect*] **5.** *a)* the impression produced on the mind of the observer or hearer, as by artistic design or manner of speaking, acting, etc. [to do something just for *effect*] *b*) something, as a design, aspect of nature, etc., that produces a particular impression [striking cloud *effects*] *c*) a scientific phenomenon [the Doppler *effect*] **6.** the condition or fact of being operative or in force [the law goes into *effect* today] **7.** [*pl.*] belongings; property [household *effects*] *–vt.* to bring about; produce as a result; cause; accomplish [to *effect* a compromise] **–give effect to** to put into practice; make operative **–in effect 1.** in result; actually; in fact **2.** in essence; virtually **3.** in operation; in force **–take effect** to begin to produce results; become operative **–to the effect** with the purport or meaning **–ef•fect'er** *n.*

1. The film had a powerful _____ on its viewers.

2. Her _____ seemed strange; she laughed when most people

   would have cried.

3. Some say that garlic has an antibiotic _____.

4. Career and family decisions that we make as young adults can

   _____ the rest of our lives.

5. It will take about thirty minutes until the drug takes _____.

prin•ci•pal (prin'sə pəl) *adj.* [OFr < L *principalis* < *princeps*: see PRINCE] **1.** first in rank, authority, importance, degree, etc. **2.** that is or has to do with PRINCIPAL (*n.* 3) *–n.* **1.** a principal person or thing; specif., *a*) a chief; head *b*) a governing or presiding officer, specif. of a school *c*) a main actor or performer *d*) either of the combatants in a duel **2.** *a*) any of the main end rafters of a roof, supporting the purlins *b*) a roof truss **3.** *Finance a*) the amount of a debt, investment, etc. minus the interest, or on which interest is computed *b*) the face value of a stock or bond *c*) the main body of an estate, etc., as distinguished from income **4.** *Law a*) a person who employs another to act as his agent *b*) the person primarily responsible for an obligation *c*) a person who commits a crime or is present as an abettor to it (cf. ACCESSORY) **5.** *Music a*) any of the principal open stops of an organ *b*) the soloist in a concert *c*) the first player of any section of orchestral instruments except the first violins *d*) the subject of a fugue (opposed to ANSWER) *–SYN.* CHIEF **–prin'ci•pally** *adv.* **–prin'ci•pal•ship'** *n.*

prin•ci•ple (prin'sə pəl) *n.* [ME, altered < MFr *principe* < *principium*: see prec.] **1.** the ultimate source, origin, or cause of something **2.** a natural or original tendency, faculty, or endowment **3.** a fundamental truth, law, doctrine, or motivating force, upon which others are based [moral *principles*] **4.** *a*) a rule of conduct, esp. of right conduct *b*) such rules collectively *c*) adherence to them;

integrity, uprightness [a man of *principle*] **5.** an essential element, constituent, or quality, esp. one that produces a specific effect [the active *principle* of a medicine] **6.** *a*) the scientific law that explains a natural action [the *principle* of cell division] *b*) the method of a thing's operation [the *principle* of a gasoline engine is internal combustion] –**in principle** theoretically or in essence –**on principle** because of or according to a principle

1. When you have extra money you can use it to reduce your mortgage

   _____ .

2. Even though I would have profited by the deal, I rejected it on

   _____ .

For explanation see pp. 6–7

Pronunciation Practice

For practice with the pronunciation guide, translate the names of these famous comedians into English spelling.

cat, āte, fäther; pen, ēvil; if, kīte; nō, ôr, fōōd, book; boil, house; up, tʉrn; chief, shell; thick, *the*; zh, treasure; ŋ, sing; ə for *a* in *about*; ' as in *able* (ā′b'l)

1. wōōp′ē gōld′bʉrg

   _____

2. rōz an′

   _____

3. jer′ē sīn′feld

   _____

4. rä′bin wil′yəmz

   _____

5. jā le′nō

   _____

6. ed′ē mʉr′fē

   _____

For explanation see pp. 2–4

Context Clues

Use the context of each sentence to figure out the meaning of the italicized word. **Do not use a dictionary.** Circle the letter of the best definition, and then write in the type of clue: definition, contrast, example, or experience.

1. The girl had to face her mother's *wrath* when it was discovered that she had taken her mother's diamond earrings without permission.

   a. joy   b. anger   c. boredom   d. laughter

   Type of clue: _____

2. Many scientists dream of receiving the *prestigious* Nobel Prize.

   a. impressive   b. depressing   c. cheap   d. expensive

   Type of clue: _____

3. *Norse* legends came from Norway and Iceland.

   a. French and Italian   b. Mexican and Guatemalan

   c. Norwegian and Icelandic   d. South African

   Type of clue: _____

4. To a Frenchman, well-prepared snails are a great delicacy, but many Americans look at a dish of snails with *aversion*.

   a. hunger   b. enjoyment   c. joy   d. disgust

   Type of clue: _____

5. "A penny saved is a penny earned" is an *adage* that recommends thrift.

   a. law   b. saying   c. war   d. fairy tale

   Type of clue: _____

6. A *neuropsychologist* is a psychologist who studies the nervous system.

   a. physician who studies the respiratory system

   b. researcher who studies the senses

   c. fortune teller who studies palmistry

   d. psychologist who studies the nervous system

   Type of clue: _____

7. Ordinary people believe many things without much proof, but scientists are trained to be more *skeptical*.

   a. doubting   b. trusting   c. stupid   d. intelligent

   Type of clue: _____

8. If you hire a personal trainer to get you in shape, you can expect a *rigorous* program of diet and exercise.

   a. easy   b. simple   c. hard   d. harmful

   Type of clue: _____

9. If you want to become a beautician, you study *cosmetology.*

   a. the work of a beautician   b. the work of a dentist

   c. the work of a nurse   d. the work of a dietician

   Type of clue: _____

10. People in certain professions are often assumed to be *unscrupulous:* for example, politicians, lawyers, and auto dealers.

    a. honest   b. caring   c. highly moral   d. not very moral

    Type of clue: _____

3 The Many Miracles of Mark Hicks

Vocabulary Preview

portfolios (pôrt fō′lē ōz′): selections of representative works, as of artists

quadriplegic (kwäd′rə plē′jik): one who is totally paralyzed from the neck down

intrigued (in trēgd′): interested

severed (sev′ərd): cut in two; divided

disarming (dis är′miŋ): removing suspicion, fear, or hostility

impassioned (im pash′ənd): filled with strong feeling

documentary (däk′yə men′tə rē): a motion picture or a television show that presents factual material in a dramatic way

excruciating (iks krōō′shē āt′iŋ): intensely painful

transpose (trans pōz′): to transfer or shift the position of

lithographs (lith′ə grafs′): prints made by a method that uses the repulsion between grease and water

wry (rī): humorous in a twisted or sarcastic way

aspirated (as′pə rāt′id): sucked or drawn in, as by inhaling

prestigious (pres tij′əs): having the power to impress as the result of having success or wealth

integrity (in teg′rə tē): the quality or state of being of high moral principle; uprightness, honesty, and sincerity

bantered (ban′tərd): joked or teased good-naturedly

cat, āte, fäther; pen, ēvil; if, kīte; nō, ôr, fōōd, book; boil, house; up, turn; chief, shell; thick, *the*; zh, treasure; ŋ, sing; ə for *a* in *about*; ′ as in *able* (ā′b′l)

Preread

STEP 1

Preview the following selection (pp. 50–53) by reading the title and the headings. Answer the following questions without looking back at the selection.

1. What is the subject?

_____

2. What is the main idea (the main thing the author is saying about the subject)?

_____

_____

3. Take a moment to think about what it would be like to be a quadriplegic and an artist. Think about what you know, what you don't know, and what you might find out from reading the selection. Make up three questions.

a. _____

b. _____

c. _____

Read

Read the selection without underlining.

Write your starting time here: _____

◆ *The Many Miracles of Mark Hicks*

Jan Stussy

Eight years ago, I was reviewing the art portfolios of applying students in my studio classroom on the campus of the University of California at Los Angeles. My secretary approached me with a special request from a quadriplegic student who wished to join my class in life drawing. "He draws by holding the pencil in his teeth," she said.

"That's crazy!" I replied. "It's tough enough to learn with skilled hands, but to try to draw with your mouth is . . . impossible. My answer is *No!*"

When I turned back to the portfolios of the waiting students—accepting some and rejecting others on the merits of their ability as draftsmen—my secretary added another student's portfolio to the pile. The work was above average in skill, and the drawings intrigued me. "Yes," I said, "I'll accept this student."

Before I could say another word, the quadriplegic flashed past me in his wheelchair, turned and stopped—facing the suddenly quiet class and a red-faced professor.

I tried not to look at him as I explained to the class (but mostly to him) that the work was going to be very hard for all of them (*especially* him) and now was the time to withdraw if anyone (*anyone!*) had second thoughts. Two students left, but those serious eyes from the wheelchair didn't even blink. I dismissed the class and asked the young man to remain.

In a soft, quiet voice, 23-year-old Mark Hicks told me that when he was 12 he fell from a tree house in his back yard in Manhattan Beach, Calif.

"It was nobody's fault," he said calmly. "I just fell." The accident severed his spinal column, causing permanent paralysis from the neck down.

Mark had drawn before his accident. Slowly, he began to sketch again (and later taught himself to paint with oils) by holding the tools clenched in his teeth. He developed very strong jaw muscles. "If all my muscles were as strong as my jaws," he remarked with disarming good humor, "I could lift up this building."

Perfecting his drawing was, for Mark, like learning to fly. Through it, he could escape from his body into the make-believe world of his mind. He worked with a tutor at home to complete high school, then went to a junior college to major in art and to develop his skill as a draftsman.

Mark did not think of himself as pitiful, so he was not embarrassed. He simply was what he was. He accepted his limitations and worked beyond his capacities, setting an example and inspiring other students. True, I was his teacher—but in a larger sense, he was mine.

His impact on me and the class was so dramatic and useful that I resolved to capture him on film. I wanted to show other people how courage and spirit can achieve great things in spite of all odds. I had never made a film, but if Mark could draw, I could make a movie.

In September 1973 I wrote an impassioned letter to my dean telling him how I wanted to make a short documentary so others could share what we found in Mark. The dean was so moved that he sent a check for $6000 from funds earmarked for special projects. It was the first of many improbable miracles.

Mark knew a student, John Joseph, in the U.C.L.A. cinema department, who wanted to make a film for his senior project. We joined forces.

Four other talented students soon joined us. We rented cameras, tripods, sound equipment and lights, and shot Mark as he lived his life. No real story, no firm plot. We filmed his father getting him out of bed, sitting him in his chair and brushing his teeth. We followed his mother cooking food and feeding it to him. We shot his attendant putting him into his van and driving him to school. We photographed him in my life-drawing class, going to exhibits, parties and back to the hospital.

The high point of the movie came about when my gallery director—unaware that Mark made his pictures with his teeth—saw his paintings and offered to give Mark a one-man exhibition. We followed Mark's van to San Francisco and documented the opening of his show, the reception party and the highly successful exhibit. Mark sat among his pictures enjoying one of the happiest moments of his life. "I reached my goal," he said. "And I did it sitting down."

At that point we ran out of money and film. In our enthusiasm, we had spent the entire $6000 and had shot 64 rolls of expensive color film. Not a dime was left to develop it. It was excruciating to have that huge stack of film and not be able to see what we had done. It was, said Mark, "like being pregnant, forever."

Hat in hand and trembling nervously, I called on Paul Flaherty, chief executive at the Technicolor laboratory. When I told him about Mark and the film project, he offered to develop and print 15 rolls as a charitable gesture. So, I sent 30. If the miracle was going to work, we might just as well go for 30.

About a month later, Flaherty called: "That film is very, very good. Can I meet Mark?"

We wheeled Mark in the next day. After 35 minutes of conversation, Flaherty promised to develop the remaining 34 rolls—again for free. The miracles were holding.

But we were still broke. We had editing to do and sound tapes to transpose and music to score and inserts and titles to make and a final print to get. We needed more money. I wrote a letter describing our project and offering one of Mark's lithographs for a $200 donation, or a set of one of his and one of mine for $500. I mailed it to everyone I ever knew. The money began to roll in, and we went back to work.

When it came time for a title, we recalled a wry observation Mark made in the movie and chose *Gravity Is My Enemy.* (It was perhaps the only enemy he ever had.)

Then the money problem struck again. The rough cut was finished but we needed a major miracle to get the final and expensive print and negative made. We had begged and borrowed from everyone. It looked like the miracles had finally run out.

At that dark moment, Mark died.

He had aspirated some food into his lung while swallowing and was unable to cough it up. It could have happened a dozen times before. But it didn't happen until he had finished his film and seen a rough cut.

Mark was gone, but we had come this far because of him and we could not stop now. We had to show others what he had been. About three weeks after Mark's funeral, I took our scratchy work print to Ray Wagner, then a vice president of M-G-M. Halfway through he turned on the lights and, with tears running down his face, told me he would make a free final print. Mark's miracles were still operating.

We sent the finished film to the prestigious San Francisco Film Festival. To our surprise it took first place in the documentary-films competition,

winning the Golden Gate Award, the top festival prize. This made it auto-
matically eligible to be nominated for an Academy Award—and to our
astonishment, it *was*. Yet another miracle!

Although we knew we hadn't a chance of winning the Oscar, it was
well worth the price of our rented tuxedos for John Joseph and me to
attend the glamorous Academy Awards. As I sat through the opening
presentations my mind drifted back to Mark and how much I wished he
could be sharing the nomination with us. Despite the realities, I really
wanted that Oscar—for Mark and U.C.L.A. and for everyone who had
made the film possible. Most of all, I wanted it to prove to other students
who want to make movies that if you do it with feeling and integrity . . .
you can win.

My mouth was dry as the moment approached for the presentation in
our category. Time passed in slow motion as Kirk Douglas and Raquel
Welch bantered before opening the envelopes. Then I heard Raquel say:
"And the winner is—*Gravity* . . ."

I have no recollection of walking up that long aisle of applauding
movie stars and reaching the podium. I meant to thank everyone, but
I froze.

Then, as in a dream, I heard myself saying, "Just finishing our film was
a miracle—and this award is another. But the greatest miracle of all was
Mark Hicks. He showed us how to live life as a hero. It's Mark's film and
his award. He can't be here tonight; he has left his wheelchair and is running free somewhere in God's Heaven." Then, I took the golden Oscar,
held it over my head and concluded: "Mark, *this* is for you."

1500 words

Write your ending time here:_____

Subtract your starting time: _____

Total time: _____

Check the Rate Chart on p. 462 to find out how many words per minute
you have read, and then record your score on the Reading Efficiency Progress
Chart on p. 463.

Analyze What You Read

Make Graphic Organizers

Although this reading is nonfiction, its structure is like that of a story.
Therefore, we will organize it according to the structure of stories: setting,
characters, plot, and theme. Fill in the chart.

The Many Miracles of Mark Hicks

Setting: (Where and when does the story take place?)	
Characters: (Who is in the story?)	
Plot: (What happens in the story?)	
Theme: (What does the story teach us about life?)	

Remember What's Important

1. To prepare for a Comprehension Check, memorize the chart. Test your-self or have someone test you on the story of Mark Hicks. Keep testing until you think you can remember everything you need to know. If necessary, review *How to Answer an Essay Question* on pp. 31–32.

2. To prepare for a Vocabulary Check, make flash cards as described on p. 12 for each of the words in the Vocabulary Preview that you do not know. Test yourself or have someone test you until you think you can remember them.

Make Use of What You Read

When you are ready, complete the Comprehension Check on p. 347 and the Vocabulary Check on p. 349. Do them from memory, without looking back at the book or your notes.

Evaluate Your Active Critical Thinking Skills

After your tests have been graded, record your scores on the Progress Chart, p. 456, and answer the questions on the Evaluation Checklist on p. 457.

Vocabulary Skills Review

For explanation see pp. 9–11

Dictionary Definitions

For practice in finding the correct meaning of a word in the dictionary, select the correct meaning of each of the following seven words from the reading. Above each entry is a sentence using the word. In the blank before the sentence, put the number of the definition that fits the way the word is used. The abbreviation under each blank tells you which part of speech the word is, so you can more easily find the proper definition.

_____   1. "When I turned <u>back</u> to the portfolios of the waiting students—
adv.   accepting some and rejecting others on the merits of their ability as draftsmen—my secretary added another student's portfolio to the pile."

back (bak) *n.* [< OE. *bæk*] **1.** the rear part of the body from the nape of the neck to the end of the spine. **2.** the backbone **3.** a part that supports or fits the back **4.** the rear part or reverse of anything **5.** *Sports* a player or position behind the front line –*adj.* **1.** at the rear **2.** remote **3.** of or for the past [*back* pay] **4.** backward –*adv.* **1.** at, to, or toward the rear **2.** to or toward a former condition, time, activity, etc. **3.** in reserve or concealment **4.** in return or requital [pay him *back*] –*vt.* **1.** to move backward **2.** to support **3.** to bet on **4.** to provide or be a back for

_____   2. "Before I could say another word, the quadriplegic <u>flashed</u> past
v.   me in his wheelchair, turned and stopped—facing the suddenly quiet class and a red-faced professor."

flash (flash) *vt.* [ME. *flashen,* to splash] **1.** to send out a sudden, brief light **2.** to sparkle **3.** to come or pass suddenly **4.** to send (news, etc.) swiftly –*n.* **1.** a sudden, brief light **2.** a brief moment **3.** a sudden, brief display **4.** a brief news item sent by radio, etc. **5.** a gaudy display –*adj.* happening swiftly or suddenly—**flash′er** *n.*

_____   3. "It's Mark's <u>film</u> and his award."
n.

film (film) *n.* [OE. *filmen*] **1.** a fine, thin skin, coating, etc. **2.** a flexible cellulose material covered with a substance sensitive to light and used in photography **3.** a haze or blur **4.** a motion picture –*vt., vi.* **1.** to cover or be covered as with a film **2.** to photograph or make a motion picture (of)

_____   4. "He developed very <u>strong</u> jaw muscles."
adj.

strong (strôŋ) *adj.* [OE. *strang*] **1.** *a*) physically powerful *b*) healthy; sound **2.** morally or intellectually powerful [a *strong* will] **3.** firm; durable [a *strong* fort] **4.** powerful in wealth, numbers, etc. **5.** of a specified number [troops 50,000 *strong*] **6.** having a powerful effect **7.** intense in degree or quality [*strong* coffee, a *strong* light, *strong* colors, etc.]

_____   5. "He <u>developed</u> very strong jaw muscles."
v.

de•vel•op (di vel′əp) *vt.* [< Fr. *dé-* apart + OFr. *voloper,* to wrap] **1.** to make fuller, bigger, better, etc. **2.** to show or work out by degrees; disclose **3.** *Photog.* to put (a film, etc.) in chemical solutions to make the picture visible **4.** to come into being or activity; occur or happen

_____   6. "He <u>simply</u> was what he was."
adv.

sim•ply (sim′plē) *adv.* **1.** in a simple way **2.** merely [*simply* trying] **3.** completely [*simply* overwhelmed]

_____   7. "The dean was so <u>moved</u> that he sent a check for $6000. . . ."
v.

move (mo͞ov) *vt.* **moved, mov′ing** [< L. *movere*] **1.** to change the place or position of **2.** to set or keep in motion **3.** to cause (*to do, say,* etc.) **4.** to arouse the emotions, etc. of **5.** to propose formally, as in a meeting **6.** to change one's residence **7.** to make progress **8.** to take action **9.** to make a formal application (*for*) **10.** to evacuate: said of the bowels **11.** *Commerce* to be sold: said of goods –*n.* **1.** act of moving **2.** an action toward some goal **3.** *Chess, Checkers,* etc. the act of moving a piece, or one's turn to move

For explanation see pp. 6–7

Pronunciation Practice

For practice with the pronunciation guide, translate these holidays into English spelling.

cat, āte, fäther; pen, ēvil; if, kīte; nō, ôr, fo͞od, book; boil, house; up, tʉrn; chief, shell; thick, *the*; zh, treasure; ŋ, sing; ə for *a* in *about*; ʼ as in *able* (āʹbʼl)

1. sānt paʹtriks dā

   _____

2. valʹən tīnzʹ dā

   _____

3. thə fôr*th*ʹ əv joo līʹ

   _____

4. mə môrʹē əl dā

   _____

5. no͞oʹyirz ēv

   _____

6. fäʹ*th*ərz dā

   _____

For explanation see pp. 4–5, 9

Etymology and Word Parts

By looking at a word's etymology in the dictionary, you can find the meaning of its roots. Here are six words from the reading that contain common roots. The roots, their meanings, and other words that can help you remember the meanings are also provided.

Word	Root	Meaning of Root	Another Word
1. quadriplegic	quad	four	quadrangle
2. request	ques	to ask or to seek	question
3. resolve	solv	to explain	solve
4. impassioned	pass	feeling	passion
5. photographed	photo	of or produced by light	photocopy
6. transpose	pos	put or place	pose

Using these roots, match the following difficult words with their definitions.

_____ 1. quadrennial

_____ 2. inquest

_____ 3. absolve

_____ 4. impassive

_____ 5. photic

_____ 6. juxtapose

a. to free from guilt (explain why someone is not guilty)

b. to put side by side

c. showing or having no feelings

d. having to do with the effect of light upon, or the production of light by, organisms

e. occurring once every four years

f. an official inquiry, usually to seek out the cause of a sudden and unexpected death

4　Superstitions: Just Whistling in the Dark

Vocabulary Preview

irrational (i rash′ə n′l): unreasonable, not logical

philosophers (fi läs′ə fərz): people who study philosophy or the principles of conduct, thought, knowledge, and the nature of the universe

Norse (nôrs): West Scandinavian: Norwegian, Icelandic

wrath (rath): intense anger

rationalized (rash′ən ə līzd′): explained or interpreted; made reasonable

incorruptibility (in′kə rup′tə bil′ə tē): state of being unable to be spoiled or made immoral

consternation (kän′stər nā′shən): great shock or fear

episode (ep′ə sōd′): event or series of events complete in itself

distorted (dis tôrt′id): twisted out of shape; misrepresented

aversion (ə vʉr′zhən): strong dislike

cat, āte, fäther; pen, ēvil; if, kīte; nō, ôr, fo͞od, book; boil, house; up, tʉrn; chief, shell; thick, *the*; zh, treasure; ŋ, sing; ə for *a* in *about*; ′ as in *able* (ā′b′l)

Preread

Preview the following selection (pp. 60–62) by reading the title and the headings. Run your eyes quickly down the page to get a general idea of what is under each heading. Answer the following questions without looking back at the selection.

1. What is the subject?

_____

2. What is the main idea (the main thing the author is saying about the subject)?

_____

3. Take a moment to think about superstitions. Think about what you know, what you don't know, and what you might find out from reading the selection. Make up three questions that might be answered by reading it.

a. _____

b. _____

c. _____

Read

Read the selection without underlining.

Write your starting time here: _____

◆ *Superstitions: Just Whistling in the Dark*

Don Boxmeyer

Why do you suppose the boss is so grumpy?
"Dunno. Maybe he got up on the wrong side of the bed."
"He'd probably feel better if you got him a cup of coffee."
"Right. Knock on wood."

One of these fellows is superstitious. He probably goes out of his way to avoid meeting black cats. He doesn't walk under ladders, step on sidewalk cracks or open umbrellas indoors, and he worries a lot if he breaks a mirror.

That makes him a trifle silly and just like almost everybody else.

A superstition is a belief based wholly on fear and not in harmony with any known law of science. How do you know the number 13 is unlucky? You just know it. How do you know that spilling salt is unlucky? It just is.

Irrational? Yes and no.

Superstitions, wrote Rabbi D. R. Brasch in his book, "How Did It Begin?" have reasons, backgrounds and practical explanations. They belonged to the social life of both the civilized and the savage.

Here are some examples.

The Unlucky Number 13

In some European countries, you can't live in house No. 13. It does not exist. No. 12 is followed by No. 12½ and then No. 14. Many office buildings in this country skip the 13th floor. Some airlines and sports arenas omit 13 as a seat number. A true triskaidekaphobiac would not start a journey on the 13th of any month (on Friday the 13th he stays right in bed with the covers pulled way up over his head), will not buy or use 13 of anything, will not wear a number 13 on a uniform or eat with 12 others.

Why? Historically, 13 represents the number of men present at the Last Supper. Greek philosophers and mathematicians scorned the number 13 as being "imperfect," and in Norse mythology, 12 gods were present when the evil spirit Loki busted a party at a good address in Valhalla and killed Balder, a very popular god.

Walking Under Ladders

This superstition has a practical application. You could get a bucket of paint on the head. But custom says if you walk under a ladder, the wrath of the gods will be on you in any case and what you ought to do is quickly cross your fingers and make a wish.

Historians have rationalized that the ladder, leaning against a wall, forms a triangle signifying the Holy Trinity. To pass through such sacred space is a punishable offense. It's flat dangerous to play with such supernatural forces; a bucket of paint on the head is nothing compared to what could be in store.

Getting out of Bed on the Wrong Side

It is written that to get out of bed on the left side is to subject your day to misfortune and misery. You are supposed to rise from the right and place your right foot on the floor first. If you err, go back to bed until you can do it correctly. This superstition has to do with the ancient belief that right was right and left was wrong.

Spilling Salt

If this happens to you, you're supposed to take a pinch of salt and toss it over your left shoulder into the face of the devil.

This superstition is rooted in the ancient and biblical importance of salt. Salt purifies; hence it became the symbol of incorruptibility. Salt on the table became the emblem of justice, and to upset it became a forewarning of injustice.

In a famous Last Supper painting by Leonardo da Vinci, the faces of Jesus and the Apostles vividly show consternation and grief. Why? Historians say because someone just dumped the salt shaker over.

Who did it? Judas, of course. But there is no confirmation of this episode; Brasch said da Vinci merely used the old superstition to dramatize his painting.

Breaking a Mirror

This is good for seven years of bad luck or it could cause a death in the family. If a mirror breaks, legend instructs you to get the pieces out of the house posthaste and bury them in the ground.

Before the invention of mirrors, man gazed at his reflection in pools, ponds and lakes. If the image was distorted, disaster was sure to strike. (Sometimes a sneaky enemy would ruin his foe's day by pitching a pebble into the water.)

Gradually water gave way to shiny metal and then glass, but man still was convinced any injury to the reflection would be visited upon the real thing, just as he thought that . . . piercing the eyes of an enemy in a picture would cause the enemy to go blind. And the seven years? It is thought that the figure stems from Roman belief that a man's body physically rejuvenated itself every seven years and he became, in effect, a new man.

Meeting a Black Cat

Custom dictates that if your path is crossed by a black cat, you're really going to be in for it unless you return home immediately.

To the Egyptians, the cat was a god and anyone who killed one was punished. Come the Middle Ages, however, and the cat was linked to witches and Satan. Everyone knows what happens when you cross the devil.

Whistling

This is a professional superstition; newsmen are not supposed to whistle in the newsroom, and actors do not whistle in the dressing room. It probably goes back to the sailor's deep aversion to whistling except at very special times.

In the days of sail, seamen believed it was possible to call up a storm by the accidental use of magic—like duplicating the noise of wind in the rigging. Whistling on board was to invite bad luck, except when the ship was becalmed, and then only by an expert who would know in which precise direction to send the whistle as an order for wind.

1000 words

Write your ending time here:_____

Subtract your starting time: _____

Total time: _____

Check the Rate Chart on p. 462 to find out how many words per minute you have read, and then record your score on the Reading Efficiency Progress Chart on p. 463.

Analyze What You Read

Make Graphic Organizers

Fill in the following chart.

Superstition	Background/Explanation
1. The unlucky number 13	
2. Walking under ladders	
3. Getting out of bed on the wrong side	
4. Spilling salt	
5. Breaking a mirror	
6. Meeting a black cat	
7. Whistling	

Remember What's Important

1. To prepare for a Comprehension Check, memorize the chart. Test yourself or have someone test you on the superstitions. Keep testing until you think you can remember everything you need to know. If necessary, review *How to Answer an Essay Question* on pp. 31–32.

2. To prepare for a Vocabulary Check, make flash cards as described on p. 12 for each of the words in the Vocabulary Preview that you do not know. Test yourself or have someone test you until you think you can remember them.

Make Use of What You Read

When you are ready, complete the Comprehension Check on p. 351 and the Vocabulary Check on p. 353. Do them from memory, without looking back at the book or your notes.

Evaluate Your Active Critical Thinking Skills

After your tests have been graded, record your scores on the Progress Chart, p. 456, and answer the questions on the Evaluation Checklist on p. 457.

Vocabulary Skills Review

| For explanation see pp. 7–9 |

Parts of Speech

For each word below and on the next page, write its part of speech. Then change it to the new part of speech. Write a sentence using the new word. Use a dictionary if you need help.

Word	Part of speech	New part of speech	New word
1. rationalize		adjective	
Sentence:			
2. aversion		adjective	
Sentence:			

Word	Part of speech	New part of speech	New word
3. distort		noun	
Sentence:			
4. philosopher		verb	
Sentence:			
5. episode		adjective	
Sentence:			
6. irrational		adverb	
Sentence:			
7. incorruptibility		adjective	
Sentence:			

For explanation see pp. 4–5

Word Parts

Here are some common word parts that will help you with this exercise.

Prefixes	Roots	Suffixes
in, im, ir = not	*tort* = twist	*ate* = become
dis = not, apart, very	*phil* = love	*ology* = study of
re = again, back	*sophos* = wise	*ible* = able to be
super = over, beyond	*juven* = young	*er* = one who
a = away	*myth* = legend	*al* = like, of
com, con, cor = together, very, with	*rupt* = break, spoil	*tion, ion* = act of, state of
	vert, vers = turn	
	firm = strong	
	rat = think	

Using these word parts as hints, match the following words with their definitions.

_____ 1. irrational

_____ 2. philosopher

_____ 3. mythology

_____ 4. supernatural

_____ 5. incorruptible

_____ 6. confirmation

_____ 7. distort

_____ 8. rejuvenate

_____ 9. aversion

a. can't be broken down or morally destroyed

b. beyond the natural or ordinary

c. twist

d. feeling of wanting to turn away because of dislike

e. act of proving or making something stronger

f. using illogical thinking

g. a person who studies because of a love of wisdom

h. legends that can be studied

i. to make young again

For explanation see pp. 2–4

Context Clues

Use the context of each sentence to figure out the meaning of the italicized word. **Do not use a dictionary.** Circle the letter of the best definition, and then write in the type of clue: definition, contrast, example, or experience.

1. Fear of public speaking is the most common *phobia,* said to be ahead of even the fear of death.

   a. leisure hobby   b. contagious illness   c. unreasonable fear

   d. superstition

   Type of clue:_____

2. *Senility,* or mental deterioration in old age, can be an inherited condition.

   a. cancerous tumors   b. viral diseases   c. birth defects

   d. mental deterioration in old age

   Type of clue:_____

3. People who want to see a very popular movie when it first comes out may have to stand in a *queue* that goes all the way around the block.

   a. line   b. race   c. contest   d. competition

   Type of clue:_____

4. The period of peace and stability was welcome after years of political *turmoil*.

   a. calm   b. upset   c. boredom   d. honesty

   Type of clue: _____

5. A *social psychologist* studies individuals in relation to groups.

   a. one who studies the brain

   b. one who studies individuals in relation to groups

   c. one who studies groups in relation to each other

   d. one who studies national identities

   Type of clue: _____

6. Although South Africa is moving in the direction of greater equality, there is still a huge contrast between the poverty of the majority and the *affluence* of the white minority.

   a. poverty   b. fear   c. wealth   d. votes

   Type of clue: _____

7. Well-known *Hispanic* artists are Velasquez and Orozco.

   a. Spanish or Latin American   b. Greek or Roman

   c. English or Irish   d. Scandinavian

   Type of clue: _____

8. A good essay is *concise* rather than long and rambling.

   a. confusing   b. complicated and boring   c. medium-sized

   d. short and clear

   Type of clue: _____

9. Some kidnappers *abduct* children for ransom; others kidnap them to hurt them.

   a. adopt   b. abuse   c. teach   d. kidnap

   Type of clue: _____

10. Security guards have to be *vigilant*.

    a. honest   b. well paid   c. watchful   d. asleep

    Type of clue: _____

5　　Saved

Vocabulary Preview

convey (kən vā′): carry; communicate by words or actions

articulate (är tik′yə lit): able to express oneself easily and clearly

hustler (hus′lər): [Slang] a person who makes money dishonestly

functional (fuŋk′shə nəl): performing or able to perform a function

emulate (em′yə lāt′): try to equal or surpass

motivation (mōt′ə vā′shən): some inner drive that causes a person to do something or act in a certain way; goal

riffling (rif′liŋ): leafing rapidly through (a book, etc.)

immensely (i mens′lē): greatly; hugely

inevitable (in ev′i tə bəl): cannot be avoided or evaded; certain to happen

circulation (sʉr′kyo͞o lā′shən): the passing of something, as money or news, from person to person or place to place

rehabilitation (re′hə bil′ə tā′shən): bringing back or restoring a person to a constructive role in society

devour (di vour′): to take in greedily with the mouth, eyes, ears, or mind

isolation (i′sə lā′shən): separation; privacy; being alone

engrossing (in grōs′iŋ): taking one's entire attention; very interesting

feigned (fānd): pretended

vistas (vis′təz): views

dormant (dôr′mənt): latent or sleeping

confers (kən fʉrz′): gives or bestows

afflicting (ə flikt′iŋ): causing pain or suffering to someone

alma mater (äl′mə mät′ər): school that one attended

cat, āte, fäther; pen, ēvil; if, kīte; nō, ôr, fo͞od, book; boil, house; up, tʉrn; chief, shell; thick, *the*; zh, treasure; ŋ, sing; ə for *a* in *about*; ′ as in *able* (ā′b′l)

Preread

STEP 1

Preview the following selection (pp. 69–72) by reading the title and the first sentence of each paragraph. Answer the following questions without looking back at the selection.

1. What is the subject?

2. What is the main idea (the main thing the author is saying about the subject)?

_____

3. Take a moment to think about Malcolm X and learning to read and write. Think about what you know, what you don't know, and what you might find out from reading the selection. Make up three questions.

   a. _____

   b. _____

   c. _____

Read

Read the selection without underlining.

Write your starting time here: _____

◆ *Saved*

Malcolm X

I became increasingly frustrated at not being able to express what I wanted to convey in letters that I wrote, especially those to Mr. Elijah Muhammad. In the street, I had been the most articulate hustler out there—I had commanded attention when I said something. But now, trying to write simple English, I not only wasn't articulate, I wasn't even functional. How would I sound writing in slang, the way I would say it, something such as, "Look, daddy, let me pull your coat about a cat, Elijah Muhammad—"

Many who today hear me somewhere in person, or on television, or those who read something I've said, will think I went to school far beyond the eighth grade. This impression is due entirely to my prison studies.

It had really begun back in the Charlestown Prison, when Bimbi first made me feel envy of his stock of knowledge. Bimbi had always taken charge of any conversation he was in, and I had tried to emulate him. But every book I picked up had few sentences which didn't contain any-where from one to nearly all of the words that might as well have been in Chinese. When I just skipped those words, of course, I really ended up with little idea of what the book said. So I had come to the Norfolk Prison Colony still going through only book-reading motions. Pretty soon,

I would have quit even these motions, unless I had received the motivation that I did.

I saw that the best thing I could do was get hold of a dictionary—to study, to learn some words. I was lucky enough to reason also that I should try to improve my penmanship. It was sad. I couldn't even write in a straight line. It was both ideas together that moved me to request a dictionary along with some tablets and pencils from the Norfolk Prison Colony school.

I spent two days just riffling uncertainly through the dictionary's pages. I'd never realized so many words existed! I didn't know *which* words I needed to learn. Finally, just to start some kind of action, I began copying.

In my slow, painstaking, ragged handwriting, I copied into my tablet everything printed on that first page, down to the punctuation marks.

I believe it took me a day. Then, aloud, I read back, to myself, everything I'd written on the tablet. Over and over, aloud, to myself, I read my own handwriting.

I woke up the next morning, thinking about those words—immensely proud to realize that not only had I written so much at one time, but I'd written words that I never knew were in the world. Moreover, with a little effort, I also could remember what many of these words meant. I reviewed the words whose meanings I didn't remember. Funny thing, from the dictionary first page right now, that "aardvark" springs to my mind. The dictionary had a picture of it, a long-tailed, long-eared, burrowing African mammal, which lives off termites caught by sticking out its tongue as an anteater does for ants.

I was so fascinated that I went on—I copied the dictionary's next page. And the same experience came when I studied that. With every succeeding page, I also learned of people and places and events from history. Actually the dictionary is like a miniature encyclopedia. Finally the dictionary's A section had filled a whole tablet—and I went on into the B's. That was the way I started copying what eventually became the entire dictionary. It went a lot faster after so much practice helped me to pick up handwriting speed. Between what I wrote in my tablet, and writing letters, during the rest of my time in prison I would guess I wrote a million words.

I suppose it was inevitable that as my word-base broadened, I could for the first time pick up a book and read and now begin to understand what the book was saying. Anyone who has read a great deal can imagine the new world that opened. Let me tell you something: from then until I left that prison, in every free moment I had, if I was not reading in the library, I was reading on my bunk. You couldn't have gotten me out of books with a wedge. Between Mr. Muhammad's teachings, my correspondence, my visitors—usually Ella and Reginald—and my reading of books, months passed without my even thinking about being imprisoned. In fact, up to then, I never had been so truly free in my life.

The Norfolk Prison Colony's library was in the school building. A variety of classes was taught there by instructors who came from such places as Harvard and Boston universities. The weekly debates between inmate teams were also held in the school building. You would be astonished to know how worked up convict debaters and audiences would get over subjects like "Should Babies Be Fed Milk?"

Available on the prison library's shelves were books on just about every general subject. Much of the big private collection that Parkhurst had willed to the prison was still in crates and boxes in the back of the library—thousands of old books. Some of them looked ancient: covers faded, old-time parchment-looking binding. Parkhurst, I've mentioned, seemed to have been principally interested in history and religion. He had the money and the special interest to have a lot of books that you wouldn't have in general circulation. Any college library would have been lucky to get that collection.

As you can imagine, especially in a prison where there was heavy emphasis on rehabilitation, an inmate was smiled upon if he demonstrated an unusually intense interest in books. There was a sizable number of well-read inmates, especially the popular debaters. Some were said by many to be practically walking encyclopedias. They were almost celebrities. No university would ask any student to devour literature as I did when this new world opened to me, of being able to read and *understand.*

I read more in my room than in the library itself. An inmate who was known to read a lot could check out more than the permitted maximum number of books. I preferred reading in the total isolation of my own room.

When I had progressed to really serious reading, every night at about ten p.m. I would be outraged with the "lights out." It always seemed to catch me right in the middle of something engrossing.

Fortunately, right outside my door was a corridor light that cast a glow into my room. The glow was enough to read by, once my eyes adjusted to it. So when "lights out" came, I would sit on the floor where I could continue reading in that glow.

At one-hour intervals the night guards paced past every room. Each time I heard the approaching footsteps, I jumped into bed and feigned sleep. And as soon as the guard passed, I got back out of bed onto the floor area of that light-glow, where I would read for another fifty-eight minutes—until the guard approached again. That went on until three or four every morning. Three or four hours of sleep a night was enough for me. Often in the years in the streets I had slept less than that. . . .

I have often reflected upon the new vistas that reading opened to me. I knew right there in prison that reading had changed forever the course of my life. As I see it today, the ability to read awoke inside me some long dormant craving to be mentally alive. I certainly wasn't seeking any degree, the way a college confers a status symbol upon its students. My homemade education gave me, with every additional book that I read, a little bit more sensitivity to the deafness, dumbness, and blindness that was afflicting the black race in America. Not long ago, an English writer telephoned me from London, asking questions. One was, "What's your alma mater?" I told him, "Books." You will never catch me with a free fifteen minutes in which I'm not studying something I feel might be able to help the black man.

900 words

Write your ending time here:_____

Subtract your starting time: _____

Total time: _____

Check the Rate Chart on p. 462 to find out how many words per minute you have read, and then record your score on the Reading Efficiency Progress Chart on p. 463.

Analyze What You Read

Make Graphic Organizers

Fill in the following chart.

Saved

Setting: (Where and when does it take place?)	
Characters: (Who is in the story?)	
Plot: (What happens in the story?)	

Plot (continued):	
Theme: (What does the story teach us about life?)	

Remember What's Important

1. To prepare for a Comprehension Check, memorize the chart. Test your-self or have someone test you on the reading selection. Keep testing until you think you can remember everything you need to know. If necessary, review *How to Answer an Essay Question* on pp. 31–32.

2. To prepare for a Vocabulary Check, make flash cards as described on p. 12 for each of the words in the Vocabulary Preview that you do not know. Test yourself or have someone test you until you think you can remember them.

Make Use of What You Read

When you are ready, complete the Comprehension Check on p. 355 and the Vocabulary Check on p. 357. Do them from memory, without looking back at the book or your notes.

Evaluate Your Active Critical Thinking Skills

After your tests have been graded, record your scores on the Progress Chart, p. 456, and answer the questions on the Evaluation Checklist on p. 457.

Vocabulary Skills Review

Dictionary Definitions

For explanation see pp. 9–11

For practice in finding the correct meaning of a word in the dictionary, select the correct meaning of each of the following six words from the reading. Above each entry is a sentence using the word. In the blank before the sentence, put the number of the definition that fits the way the word is used. The abbreviation under each blank tells you which part of speech the word is, so you can more easily find the proper definition.

_____ 1. "I became increasingly frustrated at not being able to express
n.   what I wanted to convey in <u>letters</u> that I wrote, especially those
to Mr. Elijah Muhammad."

let•ter (let′ər) *n.* [< L. *littera*] **1.** any character of the alphabet **2.** a written or printed message, usually sent by mail **3.** [*pl.*] *a*) literature *b*) learning; knowledge **4.** literal meaning –*vt.* to mark with letters

_____   2. "When I just <u>skipped</u> those words, of course, I really ended up
v.   with little idea of what the book said."

skip (skip) *vi., vt.* **skipped, skip′ping** [ME. *skippen*] **1.** to leap lightly (over) **2.** to ricochet or bounce **3.** to pass from one point to another, omitting or ignoring (what lies between) **4.** [Colloq.] to leave (town, etc.) hurriedly –*n.* a skipping; specif., a gait alternating light hops on each foot

_____   3. "I couldn't even write in a straight <u>line</u>."
n.

line (līn) *n.* [< L. *linea,* lit., linen thread] **1.** a cord, rope, wire, etc. **2.** any wire, pipe, etc., or system of these, conducting fluid, electricity, etc. **3.** a thin, threadlike mark **4.** a border or boundary **5.** a limit **6.** outline; contour **7.** a row of printed letters across a page **8.** a succession of persons or things **9.** lineage **10.** a transportation system of buses, ships, etc. **11.** the course a moving thing takes **12.** a course of conduct, action, explanation, etc. **13.** a person's trade or occupation **14.** a stock of goods **15.** a piece of information **16.** a short letter, note, etc. **17.** a verse of poetry **18.** [*pl.*] all the speeches of a character in a play **19.** the forward combat position in warfare **20.** *Football* the players in the forward row **21.** *Math.* the path of a moving point –*vt.* **lined, lin′ing 1.** to mark with lines **2.** to form a line along

_____   4. "Between what I wrote in my tablet, and writing letters, during the
n.   <u>rest</u> of my time in prison I would guess I wrote a million words."

rest (rest) *n.* [OE.] **1.** sleep or repose **2.** ease or inactivity after exertion. **3.** relief from anything distressing, tiring, etc. **4.** absence of motion **5.** what is left **6.** a supporting device **7.** *Music* a measured interval of silence between tones, or a symbol for this –*vi.* **1.** to get ease and refreshment by sleeping or by ceasing from work **2.** to be at ease **3.** to be or become still **4.** to be supported; lie or lean (*in, on,* etc.) **5.** to be found [the fault *rests* with him] **6.** to rely; depend –*vt.* **1.** to cause to rest **2.** to put at ease, etc. [*rest* your head here]

_____   5. "Anyone who has read a <u>great</u> deal can imagine the new world
adj.   that opened."

great (grāt) *adj.* [OE.] **1.** of much more than ordinary size, extent, etc. **2.** most important; main **3.** designating a relationship one generation removed [*great*-grandparent] **4.** [Colloq.] skillful (often with *at*) **5.** (Colloq.) excellent; fine –*n.* a distinguished person

_____   6. "Fortunately, right outside my door was a corridor light that
   v.   cast a glow into my room."

   cast (kast) *vt.* **cast, cast′ing** [< ON. *kasta*] **1.** to throw with force; fling;
       hurl **2.** to deposit (a ballot or vote) **3.** to direct [to *cast* one's eyes]
       4. to project [to *cast* light] **5.** to throw off or shed (a skin) **6.** to shape
       (molten metal, etc.) by pouring into a mold **7.** to select (an actor)
       for (a role or play) –*n.* **1.** a casting; throw **2.** something formed in a
       mold **3.** a plaster form for immobilizing a limb **4.** the set of actors
       in a play or movie **5.** an appearance, as of features **6.** kind; quality
       7. a tinge; shade

Word Parts

*For explanation
see pp. 4–5*

By looking at a word's etymology in the dictionary, you can find the meaning
of its roots. Here are six words from the reading that contain common roots.
The roots, their meanings, and other words that can help you remember the
meanings are also provided.

Word	Root	Meaning of Root	Another word
1. tele**vis**ion	vis	see	vision
2. **dic**tionary	dic	to say	predict
3. pro**gress**	gress	to go, walk, or step	aggression
4. tele**phon**ed	phon	sound	phonograph
5. at**ten**tion	ten	to hold	retention
6. **mot**ions	mot	to move	locomotive

Using these roots, match the following difficult words with their definitions.

_____   1. vis-à-vis   a. a place to <u>walk</u> out (exit)

_____   2. abdicate   b. capable of spontaneous <u>movement</u>

_____   3. egress   c. to <u>say</u> you're leaving a high position

_____   4. cacophony   d. the length of time something is <u>held</u>

_____   5. tenure   e. (to <u>see</u> a person) face to face

_____   6. motile   f. harsh, jarring <u>sound</u>

Parts of Speech

*For explanation
see pp. 7–9*

For each word below, write its part of speech. Then change it to the new
part of speech. Write a sentence using the new word. Use a dictionary if you
need help.

Word	Part of speech	New part of speech	New word
1. articulate		verb	
Sentence:			
2. hustler		verb	
Sentence:			
3. functional		noun	
Sentence:			
4. motivation		verb	
Sentence:			
5. immensely		adjective	
Sentence:			
6. inevitable		adverb	
Sentence:			
7. circulation		verb	
Sentence:			
8. rehabilitation		verb	
Sentence:			
9. isolation		verb	
Sentence:			
10. confer		noun	
Sentence:			

6   How to Strengthen Your Memory Power

Vocabulary Preview

cosmological (käz mə läʹjə kʼl): relating to the branch of philosophy and science that deals with the study of the universe as a whole and of its form and nature as a physical system.

retrieval (ri trēʹvʼl): the act of getting something back or recovering it

retention (ri tenʹshən): holding or keeping

distinctive (dis tiŋkʹtiv): distinguished from others; characteristic

heredity (hə redʹə tē): passing of characteristics from parent to child by means of genes

neuropsychologist (nōōʹrō sī kälʹə jist): psychologist who studies the mind and the nervous system

associative (ə sōʹshē ātʹiv, ə sōʹshə tiv): of, characterized by, or causing association, as of ideas

perception (pər sepʹshən): mental grasp of objects, qualities, and so on by means of the senses; awareness; comprehension

physiological (fizʹē ə läjʹi kʼl): bodily; physical

senility (si nilʹə tē): state typical of or resulting from old age; showing the marked deterioration often accompanying old age, especially confusion or memory loss

cat, āte, fäther; pen, ēvil; if, kīte; nō, ôr, fōōd, book; boil, house; up, tʉrn; chief, shell; thick, *the*; zh, treasure; ŋ, sing; ə for *a* in *about*; ʼ as in *able* (āʹbʼl)

Preread

STEP 1

Preview the following selection (pp. 78–81) by reading the title and the first sentence of each paragraph. Answer the following questions without looking back at the selection.

1. What is the subject?

_____

2. What is the main idea (the main thing the author is saying about the subject)?

_____

3. Take a moment to think about memory. Think about what you know, what you don't know, and what you might find out from reading the selection. Make up three questions.

a. _____

b. _____

c. _____

Read

STEP
2

Read the selection without underlining.

Write your starting time here: _____

◆ *How to Strengthen Your Memory Power*

Mary Russ

One of Albert Einstein's biographers tells a story about an encounter between the physicist and a neighborhood girl that took place as he was walking through slush and snowdrifts on his way to teach a class at Princeton. After they had chatted for a while, the girl looked down at Einstein's moccasins, which were soaking wet. "Mr. Einstein, you've come out without your boots again," she said. Einstein laughed and pulled up his trousers to show his ankles. "And I forgot my socks," he confessed.

Although you probably don't have your head in the clouds of cosmological physics, you undoubtedly experience a fair share of forgetfulness: You are introduced to someone at a party and forget the name before the handshake is over; you walk away from a department-store counter, leaving your umbrella tilted against it; you reach for the car keys only to discover that you have no idea where you left them.

Why is it that our memory sometimes lets us down? To understand this breakdown, it's important first to have an idea of how the whole process works. Memory is a set of mental abilities, more wide-ranging than the one word would seem to imply. It involves the registration, storage and retrieval of information.

Though there is disagreement over how memory actually works, many scientists believe that a memory causes a "trace" in the brain—not a physical mark or groove but rather a chemical change. It also is believed that the function of memory is divided into the two categories of short-term and long-term memory. Short-term memory has a very low retention rate, usually less than 20 seconds. Long-term memory is relatively permanent and has virtually unlimited capacity.

The nerve changes that take place in the brain are different for each type of memory. In short-term, the processing of a fact or impression involves a speedy but complex chain of events. Suppose you look up the telephone number of the local pizzeria. As you see the number, there are chemical changes on the retina of the eye. This triggers impulses in the brain that persist for a brief time and then die out as they're replaced by other patterns of activity: new facts, sights and sounds that you experience. This dying out is the reason that you forget the number practically immediately after you've dialed it and started talking.

If you don't want the pattern to fade out—if you want the fact or impression to be part of long-term memory—it must in some way be selectively maintained and reestablished as a distinctive pattern. This will happen if the impression is repeated enough or is made more vivid or important to you. For instance, you make yourself remember a good friend's telephone number by rehearsing it in your mind. As a long-term memory it is there for keeps, just waiting for the right cue to retrieve it.

Of course, some of us do a better job at remembering than others. One popular view is that certain people are simply born with better memories than others, but a number of psychologists doubt that heredity is the determining factor. Dr. Barbara Jones, a Massachusetts neuropsychologist, observes, "While heredity has something to do with it, it appears that there are certain personality styles that relate more specifically to memory. People who have more rigid personalities—who rely on routine, are well-organized, and aim toward gaining control of their lives—tend to have very good memories because they depend more on their knowledge of facts."

Is there a way to improve your memory? Can you make certain that essential information doesn't get dumped out of a short-term compartment in 20 seconds? The memory experts say yes.

"Association is the key," says Harry Lorayne, author of *The Memory Book.* You have to relate what you want to remember to something verbal or visual. Lorayne offers an example of how this works: Very few people can accurately remember the shape of foreign countries—except perhaps Italy. That's because most people have come to note that Italy is shaped like a boot. The shape of a boot is something already known and therefore hard to forget.

All human memory is associative. It involves connecting particular concepts, events, facts and principles and weaving them into systematic relation with each other. Enthusiasm, fear or anything which causes a heightening of perception can intensify this process of association. Your interest—or lack of it—in what you are seeing, hearing or learning can make all the difference.

Good organization can also assist your memory, just as an orderly street plan helps you to find your way to a particular corner in a city. Organization involves grouping items by categories and establishing a pattern to make remembering easier. For instance, if you start making a point of placing the car keys on the shelf near the door to the garage, you're not likely to lose track of them.

Failure to pay attention is frequently the real reason why we forget. We blame our memory for something that is really the fault of our concentration. At a party you may forget the names of people you met because during the introductions you were actually concentrating on the impression you were giving—and not the new names. Failure to pay attention is also the most common reason for absentmindedness—you may "forget" where you put your car keys because you were not paying a bit of attention when you put them down.

Certain physiological states can interfere with memory function. Anyone who has ever had too much to drink knows that the morning after it may be difficult to recollect what happened the night before. "People who are drunk are not processing information," says Dr. Laird Cermak, a professor and research psychologist. Since alcohol depresses the brain and the nervous system, it's particularly difficult to learn anything when you've been drinking.

There are also memory disorders that result from accidents, strokes and serious psychological stress. Following a severe head injury that produces a concussion, a person may experience a loss of memory known as amnesia. Such loss can cover periods ranging from a few minutes prior to an accident to weeks or even years before the injury. The more serious the injury, the greater the period of amnesia is likely to be. Occasionally amnesia is permanent, but usually the patient recovers most of the lost memories.

Perhaps the memory loss feared most by people is the one that begins to appear at the onset of old age. Psychologists agree that as we get older there is a very gradual loss of the ability to learn and to recall. As a person grows older, some brain cells die or are destroyed by minute injuries of various kinds. But the memory problems common among many older people should not be confused with senility, and it is dangerous to make general statements about the long-term functional changes which take place as a person ages. Professor Ian Hunter, author of *Memory,* says: "So much depends on the individual, his circumstances and interests, the sort of accomplishments he has acquired and whether he continues to use those accomplishments or not. Some people become old before their time while others continue to function at high levels of achievement into extreme old age."

Doctors are currently working on developing a drug that will help slow down or prevent memory loss due to age. Though there's no miracle pill yet, you can make your memory work better by using some of the techniques of association and organization mentioned above. Here are a few tricks to try:

One of the most famous systems for remembering a list of errands or objects is called the "link" method. According to Lorayne, it works like this: You link together the objects by associating the first to the second, the second to the third, the third to the fourth, and so on. You should make your associations as ridiculous or exaggerated as possible, so that you "see" them in your mind's eye. Let's say that one morning you want to remember to visit a sick friend at the hospital and pick up some postage stamps. Try picturing your friend lying under a giant stamp rather than a blanket. This image will be hard to forget.

Another good trick that will help you remember tasks that must be done is to make a physical change in your environment. This acts as a cue. For instance, Lorayne suggests that if you're worried about burning dinner while you watch TV, put a frying pan on the set to remind you that dinner's in the oven.

When you're introduced to lots of people at a party it can be hard to remember names. Make sure you hear the name when you're introduced. If you didn't get it, ask the person to repeat it. Then say the name over several times in your head. This repetition will help the name to stick.

1600 words

Write your ending time here:_____

Subtract your starting time: _____

Total time: _____

Check the Rate Chart on p. 462 to find out how many words per minute you have read, and then record your score on the Reading Efficiency Progress Chart on p. 463.

Analyze What You Read

STEP 3

Make Graphic Organizers

We have filled in the main points in the following outline. Go back to the reading selection and find each one. Some of them have been paraphrased.

1. Write the Roman numerals from the outline in the margin next to where the main points are located.

2. Locate the subpoints and write the capital letter from the outline in the margin next to each subpoint in the reading selection.

3. Write the subpoints next to the capital letters in the blanks below.

4. Some of the subpoints are broken down into details indicated in the outline by Arabic (regular) numbers. Write the number from the outline in the margin next to where each detail is located.

5. Write the details next to the Arabic numbers in the blanks below.

How to Strengthen Your Memory Power

   I. Memory is a set of mental abilities

      A. _____

      B. _____

      C. _____

  II. Theory that memory causes a chemical trace in the brain

 III. Function of memory divided into two categories

      A. _____

         1. _____

         2. _____

      B. _____

         1. _____

         2. _____

 IV. Ways to keep short-term memories from fading out

      A. _____

      B. _____

   V. People with rigid personalities remember better

VI. Ways to improve memory

    A. _____

        1. _____

           _____

        2. _____

           _____

    B. _____

        1. _____

        2. _____

VII. Reasons for forgetting

    A. _____

    B. _____

    C. _____

    D. _____

VIII. Memory tricks

    A. _____

    B. _____

    C. _____

Use your outline to fill in the idea map on the next page. Write the title in the circle. Write the Roman numeral headings in the rectangles starting at the top. Write the capital letter headings in the triangles, and write the Arabic number headings in the ovals.

Remember What's Important

1. To prepare for a Comprehension Check, memorize the outline and/or idea map. Test yourself or have someone test you on the reading selection. Keep testing until you think you can remember everything you need to know. If necessary, review *How to Answer an Essay Question* on pp. 31–32.

2. To prepare for a Vocabulary Check, make flash cards as described on p. 12 for each of the words in the Vocabulary Preview that you do not know. Test yourself or have someone test you until you think you can remember them.

Make Use of What You Read

When you are ready, complete the Comprehension Check on p. 359 and the Vocabulary Check on p. 362. Do them from memory, without looking back at the book or your notes.

Evaluate Your Active Critical Thinking Skills

After your tests have been graded, record your scores on the Progress Chart, p. 456, and answer the questions on the Evaluation Checklist on p. 457.

Vocabulary Skills Review

| *For explanation see pp. 11–12* |

Word Memory

There are four major ways to memorize new words: (1) make the word meaningful by using it in context, (2) make associations between the new word and a familiar word, (3) use word parts, and (4) use flash cards.

1. *Use the word in context.* Write sentences that make clear the meanings of the following words from this selection.

   a. retention _____

   b. distinctive _____

   c. perception _____

2. *Make word associations.* In the space next to each of the following words from this selection, write a familiar word that can help you remember the new one.

   a. heredity _____

   b. associative _____

   c. physiological _____

3. *Use words parts.* In the space after each word part below, write the letter of its definition. Use the dictionary if you need help. The definitions may be used more than once.

a. *cosmo* = _____   *logy* = _____   1. state or condition of
                                                2. again
b. *senil* = _____   *ity* = _____   3. mind
                                                4. study of
c. *neuro* = _____   *psycho* = _____   5. old
                                                6. one who
    log = _____   *ist* = _____   7. nerve
                                                8. find
d. *re* = _____   *trieve* = _____   9. universe

4. *Make flash cards.* Find ten words from previous readings in this book that you are having trouble remembering. On the front of a card, write the word and its pronunciation. On the back, write the definition in your own words and use the word in a sentence. Test yourself by looking at the front of the card and trying to restate the definition and a sentence. The average person needs seven self-testing sessions to thoroughly master a new word. Refer to sample flash cards on p. 12.

Analogies

A word analogy is a puzzle in which two sets of words are compared. The two words in the first set have a relationship to each other. You have to recognize the relationship in order to fill in the blank. Analogies use the mathematical symbols :, which means *is to,* and : :, which means *as.*

easy : simple : : _____ : memory

The example reads: *easy* is to *simple* as _____ is to *memory.* You must understand the relationship between *easy* and *simple.* They are synonyms; they mean the same thing. Now look at the Vocabulary Preview for this reading. Which word fits in the blank? What is a synonym for *memory*? The answer is *retention.*

For each analogy on the next page, write the word from the Vocabulary Preview that completes the analogy. Look back at the preview definitions if you need help.

neuropsychologist   associative   perception
physiological   senility   cosmology   retrieval
retention   distinctive   heredity

1. relatively : absolutely : : _____ : ordinary

2. retrieval : recovery : : _____ : awareness

3. retention : forgetting : : _____ : immaturity

4. body : mind : : _____ : psychological

5. inheritance : training : : _____ : environment

Don't Tell Jaime Escalante Minorities Can't Meet (High) Standards!

Vocabulary Preview

barrio (bä′rē ō): A chiefly Spanish-speaking community or neighborhood in a U.S. city

Hispanic (hi span′ik): of or relating to Spain or Spanish-speaking Latin America

rigorous (rig′ər əs): strict; severe; hard

demographic (dem′ə graf′ik): having to do with the study of size, growth, density, and distribution of human populations

turmoil (tʉr′moil): commotion; uproar; confusion

morale (mə ral′): the state of mind of a person or group as shown by confidence, cheerfulness, and discipline

aspirations (as′pə rā′shənz): desires for achievement

cosmetology (käz′mə täl′ə jē): the work of a beautician

sequence (sē′kwens): a related series

culminate (kul′mə nāt′): to reach the highest point or climax

skeptical (skep′ti k′l): not easily convinced; doubting; questioning

proficiency (prō fish′ən sē): skill

feat (fēt): a deed of unusual daring or skill

idiosyncratic (id′ē ə siŋ kra′tik): having to do with a personal peculiarity or mannerism

podium (po′dē əm): an elevated platform for a lecturer or conductor

cat, āte, fäther; pen, ēvil; if, kīte; nō, ôr, fo͞od, book; boil, house; up, tʉrn; chief, shell; thick, *the*; zh, treasure; ŋ, sing; ə for *a* in *about*; ′ as in *able* (ā′b′l)

Preread

Preview the following selection (pp. 89–92) by reading the title and the first sentence of each paragraph. The film *Stand and Deliver* was about Jaime Escalante. Answer the following questions without looking back at the selection.

1. What is the subject?

_____

_____

2. What is the main idea (the main thing the author is saying about the subject)?

_____

_____

3. Take a moment to think about what you know about minority achievement and math. Think about what you know, what you don't know, and what you might find out from reading the selection. Make up three questions.

a. _____

_____

b. _____

_____

c. _____

_____

Read

STEP 2

Read the selection without underlining.

Write your starting time here: _____

◆ *Don't Tell Jaime Escalante Minorities Can't Meet (High) Standards!*

David Savage

The school day starts early for students of Jaime Escalante, mathematics teacher at Garfield High School in East Los Angeles. By 7 A.M., students from Escalante's trigonometry and calculus classes are stopping by to ask his help on a difficult problem before they head off to their other classes. Some of the students are tenth graders taking math analysis or trigonometry. Others are working on second-year, college-level calculus.

These students work on mathematics afternoons, evenings, on weekends, and, for many, during the summer at a nearby community college. Ask one of them what they think of this demanding schedule, and the likely answer is, "It's fun."

Fun? And this unexpected reaction is just the beginning of the surprises at Garfield High School.

"He makes you want to work hard. He psyches you up to do it," says Frank Quezada, a Garfield senior. "He makes mathematics fun. But you also feel guilty if you don't do the work for him."

The "he" is Escalante—a Bolivian immigrant, who over the past decade has transformed a barrio high school known more for gangs than for good grades into the city's best training ground for young mathematicians. Nearly 100 percent of Garfield's students are Hispanic. And among the 50 high schools in Los Angeles, Garfield is the leader in the number of students who take and pass the College Board's rigorous advanced placement tests in algebra and calculus.

Escalante—whose achievements with his young charges have been recognized by the California State Board of Education, *Reader's Digest* magazine, and President Reagan—succeeds through a combination of drive, inspiration, and humor. And although his success story is unique, it raises an issue that goes beyond one school and one teacher.

That issue—the most difficult one facing California—is what education officials refer to, in a code of sorts, as the "demographic problem." What it boils down to, in more direct terms, is whether minority students can be expected to meet the more rigorous standards of recent education reforms.

By the year 2000, a majority of the state's schoolchildren will be minorities—Hispanic, black, and Asian. Already, Hispanic students make up more than half of the student population in the huge Los Angeles Unified School District, the nation's second largest school system. Whether the measure is grades, test scores, or college degrees, Hispanic and black students crowd at the bottom.

According to the California Commission on Postsecondary Education, for every 1,000 Hispanic ninth graders, only 661 will be graduated from high school. Black students fare only slightly better, with 667 ending up as high school graduates.

Distressingly few of those graduates move further up the educational ladder. Among Hispanic ninth graders, only 17 of that 1,000 will end up as university graduates. The picture for blacks is nearly the same: 16 will earn university degrees.

A clue to Hispanics' and blacks' low achievement record might lie in what Jaime Escalante found when he arrived at Garfield in 1974: Low grades, low morale, and low aspirations were the norm. Failure, however, doesn't fit into Escalante's frame of reference. A decade earlier, Escalante had been a highly successful mathematics teacher in Bolivia; his student teams had won national championships. When Escalante and his wife left the country because of political turmoil, he arrived in the United States unable to speak the language of the majority and with education credentials that were not recognized in California. His first job was as a busboy in a Pasadena coffee shop.

"My English was nothing, zero, an empty set," he recalls. After taking night classes to improve his English, he earned a high-paying job with the Burroughs Corp. as a computer analyst. A high salary, however, didn't satisfy him; his true love was teaching. Escalante took a big pay cut to go to work in the Los Angeles school district. And at Garfield, he found a school where most students took one math class and quit.

"I was ready to quit, too," he says. "All they were taking were Mickey Mouse courses—cosmetology, cooking. I tell them, 'You have a great future ahead—at McDonald's cooking hamburgers.'"

Escalante set out to raise students' sights and show them that minority students can succeed in a demanding academic program. He says he "scrapped the textbooks we were using" and ordered a high-level mathematics series. He spoke to the principal, his fellow math teachers, and even teachers in Garfield's junior high feeder schools about creating a new sequence of math courses that would culminate in a senior year of advanced calculus.

Many were skeptical, and a few resisted the idea of scrapping proficiency math courses in favor of algebra, trigonometry, and calculus. But the toughest sell was the students. What they needed, he told them, was not extraordinary mathematical ability, but *ganas*—a Spanish word that loosely translated means "drive" or "desire to succeed."

Giving his students *ganas*—that is, discipline, desire, determination, and the will to work—says Escalante, is his main task in the first two weeks of the school year.

"I have a heart-to-heart talk with students. We talk about money and about success. Everyone wants to play football, be a big star. I ask them, 'How many Garfield students have become pro football players and make big money?' They don't know the answer, but I do. Zero.

"Then I tell them the money is in computers and physics and chemistry and biology. And they want you out there. But you have to speak their language first, and the language is math."

Though his classes have 50 students or more, Escalante sits down with each tenth grader and goes over a learning contract. The students and their parents must sign the contracts, committing themselves to a program of hard work in school and at home. For most, the commitment is a stiff challenge.

But Escalante has found potential among Garfield students. In May 1982, 14 of his students achieved a top score on the College Board's advanced placement examination in calculus, an extraordinary feat for such a school. The accomplishment was noticed first, however, because the Educational Testing Service (E.T.S.) questioned the scores. Examiners had noted that the students had worked problems in a similar, idiosyncratic way.

Many in the Hispanic community suspected that E.T.S. questioned the scores only because the students came from a barrio school. E.T.S. officials denied the charge.

"We followed the same procedures in this case as in any other. The graders don't know the names or schools of the papers they are grading," says Frank Romero, director of the E.T.S. office in Los Angeles.

Escalante put the controversy to rest by rounding up his students in August and having E.T.S. officials administer the test to them again. Once again, all 12 (two had already left the city) achieved passing scores on the rigorous exam, despite having virtually no time for preparation.

"It was clear that the students did know calculus. It was a credit to Mr. Escalante," said Romero.

Since then, Escalante's program—and its reputation—have grown steadily. Last year, 102 of his seniors took the advanced placement (A.P.) calculus exam, and more than three-fourths got passing grades, an achievement that will earn them a year's worth of college credit in math. This year, he has 150 students enrolled in courses to prepare for the A.P. exams. And his success has created a farm system in the junior high schools of East Los Angeles, as teachers and students upgrade to get ready for Escalante's major league program.

Escalante's high expectations, however, tell only part of the reason for his success. The rest, as with any outstanding teacher, lies in his approach to teaching. In front of his class, Escalante is part tough taskmaster and part comedian. Each class begins with a five-minute quiz. Students pick up the quizzes on their way into the room and work the problems quietly. When Escalante sounds a bell, selected students collect the papers. The teacher has yet to say a word.

But as he moves through a set of problems in rapid-fire style, Escalante the actor emerges. Under his podium, he keeps a collection of dolls and stuffed animals, each of which has a meaning to the students. He wanders through the aisles as he talks, offering a mock karate chop to those who stumble on a question. Their eyes follow him wherever he moves. He can turn suddenly and whisper an answer that can be heard throughout the small auditorium.

"You need the skill of an actor to keep their attention," he says. "You need to show that energy to attract people. The teacher also needs the patience of a doctor to show love to the kids."

1500 words

Write your ending time here:_____

Subtract your starting time: _____

Total time: _____

Check the Rate Chart on p. 462 to find out how many words per minute you have read, and then record your score on the Reading Efficiency Progress Chart on p. 463.

Analyze What You Read

STEP 3

Make Graphic Organizers

Fill in the following chart.

Don't Tell Jaime Escalante Minorities Can't Meet (High) Standards!

Setting: (Where and when does the story take place?)	
Characters: (Who is in the story?)	
Plot: (What happens in the story?)	

Theme:
(What does the story
teach us about life?)

Remember What's Important

1. To prepare for a Comprehension Check, memorize the chart. Test yourself or have someone test you on the reading selection. Keep testing until you think you can remember everything you need to know. If necessary, review *How to Answer an Essay Question* on pp. 31–32.

2. To prepare for a Vocabulary Check, make flash cards as described on p. 12 for each of the words in the Vocabulary Preview that you do not know. Test yourself or have someone test you until you think you can remember them.

Make Use of What You Read

When you are ready, complete the Comprehension Check on p. 363 and the Vocabulary Check on p. 365. Do them from memory, without looking back at the book or your notes.

Evaluate Your Active Critical Thinking Skills

After your tests have been graded, record your scores on the Progress Chart, p. 456, and answer the questions on the Evaluation Checklist on p. 457.

Vocabulary Skills Review

For explanation
see pp. 7–9

Parts of Speech

For each word on the next page, write the part of speech. Then change it to the new part of speech. Write a sentence using the new word. Use a dictionary if you need help.

Word	Part of speech	New part of speech	New word
1. rigorous		noun	
Sentence:			
2. proficiency		adjective	
Sentence:			
3. aspiration		verb	
Sentence:			
4. idiosyncratic		noun	
Sentence:			
5. skeptical		adverb	
Sentence:			

For explanation see p. 86

Analogies

Write the word from the Vocabulary Preview that completes each analogy below.

1. mock : fake : : _____ : strict

2. minority : majority : : _____ : peace

3. huge : tiny : : _____ : sure

4. extraordinary : average : : _____ : begin

5. aspirations: goals : : _____ : platform

9 Obstacles to Creativity—and How You Can Remove Them

Vocabulary Preview

novel (näv′əl): new and unusual; esp., being the first of its kind

compiled (kəm pīld′): gathered and put together (statistics, facts, etc.) in an orderly form

jettison (jet′ə sən, -zən): to discard (something) as useless or a burden

relentlessly (ri lent′lis lē): persistently; unremittingly

impulsive (im pul′siv): resulting from a sudden impulse

phenomenon (fə näm′ə nən′, -nän): any event, circumstance, or occurrence that can be experienced and described

blatant (blāt′′nt): glaringly conspicuous

opportune (äp′ər tōōn′, -tyōōn′): happening or done at the right time; seasonable; well-timed; timely

viable (vī′ə bəl): workable and likely to survive or to have real meaning, pertinence, etc. [a *viable* economy, *viable* ideas]

debris (də brē′): bits and pieces of rubbish; litter

scrutinize (skrōōt′′n īz′): to look at very carefully; examine closely; inspect minutely

status quo (stat′əs kwō′): the existing state of affairs (at a particular time)

analogy (ə nal′ə jē): the likening of one thing to another on the basis of some similarity between the two

realm (relm): a region; sphere; area [the *realm* of thought]

formalize (fôr′mə līz′): to give definite form to

innovation (in′ə vā′shən): something newly introduced; new method, custom, device, etc.; change in the way of doing things

syndrome (sin′drōm′): any set of characteristics regarded as identifying a certain type, condition, etc.

superficial (sōō′pər fish′əl): concerned with and understanding only the easily apparent and obvious; not profound; shallow

tangible (tan′jə bəl): capable of being touched or felt by touch; having actual form and substance

facilitate (fə sil′ə tāt′): to make easy or easier

cat, āte, fäther; pen, ēvil; if, kīte; nō, ôr, fōōd, book; boil, house; up, turn; chief, shell; thick, *the*; zh, treasure; ŋ, sing; ə for *a* in *about*; ′ as in *able* (ā′b′l)

Preread

Preview the following selection (pp. 97–106) by reading the title and the headings. Answer the following questions without looking back at the selection.

1. What is the subject?

   _____

2. What is the main idea (the main thing the author is saying about the subject)?

   _____

3. Take a moment to think about creativity. Think about what you know, what you don't know, and what you might find out from reading the selection. Make up three questions.

   a. _____

   b. _____

   c. _____

Read

Read the selection without underlining.

Write your starting time here: _____

◆ 9 Obstacles to Creativity—and How You Can Remove Them

Alexander Hiam

I'm often asked to come into an organization as a consultant or trainer to help people "get out of the box" and find new solutions. Whether they're new product concepts, new business strategies, or new ways to cut errors or improve employee performance, I am usually surprised to find I can suggest many novel approaches. Surprised because I'm not necessarily smarter than my clients are, and I rarely know their industries as well as they do. But I can see all sorts of alternatives that they can't because they are failing to "do" creativity in the first place. They are making some of those obvious errors that trap you in routine thinking and close off creative avenues that seem fairly obvious to most outsiders.

Employees often know precisely what their organization's problems are, and how to solve them, but they find that their senior managers are quite unable to see the obvious. Customers often offer brilliant insights when given half a chance—"brilliant" to the managers, but painfully obvious to the customers!

These sorts of experiences have led me to believe that a foundational attack on the corporate creativity problem is sometimes more valuable than the sophisticated "upper story" approaches taken by most experts. As a result, I have gradually compiled a list of the most common errors—things that routinely block creativity in organizations and for many individuals, as well. The resulting list might be called *Creativity for Dummies*, except that the reality is that we all make these dumb mistakes—and far too often. They are embedded in our organizational cultures and in our individual training as students and employees. They may even have some value under circumstances in which creativity is not required. But the vast majority of us live and work in circumstances that demand creativity, and so we all need to jettison these nine bad habits:

1. Failure to Ask Questions

Unless you ask lots of "why" questions, you won't generate creative insights. To avoid this most common of creativity errors, be sure to peek under all the carpets, including your own. Don't take anything for granted, especially success.

• Get in the good habit of asking yourself and those around you to question more things more often. If you aren't sure how to do this, just spend a little time with a four-year-old. Children around this age not only question you relentlessly (why *is* the sky blue, anyway?), but also question their *environment* by constantly manipulating it. (What happens if you try to stack these blocks really high? Oh, they fall down. Cool!) Or try watching a teenager explore a new software program. Kids at this age do the same thing: poke something every way they can to find out how it works. In the process, they discover many relationships that adults wouldn't find without a user's manual.

When was the last time you "poked" your own work processes in the same way a kid does a new computer game? It's hard to remember, isn't it? That means you're probably not asking those loosely defined, impulsive questions that so often give birth to creative insight.

Don't feel bad—you're not alone. The failure to ask questions is a widespread social phenomenon; in fact, most of our social institutions seem designed to limit, if not discourage, creative inquiry. Many of the processes used in organizations are just as bad, if not worse. The typical staff meeting is the most blatant example of an uncreative process. At every staff meeting

I attend or see transcripts of, its leader unwittingly fails to ask for creative ideas, even at the most opportune points. A formal, professional atmosphere is combined with a structured conversation path or meeting agenda to keep people "on track," or "focused." Buy why meet in the first place if you don't take advantage of the group's unique creative potential? One person's question or comment can easily stimulate another's imagination—if you ask for imaginative thinking. Thus, no business meeting should reach its end without the leader asking for creative ideas.

Now that you're aware of this uncreative habit, you can start rattling its chains. Try looking at the world through more-inquisitive eyes; try getting ideas in motion; try asking the all-important question: "Why?" See what happens!

2. Failure to Record Ideas

This is a really big problem. I recently attended a retreat for generating new product ideas with an employee group from a large, mature consumer-products company. The event was part of a long, costly effort to find a dozen concepts worthy of test marketing—a goal that required generating hundreds of ideas. During a break, one company veteran told me, "As I listen to all these new ideas, I keep hearing things that we've already considered at one time or another. We've had so many people working on product development for so many decades that there actually are no new ideas." I took that as a personal challenge, of course, and made sure the final report included plenty of surprises for him. But I also felt a pang of regret. Undoubtedly, thousands of good ideas had been developed over the course of that company's history, some going on to formal testing, some introduced to the market, but most—probably more than 90%—simply forgotten. They hadn't been *recorded.*

Maybe they weren't good ideas, but in the world of creativity, there's no such thing as a bad idea. The more blocks you have and the more varied they are, the more things you can make; and you don't toss out the blocks you haven't used today, because you never know what you'll want or need to build tomorrow. This company (like many others) wasted its most valuable asset by throwing out the "unused blocks." If someone had only kept a simple index-card file of each and every idea over the years, the sessions would have been more efficient and maybe more productive.

If you keep a record of your ideas, then, when you need new ideas, you can start by reexamining the old ones. Some that seemed crazy a decade ago might now be viable. Others might always be crazy but serve as the spark you need to come up with more valuable concepts.

This is an important practice for the individual as well as for the organization. I don't keep a formal journal because I have trouble maintaining it on a daily basis. (You can try this approach, though, and see if it works for you.) I find it much simpler to keep an informal log or file of ideas. You can do so in a number of ways:

- Record the ideas in a notebook or journal; on scraps of paper (just label a folder "Ideas" and the scraps will find their way into it); in the margins of the books and reports you read; or in electronic files. (How about an idea database?)

- Use pocket message recorders: Log ideas on these handy audio devices for recording "to do" items; then write down the ideas later.

- Leave yourself voice mail. I often call my office at night and leave idea messages so I don't have to worry about forgetting them overnight.

- Use e-mail. You can create an idea address and send yourself ideas—as well as scoot others' idea-oriented e-mail into that file. Periodically, you can move the ideas into long-term storage, either on disk or on printouts of your idea file. Of course, you can also come up with your own approach to capturing ideas—something new and creative!

Countless ideas occur to you each month, but many are lost. If you just double the number you save, your raw material for any thinking job will be enriched by 100%.

3. Failure to Revisit Ideas

Whether you keep a formal record of ideas or not, you leave behind, in the wake of your daily work, many ideas and assumptions. As the path is rarely straight, you often recross your wake, but do you notice what's there? Do you learn from it? That's much easier said than done.

One way to revisit old ideas is to schedule yourself a little time for rambling through the debris of past projects. Every month or two, give yourself an hour to dig out old reports, peek into old working files, and leaf through old appointment books—whatever is necessary to resurface old ideas and bring into focus the context of prior decisions.

When revisiting ideas, you want to do two things:

1. Give old ideas a second chance.
2. Make yourself more aware of old assumptions.

I know it may sound confusing to divide revisiting into two separate areas—ideas and assumptions—but they have a distinct relationship to each other: We can think of ideas as the opposites of assumptions. Let me explain.

Ideas represent activity: To generate them, we have to focus attention on something, think hard about it, get the mental gears in motion. Assumptions, on the other hand, represent passivity: We don't really generate assumptions so much as fall (or ease) into them, choosing not to think, whether we're conscious of making that choice or not. Either we think hard about something, coming up with ideas and insights, or we don't—and when we don't, we've entered the area of assumptions.

When revisiting, you often find that assumptions are more striking than ideas. You may see places where opportunities for improvement have been oddly overlooked or underdeveloped; where the validity or reliability of something—a process step, a planning tool, a vendor's practices—is more trusted than proved; where good, hard questions have been raised one day, only to be disregarded and shelved the next; where individuals have simply—and dangerously—based decisions on suppositions. If you scrutinize these places, you'll notice how assumptions tend to build a "comfort zone" around us, giving us permission to keep avoiding thought and creative alternatives to the status quo.

Most organizations have powerful social mechanisms working against revisiting. Executives don't want their past decisions questioned. Team leaders and supervisors don't want to put back on the agenda an item they managed to get off it last month. Employees inevitably resist the feeling of backward motion that a reexamination of ideas brings with it. Add to that the danger of someone using revisiting as an excuse for playing the "blame game," and you may find that revisiting causes a level of anxiety that hinders productivity.

In such a case, you have to sell the idea of revisiting from the top down before it can be practiced successfully in the ranks of an organization. That's a lengthy process, as is any that requires a change of habit by top managers, but in the meantime, you can certainly begin to practice revisitation on your own. Like other creativity practices, this can be done alone or in groups. If enough people become "closet creators" in a company, then organizational change is sure to follow.

4. Failure to Express Ideas

If you have an idea—any idea—you should express it right away. Tell it to yourself if you are alone; tell it to others if you are in a group.

That sounds simple, even obvious, but the principle is rarely followed. Most ideas are cut short by our automatic self-censorship. We never give them enough thought to figure out if they're worthwhile; nor do we share them with others. Stray ideas are treated like weeds—minor irritants to be uprooted as quickly as possible. An orderly mind has few weeds, but an orderly mind is not creative. If you want creativity, you must attend to those weeds and treat each one as a potentially valuable new crop.

The weed analogy has an especially rich meaning for me. It brings to mind how my daughter, when she was four, would grill me with questions as she helped me tend our garden. She just couldn't figure out what weeds were and why they should be pulled out. "Is this a weed?" she'd ask. "What about this? Why is this a weed, but not that?" And so on, relentlessly. Finally I had to admit an essential truth about the "weeds" category: It has no botanical significance; there is no such thing as a weed from a scientific perspective. A weed is really just a plant you don't want growing in a particular place. The vegetable garden's weed may be the wildflower garden's specialty. No wonder my daughter found the category endlessly puzzling!

The same is true of ideas. We dismiss many as weeds on the assumption that they're not worth growing in our mental garden. But in doing that, we miss many potentially useful thoughts. Some mental gardens yield no crop of lasting value except the weeds—if the owners had the foresight to attend to them. One very good way to attend to them is to express them.

Write down your stray thought, your "weed idea." Say it. Get it out of your head and into the realm of communication. That gives you the opportunity to consider it more carefully and fully—maybe to find a practical use for it as well. It also gives the thought a chance to grow and develop, possibly into other valuable ideas.

If you get in the habit of expressing your weed ideas, you'll be surprised how easily they seed other people's imaginations. It just takes one person to get everyone in an office thinking, perhaps because they figure out that the creative thinker is having more fun than they are and that they can easily join the game by paying more attention to their own ideas.

5. Failure to Think in New Ways

You don't get out of the box by doing what you've always done. If you usually sit down and write a list of pros and cons before adopting an alternative, then you have to try a new thinking strategy to come up with anything creative. Jettison that pro-and-con analysis as quickly as possible. (Of course, if you never use a pro-and-con analysis, then by all means give it a try.)

Visual thinking is usually a good choice. Draw a diagram or picture of the problem you're working on, or think up visual analogies by asking yourself to name 10 things the problem looks like. Then seek ways of generating fresh perspectives by analyzing these images: Ask yourself why the problem looks like that thing.

Such thought patterns are novel, so they bring you quickly into unfamiliar territory. They draw much of their power from their novelty. So be creative about how you think about creativity. Try new and different strategies, and encourage others to do so as well.

It pays to discuss not just *what* you think, but *how* you think. In any project team, office, or conference room, there are people who think in radically different ways. If you ask people how they think through a problem or issue, you may stumble upon a new approach for generating fresh ideas. You can even formalize the process by running an idea-generation session. Ask people to take turns sharing their approach to the task and leading the group through the thought process they favor. That way, everyone gets a chance to try thinking about the topic in many different ways—and all are forced to articulate their mental strategies, which helps make them more conscious of how they think and thus better able to take control of their thought processes.

6. Failure to Wish for More

If you're content with the current state of things, you won't feel that creative itch. Creativity is nurtured by optimistic speculation: "Wonder if we could solve that problem"; "Wish there was some way to do that." The failure to wish for more—for the currently unattainable—is a common way to mess up creativity.

Inventors, it seems to me, are like ordinary people in all respects but one: They always wish there were a better way. When they tie their shoes, they wish they didn't have to tie them, so they think of using buckles, snaps, elastic, Velcro, or magnets. When they cook dinner, they wish there were some way to avoid scrubbing the saucepans, so they develop stick-free coatings for pans or disposable liners. When they return to the office and listen to their voice mail, they wish there were some way they could avoid missing important messages, so they develop pagers. All such innovations arise from the wish to improve upon the status quo.

Yet it is far too easy for us as employees to fall into the deadening routines of our busy work lives and to slowly lose that knack of wishful thinking. It seems that life is lived at too fast a pace for any such habits to persist unless we recognize their value and make a special practice of them. Most of use don't stop to think that wishful thinking is in fact a very valuable thing.

7. Failure to Try Being Creative

Many people feel they're not creative and therefore don't try to be. They don't see how simple it is: You are creative if you engage in creative thinking, and you aren't if you don't. Failing to try is the quickest way to derail your creativity. Fortunately, a little effort is the easiest way to get it back on track.

8. Failure to Keep Trying

Most of us don't generate brilliant, "breakthrough" ideas when we first sit down to do creative thinking. In fact, it's easy to generate dozens of ideas and find that all are throwaways.

While it is easy to stimulate creative thought in yourself and others, there is absolutely no guarantee that it will be productive in any practical sense. It often isn't—at least not at first—so we tend to abandon creative lines of thought prematurely, discouraged by their lack of fruitfulness. But that is a big mistake—another way in which we all mess up creativity from time to time.

No group can reliably produce valuable, profitable concepts unless they generate ideas in the hundreds. In my personal life, I'm often startled by the number of times I have to revisit a topic before hitting on that breakthrough idea I need. Creativity sometimes requires a great deal of heat to produce any light.

If you know this before you start, you won't be discouraged by initial failure. You'll have faith in the creative process and keep working at creative thinking until you get something useful for your trouble. It might take a minute or a hundred hours to achieve the kind of breakthrough you need—but either way, you can do it.

I feel like I'm giving a pep talk here, and I guess I am; but I've seen the syndrome too many times. People think they're "stuck" when they've invested only a few minutes of thought in a problem. Organizations often accept the alternatives on the table after investing only a few meetings or work sessions in them. Yet this is the easiest mistake to avoid. All you have to do is try doubling or tripling your thinking time and see what happens. If you get good results, then increase your thinking time again: The results will get even better.

The more familiar you become with the process of creative thinking, the better you'll get at estimating the time required to complete specific "thinking tasks." You'll have more realistic expectations, so you'll be less apt to abandon such tasks prematurely. To start you off with a guideline, I suggest budgeting at least five hours for a major thinking task.

You must also, with any thinking task, give yourself time for incubation—the idea development that occurs when you "sit on a problem" for a while. Incubation is an important, even amazing, part of creative thinking, for in relaxing your focus on a problem you create the conditions needed for fresh perspectives on the problem to develop.

The secret to incubating ideas is revisiting the problem and doing so often. You have to keep working at it, renewing your focus and reintensifying your efforts with each return visit. This is vital because you must not lose touch with the problem. You should always have a low-level awareness of it and be able to "feel" its presence in your mind. That only happens if you put significant mental energy into the problem beforehand. Just toying with a problem is a superficial activity: Nothing sinks into your mind, so when you set the problem aside, there's nothing to incubate!

In creativity, effort counts. Thomas Edison had a reason for saying "Genius is 1% inspiration and 99% perspiration": As an inventor, he knew it was the plain truth. So break the bad habit of thinking there are shortcuts to breakthrough ideas. Keep trying until you finally achieve that "Aha" experience you've been waiting for.

9. Failure to Tolerate Creative Behavior

Creative people are a bit weird. I say this even though I don't believe in the myth of the creative person; that is, I don't believe that some of us are creative and the rest aren't. What I've found is that, when people are being creative, their behavior seems a bit weird to others. Therefore, tolerance of creative behavior—yours or others'—is a must if you want to profit from creative thinking.

Most supervisors communicate a "Stop thinking and get back to work" message to workers. If you aren't visibly producing something tangible, then you're wasting the company's money. But ideas by their nature are invisible and intangible. So when and where can the poor employees think?

When I visit organizations to facilitate creativity processes. I sometimes suspect that this will be the only opportunity most of the attendees will get for focusing fully on creative thinking. Even if my visit is a two-day affair, I can't help wondering how the company will get along on only two days of creative thinking in an entire year of work.

If that's the case—if creative thinking is reserved for special occasions when you bring in a "creativity expert" to lead a thinking session—then your organization and its managers are making the tolerance error. And the retreat—that often-used term for those one- or two-day brainstorming sessions—is aptly named.

For it is a brief retreat from an intolerant environment that does not recognize creative thinking as a valid employee activity. And the prescription for any environment from which retreat is necessary is to begin "doing" creativity at work, right in the face of such intolerance. Organizations cannot profit from employees' creative potential until their supervisors encourage and ask for creativity instead of censoring it.

3700 words

Write your ending time here:_____

Subtract your starting time: _____

Total time: _____

Check the Rate Chart on p. 462 to find out how many words per minute you have read, and then record your score on the Reading Efficiency Progress Chart on p. 463.

Analyze What You Read

Make Graphic Organizers

Fill in the following idea map.

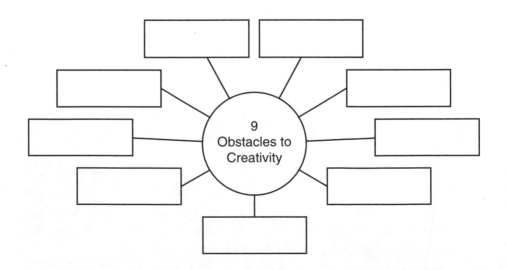

Remember What's Important

1. To prepare for a Comprehension Check, memorize the idea map. Test yourself or have someone test you on the reading selection. Keep testing until you think you can remember everything you need to know. If necessary, review *How to Answer an Essay Question* on pp. 31–32.

2. To prepare for a Vocabulary Check, make flash cards as described on p. 12 for each of the words in the Vocabulary Preview that you do not know. Test yourself or have someone test you until you think you can remember them.

Make Use of What You Read

When you are ready, complete the Comprehension Check on p. 367 and the Vocabulary Check on p. 368. Do them from memory, without looking back at the book or your notes.

Evaluate Your Active Critical Thinking Skills

After your tests have been graded, record your scores on the Progress Chart, p. 456, and answer the questions on the Evaluation Checklist on p. 457.

Vocabulary Skills Review

Dictionary: Confused Words

The following five pairs of words are often confused. Fill in the blanks with the correct word from the pair that precedes each group of sentences.

> **phase** (fāz) *n.* [ModL. *phasis* < Gr. *phasis* < *phainesthai,* to appear, akin to *phainein:* see FANTASY] **1.** any of the recurring stages of variation in the illumination and apparent shape of the moon or a planet **2.** any of the stages or forms in any series or cycle of changes, as in development **3.** any of the ways in which something may be observed, considered, or presented; aspect; side; part [a problem with many *phases*] **4.** *Chem.* a solid, liquid, or gaseous homogeneous form existing as a distinct part in a heterogeneous system [ice is a *phase* of H$_2$O] **5.** *Physics* the fractional part of a cycle through which a periodic wave, as of light, sound, etc., has advanced at any instant, measured from an arbitrary starting point or assumed moment of starting **6.** *Zool.* any of the characteristic variations in color of the skin, fur, plumage, etc. of an animal, according to season, age, etc. *–vt.* **phased, phas′ing 1.** to plan, introduce, carry out, etc. in phases, or stages (often with *in, into,* etc.) **2.** to put in phase *–vi.* to move by phases **–in** (or **out of**) **phase** in (or not in) a

state of exactly parallel movements, oscillations, etc.; in (or not in) synchronization –☆**phase out** to bring or come to an end, or withdraw from use, by stages **–pha•sic** (fā′zik) *adj. SYN.* **–phase** applies to any of the ways in which something may be observed, considered, or presented, and often refers to a stage in development in a cycle of changes, etc. [the *phases* of the moon]

faze (fāz′) *vt.* **fazed, faz′ing** [var. of FEEZE] to disturb; disconcert *–SYN.*
EMBARRASS

1. I hope my daughter's selfish behavior is just a _____ she's going through.

2. The larval _____ is part of the development of a butterfly.

3. She was able to be a nonconformist because the disapproval of other people didn't _____ her.

4. The waxing crescent is one _____ of the moon; the others are first quarter, waxing gibbous, full moon, waning gibbous, last quarter, and waning crescent.

5. Because teenagers are so self-conscious, the slightest criticism can

_____ them.

com•ple•ment (käm′plə mənt; *for v.,* -ment′) *n.* [ME < L *complementum,* that which fills up or completes < *complere:* see COMPLETE] **1.** that which completes or brings to perfection **2.** the amount or number needed to fill or complete **3.** a complete set; entirety **4.** something added to complete a whole; either of two parts that complete each other **5.** *Gram.* a word or group of words that, with the verb, completes the meaning and syntactic structure of the predicate (Ex.: *foreman* in "make him foreman," *paid* in "he expects to get paid") **6.** *Immunology* any of a group of proteins in the blood plasma that act with specific antibodies to destroy corresponding antigens, as bacteria or foreign proteins **7.** *Math. a)* the number of degrees that must be added to a given angle or arc to make it equal 90 degrees *b)* the subset which must be added to any even subset to yield the original set **8.** *Music* the difference between a given interval and the complete octave **9.** *Naut.* all of a ship's personnel, including the officers, required to operate a ship *–vt.* to make complete; be a complement to

com•pli•ment (käm′plə mənt; for *v.,* -ment′) *n.* [Fr < It *complimento* < Sp *cumplimiento* < *cumplir,* to fill up < VL **complire,* for L *complere,* to COMPLETE] **1.** a formal act or expression of courtesy or respect **2.** something said in admiration, praise, or flattery **3.** courteous greetings; respects [send with our *compliments*] **4.** [Now Chiefly Dial.] a gift given for services; tip *–vt.* **1.** to pay a compliment to; congratulate **2.** to present something to (a person) as an act of politeness or respect

1. John and Martha _____ each other; her personality is outgoing and emotional, while his is quiet and thoughtful.

2. Most people feel good when you give them a _____ .

al•lu•sion (ə lōō′zhən, a-) *n.* [LL *allusio,* a playing with < *allusus,* pp. of *alludere:* see ALLUDE] **1.** the act of alluding **2.** an indirect reference; casual mention

il•lu•sion (i lōō′zhən) *n.* [ME *illusioun* < OFr *illusion* < L *illusio,* a mocking (in LL(Ec), deceit, illusion) < *illusus,* pp. of *illudere,* to mock, play with < *in-,* on + *ludere,* to play: see LUDICROUS] **1.** a false idea or conception; belief or opinion not in accord with the facts **2.** an unreal, deceptive, or misleading appearance or image [a large mirror giving the *illusion* of space in a small room] **3.** *a)* a false perception, conception, or interpretation of what one sees, where one is, etc. *b)* the misleading image resulting in such a false impression **4.** HALLUCINATION **5.** a delicate, gauzy silk tulle used for veils, etc. *–SYN.* DELUSION *–***il•lu′sion•al** or **il•lu′sion•ar′y** *adj.*
il•lu•sion•ism (-iz′əm) *n.* the use of illusions in art *–***il•lu′sion•is′tic** *adj.*

1. A mirage is an optical _____ .

2. The character in the play made an _____ to Shakespeare.

loath (lōth, lōth) *adj.* [ME *loth* < OE *lath,* hostile, hateful, akin to Ger *leid,* sorrow (orig. *adj.*) < IE base **leit-,* to detest, abhor > Gr *aleitēs,* sinner] unwilling, reluctant: usually followed by an infinitive [to be *loath* to depart] *–SYN.* RELUCTANT *–***nothing loath** not reluctant(ly); willing(ly) *–***loath′ness** *n.*

loathe (lōth) *vt.* **loathed, loath′ing** [ME *lothen* < OE *lathian,* to be hateful < base of *lath:* see prec.] to feel intense dislike, disgust, or hatred for; abhor, detest *–SYN.* hate *–***loath′er** *n.*

1. I am _____ to get injections.

2. I _____ spiders.

elic•it (ē lis′it, i-) *vt.* [< L *elicitus,* pp. or *elicere,* to draw out < *e-,* out + *lacere,* to entice, akin to *laqueus:* see LACE] **1.** to draw forth; evoke [to *elicit* an angry reply] **2.** to cause to be revealed [to *elicit* facts] *–SYN.* EXTRACT *–***elic′it•able** *adj.* *–***elic′i•ta′tion** *n.* *–***elic′i•tor** *n.*

il•lic•it (il lis′it, i lis′-) *adj.* [Fr *illicite* < L *illicitus*, not allowed: see IN-² & LICIT] not allowed by law, custom, rule, etc.; unlawful; improper; prohibited; unauthorized **–il•lic′itly** *adv.* **–il•lic′it•ness** *n.*

1. The teacher tried to _____ the students' opinions.

2. Cocaine is an _____ drug.

Word Memory

<table>
<tr><td>

For explanation see pp. 2–4

</td><td>

1. *Use the word in context.* Write sentences that make clear the meanings of each of the following words:

  a. impulsive _____

  _____

  b. realm _____

  _____

  c. facilitate _____

  _____

</td></tr>
<tr><td>

For explanation see pp. 11–12

</td><td>

2. *Make word associations.* In the space next to each of the following words from this reading selection, write a familiar word or phrase that can help you remember the new one.

  a. formalize _____

  b. opportune _____

  c. compile _____

</td></tr>
<tr><td>

For explanation see pp. 4–5

</td><td>

3. *Use word parts.* Write the correct word part from the following list in each blank on the next page. Make sure the words match their definitions. Use the dictionary if you need help. The word parts may be used more than once.

</td></tr>
</table>

Word Part	Example
nov = new	novice (newcomer)
com = together	compact (packed together)
jet (jec) = throw	reject (throw back)
stat = stand	statue (a standing sculpture)
syn = together	synthetic (put together out of parts)

Word	Definition
a. __ __ __ __ us quo	how things <u>stand</u> at present
b. in __ __ __ ation	something <u>newly</u> introduced
c. __ __ __ drome	a set of characteristics grouped <u>together</u>
d. __ __ __ el	<u>new</u> and unusual
e. __ __ __ pile	gathered <u>together</u>

For explanation see p. 12

4. *Make flash cards.* Find ten words from this or previous reading selections that you have trouble remembering. On the front of the card, write the word and its pronunciation. On the back, write the definition in your own words and use the word in a sentence. Test yourself by looking at the front of the card and trying to restate the definition and a sentence. The average word requires seven self-testing sessions to be memorized.

9   Improving Test-Taking Strategies

Vocabulary Preview

format (fôr′mat): general arrangement or plan
cognitive (käg′nə tiv): having to do with thinking, knowing, remembering
adage (ad′ij): an old saying
empirical (em pir′i kəl): based on practical experience rather than theory
explicit (eks plis′it): clearly stated; leaving nothing implied
implausible (im plô′zə bəl): not likely to be true
generalization (jen′ər əl i zā′shən): a general, unspecific idea, statement, etc.
vigilant (vij′ə lənt): watchful; alert
assertion (ə sʉr′shən): positive statement; declaration
concise (kən sīs′): brief and to the point; short and clear

**cat, āte, fäther; pen, ēvil; if, kīte; nō, ôr, fo͞od, book; boil, house; up,
tʉrn; chief, shell; thick, *the*; zh, treasure; ŋ, sing; ə for *a* in *about*; ′ as
in *able* (ā′b′l)**

STEP
1

Preread

Preview the following selection (pp. 113–117) by reading the title, the headings, and the first sentence of each paragraph, and by looking at the illustrations. Answer questions 1 and 2 without looking back at the selection.

1. What is the subject?

   _____

2. What is the main idea (the main thing the author is saying about
   the subject)?

   _____

3. Look at Figures 1 and 2 and read the captions.

   a. What is the subject of Figure 1?

   _____

   b. What is the main idea of Figure 1 (the main thing the illustration is
      telling you about the subject)?

   _____

c. What is the subject of Figure 2?

_____

_____

d. What is the main idea of Figure 2?

_____

_____

e. What inference can you make from Figures 1 and 2?

_____

_____

4. Take a moment to think about test-taking strategies. Think about what you know, what you don't know, and what you might find out from reading the selection. Make up three questions.

a. _____

b. _____

c. _____

Read

STEP
2

Read the selection without underlining.

Write your starting time here: _____

◆ *Improving Test-Taking Strategies*

Wayne Weiten

Let's face it—some students are better than others at taking tests. *Testwiseness* is the ability to use the characteristics and format of a cognitive test to maximize one's score. Students clearly vary in testwiseness, and such variations are reflected in performance on exams. Testwiseness is not a substitute for knowledge of the subject matter. However, skill in taking tests can help you show what you know when it is critical to do so.

A number of myths exist about the best way to take tests. For instance, it is widely believed that students shouldn't go back and change their answers to multiple-choice questions. Benjamin, Cavell, and Shallenberger (1984) found this to be the dominant belief among college faculty as well as students (see Figure 1). However, the old adage that "your first hunch is

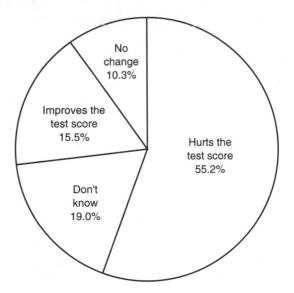

Figure 1   Beliefs about the effects of answer changing on tests.
Benjamin et al. asked 58 college faculty whether changing answers on tests is a good idea. Like most students, the majority of the faculty felt that answer changing usually hurts a student's test score, even though the evidence contradicts this belief (see Figure 2).

your best hunch on tests" has been shown to be wrong. Empirical studies clearly and consistently indicate that, over the long run, changing answers pays off. Benjamin and his colleagues reviewed 20 studies on this issue; their findings are presented in Figure 2. As you can see, answer changes that go from a wrong answer to a right answer outnumber changes that go from a right answer to a wrong one by a sizable margin. The popular belief that answer changing is harmful is probably attributable to painful memories of right-to-wrong changes. In any case, you can see how it pays to be familiar with sound test-taking strategies.

General Tips

- If efficient time use appears crucial, set up a mental schedule for progressing through the test. Make a mental note to check whether you're one-third finished when a third of your time is gone.

- Don't waste time pondering difficult-to-answer questions excessively. If you have no idea at all, just guess and go on. If you need to devote a good deal of time to the question, skip it and mark it so you can return to it later if time permits.

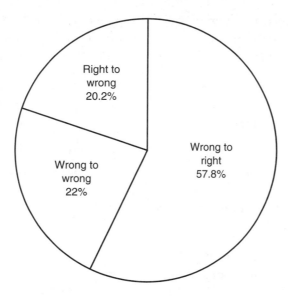

Figure 2   Actual effects of changing answers on multiple-choice tests.
When the data from all the relevant studies are combined, they indicate that answer changing on tests generally does not reduce students' test scores. It is interesting to note the contrast between beliefs about answer changing (see Figure 1) and the actual results of this practice.

- Adopt the appropriate level of sophistication for the test. Don't read things into questions. Sometimes students make things more complex than they were intended to be. Often, simple-looking questions are just what they appear to be.

- Unless it is explicitly forbidden, don't hesitate to ask the examiner to clarify a question when necessary. Many examiners will graciously provide a great deal of useful information.

- If you complete all of the questions and still have some time remaining, review the test. Make sure that you have recorded your answers correctly. If you were unsure of some answers, go back and reconsider them.

Tips for Multiple-Choice Exams

Sound test-taking strategies are especially important with multiple-choice (and true-false) questions. These types of questions often include clues that may help you converge on the correct answer. You may be able to improve your performance on such tests by considering the following advice:

- As you read the stem of each multiple-choice question, anticipate the answer if you can, before looking at the options. If the answer you anticipated is among the options, it is likely to be the correct one.

- Always read each question completely. Continue reading even if you find your anticipated answer among the options. There may be a more complete option farther down the list.

- Learn how to eliminate quickly those options that are highly implausible. Many questions have only two plausible options, accompanied by "throwaway" options for filler. You should work at spotting these implausible options so that you can quickly discard them and narrow your task.

- Be alert to the fact that information relevant to one question is sometimes given away in another test item.

- On items that have "all of the above" as an option, if you know that just two of the options are correct, you should choose "all of the above." If you are confident that one of the options is incorrect, you should eliminate this option and "all of the above" and choose from the remaining options.

- Options that represent broad, sweeping generalizations tend to be incorrect. You should be vigilant for words such as *always, never, necessarily, only, must, completely, totally,* and so forth that create those improbable assertions.

- In contrast, options that represent carefully qualified statements tend to be correct. Words such as *often, sometimes, perhaps, may,* and *generally* tend to show up in these well-qualified statements.

Tips for Essay Exams

There is little research on testwiseness as it applies to essay exams. This is because there are relatively few clues to take advantage of in the essay format. Nonetheless, various books offer tips based on expert advice, including the following:

- Time is usually a crucial factor on essay tests. Therefore, you should begin by looking over the questions and making time allocations on the basis of (1) your knowledge, (2) the time required to answer each question, and (3) the points available for answering each question. Usually it's a good idea to answer the questions that you know best first.

■ Many students fail to appreciate the importance of good organization in their essay responses. If your instructor can't follow where you are going with your answers, you won't get many points. Test essays are often poorly organized because students feel pressured for time and plunge into answering questions without any planning. It's a good idea to spend a minute getting organized first. Also, many examiners appreciate it if you make your organization quite explicit by using headings or by numbering the points you're making.

■ In writing essays, the trick is to be concise while being complete. You should always try to get right to the point, and you should never pad your answer. Many examiners get cross when they have to wade through excess padding to track down the crucial ideas they're looking for. However, you should avoid writing in such a "shorthand" manner that you leave things ambiguous.

■ In many courses you'll learn a great deal of jargon or technical terminology. Demonstrate your learning by using this technical vocabulary in your essay answers.

1000 words

Write your ending time here:_____

Subtract your starting time: _____

Total time: _____

Check the Rate Chart on p. 462 to find out how many words per minute you have read, and then record your score on the Reading Efficiency Progress Chart on p. 463.

Analyze What You Read

STEP 3

Make Graphic Organizers

We have filled in the main points in the following outline. Go back to the reading selection and find each one.

1. Write the Roman numerals from the outline in the margin next to where the main points are located.

2. Locate the subpoints and write the capital letter from the outline in the margin next to each subpoint in the reading selection.

3. Write the subpoints next to the capital letters in the blanks on the next page.

Improving Test-Taking Strategies

I. General tips

    A. _____

    B. _____

    C. _____

    D. _____

    E. _____

II. Tips for multiple-choice exams

    A. _____

        _____

    B. _____

        _____

    C. _____

        _____

    D. _____

        _____

    E. _____

        _____

    F. _____

        _____

    G. _____

        _____

III. Tips for essay exams

    A. _____

        _____

        _____

    B. _____

        _____

    C. _____

        _____

    D. _____

        _____

Use the outline to fill in the idea map below. Write the title in the circle. Write the Roman numeral headings in the rectangles. Write the capital letter headings in the triangles.

Remember What's Important

1. To prepare for a Comprehension Check, memorize the outline and/or idea map. Test yourself or have someone test you on the reading selection. Keep testing until you think you can remember everything you need to know. If necessary, review *How to Answer an Essay Question* on pp. 31–32.

2. To prepare for a Vocabulary Check, make flash cards as described on p. 12 for each of the words in the Vocabulary Preview that you do not know. Test yourself or have someone test you until you think you can remember them.

Make Use of What You Read

When you are ready, complete the Comprehension Check on p. 371 and the Vocabulary Check on p. 373. Do them from memory, without looking back at the book or your notes.

Evaluate Your Active Critical Thinking Skills

After your tests have been graded, record your scores on the Progress Chart, p. 456, and answer the questions on the Evaluation Checklist on p. 457.

Vocabulary Skills Review

Dictionary: Confused Words

The following five pairs of words are often confused. Fill in the blanks with the correct word from the pair that precedes each group of sentences.

> **aes•thet•ic** (es thet´ik) *adj.* [Gr *aisthētikos*, sensitive < *aisthanesthai*, to perceive < IE base **awis-* > L *audire*, to hear] **1.** of or in relation to aesthetics **2.** of beauty **3.** sensitive to art and beauty; showing good taste; artistic Also **aes•thet´i•cal** –*n.* an aesthetic theory or viewpoint

> **as•cet•ic** (ə set´ic) *adj.* [Gr(Ec) *askētikos*, austere < Gr, laborious, exercised < *askein*, to exercise, train (for athletic competition)] of or characteristic of ascetics or asceticism; self-denying; austere Also **as•cet´i•cal** –*n.* [< Gr *awkētēs*, monk, hermit] **1.** a person who leads a life of contemplation and rigorous self-denial for religious purposes **2.** anyone who lives with strict self-discipline and without the usual pleasures and comforts –*SYN.* SEVERE **–as•cet´i•cal•ly** *adv.*

1. A yogi who lives in a cave is an _____.

2. Most people agree that Rembrandt's paintings have great

   _____ value.

> **em•i•nent** (em´ə nənt) *adj.* [ME < L *eminens:* see EMINENCE] **1.** rising above other things or places; high; lofty **2.** projecting; prominent; protruding **3.** standing high by comparison with others, as in rank or achievement; renowned; exalted; distinguished **4.** outstanding; remarkable; noteworthy [a man of *eminent* courage] –*SYN.* FAMOUS **–em´i•nent•ly** *adv.*

> **im•mi•nent** (im´ə nənt) *adj.* [L *imminens*, prp. of *imminere*, to project over, threaten < *in-*, on + *minere*, to project: see MENACE] likely to

happen without delay; impending; threatening: said of danger, evil, misfortune **–im′mi•nent•ly** *adv.*

1. Sigmund Freud was an _____ psychologist.

2. The next election is _____ .

> **flaunt** (flônt) *vi.* [15th & 16th c., prob. < dial. *flant,* to strut coquettishly, akin to Norw *flanta* < ON *flana,* run back and forth < IE **plano-* < base **pla-,* broad, flat, spread out > Gr *planos,* wandering] **1.** to make a gaudy, ostentatious, conspicuous, impudent, or defiant display **2.** to flutter or wave freely *–vt.* **1.** to show off proudly, defiantly, or impudently [to *flaunt* one's guilt] **2.** FLOUT: usage objected to by many *–n.* [Archaic] the act of flaunting *–SYN.* SHOW **–flaunt′ingly** *adv.*

> **flout** (flout) *vt.* [prob. special use of ME *flouten,* to play the flute, hence, whistle (at)] to mock or scoff at; show scorn or contempt for *–vi.* to be scornful; show contempt; jeer; scoff *–n.* a scornful or contemptuous action or speech; mockery; scoffing; insult **–flout′er** *n.* **–flout′ing•ly** *adv.*

1. Actresses and models are often asked to _____ their

   sex appeal.

2. Old-style beatniks and hippies were people who liked to

   _____ conventional values.

> **hoard** (hōrd) *n.* [ME *hord* < OE, akin to Ger *hort,* Goth *huzd* < IE **keus-* < base **(s)keu-,* to cover, conceal > HIDE[1], Gr *skylos,* animal's skin] a supply stored up and hidden or kept in reserve *–vi.* to get and store away money, goods, etc. *–vt.* to accumulate and hide or keep in reserve **–hoard′er** *n.* **–hoard′ing** *n.*

> **horde** (hōrd) *n.* [Fr < Ger, earlier *horda* < Pol < Turk *ordū,* a camp < Tat *urdu,* a camp, lit., something erected < *urmak,* to pitch (a camp)] **1.** a nomadic tribe or clan of Mongols **2.** any wandering tribe or group **3.** a large, moving crowd or throng; swarm *–vt.* **hord′ed, hord′ing** to form or gather in a horde *–SYN.* CROWD[1]

1. A whole _____ of customers showed up at the garage sale.

2. Misers like to _____ their wealth.

> **li•able** (lī′ə bəl; *often, esp. for 3,* lī′bəl) *adj.* [prob. via Anglo-Fr < OFr *lier,* to bind < L *ligare,* to bind (see ligature) + -ABLE] **1.** legally bound or obligated, as to make good any loss or damage that occurs in a transaction; responsible **2.** likely to have, suffer from, etc.; exposed

to or subject to [*liable* to heart attacks] **3.** subject to the possibility of; likely (*to* do, have, get, etc. something unpleasant or unwanted) [*liable* to cause hard feelings] –*SYN.* LIKELY

li•bel (li′bəl) *n.* [ME, little book < OFr < L *libellus*, little book, writing, lampoon, dim. of *liber*, a book: see LIBRARY] **1.** any false and malicious written or printed statement, or any sign, picture, or effigy, tending to expose a person to public ridicule, hatred, or contempt or to injure a person's reputation in any way **2.** the act of publishing or displaying publicly such a thing **3.** anything that gives an unflattering or damaging picture of the subject with which it is dealing **4.** in ecclesiastical law and formerly in maritime law, a written statement containing the plaintiff's grievances; initial pleading –*vt.* **-beled** or **-belled, -bel•ing** or **-bel•ling 1.** to publish or make a libel against **2.** to give an unflattering or damaging picture of **3.** to bring suit against by presenting a LIBEL (*n.* 4)

1. If you start false rumors about someone, you can be sued for

   _____ .

2. If you don't turn in assignments, you are _____ to fail

   the class.

*For explanation
see pp. 2–4*

Context Clues

Use the context of each sentence to figure out the meaning of the italicized word. **Do not use a dictionary.** Circle the letter of the best definition, and then write in the type of clue: definition, contrast, example, or experience.

1. The Americans with Disabilities Act requires public buildings to be *accessible* to disabled people.

   a. closed   b. free   c. available   d. hidden from

   Type of clue: _____

2. Although most of the senators voted in the negative, a few voted in the *affirmative*.

   a. final stage   b. way they were told   c. same direction   d. positive

   Type of clue: _____

3. Over the years I have collected paintings, sculptures, and other *objets d'art*.

   a. investments   b. rare stamps   c. coin collections   d. art objects

   Type of clue: _____

4. *Socioeconomic* standing depends both on social class and on money.

   a. social and economic   b. intellectual and creative

   c. power and influence   d. old wealth

   Type of clue: _____

5. If you want to be a doctor or nurse, you have to get over *squeamishness* at the sight of blood and guts.

   a. enjoyment   b. matter-of-fact feelings   c. sick feelings   d. anger

   Type of clue: _____

6. For some women, childbirth is easy; for others it is *an ordeal.*

   a. enjoyable   b. a painful experience   c. an experience to remember

   d. hard to remember

   Type of clue: _____

7. The *stereotype* of the computer genius is a geek who wears peculiar clothes, thick glasses, and a pocket protector.

   a. popular idea   b. actual truth   c. deliberate lie   d. movie role

   Type of clue: _____

8. Some of the world's greatest artists were famous in their lifetimes; others remained *obscure* until long after their deaths.

   a. well-known   b. wealthy   c. sick   d. unknown

   Type of clue: _____

9. "Compos mentis" is Latin for "*sound mind.*"

   a. crazy   b. stupid   c. sane   d. asleep

   Type of clue: _____

10. Now that checks and credit cards have been invented, there is little need to carry bills in *denominations* larger than $100.

    a. coins   b. money orders   c. letters of credit   d. units of value

    Type of clue: _____

10 Conflict and Communication: Learning How to Disagree

Vocabulary Preview

confrontation (kän frun tā'shən): a face-to-face meeting, esp. in opposition or defiance

accommodation (ə käm'ə dā' shən): adaptation; adjustment of oneself to fit the circumstances

martyrdom (märt'ər dəm): severe, long-continued suffering; torment; torture

preceding (prē sēd'iŋ, pri-): going or coming before

integration (in' tə grā'shən): the bringing together and resolving of differences

disparages (di spar'ij iz): shows disrespect for; belittles

suppressed (sə prest'): kept back; restrained; checked

chronic (krän'ik): lasting a long time or recurring often

divergent (di vʉr'jənt): varying from one another or from a norm; deviating; different

defensive (dē fen'siv, di-): feeling under attack and hence quick to justify one's actions

stance (stans): the attitude adopted in confronting or dealing with a particular situation

passive aggression (pas'iv ə gresh'ən): when anger is denied but acted out

attributes (a'trə byo͞ots'): characteristics or qualities of a person or thing

alienate (āl'yən āt', āl'ē ən-): to make unfriendly; estrange [his behavior *alienated* his friends]

empathy (em'pə thē): ability to share in another's emotions, thoughts, or feelings

subtle (sut''l): delicately suggestive; not grossly obvious [a *subtle* hint]

responsive (ri spän'siv): reacting easily or readily

diplomacy (də plō'mə sē): skill in dealing with people; tact

invariably (in ver'ē ə blē): without variation or exception

inhibited (in hib'it id): held back; not freely expressive; restrained

cat, āte, fäther; pen, ēvil; if, kīte; nō, ôr, fo͞od, book; boil, house; up, tʉrn; chief, shell; thick, *the*; zh, treasure; ŋ, sing; ə for *a* in *about*; ' as in *able* (ā'b'l)

Preread

Preview the following selection (pp. 125–130) by reading the title and the boldface and italic headings. Answer the following questions without looking back at the selection.

1. What is the subject?

_____

2. What is the main idea (the main thing the author is saying about the subject)?

_____

3. Think about what you know about communication, what you don't know, and what you might find out from reading the selection. Make up three questions.

a. _____

b. _____

c. _____

Read

Read the selection without underlining.

Write your starting time here: _____

◆ *Conflict and Communication: Learning How to Disagree*

Brian K. Williams and Sharon M. Knight

Why can't couples get along better? Must there always be conflict in intimate relationships?

Conflict: Most People Adopt One of Five Styles of Dealing With Conflict

Researchers have identified five styles of dealing with conflict, one of which is probably closest to yours.

1. Avoidance: "Maybe It Will Go Away."

People who adopt this style find dealing with conflict unpleasant and uncomfortable. They hope that by ignoring the conflict or by avoiding confrontation the circumstances will change and the problem will magi-cally disappear. Unfortunately, avoiding or delaying conflict usually means the situation will have to be dealt with later, at which point it may have worsened.

2. Accommodation: "Oh, Have It Your Way!"

Accommodation does not mean compromise; it means simply giving in, although it does not really resolve the matter under dispute. People who adopt a style of easy surrender are, like avoiders, uncomfortable with conflict and hate disagreements. They are also inclined to be "people pleasers," worried about the approval of others. However, giving in does not really solve the conflict. If anything it may aggravate the situation over the long term because accommodators may be deeply resentful that the other person did not listen to their point of view. Indeed, the resentment may even develop into a role of martyrdom, irritating the partner.

3. Domination: "Only Winning Matters."

The person with a winning-is-everything, dominating style should not be surprised if he or she some day finds an "I've moved out" note from the partner. The dominator will go to any lengths to emerge triumphant in a disagreement, even if it means being aggressive and manipulative. However, winning isn't what intimate human relationships are about; that approach to conflict only produces hostility.

4. Compromise: "I'll Meet You Halfway."

Compromise seems like a civilized way of dealing with conflict, and it is definitely an improvement over the preceding styles. People striving for compromise recognize that partners have different needs and try to negotiate to reach agreement. Even so, they may still employ some gamesmanship, such as manipulation and misrepresentation, in an attempt to further their own ends. Thus, the compromise style is not as effective in resolving conflict as the integration style.

5. Integration: "Let's Honestly Try to Satisfy Both of Us."

Compromisers view solutions to conflict as a matter of each party meeting the other half way. The integration style, on the other hand, attempts to find a solution that will achieve satisfaction for both partners. Integration has several parts to it:

- *Openness for mutual problem solving:* The conflict is seen not as a game to be won or negotiated but as a problem to be solved for mutual benefit. Consequently, manipulation and misrepresentation have no place; honesty and openness are a necessary part of reaching the solution. This also has the benefit of building trust that will carry over to the resolution of other conflicts.

■ *Disagreement with the ideas, not the person:* An important part of integration, which we expand on below, is that partners criticize each other's ideas or specific acts rather than each other as persons. It is one thing, for instance, to say "You drink too much" and another to say "I feel you drank too much last evening." The first disparages character, the second states unhappiness with a particular incident.

■ *Emphasis on similarities, not differences:* Integration requires more work than other styles of dealing with conflict (although the payoffs are better) because partners must put a good deal of effort into stating and clarifying their positions. To maintain the spirit of trust and problem solving, the two should also emphasize the similarities in their positions as they work toward a mutually satisfactory solution.

Communication: There Are Ways to Learn How to Disagree

Conflict is practically always present in an ongoing relationship between two people. That does not mean it is bad or that it should be suppressed. When handled constructively, researchers point out, conflict may "(1) bring problems out into the open, where they can be solved, (2) put an end to chronic sources of discontent in a relationship, and (3) lead to new insights through the clashing of divergent views." The key to intimacy is the ability to handle conflict well, which means the ability to communicate well.

Bad Communication

Most of us *think* communication is easy, points out psychiatrist David Burns, because we've been talking since childhood. However, it's when we have a conflict that we find out if we communicate well.

Bad communication, says Burns, author of *The Feeling Good Handbook,* has two characteristics:

■ *You become argumentative and defensive:* The natural tendency of most of us when we are upset is to argue. The habit of contradicting others, however, is self-defeating, for it creates distance between you and them and prevents intimacy. Moreover, in this stance you show you are not interested in listening to the other person or understanding his or her feelings.

- *You deny your own feelings and act them out indirectly:* You may become sarcastic, or pout, or storm out of the room slamming doors. This kind of reaction, known as *passive aggression,* can sometimes be as destructive as *active aggression,* in which you make threats or tell the other person off.

Good Communication

"Most people want to be understood and accepted more than anything else in the world," says Burns. Knowing that is a first step toward good communication.

Good communication, according to Burns, has two attributes:

- *You listen to and acknowledge the other person's feelings:* Instead of showing that you are only interested in broadcasting your feelings and insisting that the other agree with you, you encourage the other to express his or her feelings. You try to listen to and understand what the other person is thinking and feeling.

- *You express your own feelings openly and directly:* If you only listen to the other person's feelings and don't express your own, you will end up feeling shortchanged, angry, and resentful. When you deny your feelings, you end up acting them out indirectly. The trick, then, is to express your feelings in a way that will not alienate the other person.

Becoming Expert at Listening

Besides the Burns book, perhaps one of the best books on communication is *Love Is Never Enough* by Aaron Beck.

Some listening guidelines Beck suggests:

- *Tune in to your partner's channel:* Imagining how the other person might be feeling—putting yourself in the other's shoes—is known as *empathy,* trying to experience the other's thoughts and feelings.

- *Give listening signals:* Use facial expressions, subtle gestures, and sounds such as "uh-huh" and "yeah" to show your partner you are really listening. Beck particularly urges this advice on men, since studies find that women are more inclined to send responsive signals.

- *Don't interrupt:* Although interruptions may seem natural to you, they can make the other person feel cut off. Men, says Beck, tend to interrupt more than women do, although they interrupt other men as often as they do women.

■ *Ask questions skillfully:* Asking questions can help you determine what the other person is thinking and keep the discussion going—provided the question is not a *conversation stopper.* "Why" questions can be conversation stoppers ("Why were you home late?"). So can questions that can have only a yes-or-no answer. Questions that ask the other's opinion can be *conversation starters* ("What do you think about always having dinner at the same time?"). Questions that reflect the other's statements ("Can you tell me more about why you feel that way?") help convey your empathy. The important thing is to ask questions *gently,* never accusingly.

■ *Use diplomacy and tact:* Everyone has sensitive areas—about their appearance or how they speak, for example. This is true of people in intimate relationships as much as people in other relationships. *Problems in relationships invariably involve feelings.* Using diplomacy in your responses will help build trust to talk about difficulties.

An especially wise piece of advice about listening comes from David Burns: find *some* truth in what the other person is saying and agree with it, even if you feel convinced that what he or she is saying is totally wrong, unreasonable, irrational, or unfair. This technique, known as *disarming,* works especially well if you're feeling criticized and attacked. If you resist the urge to argue or defend yourself and instead agree with the other person, it takes the wind out of the other person's sails and has a calming effect. That person will then be more open to your point of view. Adds Burns: "When you use the disarming technique, you must be genuine in what you say or it will backfire. You can always find some valid way to agree, no matter how illogical the person's accusations might seem to you. If you agree with them in a sincere way, they will generally soften and will be far more willing to listen to you."

Becoming Expert at Expressing Yourself

In expressing yourself, there are two principal points to keep in mind:

■ *Use "I feel" language:* It's always tempting to use accusatory language during the heat of conflict ("You make me so mad!" or "You never listen to what I say!"), but this is sure to send the other person stomping out of the room. By using the simple method of saying "I feel" followed by the word expressing your feelings ("frustrated," "ignored," "attacked," "nervous," "unloved"), you don't sound blaming and critical, as you would by saying "You make me . . ." or "You never . . ." By telling your partner how you feel, rather than defending the "truth" of your position, you are able to express your feelings without attacking the other person.

■ *Express praise and keep criticism specific:* In any conflict, we may disagree with a person's *specific act or behavior,* but we need not reject the other as a person. For example, to express criticism alone, you might say, "When we make love you seem so inhibited." Better to combine criticism with praise by saying, "I appreciate the way you respond to me when we make love, and I think it could be even better if you would take the initiative sometimes. Does this seem like a reasonable request?"

1600 words

Write your ending time here:_____

Subtract your starting time: _____

Total time: _____

    Check the Rate Chart on p. 462 to find out how many words per minute you have read, and then record your score on the Reading Efficiency Progress Chart on p. 463.

Analyze What You Read

STEP
3

Make Graphic Organizers

Go back to the reading selection and find the points in the following outline.

1. Write the Roman numerals from the outline in the margin next to the two major headings.

2. Write the capital letters from the outline in the margin next to the minor headings.

3. Write the Arabic numbers from the outline in the margin next to the italic headings.

4. Use what you have written in the margin to fill in the outline below.

Conflict and Communication: Learning How to Disagree

I. _____

    A. _____

    B. _____

    C. _____

    D. _____

E. _____

    1. _____

    2. _____

    3. _____

II. _____

  A. _____

    1. _____

    2. _____

  B. _____

    1. _____

    2. _____

  C. _____

    1. _____

    2. _____

    3. _____

    4. _____

    5. _____

  D. _____

    1. _____

    2. _____

Remember What's Important

1. To prepare for a Comprehension Check, memorize the outline. Test yourself or have someone test you on the reading selection. Keep testing until you think you can remember everything you need to know. If necessary, review *How to Answer an Essay Question* on pp. 31–32.

2. To prepare for a Vocabulary Check, make flash cards as described on p. 12 for each of the words in the Vocabulary Preview that you do not know. Test yourself or have someone test you until you think you can remember them.

Make Use of What You Read

When you are ready, complete the Comprehension Check on p. 375 and the Vocabulary Check on p. 377. Do them from memory, without looking back at the book or your notes.

STEP 6

Evaluate Your Active Critical Thinking Skills

After your tests have been graded, record your scores on the Progress Chart, p. 456, and answer the questions on the Evaluation Checklist on p. 457.

Vocabulary Skills Review

Word Memory

For explanation see pp. 2–4

1. *Use the word in context.* Write sentences that make clear the meanings of each of the following words:

   a. disparage _____

   _____

   b. inhibit _____

   _____

   c. stance _____

   _____

For explanation see pp. 11–12

2. *Make word associations.* In the space next to each of the following words from this reading selection, write a familiar word or phrase that can help you remember the new one.

   a. confront _____

   b. responsive _____

   c. invariably _____

   d. defensive _____

For explanation see pp. 4–5

3. *Use word parts.* Write the correct word part from the following list in each blank. Make sure the words match their definitions. Use the dictionary if you need help. The word parts may be used more than once.

Word Part	Example
pre = before	preview (to see before)
al = other, strange	alien (from another place; stranger)
path = feel	sympathy (feeling for another)
press = squeeze, press	pressure (squeezing, pressing)
verg or vers = turn	versus (turned against)
chron = time	chronicle (history; order of events in time)
var = change	variety (change)

Word	Definition
a. __ __ __ cede	to go or come <u>before</u>
b. sup __ __ __ __ __	to check (<u>press</u> back or down)
c. __ __ __ __ __ ic	lasting a long <u>time</u>
d. di __ __ __ __ent	different (<u>turning</u> away from the norm)
e. __ __ ienate	to e<u>strange</u>; make unfriendly
f. em __ __ __ __ y	<u>feeling</u> with another person
g. in __ __ __ iably	without <u>changing</u>

For explanation see p. 12

4. *Make flash cards.* Find ten words from this or previous reading selections that you have trouble remembering. On the front of the card, write the word and its pronunciation. On the back, write the definition in your own words and use the word in a sentence. Test yourself by looking at the front of the card and trying to restate the definition and a sentence. The average word requires seven self-testing sessions to be memorized.

For explanation see p. 86

Analogies

For each analogy below, write the word from the Vocabulary Preview that completes the analogy. Look back at the preview definitions if you need help.

confrontation   blatant   disparage   chronic   divergent

stance   attributes   alienate   subtle   invariably

preceding   inhibited   suppressed

1. chronic : regular : : _____ : different

2. invariably : never : : _____ : blatant

3. confrontation : avoidance : : _____ : following

4. suppressed : controlled : : _____ : shy

5. stance : posture : : _____ : characteristics

6. alienate : attract : : _____ : praise

UNIT III

Textbook Learning with the ACT Method

Creating a Study System Using the ACT Method

Good students use a study system. A study system does three things. First, it helps you figure out what will be on a test so that you know what to study. Second, it gives you a way to study that leads to success. Third, it takes as little time as possible. The six-step ACT system accomplishes all three purposes.

Preread

As you remember from Unit II, prereading increases your comprehension in two ways. First, it sets up mental categories to increase comprehension. In psychology, these categories are called *advance organizers.* Second, the process of activating your background knowledge and generating questions sets the stage for active rather than passive reading.

Prereading Textbooks

When you first buy your books, take five or ten minutes to preview each one. First, look at the front matter: author, title, date of publication, table of contents, preface, foreword, or introduction. Second, look at the back matter: is there a glossary, appendix, index, bibliography? Then flip through the book, noting its organization. Are there chapter objectives or outlines, chapter summaries, review questions at the ends of the chapters? Are there clear headings? Are there many illustrations? This preview lets you know what is in the book and how it is organized. It also lets you know whether there are any study aids.

Prereading Chapters

When a chapter is assigned, take a few minutes to preview it before reading. Read the chapter title, the outline if there is one, and all the headings and subheadings. If there are illustrations, read the caption of each one and try to figure out the main idea by looking at the illustration. Read the summary or review questions at the end of the chapter, if they are included. This preview will give you an overview of all the main ideas in the chapter, and it will increase your comprehension, memory, and speed.

Next, take a moment to activate your mind. Think about what you know and don't know about the topic. Make up some questions that you think might be answered by the reading.

Read

If the chapter is long, break it into logical sections. Use the headings as guides to the sections. Take the first section and read *with your pencil down.* Do not underline or highlight at this point. Just try to understand what you are reading and find answers to your questions. There are several things you can do if you find material you don't understand. First, mark what you don't understand. Then look for an explanation. You can ask your instructor in class or during his or her office hours. You can ask other students. You can also find books, tapes, or computer programs that cover the same subject using different explanations and/or different examples. Sometimes, especially in math, the problem isn't really that you don't understand it. It's that you just need more practice. So, for example, if you have problems with percentages, find an extra textbook or workbook that you can use to get the practice you need. The same goes for grammar or any other subject that requires practice. One way or another, do what you need to make sure you understand the material.

Analyze What You Read—Create a Study Guide

First, find out whatever you can about the test. You can ask the instructor which chapters and lectures will be covered, how much time you will have, and the number and types of questions. There are four different types of test questions: objective, essay, application, and problem-solving. The study guide you create will depend on the type. You can also ask other students who have taken the class about the tests. If you can obtain copies of old tests, so much the better.

Second, you must predict the questions. This may sound hard to do, but it really isn't. Put yourself in the instructor's place. What you (the instructor) really want to do is find out who learned the material and who didn't so you can assign grades. You hope the students do well on the test, because that means you did a good job teaching them. Therefore, most instructors will test the students on the most important material and skip what is less important.

Review both the text and the lecture notes. Pay attention to the topics your instructor stressed in class. Let's say the test will cover five chapters and will have fifty objective items (true-false, multiple choice, matching, and or completion/short answer). The test will probably cover the fifty most obvious items. If you pick the seventy most obvious items to memorize, you will probably get an A. If the test will have five essay questions, and you pick the ten most obvious ones to memorize, you should score very well.

Study Guide for Objective Tests

Underline: Let's say you have just finished reading the first section of a chapter as described in Step 2. Look it over, thinking about what is likely to be on the test and which of those things you might have trouble remembering. Underline or highlight *only those things.* Do not underline too much. The purpose of underlining is quick review for tests. If you underline too much, you will defeat your purpose.

Make Marginal Notes: In the margin, next to each idea you have underlined, write a note that you can use to test your memory. Don't write a summary. Write something you can use as a question. Another way of thinking about it is to consider the marginal note as the subject and the underlining as the main idea. Look at this example:

3 types of
insomnia

> It is convenient to distinguish three main types of insomnia. People with onset insomnia have trouble falling asleep. Those with termination insomnia awaken early and cannot get back to sleep. Those with maintenance insomnia awaken frequently during the night, though they get back to sleep each time. (From James Kalat, *Introduction to Psychology*, 4th Ed., Brooks/Cole, 1996, p. 195.)

Notice that the marginal note doesn't give a definition. It only lets you test your memory.

Flash Cards: Instead of, or in addition to, marking in your book, you can use flash cards. On the front of the flash card, write what you *would* have put in the margin (the subject). On the back, write what you would have underlined (the main idea). Here is an example:

Front

> 3 types
> of insomnia

Back

> 1. Onset insomnia
> 2. Termination insomnia
> 3. Maintenance insomnia

Flash cards can easily be carried in a pocket or purse. One secret of successful study is to use small bits of time instead of waiting until you have a few hours free. For example, while you are eating lunch alone, standing in line, or riding the bus, you could be memorizing your flash cards. Look at the topic on the front, and test yourself to see if you remember what's on the back. If you get your memorization done in advance, you won't have much to worry about just before the exam.

Study Guide for Essay Tests

Essay questions are broader and more general than most objective questions. Therefore, you will have to look for important ideas rather than details when you predict the questions.

After you have predicted the questions, you have to put the answers in a form that can be memorized. This means making up pictures, or *graphic organizers*. A graphic organizer can be an outline, a study map, a chart, a time line, or whatever other visual format you can think of. They are just like the ones you already used in Unit II. You can put them on flash cards or paper, depending on the amount of room you need. Put the subject on the front and the graphic organizer on the back. If your graphic organizers are small enough to carry with you, you can use them like flash cards to take advantage of small bits of time you would otherwise waste.

Study Guide for Problem-Solving or Application Exams

Problem-solving tests often occur in mathematics and science courses. Application tests occur when you have to *use* what you've learned, as in foreign languages or music. In either case, try to predict the types of problems or performance that will be tested. Then make a plan to make sure you get enough practice to reach the level of mastery you need. For example, if you know the test will cover decimals, schedule enough time to practice decimals until you feel confident. If the test requires swimming the backstroke, schedule the number of practice sessions you will need.

Some tests require more than one type of preparation. For example, a Spanish test might require memorization of flash cards for vocabulary and grammar. It might also require application; it could test your reading or listening comprehension or your speaking ability in Spanish. Many classes have both objective and essay questions on tests. Also, some objective questions can test application or problem-solving ability. Here are some examples:

True or false: The product of 2 and 2 is 4. **(True)**

Multiple choice: Which of the following is a complete sentence?

a. Hurry up!

b. Having a good day.

c. Jimmy and his brother.

d. All of the above. **(The answer is a.)**

Learning Style

During your years in school, you probably liked some subjects better than others. The ones you liked were probably easier for you. Part of the reason is your learning style. For example, some people understand the logic of mathematics and science. Others enjoy the creativity of literature or art. Some people find it easy to memorize facts, but they hate to write essays. Others enjoy expressing themselves in words, but they hate to memorize. Some learn best from reading; they understand things better when they see them. Others learn best from lectures and discussions; they learn better from hearing.

Just as you have a learning style, each of your instructors also has a teaching style. Some prepare well-organized lectures and assignments. Others come to class without notes and teach through informal discussion. Some give tests that focus on memorizing facts. Others give tests that require you to analyze information and draw conclusions.

You will probably have little trouble when your learning style matches your instructor's teaching style. You are more likely to have problems when there is a mismatch. One of the best things you can do in that case is join a study group with people whose learning styles are more like the instructor's. For example, let's say you are studying for a history exam that will require analysis, and you have trouble with analysis. Try to find other students who can help you predict questions. Then you can make your graphic organizers and memorize.

Remember What's Important

In this step you memorize what is on your study guides for essay and objective tests, or you practice what is on your study guides for problem-solving and application tests.

Remembering

Some students try to memorize by reading the material they have underlined over and over, hoping something will stick. A better way to memorize is by self-testing. Test yourself the first time immediately after Step 3. If you cannot remember the material at this point, you probably won't remember it for a test.

If your study guide consists of underlining and marginal notes, cover the page and use the marginal notes to test your memory of what you have underlined. Pay attention to any points you miss. Keep self-testing until you remember everything.

If you are using flash cards, test yourself on the subject written on the front of the card. Put the cards away as you memorize them, so you don't keep retesting on those you already know. Try to have no more than ten to twenty cards to work on at one time. The night before the exam you should have just a few that still need reviewing. Review them before going to bed, get a good night's sleep, and review them again just before the test.

If you have broken the chapter into sections for Steps 2, 3, and 4, repeat the steps for each section until you reach the end of the chapter.

When you have finished a chapter, retest yourself on the marginal notes or flash cards for the whole chapter. Concentrate on what is most difficult, and keep testing until you reach mastery. If you are using graphic organizers, self-test the same way you would with flash cards. If you need to, you can draw each graphic organizer from memory and make sure it matches the original. If there are any study questions at the end of the chapter, answer them. Check your answers by looking back at the chapter. Review again about one week later and then as often as needed until the test. The more difficult the chapter, the more frequent the review should be. That way you won't have to cram for the test.

Practicing

If your study guide contains a plan or schedule for practicing for application or problem-solving tests, follow the study guide. Keep practicing until you reach mastery. For example, if you have to master the backstroke, schedule enough pool sessions. If you have to master decimals, schedule enough decimal problems.

Make Use of What You Read—Take the Test

The following suggestions are good for taking all types of tests:

1. Arrive at the test on time. Bring pencils, blue books, a calculator, or whatever you need.

2. Look the test over and then look at the clock. Make a schedule that will give you the most points. For example, if you have to answer fifty multiple-choice questions in fifty minutes, make sure that after twenty-five minutes have gone by, you are somewhere near the twenty-fifth question. If there is an essay worth fifty points and fifty objective questions worth one point each, make sure you spend approximately half your time on the essay. Allow enough time to review the test before you turn it in.

3. Answer the easy questions first. Mark those you don't know and come back to them later. Unless there is a penalty for guessing, don't leave anything blank. If there is a penalty, find out what it is and figure out mathematically when you should guess. For example, let's say there are five multiple choices and 25 percent is deducted for each wrong answer (as on the SAT test). If you have absolutely no idea which choice is right, you have a 20 percent (one-fifth) chance of being right by making a wild guess. However, 25 percent (one-fourth of a point) is deducted if you're wrong. In that case, don't guess. If, however, you can eliminate one of the choices that you are sure is wrong, then you have a 25 percent chance of being right by guessing among the remaining four. Your reward for being right is equal to your penalty for being wrong. If you can eliminate two choices, then your odds increase to 33 percent (one-third). In that case, you should definitely guess.

Essay Tests

In addition to the skills described above, there are some special skills you need for essay tests.

1. *Follow the directions.* The topics you memorized by using your graphic organizers will be turned into test questions by your instructor. You will have to direct your answers in such a way that they answer what is asked. The following words are often used in the directions for essay tests. Review them carefully and be sure you know what they mean so you can do exactly what they say when you take a test:

List = make a list

Compare = show similarities

Contrast = show differences

Discuss = give an overview

Outline = make an outline

Enumerate = list with numbers

Trace = describe in order

Summarize = write the major ideas in a few words

Diagram = draw an illustration

Criticize = say what's wrong with it

Evaluate = give good and bad points

2. *Organize.* Before writing an essay, draw the outline, map, or other graphic organizer from your study guide. **Write the essay from your graphic**

organizer, and use an introduction, conclusion, and signal words (*first, most important, finally*). If your essay is disorganized, the instructor will think you don't know the answer. If you really don't know the answer, write anything that comes to mind in the hopes that you will pick up a few points.

Application and Problem-Solving Tests

Follow the general directions given earlier. As with essay tests, if you don't know an answer or have not mastered a skill, and if credit is given for partial mastery, do whatever you can in the hopes of picking up a few points.

Evaluate Your ACT Skills—Analyze Test Results

When you get your test back, first make sure you understand your mistakes. Then analyze your test-taking skills. Answering the following questions will help you do better next time.

- Did you find out enough about the test? For example, did you study the right chapters, did you prepare for the right number and types of questions (essay, objective, problem-solving)? If not, ask more questions next time.

- Did you predict the right questions? If there were any questions you didn't expect, go back to the book and find out why you didn't anticipate them.

- Did you use good test-taking skills? Did you arrive on time with the right materials? Did you organize your time so you were able to answer all the questions and check them over before turning in the test?

- Did you remember the material you studied? If not, make better use of marginal notes, flash cards, and graphic organizers for self-testing.

- If there were essay questions, did you follow directions and organize your answers before beginning to write?

- If there were problem-solving or application questions, did you practice enough?

At first the ACT system might seem uncomfortable because it is new, but keep trying. By the end of this unit, you will find that your time and effort have been well spent.

11 The Stages of Death and Loss

Vocabulary Preview

psychologist (sī käl′ə jist): one who studies the mind and mental and emotional processes

psychiatrist (sī kī′ə trist, si-): a doctor of medicine specializing in disorders of the mind

sociologist (sō′sē äl′ə jist): one who studies the science of human society and of social relations, organization, and change

taboo (tə bōō′, ta-): prohibited or forbidden by convention or tradition

seminar (sem′ə när′): an advanced discussion course

contemporary (kən tem′pə rer′ē): of or in the style of the present or recent times; modern

universal (yōōn′ə vʉr′səl): understood by all

impending (im pend′iŋ): coming; about to happen

resolution (rez′ə lōō′shən): the act or process of resolving something; arriving at an acceptable end

delineate (di lin′ē āt′): to depict in words; describe

compartmentalize (käm′pärt men′tə līz): to put or separate into compartments, divisions, or categories

displaced (dis plāst′): placed on the wrong object

essence (es′əns): fundamental nature or most important quality (of something)

remission (ri mish′ən): a relatively prolonged lessening or disappearance of the symptoms of a disease

subjected (səb jekt′id): caused to undergo or experience some action or treatment

chemotherapy (kē′mō ther′ə pē): the prevention or treatment of disease by the administration of drugs

depleting (dē plēt′iŋ): making less by gradually using up (resources, funds, strength, etc.)

serenity (sə ren′ə tē): calmness; tranquillity

devoid (di void′): completely without; empty or destitute (*of*)

dehumanizing (dē hyōō′mə nīz′iŋ): depriving of human qualities or individuality

cat, **ā**te, **fä**ther; pen, **ē**vil; if, **kī**te; n**ō**, **ô**r, f**ōō**d, book; boil, house; up, tʉrn; chief, shell; thick, *the*; zh, treasure; ŋ, sing; ə for *a* in *about*; ′ as in *able* (ā′b′l)

Preread

Preview the following selection by reading the title and the headings. Answer the following questions without looking back at the reading.

1. What is the subject?

_____

2. What is the main idea?

_____

3. Take a moment to think about the stages of death and loss. Think about what you know, what you don't know, and what you might find out from reading the selection. Make up three questions.

   a. _____

   b. _____

   c. _____

Read

Read the selection without underlining. Ignore the notes written in the margin.

Write your starting time here: _____

◆ *The Stages of Death and Loss*

Gerald Corey and Marianne Schneider Corey

Death and dying have become topics of widespread discussion among psychologists, psychiatrists, physicians, sociologists, ministers, and researchers. Whereas these topics were once taboo for many people, they are now the focus of seminars, courses, and workshops, and a number of books give evidence of this growing interest.

Dr. Elisabeth Kübler-Ross is a pioneer in the contemporary study of death and dying. In her widely read books *On Death and Dying* (1969) and *Death: The Final Stage of Growth* (1975), she discusses the psychological and sociological aspects of death and the experience of dying. In a more recent book, *AIDS: The Ultimate Challenge*, Kübler-Ross (1993) applies the stages of dying to people with AIDS. Thanks to her efforts, many people have become aware of the almost universal need the dying have to talk about their impending death and to complete their business with the important

expert on death and dying

people in their lives. She has shown how ignorance of the dying process and of the needs of dying people—as well as the fears of those around them—can rob the dying of the opportunity to fully experience their feelings and arrive at a resolution of them.

2 reasons to study dying

5 stages

A greater understanding of dying can help us come to an acceptance of death, as well as be more helpful and present to those who are dying. For this reason, we describe the five stages of dying that Kübler-Ross has delineated, based on her research with terminally ill cancer patients. She emphasizes that these are not neat and compartmentalized stages that every person passes through in an orderly fashion. At times a person may experience a combination of these stages, perhaps skip one or more stages, or go back to an earlier stage he or she has already experienced. In general, however, Kübler-Ross found this sequence: denial, anger, bargaining, depression, and acceptance.

To make this discussion of the stages of dying more concrete, we will examine these stages as they relate to Ann, a 30-year-old cancer patient. Ann was married and the mother of three children in elementary school. Before she discovered that she had terminal cancer, she felt she had much to live for, and she enjoyed life.

denial

Denial

Ann's first reaction to being told she had only about a year to live was shock. She refused to believe that the diagnosis was correct. Even after obtaining several other medical opinions, she still refused to accept that she was dying. In other words, her initial reaction was one of *denial*.

Even though Ann was attempting to deny the full impact of the reality, it would have been a mistake to assume that she didn't want to talk about her feelings. Her husband also denied her illness and was unwilling to talk to her about it. He felt that talking bluntly might only make her more depressed and lead her to lose all hope. He failed to recognize how important it would have been to Ann to feel that she *could* bring up the subject if she wished. On some level she knew that she could not talk about her death with her husband.

how to help

During the stage of denial, the attitudes of a dying person's family and friends are critical. If these people cannot face the fact of their loved one's dying, they cannot help him or her move toward an acceptance of death. Their own fear will blind them to signs that the dying person wants to talk about his or her death and needs support. In the case of Ann it would not necessarily have been a wise idea to force her to talk, but she could have been greatly helped if those around her had been available and sensitive to her when she stopped denying her death and showed a need to be listened to.

Anger

anger

As Ann began to accept that her time was limited by an incurable disease, her denial was replaced by anger. Over and over she wondered why she— who had so much to live for—had to be afflicted with this dreadful disease. Her anger mounted as she thought of her children and realized that she would not be able to see them grow and develop. During her frequent visits to the hospital for radiation treatments, she directed some of her anger toward doctors "who didn't seem to know what they were doing" and toward the "impersonal" nurses.

During the stage of anger it's important that others recognize the need of dying people to express their anger, whether they direct it toward their doctors, the hospital staff, their friends, their children, or God. If this dis- placed anger is taken personally, any meaningful dialogue with the dying will be cut off. Moreover, people like Ann have reason to be enraged over having to suffer in this way when they have so much to live for. Rather than withdrawing support or taking offense, the people who surround a dying person can help most by allowing the person to fully express the pent-up rage inside. In this way they help the person to ultimately come to terms with his or her death.

how to help

Bargaining

bargaining

Kübler-Ross (1969) sums up the essence of the bargaining stage as follows: "If God has decided to take us from this earth and he did not respond to any angry pleas, he may be more favorable if I ask nicely." Basically, the stage of bargaining is an attempt to postpone the inevitable end.

Ann's ambitions at this stage were to finish her college studies and graduate with her bachelor's degree, which she was close to obtaining. She also hoped to see her oldest daughter begin junior high school in a little over a year. During this time she tried any type of treatment that offered some hope of extending her life.

Depression

depression

Eventually Ann's bargaining time ran out. No possibility of remission of her cancer remained, and she could no longer deny the inevitability of her death. Having been subjected to radiation treatments, chemotherapy, and a series of operations, she was becoming weaker and thinner, and she was able to do less and less. Her primary feelings became a great sense of loss and a fear of the unknown. She wondered about who would take care of her children and about her husband's future. She felt guilty because she was demanding so much attention and time and because the treatment of her illness was depleting the family income. She felt depressed over losing her hair and her beauty.

how to help

It would not have been helpful at this stage to try to cheer Ann up or to deny her real situation. Just as it had been important to allow her to fully vent her anger, it was important now to let her talk about her feelings and to make her final plans. Dying people are about to lose everyone they love, and only the freedom to grieve over these losses will enable them to find some peace and serenity in a final acceptance of death.

acceptance

Acceptance

Kübler-Ross found that if patients have had enough time and support to work through the previous stages, most of them reach a stage at which they are neither depressed nor angry. Because they have expressed their anger and are mourning the impending loss of those they love, they are able to become more accepting of their death. Kübler-Ross comments: "Acceptance should not be mistaken for a happy stage. It is almost devoid of feelings. It is as if the pain has gone, the struggle is over, and there comes a time for 'the final rest before the long journey,' as one patient phrased it."

Of course, some people never achieve an acceptance of their death, and some have no desire to. Ann, for example, never truly reached a stage of acceptance. Her final attitude was more one of surrender, a realization that it was futile to fight any longer. Although she still felt unready to die, she did want an end to her suffering. It may be that if those close to her had been more open to her and accepting of her feelings, she would have been able to work through more of her anger and depression.

how to use
the stages

The Significance of Kübler-Ross's Stages

Kübler-Ross's description of the dying process is not meant to be rigid and should not be interpreted as a natural progression that is expected in most cases. just as people are unique in the way they live, they are unique in the way they die. It is a mistake to use these stages as the standard by which to judge whether a dying person's behavior is normal or right. The value of the stages is that they describe and summarize in a general way what many patients experience and therefore add to our understanding of dying. Sometimes practitioners who work with the terminally ill forget that the stages of dying do not progress neatly, even though they cognitively know this reality. One practitioner told us: "Although I had read Kübler-Ross's book and knew the stages that a dying person was supposed to go through, many of my terminal patients had not read the same book!"

Patients who do not make it to the acceptance stage are sometimes viewed as failures. For example, some nurses get angry at patients who take "backward" steps by going from depression to anger, or they question patients about why they have "stayed so long in the anger stage." People die in a variety of ways and have a variety of feelings during this process: hope, anger, depression, fear, envy, relief, and anticipation. Those who are dying move back and forth from mood to mood. Therefore, these stages should not be used as a method of categorizing, and thus dehumanizing, the dying; they are best used as a frame of reference for helping them.

1700 words

Write your ending time here:_____

Subtract your starting time: _____

Total time: _____

Check the Rate Chart on p. 462 to find out how many words per minute you have read, and then record your score on the Reading Efficiency Progress Chart on p. 464.

Analyze What You Read—Create a Study Guide

Objective Questions

Go back to the reading selection and think about what would likely be on a test. Then think about whether or not you will remember it. Underline or highlight only (1) what you believe will be on a test and (2) what you don't think you will remember. Since this is your first selection for study reading, we have written the marginal self-test notes for you. You can use the notes as a guide to what should be underlined. Remember that the notes are like the subject and the underlining is like the main idea. If you prefer, you may write each self-test note on the front of a flash card and write what you would have underlined (change it into your own words) on the back.

Essay/Application Questions

Predict Essay Questions: There is only one topic in this reading selection important enough for an essay. Write it here:

_____

Make Graphic Organizers: Fill in the following idea map.

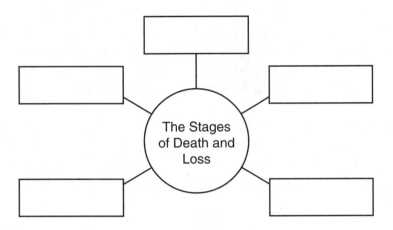

The Stages of Death and Loss

Skill Development: Summarizing

You have already been writing essays in Unit II. The main difference between essays and summaries is that the summary covers all the important ideas in a reading selection, while the answer to an essay question covers only what is asked. Depending on the question, the essay may be the same as the summary, or it may cover only part of the summary.

Summarizing, essays, and most other types of writing are easy if you have a graphic organizer. Writing is much harder if you don't. For this reading you have two graphic organizers. The first one consists of the underlining and notes in the margin of the reading selection. The second one consists of the idea map. Here is how to summarize using each of them:

1. To summarize using the underlining and marginal notes: First, write the main idea in a complete sentence. Then turn each marginal note into a complete sentence, using the underlining as needed. Use paragraph form, not outline form. Use signal or transition words, such as *first, finally, therefore*, etc., to make it easier for the reader to follow your ideas. For example, you might say, "Dr. Kübler-Ross has identified five stages of dying."

2. To summarize using the idea map above, do the same thing. Start with the main idea. Turn the topics into sentences using paragraph form. Use signal words. Now write your summary on a separate piece of paper.

Remember What's Important

Use the marginal self-test notes or the flash cards and the graphic organizer to memorize the material.

To use the marginal self-test notes, cover the page with your hand, look at the note, and see if you can give the answer. Remove your hand and check your answer. If it is not correct, do it again until it is correct.

To use the flash cards, look at the topic on the front and try to give the answer. Check the answer on the back. If it is not correct, keep self-testing until you can remember it.

You can use the graphic organizer (idea map) by trying to draw it from memory. Check your answer and do it again until it is correct.

If it's easier or more fun for you to have someone else test you, that's fine. Remember to keep testing until you think you can remember everything for the Comprehension Check.

Memorize the Vocabulary Preview words as needed for the Vocabulary Check.

Make Use of What You Read

When you are ready, complete the Comprehension Check on p. 379 and the Vocabulary Check on p. 381. Do not look back at the reading selection or study guides.

Evaluate Your Active Critical Thinking Skills

After your tests have been graded, record your scores on the Progress Chart, p. 456, and answer the questions on the Evaluation Checklist on p. 457.

<table>
<tr><td>**12**</td><td># Intellectual Health: Critical Thinking and the Art of Living</td></tr>
</table>

Vocabulary Preview

prevail (prē vāl′, pri-): to be effective; succeed

pornography (pôr näg′rə fē): writings, pictures, etc. intended primarily to arouse sexual desire

faculties (fak′əl tēz): powers or abilities to do some particular thing; special aptitudes or skills

prospective (prō spek′tiv, prə-; also prä-): expected; likely; future

alleviate (ə lē′vē āt′): to reduce or decrease

unprecedented (un pres′ə den′tid): having no precedent or parallel; unheard-of; novel

debunker (dē buŋk′ər): one who exposes false or exaggerated claims

paranormal (par′ə nôr′məl): having to do with psychic or mental phenomena outside the range of the normal

absurdity (ab sʉr′də tē, -zʉr′-; əb-): an absurd idea or thing; nonsense

conversely (kən vʉrs′lē): on the other hand; having any opposite or contrary position

subconscious (sub kän′shəs): occurring without conscious perception, or with only slight perception, on the part of the individual: said of mental processes and reactions

deductive (dē dukt′iv, di-): *Logic* a type of reasoning based on deducing; reasoning from the general to the specific, or from premises to a logically valid conclusion

inductive (in duk′tiv): *Logic* a type of reasoning from particular facts or individual cases to a general conclusion

premise (prem′is): a previous statement or assertion that serves as the basis for an argument

anecdote (an′ik dōt′, -ek-): a short, entertaining account of some happening, usually personal or biographical

exposition (eks′pə zish′ən): a setting forth of facts, ideas, etc.; detailed explanation

logician (lō jish′ən): an expert in logic

fallacy (fal′ə sē) *a)* an error in reasoning; flaw or defect in argument *b) Logic* an argument which does not conform to the rules of logic, esp. one that appears to be sound

non sequitur (nän′ sek′wi tər): *Logic* a conclusion or inference which does not follow from the premises: abbrev. **non seq.**

causal (kôz′əl): relating to cause and effect

cat, āte, fäther; pen, ēvil; if, kīte; nō, ôr, fo͞od, book; boil, house; up, tʉrn; chief, shell; thick, *the*; zh, treasure; ŋ, sing; ə for *a* in *about*; ’ as in *able* (ā′b’l)

STEP 1

Preread

Preview the following selection by reading the title, the headings, and the subheadings. Answer the following questions without looking back at the selection.

1. What is the subject?

 ____

2. What is the main idea (the main thing the author is saying about the subject)?

 ____

3. Take a moment to think about critical thinking. Think about what you know, what you don't know, and what you might find out from reading the selection. Make up three questions.

 a. ______________________________

 b. ______________________________

 c. ______________________________

STEP 2

Read

Read the selection without underlining. Ignore the lines written in the margin.

Write your starting time here: ______________________________

◆ *Intellectual Health: Critical Thinking and the Art of Living*

Brian K. Williams and Sharon M. Knight

What, finally, will make the difference as to whether you prevail in life? Your drive? discipline? good nature? faith? It might be all of these, and then something else: your intellect.

State whether you agree or disagree with the following by answering yes or no.

_____ 1. Since it's clear that traditional Western medicine is not always able to cure various kinds of cancer, you might as well see what the alternative therapies have to offer.

_____ 2. Because condoms sometimes break, there's no point in using them to protect against HIV.

_____ 3. I wouldn't want a doctor who was rumored to like child pornography to be my surgeon; he or she couldn't be very good at performing surgery.

_____ 4. If we allowed marijuana to become legal, sooner or later there would be a lot more people ending up on hard drugs.

The answers to all of these should be no, for all of these statements are examples of incorrect reasoning, as follows: (1) jumping to conclusions; (2) irrelevant reason; (3) irrelevant attack on a person; (4) slippery slope. We explain these concepts below.

Intellectual health has to do with thinking or cognition and covers such activities as speaking, writing, analyzing, and judgment. It is one of the five dimensions of the definition of health (the others being physical, emotional, social, and spiritual). Developing the faculties of your intellectual health is crucial in helping to evaluate the claims of prospective healers, whether traditional or alternative.

A good way to expand your range intellectually is to learn to think critically. Critical thinking means actively seeking to understand, analyze, and evaluate information in order to solve specific problems. *Critical thinking*, in other words, is simply clear thinking. "Clear thinkers aren't born that way. They work at it," says one writer. "Before making important choices, they try to clear emotion, bias, trivia and preconceived notions out of the way so they can concentrate on the information essential to making the right decision."

1. _____
   _____
   _____

2. _____
   _____
   _____

3. _____
   _____
   _____

The Hazards of Uncritical Thinking

Uncritical thinking is all around us. People run their lives on the basis of horoscopes, numerology, and similar nonsense. They pick lottery tickets based on their spouse's birth date. They believe in "crystal healing" and "color therapy." They think so-called outside experts—actually, cranks or quacks—will do what medicine cannot: cure cancer with apricot-pit extract, alleviate arthritis with copper bracelets, end blindness with prayer.

These are not just bits of harmless goofiness, like wearing your "lucky" shirt to your final exam. "We live in a society that is enlarging the boundaries of knowledge at an unprecedented rate," points out James Randi, a debunker of claims made by supporters of the paranormal, "and we cannot keep up with more than a small portion of what is made available to us. To mix our data input with childish notions of magic and fantasy is to cripple our perception of the world around us. We must reach for the truth, not for the ghosts of dead absurdities."

4. _____
_____
_____

By the time we are grown up, our minds have become "set" in various patterns of thinking that affect the way we respond to new situations and new ideas. These mindsets are the result of our personal experiences and the various social environments in which we grew up. Such mindsets determine what ideas we think are important and, conversely, what ideas we ignore. "Because we can't pay attention to all the events that occur around us," points out one book on clear thinking, "our minds filter out some observations and facts and let others through to our conscious awareness." Herein lies the danger: ". . . we see and hear what we subconsciously want to, and pay little attention to facts or observations that have already been rejected as unimportant."

The Reasoning Tool: Deductive and Inductive Arguments

The tool for breaking through the closed habits of thought called mindsets is reasoning. *Reasoning*—giving reasons in favor of this assertion or that—is essential to critical thinking and solving life's problems. Reasoning is put in the form of *arguments,* which consist of one or more *premises,* or reasons, logically supporting a result or outcome called a *conclusion.*

5. _____
_____
_____

6. _____
_____
_____

An example of an argument is as follows:

Premise 1: All students must pass certain courses in order to graduate.

Premise 2: I am a student who wants to graduate.

Conclusion: Therefore, I must pass certain courses.

Note the tip-off word "Therefore," which signals that a conclusion is coming. In real life, such as arguments of radio and TV shows, in books and magazines and newspapers, and the like, the premises and conclusions are not so neatly labeled. Still, there are clues: the words *because, since,* and *for* usually signal premises. The words *therefore, hence,* and *so* signal conclusions. Not all groups of sentences form arguments. Often they form anecdotes or other types of exposition or explanation.

7. _____
_____
_____

8. _____
   _____
   _____

The two main kinds of correct or valid arguments are inductive and deductive:

■ *Deductive argument:* A deductive argument is defined as follows: *If its premises are true, then its conclusions true also.* In other words, if the premises are true, the conclusions cannot be false.

■ *Inductive argument:* An inductive argument is defined as follows: *If the premises are true, the conclusions are PROBABLY true, but the truth is not guaranteed.* An inductive argument is sometimes known by logicians as a "probability argument."

An example of a *deductive argument* is as follows:

Premise 1: All students experience stress in their lives.

Premise 2: Reuben is a student.

Conclusion: Therefore, Reuben experiences stress in his life.

This argument is deductive—the conclusion is *definitely* true if the premises are *definitely* true.

An example of an *inductive argument* is as follows:

Premise 1: Stress can cause illness.

Premise 2: Reuben experiences stress in his life.

Premise 3: Reuben is ill.

Conclusion: Therefore, stress may be the cause of Reuben's illness.

Note the word *may* in the conclusion. This argument is inductive—the conclusion is not stated with absolute certainty; rather, it only suggests that stress *may* be the cause. The link between premises and conclusion is not definite because there may be other reasons for Reuben's illness.

Some Types of Incorrect Reasoning

9. _____
   _____
   _____

Patterns of incorrect reasoning are known as *fallacies.* Learning to identify fallacious arguments will help you avoid patterns of faulty thinking in your own writing and thinking and identify it in others'.

Jumping to Conclusions

10. _____
    _____
    _____

Also known as *hasty generalization*, the fallacy called *jumping to conclusions* means that a conclusion has been reached when not all the facts are available.

Example: You might believe that, because traditional Western medicine is not always able to cure various kinds of cancer, you might as well see what the alternative therapies (such as promoters of apricot-pit extracts) have to offer. However, what you don't know is that alternative therapies have an even *worse* record at curing cancer than high-tech medicine does.

Irrelevant Reason or False Cause

The faulty reasoning known as *non sequitur* (Latin for "it does not follow") might be better called *false cause* or *irrelevant reason*. Specifically, it means that the conclusion does not follow logically from the supposed reasons stated earlier. There is no *causal* relationship.

11. _____
_____
_____

> *Example:* Because you know that condoms sometimes break, you think there's no point in using them to protect against HIV. This is irrelevant, because condoms do not *always* break and, in your case, may *never* break while you are using them.

Irrelevant Attack on a Person or an Opponent

Known as an *ad hominem* argument (Latin for "to the person"), the *irrelevant attack on an opponent* attacks a person's reputation or beliefs rather than his or her argument.

12. _____
_____
_____

> *Example:* You may decide you wouldn't want a surgeon who was rumored to be interested in child pornography because you think he or she couldn't be very good at surgery. However, the interest in pornography may have no bearing on his or her present ability to do surgery.

Slippery Slope

The *slippery slope* is a failure to see that the first step in a possible series of steps does not lead inevitably to the rest.

13. _____
_____
_____

> *Example:* Believing that, if we allowed marijuana to become legal, sooner or later there would be a lot more people ending up on hard drugs is a slippery-slope argument. Although it *may* be true that marijuana is a "gateway drug" that could lead some users to progress to stronger and more dangerous narcotics, it is not inevitable.

Appeal to Authority

The *appeal to authority* argument (known in Latin as *argumentum ad verecundiam*) uses an authority in one area to pretend to validate claims in another area in which the person is not an expert.

14. _____
_____
_____

> *Example:* You see the appeal-to-authority argument used all the time in advertising. But what, for example, does an Olympic skating star know about nutrition?

Circular Reasoning

15. _____
_____
_____

The *circular reasoning* argument rephrases the statement to be proven true and then uses the new, similar statement as supposed proof that the original statement is in fact true.

> *Example:* You declare that you can drive safely at high speeds with only inches separating you from the car ahead because you have driven this way for years without an accident.

Straw Man Argument

16. _____
_____
_____

The *straw man argument* is when you misrepresent your opponent's position to make it easier to attack, or when you attack a weaker position while ignoring a stronger one. In other words, you sidetrack the argument from the main discussion.

> *Example:* Saying "You don't care about being spontaneous" is a way of misrepresenting a person who is concerned about using condoms as protection.

Appeal to Pity

17. _____
_____
_____

The *appeal to pity* argument appeals to mercy rather than making an argument on the merits of the case itself.

> *Examples:* The joke of the boy who kills his parents and then throws himself on the mercy of the court because he is an orphan is one example. So is the appeal to the dean not to expel you for cheating because your parents are poor and made sacrifices to put you through college.

Questionable Statistics

18. _____
_____
_____

Statistics can be misused in many ways as supporting evidence. The statistics may be unknowable, drawn from an unrepresentative sample, or otherwise suspect.

> *Examples:* Stating that in the past 10,000 years people have been far less happy or healthy than they are today is an example of unknowable or undefined use of statistics. Stating how much money is lost to taxes because of illegal drug transactions is speculation because such transactions are hidden or underground.

> *1700 words*

Write your ending time here:_____

Subtract your starting time: _____

Total time:_____

Check the Rate Chart on p. 462 to find out how many words per minute you have read, and then record your score on the Reading Efficiency Progress Chart on p. 464.

Analyze What You Read—Create a Study Guide

Objective Questions

Go back to the reading and underline or highlight what you think will be asked on a test. Then fill in the missing marginal notes to test your memory of what you have underlined. To make this easier, we have written the self-test notes in random order below. Write each one on its correct line in the reading. If you prefer, you may write each self-test note on the front of a flash card and what you would have underlined on the back.

Components of arguments

Irrelevant reason or false cause

Definition of critical thinking

Questionable statistics

Definition of reasoning

Circular reasoning

Definition of fallacy

Jumping to conclusions

Irrelevant attack on a person or opponent

Appeal to pity

Five dimensions of the definition of health

Appeal to authority

Hazards of uncritical thinking

Signal words

Two main kinds of valid arguments

Slippery slope

Straw man argument

What intellectual health covers

Essay/Application Questions

Predict Essay Questions: There are three topics in this reading selection important enough for an essay question. Write them here:

1. _____

2. _____

3. _____

Make Graphic Organizers: Fill in.

1. Hazards of uncritical thinking: _____

   _____

   _____

   _____

2. Fill in the blanks in the chart.

Two main types of valid arguments	Definition	Example
Deductive reasoning		
Inductive reasoning		

3. Fill in the blanks in the chart on the next page.

Types of incorrect reasoning	Definition	Example
Jumping to conclusions (hasty generalization)		
Irrelevant reason or false cause (non sequitur)		
Irrelevant attack on a person or opponent (ad hominem)		
Slippery slope		
Appeal to authority (argumentum ad verecundiam)		
Circular reasoning		
Straw man		
Appeal to pity		
Questionable statistics		

*For explanation
see p. 150*

Skill Development: Summarizing

For this reading you have two graphic organizers. The first one consists of the underlining and notes in the margin of the reading selection. The second one consists of graphic organizers 1–3 on pp. 160–161. Here is how to summarize using each of them:

1. To summarize using the underlining and marginal notes: First, write the main idea in a complete sentence. Then turn each marginal note into a complete sentence, using the underlining as needed. Use paragraph form, not outline form. Use signal or transition words, such as *first, finally, therefore,* etc., to make it easier for the reader to follow your ideas. For example, you might say, "The author identifies two main types of correct reasoning and nine common types of fallacious reasoning."

2. To summarize using the graphic organizers 1–3 on pp. 160–161, do the same thing. Start with the main idea. Turn the topics into sentences using paragraph form. Use signal words.

Write your summary on a separate piece of paper.

Remember What's Important

Use the marginal notes or the flash cards and the graphic organizers for self-testing. Keep testing or have someone test you until you know the material. Test yourself as needed on the Vocabulary Preview words.

Make Use of What You Read

When you are ready, complete the Comprehension Check on p. 383 and the Vocabulary Check on p. 384. Do them from memory, without looking back at the reading selection or the study guide.

Evaluate Your Active Critical Thinking Skills

After your tests have been graded, record your scores on the Progress Chart, p. 456, and answer the questions on the Evaluation Checklist on p. 457.

13   **Shared Characteristics of Life**

Vocabulary Preview

emerge (ē murj′, i-): to develop or evolve

convergence (kən vur′jəns): coming together

initially (i nish′əl ē): at the beginning; at first

secretion (si krē′shən): a process in which a gland, tissue, etc. releases a biochemical for use by the organism

hormone (hôr′mōn′): a substance formed in some organ of the body and carried by a body fluid to another organ or tissue, where it has a specific effect

tolerable (täl′ər ə bəl): that can be tolerated or borne; endurable

drastic (dras′tik): severe; harsh; extreme

sabotage (sab′ə täzh′): damage

predator (pred′ə tər): an animal that lives by capturing and feeding on other animals

variant (ver′ē ənt): varying, different

cat, āte, fäther; pen, ēvil; if, kīte; nō, ôr, fōōd, book; boil, house; up, turn; chief, shell; thick, *the*; zh, treasure; ŋ, sing; ə for *a* in *about*; ′ as in *able* (ā′b'l)

Preread

STEP 1

Preview the following selection by reading the title, the headings, and the illustrations. Answer the first two questions without looking back at the reading.

1. What is the subject?

   _____

2. What is the main idea?

   _____

3. Look at Figure 1.

   a. What is the subject?

      _____

   b. What is the main idea?

      _____

4. Look at Figure 2.

   a. What is the subject?

   _____

   b. What is the main idea?

   _____

   _____

5. Take a moment to think about shared characteristics of life. Think about what you know about the subject, what you don't know, and what you might find out from reading this selection. Make up three questions.

   a. _____

   b. _____

   _____

   c. _____

Read

STEP 2

Read the selection without underlining. Ignore the lines in the margin.

Write your starting time here: _____

◆ *Shared Characteristics of Life*

Cecie Starr

Levels of Biological Organization

1. _____

2. _____

3. _____

4. _____

5. _____

Picture a frog on a rock, busily croaking. Without even thinking about it, you know that the frog is alive and the rock is not. And yet, at a deeper level, the difference between them blurs. Both consist of the same particles (protons, electrons, and neutrons), organized as atoms according to the same physical laws. At the heart of those laws is something called **energy**—a capacity to make things happen, to do work. Energetic interactions bind atom to atom in orderly patterns, giving rise to the structured bits of matter we call molecules. Energetic interactions among molecules hold rocks together. And they hold frogs—and all other organisms—together.

A special type of molecule—deoxyribonucleic acid, or **DNA**—sets living things apart from the nonliving world. No chunk of granite or quartz has it. DNA has instructions for assembling organisms from "life-less" molecules that contain carbon and a few other kinds of atoms. By analogy, with proper instructions and a little effort, you can turn a heap of just two kinds of ceramic tiles into ordered patterns such as these:

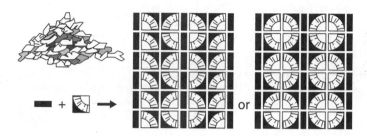

By itself, DNA—"the molecule of life"—is not alive. As Figure 1 indicates, the properties of life emerge in individual cells. The **cell** is an organized unit that can survive and reproduce on its own, given DNA instructions, raw materials, and inputs of energy. Clearly this definition fits a free-living, single-celled organism such as an amoeba. Does it fit a **multicelled organism,** which has specialized cells organized as tissues and organs? Yes. You may find this a strange answer. After all, your own cells could never live all by themselves in nature; body fluids must con-tinuously bathe them. Yet even isolated human cells can be kept alive under controlled laboratory conditions. In fact, researchers throughout the world routinely maintain human cells for use in important experiments, including cancer studies.

The next level of organization is the **population,** a group of organisms of the same kind, such as a colony of Emperor penguins. Next is the **community**—all of the populations of all species living in the same area (such as Antarctica's penguins, seals, birds, and so on). The next level, the **ecosystem,** includes the community *and* its physical and chemical environ-ment. Finally, the **biosphere** includes all parts of the earth's waters, crust, and atmosphere in which organisms live. Astoundingly, *this globe-spanning organization starts with the convergence of energy, materials, and DNA in tiny, individual cells.*

Metabolism: Life's Energy Transfers

The metabolic activities of single cells and multicelled organisms maintain the great pattern of organization in nature. **Metabolism** refers to the capacity of the cell to (1) extract and convert energy from its surroundings

6. _____

7. _____
   _____

8. _____

9. _____

10. _____

11. _____

12. _____

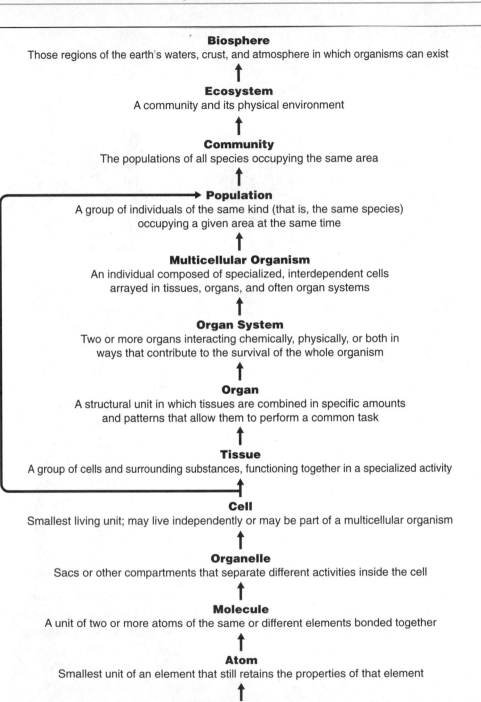

Biosphere
Those regions of the earth's waters, crust, and atmosphere in which organisms can exist

↑

Ecosystem
A community and its physical environment

↑

Community
The populations of all species occupying the same area

↑

Population
A group of individuals of the same kind (that is, the same species) occupying a given area at the same time

↑

Multicellular Organism
An individual composed of specialized, interdependent cells arrayed in tissues, organs, and often organ systems

↑

Organ System
Two or more organs interacting chemically, physically, or both in ways that contribute to the survival of the whole organism

↑

Organ
A structural unit in which tissues are combined in specific amounts and patterns that allow them to perform a common task

↑

Tissue
A group of cells and surrounding substances, functioning together in a specialized activity

↑

Cell
Smallest living unit; may live independently or may be part of a multicellular organism

↑

Organelle
Sacs or other compartments that separate different activities inside the cell

↑

Molecule
A unit of two or more atoms of the same or different elements bonded together

↑

Atom
Smallest unit of an element that still retains the properties of that element

↑

Subatomic particle
An electron, proton, or neutron; one of the three major particles of which atoms are composed

Figure 1   Levels of organization in nature.

and (2) use energy to maintain itself, grow, and make more cells. Simply put, it means *energy transfers.*

　　Think of a food-producing cell inside a leaf of a tree. By the process of **photosynthesis,** it traps energy from the sun and uses it to produce molecules of an energy carrier, called **ATP.** Then ATP transfers energy to sites inside the cell where "metabolic workers" (enzymes) put together sugars, starch, and other substances. The cell even stores some energy. By the process of **aerobic respiration,** it can later release some stored energy and produce ATP molecules—which transfer the energy that drives hundreds of different cellular activities.

13. _____

14. _____

15. _____

　　_____

Interdependencies Among Organisms

Plants and other photosynthetic organisms are the main entry point for an immense flow of energy into the world of life. They are the food **producers.** Animals are **consumers.** Directly or indirectly, they feed on energy that has been stored in tissues of the photosynthesizers. For example, some energy is transferred to elephants after they eat leaves. Energy is transferred again when lions eat a baby elephant that wandered away from its herd. And it is transferred again to fungi and bacteria that are **decomposers.** When decomposers feed on the tissues or remains of elephants, lions, or any other organism, they break down sugars and other biological molecules to simple materials—which may be cycled back to the producers. In time, all of the energy that the producers initially captured from the sun flows back to the environment, but that's another story.

16. _____

17. _____

18. _____

　　For now, keep in mind that interdependencies link organisms together, owing to a one-way flow of energy *through* them and a cycling of materials *among* them (Figure 2). Such interactions influence the structure, size, and composition of populations and communities. They influence ecosystems, even the biosphere. Understand the extent of these interactions and you will gain insight into amplification of the greenhouse effect, acid rain, and other modern-day problems.

19. _____

Sensing and Responding to the Environment

It is often said that only organisms can respond to the environment. Yet even a rock shows responsiveness, as when it yields to the force of gravity and tumbles down a hill or changes shape slowly under the battering of wind, rain, or tides. The difference is this: *Organisms can sense changes in their surroundings, then make controlled, compensating responses to them.* How? Each organism has **receptors,** which are certain molecules and structures

20. _____

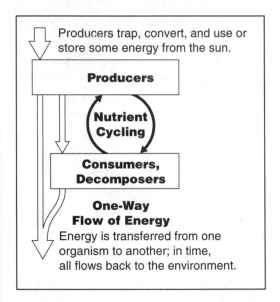

Figure 2 Energy flow and cycling of materials through the biosphere.

that can detect specific kinds of information about the environment. When cells receive signals from receptors, their metabolic activities shift in ways that bring about a suitable response. When your brain receives signals from receptors inside your body or near its surface, it rapidly sends out commands to muscles or glands that can execute a suitable response.

For example, an organism's body can withstand only so much heat or cold. It must rid itself of harmful substances. It requires certain foods, in certain amounts. Yet temperatures do shift, harmful substances might be encountered, and food is sometimes plentiful or scarce.

Think about what happens after you finish a snack. Simple molecules, including sugars, leave your gut and enter your bloodstream. Blood is part of the body's "internal environment" (the other part is tissue fluid that bathes your cells). The sugar absorbed from the gut raises the concentration of sugar in the blood. Now cells in a glandular organ called the pancreas step up their secretion of insulin. As it happens, most cells in your body have receptors for insulin—a hormone that stimulates them to take up sugar molecules from the internal environment. When an enormous number of cells do this, the blood concentration of sugar returns to normal.

Suppose you skip breakfast, then lunch. The blood concentration of sugar starts to decrease. Now a different hormone goes into action. It stimulates liver cells to dig into their stores of energy-rich molecules and break them down to simple sugars. The cells release sugars, which enter the bloodstream. There they help return the blood concentration of sugar to normal.

Usually, the range of physical and chemical conditions inside an organism remains fairly constant. When the internal operating conditions stay within tolerable limits, we call this a state of **homeostasis.**

21. _____

Continuity and Change—The Nature of Inheritance

Perpetuating Heritable Traits

We humans tend to think we enter the world rather abruptly and leave it the same way. Yet we and all other organisms are more than this. *We are part of an immense journey that began billions of years ago.*

Think of the first cell of a new individual, produced when a human sperm fertilizes an egg. It would not even exist if the sperm and egg had not formed earlier, according to DNA instructions that were passed down through countless human generations. With those time-tested instructions, a new individual may develop, grow, and then eventually engage in **reproduction**—that is, the production of offspring. By this process, life's journey continues.

22. _____

Or think about a moth. Is it just a winged insect? What of the fertilized egg deposited upon a leaf by a female moth? Inside that small egg are instructions for becoming an adult. They guide the egg's development into a caterpillar, a larval stage adapted for rapid feeding and growth. The caterpillar eats and grows until an internal "alarm clock" goes off. Then its body enters a pupal stage, when tissues undergo drastic remodeling. Many cells die; others multiply and become organized in different patterns. In time an adult emerges that is adapted for reproduction. It has organs that house eggs or sperm. Its wings are brightly colored and flutter at a frequency suitable for attracting a mate.

None of these stages is "the insect." The insect is a series of organized stages, from one fertilized egg to the next. Each stage is vital for the ultimate production of new moths. Instructions for each stage were written into moth DNA long before each moment of reproduction—and so the ancient moth story continues.

Mutations—Source of Variations in Heritable Traits

Reproduction is possible because of a process known as **inheritance.** The word means that parent organisms transmit specific DNA instructions for duplicating their traits to offspring. Why does a baby stork look like its

23. _____

parents and not like pelicans? It inherited stork DNA—which is not exactly the same as pelican DNA.

24. _____
_____

DNA has two striking qualities. Its instructions assure that offspring will resemble their parents—yet they also permit *variations* in the details of most traits. For example, having five fingers on each hand is a human trait. Yet some humans are born with six fingers on each hand instead of five! This is an outcome of a **mutation**—a molecular change in the DNA. Mutations are the original source of variations in heritable traits.

25. _____

Many mutations are harmful. A change in even a tiny bit of DNA may be enough to sabotage the body's growth, development, or functioning. One such mutation causes hemophilia A, a blood-clotting disorder. After even a small cut or bruise, an abnormally long time passes before a clot forms and stops the bleeding. Yet some variations are harmless or even beneficial under conditions that happen to prevail in the environment. A classic case is a mutation in lightly colored moths that results in dark offspring. Moths fly at night and rest during the day, when birds that eat them are active. When a light-colored moth rests on a light tree trunk, it is camouflaged—it "hides in the open"—so birds tend not to see it. Suppose people build coal-burning factories nearby. Over time, soot-laden smoke darkens the tree trunks. Now the dark moths are less conspicuous to predators—so they have a better chance of living long enough to reproduce. Under sooty conditions, the variant form of the trait is more adaptive.

26. _____
_____

An **adaptive trait** simply is any trait that helps an organism survive and reproduce under a given set of environmental conditions.

2100 words

Write your ending time here:_____

Subtract your starting time: _____

Total time: _____

Check the Rate Chart on p. 462 to find out how many words per minute you have read, and then record your score on the Reading Efficiency Progress Chart on p. 464.

Analyze What You Read—Create a Study Guide

STEP 3

Objective Questions

Go back to the article and underline or highlight what you think will be asked on a test. Then fill in the missing marginal notes to test your memory of what you have underlined. We have provided the lines for the notes, but you will have to figure out the topics to write on the lines. If you prefer, you may write each self-test note on the front of a flash card and what you would have underlined on the back.

Essay/Application Questions

Predict Essay Questions: What are the two most likely topics for essay questions?

1. _____

2. _____

Make Graphic Organizers:

1. Fill in the following idea map for the six shared characteristics of life.

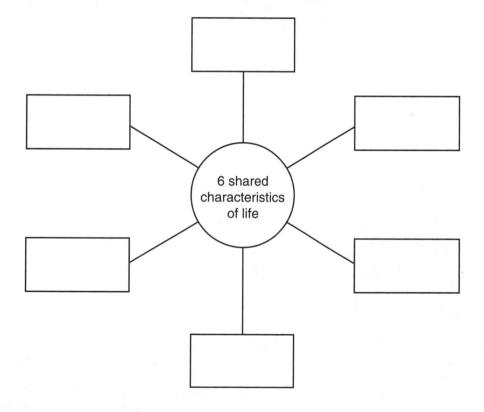

2. Use Figure 1 as a graphic organizer for the thirteen levels of organization in nature.

Skill Development: Mnemonic Devices

When you have lists of material to memorize, it helps to use *mnemonic devices*, or memory tricks. To memorize the six shared characteristics of life you can use the first letter of each item on the idea map to make up a nonsense sentence that's easy to remember, such as *Don's Mother Irene Serves Red Meat*. To make it easier to remember the thirteen levels of organization in nature, you could group them as follows:

1. Living and nonliving: SAM (Subatomic particle, Atom, Molecule)

2. Living organisms: OCTOOM (Organelle, Cell, Tissue, Organ, Organ system, Multicellular organism)

3. Groups of organisms: PCEB (Population, Community, Ecosystem, Biosphere)

   For practice, make up a nonsense sentence to remember the order of the planets from the sun outwards (*Mercury, Venus, Earth, Mars, Jupiter, Saturn, Uranus, Neptune, Pluto*).

1. _____

2. Now group the following shopping list into four categories: hamburger, lettuce, hamburger buns, ketchup, tomatoes, mustard, onions, muffins, bacon

   a. _____

   b. _____

   c. _____

   d. _____

For explanation see p. 150

Skill Development: Summarizing

Use the underlining and marginal notes and/or the idea map to summarize this reading selection. Use a separate piece of paper.

Remember What's Important

STEP 4

Use the marginal notes or flash cards, the graphic organizers, and mnemonic devices for self-testing. Keep testing or have someone test you until you know the material. Test yourself as needed on the Vocabulary Preview words.

Make Use of What You Read

When you are ready, complete the Comprehension Check on p. 387 and the Vocabulary Check on p. 389. Do them from memory, without looking back at the reading selection or the study guide.

Evaluate Your Active Critical Thinking Skills

After your tests have been graded, record your scores on the Progress Chart, p. 456, and answer the questions on the Evaluation Checklist on p. 457.

14   Interpersonal Attraction: Liking and Loving

Vocabulary Preview

dynamics (dī nam′iks): the various forces operating in a field

social psychologist (sō′shəl sī kâl′ə jist): one who studies individuals in relation to other people

proximity (präks im′ə tē): nearness

reciprocity (res ə präs′ə tē): mutual action or exchange

spatial (spā′shəl): happening or existing in space

arbitrary (ar′bə trer′ē): chance

evolve (ē välv′): to develop gradually, unfold

hypothesis (hī päth′ə sis): an unproved theory used as a basis for further investigation

illicit (il lis′it): unlawful or improper

self-concept (self kän′sept): the image one has of oneself

status (stat′əs): position, rank, standing

ethnicity (eth nis′ə tē): cultural background

repulsion (ri pul′shən): strong dislike

disdain (dis dān′): scorn

idealize (ī dē′əl īz): regard as ideal or perfect or more nearly perfect than is true

cat, āte, fäther; pen, ēvil; if, kīte; nō, ôr, fōod, book; boil, house; up, turn; chief, shell; thick, *the*; zh, treasure; ŋ, sing; ə for *a* in *about*; ′ as in *able* (ā′b′l)

Preread

Preview the following selection by reading the title and the headings. Answer the first two questions without looking back at the reading.

1. What is the subject?

_____

2. What is the main idea?

_____

3. Take a moment to think about interpersonal attraction. Think about what you know about it, what you don't know, and what you might find out from reading the selection. Make up three questions.

a. _____

b. _____

c. _____

Read

STEP 2

Read the selection without underlining.

Write your starting time here: _____

◆ *Interpersonal Attraction: Liking and Loving*

Wayne Weiten

"I just don't know what she sees in him. She could do so much better for herself. I suppose he's a nice guy, but they're just not right for each other." You've probably heard similar remarks on many occasions. These comments illustrate people's interest in analyzing the dynamics of attraction. *Interpersonal attraction refers to positive feelings toward another.* Social psychologists use this term to include a variety of experiences, including liking, friendship, admiration, lust, and love.

Key Factors in Attraction

Many factors influence who is attracted to whom. Here we'll discuss factors that promote the development of liking, friendship, and love. Although these are different types of attraction, the interpersonal dynamics at work in each are surprisingly similar. Each is influenced by proximity, physical attractiveness, similarity, and reciprocity.

Proximity Effects

It would be difficult for you to develop a friendship with someone you never met. It happens occasionally (among pen pals or users of on-line computer services, for instance). But attraction usually depends on people being in the same place at the same time. *Proximity* **refers to geographic, residential, and other forms of spatial closeness** (classroom seating, office arrangements, and so forth). Generally, people become acquainted with, and attracted to, people who live, work, shop, and play nearby. The importance of spatial factors in living arrangements was apparent in a classic study of friendship patterns among married graduate students living in university housing projects. The closer people's doors were, the more likely they were to become friends.

Proximity effects may seem self-evident, but it's sobering to realize that your friendships and love interests are shaped by arbitrary office desk arrangements, dormitory floor assignments, and traffic patterns in apartment complexes. In spite of the increasing geographic mobility in modern society, people still tend to marry someone who grew up nearby.

Physical Attractiveness

People often say that "beauty is only skin deep." But the evidence suggests that most people don't really believe it. The importance of physical attractiveness was demonstrated in a recent study of college students. Unacquainted men and women were sent off on a "get-acquainted" date. The investigators were mainly interested in how communication might affect the process of attraction. However, they also measured subjects' perceptions of their dates' physical attractiveness and similarity to themselves. They found that the quality of communication during the date did have some effect on females' interest in friendship. However, the main thing that determined romantic attraction for both sexes was the physical attractiveness of the other person. Many other studies have shown the importance of physical attractiveness in the initial stage of dating. It continues to influence how committed the couples are as dating relationships evolve. In the realm of romance, being physically attractive appears to be more important for females than for males.

Although people prefer physically attractive partners in romantic relationships, they may consider their own level of attractiveness in pursuing dates. **The *matching hypothesis* proposes that males and females of approximately equal physical attractiveness are likely to select each other as partners.** The matching hypothesis is supported by evidence that married couples tend to be very similar in level of physical attractiveness. However, there's some debate about whether people match up by their own choice. Some theorists believe that people mostly look for very attractive partners. They think that the matching occurs because people are rejected by those who are more attractive.

Most of the studies of physical beauty and attraction have focused on dating relationships. Only a few have looked at friendships. However, the studies of friendship suggest that people prefer attractive opposite-sex friends as well as dates. Researchers have also found evidence for matching effects in same-sex friendships. Interestingly, this same-sex matching appears to occur among male friends but not among female friends.

Similarity Effects

Is it true that "birds of a feather flock together," or do "opposites attract"? Research provides far more support for the idea that like attracts like. Married and dating couples tend to be similar in age, race, religion, social class, personality, education, intelligence, physical attractiveness, and attitudes. Married couples who have similar personalities seem to have happier marriages. Similarity is also seen among friends. For instance, adolescent friends are more similar than nonfriends in educational goals and performance, political and religious activities, illicit drug use, and self-concept. Adult friends also tend to be relatively similar in terms of income, education, occupational status, ethnicity, and religion.

The most obvious explanation for these findings is that similarity causes attraction. Laboratory experiments on *attitude similarity* suggest that similarity does cause liking. In these studies, subjects who have previously provided information on their own attitudes are led to believe that they'll be meeting a stranger. They're given information about the stranger's views that has been manipulated to show various degrees of similarity to their own views. As attitude similarity increases, subjects' ratings of the likability of the stranger increase. This evidence supports the notion that similarity promotes attraction. However, it's also consistent with a somewhat different explanation proposed by Rosenbaum.

Rosenbaum has obtained evidence suggesting that similarity effects occur in attraction not because similarity fosters liking but because *dissimilarity* leads to *dislike* of others. In one study of his "repulsion hypothesis," Rosenbaum found that Democrats did not rate other Democrats (similar others) higher than controls. They rated Republicans (dissimilar others) lower than controls. Rosenbaum acknowledges that similarity sometimes causes liking, but he maintains that *dissimilarity causes disdain* more frequently. Thus, there is reason to believe that liking is influenced by *both* similarity and dissimilarity in attitudes.

Reciprocity Effects

In his book *How to Win Friends and Influence People,* Dale Carnegie suggested that people can gain others' liking by showering them with praise and flattery. However, we've all heard that "flattery will get you nowhere." Which advice is right? The evidence suggests that flattery will get you somewhere, with some people, some of the time. In interpersonal attraction, **reciprocity involves liking those who show that they like you.** In general, research indicates that we tend to like those who show that they like us. We also tend to see others as liking us more if we like them. Thus, it appears that liking breeds liking and loving promotes loving.

A recent study suggests that in romantic relationships this reciprocity effect even extends to partners "idealizing" each other. Murray, Holmes, and Griffin asked 180 married or dating couples to rate themselves, their partners, and their ideal partners on a variety of traits and to rate their satisfaction with their relationships. Common sense would suggest that an accurate view of one's partner would be the best foundation for a stable, satisfying intimate relationship. However, this is not what the investigators found. Instead, they discovered that most people viewed their partners more favorably than the partners viewed themselves. Individuals' perceptions of their romantic partners seemed to reflect their ideals for a partner more than reality. Moreover, the data showed that people were happier in their relationship when they idealized their partners and when their partners idealized them. A follow-up study found that relationships were more likely to persist—even in the face of conflicts and doubts—when partners idealized one another. These results mesh well with the finding that small positive illusions may be good for people's mental and physical well-being. Apparently, they are good for healthy romantic relationships as well.

1200 words

Write your ending time here:_____

Subtract your starting time: _____

Total time: _____

Check the Rate Chart on p. 462 to find out how many words per minute you have read, and then record your score on the Reading Efficiency Progress Chart on p. 464.

Analyze What You Read—Create a Study Guide

Objective Questions

Go back to the reading and underline or highlight what you think will be on the test. For each idea that you underline, write a note in the margin that you can use to test yourself on the idea. If you prefer, you may write each self-test note on the front of a flash card and what you would have underlined on the back.

Essay/Application Questions

Predict Essay Questions: What is the most likely topic for an essay question?

_____

Make Graphic Organizers: Fill in the blanks in the following idea map.

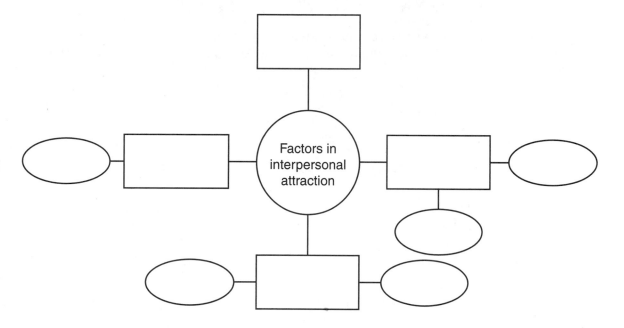

For explanation see p. 172

Skill Development: Mnemonic Devices

Make up a nonsense phrase or sentence in which each word begins with the first letter of one of the four factors in interpersonal attraction.

_____

For explanation see p. 150

Skill Development: Summarizing

Use the underlining and marginal notes and the idea map to write a summary of this reading selection. Use a separate piece of paper.

Remember What's Important

Use the marginal notes or the flash cards and the graphic organizers for self-testing. Keep testing or have someone test you until you know the material. Test yourself as needed on the Vocabulary Preview words.

Make Use of What You Read

When you are ready, complete the Comprehension Check on p. 391 and the Vocabulary Check on p. 392. Do them from memory, without looking back at the reading selection or the study guide.

Evaluate Your Active Critical Thinking Skills

After your tests have been graded, record your scores on the Progress Chart, p. 456, and answer the questions on the Evaluation Checklist on p. 457.

15   Safer Sex

Vocabulary Preview

promiscuous (prō mis′kyo͞o əs, prə-): characterized by a lack of discrimination; specif., engaging in sexual intercourse indiscriminately or with many persons

antibody (an′ti bäd′ē, -tə-): a specialized protein that neutralizes, thus creating immunity to, specific antigens; immunoglobulin

casualty (kazh′o͞o əl tē): anything lost, destroyed, or made useless by some unfortunate happening

hypothetically (hī pō thet′i klē, -pə-): based on, involving, or having the nature of a hypothesis; assumed; supposed

respondent (ri spän′dənt): a person who responds, answers, or replies

presumably (prē zo͞om′ə blē, -zyo͞om′-; pri-): that may be presumed, or taken for granted; probable

anonymous (ə nän′ə məs): by a person whose name is withheld or unknown

mandatory (man′də tôr′ē): authoritatively commanded or required; obligatory

divulge (də vulj′): to make known; disclose; reveal

stringent (strin′jənt): rigidly controlled, enforced, etc.; strict; severe

vulnerability (vul′nər ə bil′ə tē): ability to be hurt or injured

cohabiting (kō hab′it iŋ): living together as husband and wife, esp. when not legally married

euphemism (yo͞o′fə miz′əm): the use of a word or phrase that is less expressive or direct but considered less distasteful, less offensive, etc. than another

breach (brēch): a failure to observe the terms, as of a law or promise, the customary forms, etc.; violation; infraction

enhance (en hans′, -häns′; in-): to improve the quality or condition of

cat, āte, fäther; pen, ēvil; if, kīte; nō, ôr, fo͞od, book; boil, house; up, turn; chief, shell; thick, *th*e; zh, treasure; ŋ, sing; ə for *a* in *about*; ′ as in *able* (ā′b′l)

Preread

Preview the following selection by reading the title, the headings, and the illustrations. Answer the following questions without looking back at the reading.

1. What is the subject?

   _____

2. What is the main idea?

   _____

3. Look at Figure 1.

   a. What is the subject?

      _____

   b. What is the main idea?

      _____

      _____

      _____

4. Look at Table 1.

   a. What is the subject?

      _____

   b. What is the main idea?

      _____

5. Look at Figure 2.

   a. What is the subject?

      _____

   b. What is the main idea?

      _____

      _____

6. Think about what you know about safer sex, what you don't know, and what you might find out from reading the selection. Make up three questions.

   a. _____

   b. _____

   c. _____

Read

STEP
2

Read the selection without underlining.

Write your starting time here: _____

◆ *Safer Sex*

Brian K. Williams and Sharon M. Knight

Know your sexual partner, medical authorities advise. Many college students have taken the advice to heart. Unfortunately, says psychologist Jeffrey D. Fisher, they may go about it the wrong way. Rather than try to determine directly whether a prospective partner has been infected with the AIDS virus—**HIV,** the **human immunodeficiency virus**—or another sexually transmitted disease, they ask about home town, family, and major. Using those useless and irrelevant facts, says Fisher, they draw a conclusion about how safe it is to have sex with that person.

Other young adults make similar kinds of decisions. They decide whether to use condoms on the basis of the other person's perceived *social class,* judging a person who seems "lower class" to be more promiscuous or more risky. Or they base their risk assessment on *appearance,* considering a person who is attractive and well educated to be less risky. Do such external clues work? No, says Fisher. To use them as guides to safe sex, he says, is to believe in superstition.

How can you be *sure* that sex is really safe? The answer is: you can't. However, there are things that you can do to reduce your risks.

Unsafe Sex and Knowing Your Partner

To reduce your risk of exposure to sexually transmitted organisms such as HIV, you need to ask the right kinds of questions of prospective sexual partners, although the answers are no guarantees. The law may also require partner notification about sexual disease.

AIDS, or **acquired immunodeficiency syndrome,** the final and fatal stages of infection from HIV, has been in North America since at least 1975. In the years following, it has become more and more apparent that it is not a disease limited to male homosexuals and intravenous drug users. Indeed, the fastest-growing group of HIV-infected people worldwide is heterosexual women. Women account for half of new AIDS cases, and an official for the World Health Organization (WHO) says that by the year 2000 most new AIDS infections worldwide will be among women. "To put it simply, AIDS is becoming a heterosexual disease," says Michael Merson, director of WHO's Global Program on AIDS. Even in the United States, "the greatest rate of increase is among heterosexuals," he says.

The Concerns About Unsafe Sex

The message about the dangers of unprotected sex seems to have gotten through to many people, but clearly more must be done. For instance, even some students in a Stanford survey who used condoms said they tended to rely on them more to prevent pregnancy than to avoid sexually transmitted diseases. Other studies show that teenagers who use condoms are swayed less by health concerns than by the popularity of condoms among peers and by their ease of use. A 1992 survey of 10,000 heterosexual Americans ages 18–75 found that the vast majority of those with multiple partners were engaging in sexual intercourse without condoms. One author of the study, Joseph Catania, said the situation might reflect "a denial of personal risk" by a segment of the population that "still believes [AIDS] is a gay disease."

It's time to "Get real!", as the expression goes. AIDS is only one of several sexually transmitted diseases (STDs) that have shown an alarming rise. The rates are up for syphilis, chlamydia, genital warts, genital herpes, and other STDs. Gonorrhea, pelvic inflammatory disease, genital warts, and hepatitis B continue to pose serious problems. Indeed, according to a 1993 report by the Alan Guttmacher Institute, *more than one in five of all Americans is infected by a sexually caused viral disease.* About 12 million new sexually transmitted infections occur every year, two-thirds of them to people under 25, one-quarter in teenagers.

The sexually transmitted diseases caused by viruses—such as hepatitis B, genital herpes, genital warts, and HIV infection—cannot be cured, although they can in many cases be controlled. Some, such as genital warts, have been linked with an increased risk of cervical cancer in women. STDs caused by bacteria (such as gonorrhea, chlamydia, and syphilis) can be cured, but unfortunately many have no obvious symptoms and so they can continue to develop. Thus, they pose special threats to women of childbearing age as well as to men because, if not treated, they can lead to serious complications (infertility, tubal pregnancies, and chronic pain).

Asking Partners About Their Sexual History

However embarrassing the conversation, it can be helpful for people to explore their prospective partners' sexual histories before getting involved. Here are some questions to ask:

- *STD tests:* "Have you ever been tested for HIV or for other STDs? Would you be willing to have an HIV test done?"

- *Previous partners:* "How many sexual partners have you had?" (The more partners, the higher the STD risk.)

- *Prostitution:* "Have you ever had sex with a prostitute?" (If so, was protection used?)

- *Bisexuality:* For a woman to ask a man: "Have you ever had a male sexual partner?" For a man to ask a woman: "Have you ever had a sexual partner who was bisexual?"

- *IV drug use:* "Have you—*or your sexual partners*—ever injected drugs?" (A previous sexual partner can transmit AIDS or hepatitis by sharing needles.)

- *Blood transfusion:* "Have you ever had a transfusion of blood or blood products?" (This fact is particularly important if it occurred before 1985, when blood wasn't screened for HIV.)

Even if you ask all the right questions, however, you still can't be sure of the answers. Someone may look at you and state with absolute honesty and sincerity that he or she is "clean," yet may have an infection and not know it. Even people who flash a card showing they visited a county health department for an HIV test can't actually offer proof of lack of infection. The test measures the presence of antibodies (which fight the HIV infection) that can take up to 6 months to develop, and there's no guarantee the person hasn't been infected since the test. Indeed, a person can have HIV and be able to infect others during the 2 weeks to 6 months necessary to show antibodies.

Blood-donor cards are equally suspect: though the cards show the bearer has given blood that was subsequently screened for HIV infection, they do not prove that one hasn't been infected after the donation and is a safe partner.

Dating and Sexual Honesty

Truth is the first casualty in war, it is said. Some think it is also the first casualty in sexual behavior.

A survey by psychologists Susan Cochran and Vickie Mays of 422 sexually active college students found that 60% of the women and 47% of the men said that someone had lied to them in order to have sex. In turn, 10% of the women and 30% of the men said that they had told a lie to obtain sex. And 42% of the women and 47% of the men said that, if asked, they would understate the number of previous sexual partners they had had. Finally, asked hypothetically if they would lie about having tested positive for HIV, 4% of the women and 20% of the men said they would not reveal they were HIV positive.

Although male respondents were more willing to lie than women, Cochran says it would be a mistake to say that men are more dishonest about sex. Rather, "women will lie in order to achieve a relationship, while men will lie for both sex and relationships," she says. Clearly, the bottom line, as Cochran points out, is that simply "asking one's partner about AIDS is a risky technique" and does not by itself guarantee safer sex.

Partner Notification of Sexually Transmitted Diseases

In recent years, *partner notification* has become a major issue. There are two kinds of partner notification:

1. *Notification in advance by one partner to another*: Some persons have been sued or prosecuted for failing to inform a sexual partner before having sex that they had an STD, or for not wearing a condom when they presumably knew they were infected and could transmit the disease. Some people being sued have claimed they were not even aware themselves that they were infected at the time, but the Courts have still made them pay damages (up to $150,000 in one case) to the person they infected. Most of the court cases were brought by victims of herpes (a nonfatal STD that is treatable but not curable).

2. *Partner notification afterward by health authorities:* The question of partner notification may also arise later, after people have been tested to see if they have been infected with an STD, particularly HIV. An important concern is whether states should allow anonymous testing for the AIDS virus. Such policies enable people to find out whether they have become infected but maintain their privacy, since the results of their tests are not reported to any health agencies. Or, should states require all people whose tests show they are HIV infected to be identified so that their sexual partners, past and present, can be warned?

Several states have various forms of "mandatory name reporting." (*See Figure 1.*) This means that when people test positive for the AIDS virus, their names are reported to the state health department. They are then contacted and asked to *voluntarily* provide the names of their sexual partners, so that the partners can be notified by health officials. It's important to note that no state so far forces people to divulge partners' names. In addition, stringent precautions are taken by health officials to prevent partners from finding out the identity of the person who may have infected them.

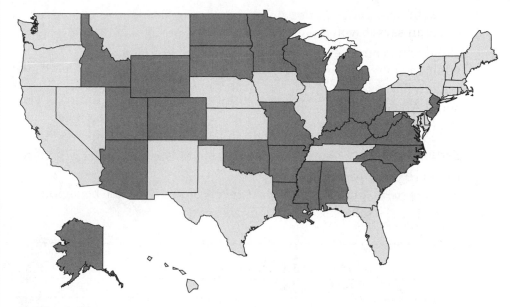

Explanation

▪ States with mandatory name reporting of people who test positive for the AIDS virus.

▪ States with mixed name reporting that allows some anonymous testing.

☐ Most of the other states rely on anonymous testing entirely or require name reporting only in special cases.

Figure 1   States with mandatory, mixed, or no reporting of people testing positive for HIV.   States with mandatory reporting are required to contact infected persons and ask for their cooperation in providing the names of sexual partners, who are then notified of their possible infection (without identifying who may have infected them).

Reducing Risks of Acquiring Sexually Transmitted Diseases

The safest form of sex for preventing transmission of STDs is abstinence and other behavior in which body fluids are not exchanged. The next least risky is protected sex, such as that using condoms and dental dams. High-risk behavior involves sexual exchange of body fluids or use of intravenous needles. Long-term mutually monogamous relationships are an especially important consideration.

So how *should* one pursue sexual relationships? There are two principal pieces of advice:

1. *Use precautions universally*: If you choose to have sex, then CONSISTENTLY use safer-sex measures (such as a condom) with ALL partners. This means *all* sexual partners, not just those you don't know well or those you think may be higher risk.

2. *Keep your head clear*: Be careful about using alcohol and other drugs with a prospective sexual partner. They may cloud your judgment, placing you in a position of increased vulnerability.

No doubt you have heard the phrase "safe sex." However, only abstinence is considered safe—that is, no sexual contact at all, or no contact with a partner's body fluids, including semen, vaginal secretions, saliva, or blood. Actually, even if no body fluids are exchanged, some STDs, such as genital herpes or pubic lice, can still be transmitted under certain conditions by skin-to-skin contact.

In general, then, there are three levels of risk in sexual behavior: "saved sex," "safer sex," and high-risk sex. (*See Table 1.*)

Table 1
Relative risks of various sexual behaviors

Level of risk	Behavior
Lower risk	Abstinence Massage Hugging Rubbing bodies Dry kissing (not exchanging saliva) Masturbation Mutual manual stimulation of genitals (avoiding contact with body fluids)
Somewhat risky	Deep (French) kissing Vaginal intercourse, using latex condoms with the spermicide nonoxynol-9 Oral sex, with the male wearing a condom Oral sex, with a nonmenstruating female using a latex dental dam
Very risky	Vaginal or anal intercourse without a condom Oral sex without a condom Oral sex without a dental dam Oral-anal contact Semen in the mouth Contact with a partner's blood, including menstrual blood Sexual behavior leading to bleeding or tissue damage Behavior involving shared IV needles Sexual contact with an IV user Sexual contact with someone whose previous partner was an IV user Sexual contact with someone who sells or buys sex

Lower Risk: "Saved" Sex, Including Abstinence

The safest kind of sex avoids the exchange of semen, vaginal secretions, saliva, or blood. The principal kind of "saved sex" is **abstinence,** defined as the voluntary avoidance of sexual intercourse. Saved sex also includes massage, hugging, rubbing of bodies, dry kissing (not exchanging saliva), masturbation, and mutual manual stimulation of the genitals (if contact with body fluids is avoided).

Thus, abstinence can be taken to mean anything from avoiding all forms of sexual activity to avoiding only those, such as intercourse or oral sex, in which fluids are exchanged in a way that can transmit disease. Of course, if you *do* want to practice only safe sexual behaviors, the trick is not to get swept away and end up practicing unsafe sex in spite of yourself.

Some people are more comfortable being with dates, potential mates, and just plain friends who do nothing more than kiss and cuddle. In other words, practicing abstinence is becoming increasingly acceptable.

Somewhat Risky: "Safer" Sex, Including Use of Condoms

Abstinence may be unrealistic for some people. The next best step to ensuring safe sex—actually, only *safer* sex—is to use *latex:* condoms and dental dams. "Safer" sex is still somewhat risky, but at least it minimizes the exchange of body fluids (semen, vaginal secretions, saliva, or blood). Examples of safer-sex behavior include dry kissing, vaginal intercourse using latex condoms with the spermicide nonoxynol-9 (which kills STD organisms), oral sex with the male wearing a condom, and oral sex with a nonmenstruating female using a latex dental dam. Let us consider the two principal means of protection, condoms and dental dams:

- *Condoms*: A **condom** ("prophylactic," "rubber," "safe," "French letter") is a thin sheath made of latex rubber or lamb intestine (called "natural skin," but only latex is recommended for HIV protection). Packaged in rolled-up form, the condom is unrolled over a male's erect penis, leaving a little room at the top to catch the semen. Some condoms are marketed with a "reservoir" at the end for this purpose.

  The purpose of a condom is to provide protection for both partners during vaginal, oral, or anal intercourse. On the one hand, it keeps semen from being transmitted to a man's sexual partner and shields against contact with any infectious problem on his penis. On the other hand, the condom also protects the male's penis and urethra from contact with his partner's secretions, blood, and saliva.

- *Dental dams*: Every major sexually transmitted disease can be acquired during oral sex, although not as easily as during intercourse. Males receiving oral sex should wear a condom. If a female is the recipient, she should use a **dental dam.** Sold in medical supply stores and pharmacies, a dental dam (designed for use in dental surgery) is a flat 5-inch-square piece of latex that may be placed over the vaginal opening and surrounding area. Some people use plastic wrap (for example, Saran Wrap) for the same purpose, although this has not been tested to see how well it protects.

Unfortunately, *condoms are not perfect protection*. They only *reduce* the risk of acquiring HIV infections and other STDs. Note that *reducing the risk is not the same as eliminating the risk.* If the condom slips off or breaks during intercourse or is flawed to begin with, there is, obviously, 100% exposure—possibly to a disease that is 100% fatal.

How often do condoms come off or tear during intercourse? One way to judge is that there are typically 12 pregnancies per 100 women using condoms during the first year of use. A nonprofit family-planning research agency in North Carolina, Family Health International, conducted a 2-year study in nine countries and found that married or cohabiting couples broke only 1–2% of the condoms they used. However, among other couples, such as those having casual sex or extramarital affairs or lovers not living together—people who actually need the highest protection—there was a higher breakage rate: 3–5%. About 1 couple in 20 broke condoms 20% of the time, according to the study. Condoms break most frequently when couples use oil-based lubricants, attempt their own "quality testing" (such as blowing up condoms to test for leaks), or engage in prolonged sex. There are several precautions people can take to ensure that condoms are used properly. *(See Figure 2.)*

Condoms, whether made by U.S. or overseas manufacturers, are tested for leakage by the Food and Drug Administration. As of February 1988, 12% of the samples of domestically produced condoms and 21% of foreign-made condoms failed the FDA tests. In March 1989, Consumers Union tested condoms and listed 43 brands and models in terms of their features and performance in resisting breakage. Your physician, health department, or campus student health service can provide additional information. Planned Parenthood will also answer questions about condoms.

Very Risky: Unprotected Sex and Other Behavior

Behavior that is high-risk for the transmission of STDs includes unprotected sex plus any behavior that involves sharing intravenous needles. This includes vaginal or anal intercourse without a condom, oral sex without a condom or without a dental dam, and unprotected oral-anal

---

How to Buy

Materials: Buy latex, not natural membrane or lambskin. Latex is less apt to leak and better able to protect against HIV transmission. Inexpensive foreign brands are suspect.

Sizes: The Food and Drug Administration (FDA) says condoms must be between 6 and 8 inches in length when unrolled. (The average erect penis is 6½ inches.)

Condoms labeled *Regular* are 7½ inches.

Instead of "Small" for condoms under 7½ inches, manufacturers use labels such as *Snug Fit.*

Instead of "Large" for condoms over 7½ inches, manufacturers use labels such as *Max* or *Magnum.*

Shapes: Most condoms are *straight-walled.* Some are labeled *contoured,* which means they are anatomically shaped to fit the penis and thus are more comfortable.

Tips: Some condoms have a *reservoir* at the end to catch semen upon ejaculation. Others do not have a reservoir, in which case they should be twisted at the tip after being put on.

Plain or Lubricated: Condoms can be purchased *plain* (unlubricated) or *lubricated,* which means they feel more slippery to the touch. There are four options:

1. Buy a plain condom and don't use a lubricant.

2. Buy a plain condom and use your own lubricant, preferably water-based (such as K-Y Jelly or Astroglide).

3. Buy a lubricated condom pregreased with silicone-, jelly-, or water-based lubricants.

4. Buy a *spermicidally lubricated* condom, which contains *nonoxynol-9,* a chemical that kills sperm and HIV. This is probably the best option.

Figure 2 How to buy and use condoms.

contact. It includes all forms of sex in which body fluids may be exchanged: semen in the mouth, contact with a partner's blood (including menstrual blood), and any sexual behavior that leads to bleeding or tissue damage.

Finally, the category of high risk has to be extended to people or behavior that involves the exchange of blood, especially by means of injectable drugs or any other situation in which blood-contaminated needles or other objects may be shared (tattooing, ear-piercing, shaving, and so on). Thus, you should not only not share IV needles yourself but should avoid sexual contact with someone who is an IV drug user or whose previous partner was an IV drug user. And you should avoid having sexual contact with people who sell or buy sex, who are often IV drug users.

Mutual Monogamy

Most men and women in the United States have more than one sexual partner during their lifetime. Indeed, two-thirds of all American women who have ever had intercourse have had more than one partner, and some young women have more than one partner within a short time.

Having multiple sexual partners is one of the leading risk factors for the transmission of STDs. Clearly, mutual monogamy is one way to avoid infection. However, in "this day and age" (as the euphemism goes for the Age of AIDS), even apparent monogamy *may* have its risks:

- *"Cheating hearts":* If one partner is having sexual contacts (whether heterosexual, bisexual, or homosexual) outside the supposedly monogamous relationship and is not using condoms—and is not telling his or her principal partner about such activities—it does not just breach a trust. It endangers the other's life. AIDS makes this old problem much more agonizing than, say, 15 years ago, when there was a possibility of passing along herpes, syphilis, or gonorrhea, diseases that are serious but, in North America today, not usually fatal.

- *The AIDS time bomb:* The AIDS virus can be present in a person for perhaps 1 0 years before AIDS itself begins to appear. *And there may be no outward signs or symptoms at all during that time.* This poses a real dilemma, for you could be in a monogamous relationship with someone but have no idea if he or she was previously infected with HIV. Only by waiting 6 months while remaining faithful to each other and then taking a test to see if AIDS virus antibodies are present can one be reasonably sure that the partner is free of HIV infections.

Having extramarital affairs or otherwise "cheating" outside the relationship means, of course, that the commitment is not truly monogamous. The world has changed, but many of our cultural images have not: movies and magazines still celebrate the glories of passion, of losing oneself in sexual ecstasy, of having relationships with exciting strangers. Still, the best strategy for living includes acknowledging the risks associated with sexual behavior, making rational, informed choices that enhance your well-being, and using universal precautions during sexual activity.

800-HELP

AIDS Hotline. 800-533-AIDS (in Canada, 800-668-AIDS)

AIDS Information Hotline. 800-342-AIDS

STD National Hotline. 800-634-3662 (in California, 800-982-5883)

3200 words

Write your ending time here:_____

Subtract your starting time: _____

Total time: _____

Check the Rate Chart on p. 462 to find out how many words per minute you have read, and then record your score on the Reading Efficiency Progress Chart on p. 464.

Analyze What You Read—Create a Study Guide

Objective Questions

Go back to the reading and underline what you think might be on a test. Make marginal self-test notes to remember what you have underlined. If you prefer, you may write each self-test note on a flash card and paraphrase the underlining on the back.

Essay/Application Questions

Predict Essay Questions: There are two main topics that would most likely be asked on an essay test. What are they?

1. _____

2. _____

Make Graphic Organizers: Fill in the charts.

Questions to ask your prospective sexual partner:
1.
2.
3.
4.
5.
6.

Level of risk of various sexual behaviors	Examples of behaviors
1.	

continued

Level of risk of various sexual behaviors	Examples of behaviors
2.	
3.	

For explanation
see p. 150

Skill Development: Summarizing

Use the underlining and marginal notes and the two charts to write a summary of this reading selection. Use a separate piece of paper.

Remember What's Important

Use the marginal notes or the flash cards and the graphic organizers for self-testing. Keep testing or have someone test you until you know the material. Test yourself as needed on the Vocabulary Preview words.

Make Use of What You Read

When you are ready, complete the Comprehension Check on p. 395 and the Vocabulary Check on p. 397. Do them from memory, without looking back at the reading selection or the study guide.

Evaluate Your Active Critical Thinking Skills

After your tests have been graded, record your scores on the Progress Chart, p. 456, and answer the questions on the Evaluation Checklist on p. 457.

16 Choosing an Occupation or a Career

Vocabulary Preview

implement (im′plə mənt): to carry into effect; fulfill; accomplish

compelled (kəm peld′): forced or constrained, as to do something

implication (im′pli kā′shən): something implied, from which an inference may be drawn

procrastination (prō kras′tə nā′shən, prə-): putting off doing (something unpleasant or burdensome) until a future time; esp., postponing (such actions) habitually

envision (en vizh′ən, in-): to imagine (something not yet in existence); picture in the mind

differential (dif′ər en′shəl): of, showing, or depending on a difference or differences [*differential* rates]

aptitude (ap′tə tōōd′, -tyōōd′): quickness to learn or understand

competence (käm′pə təns): ability; fitness

integral (in′tə grəl; often, for adj., in teg′rəl): necessary for completeness; essential [an *integral* part]

component (kəm pō′nənt): serving as one of the parts of a whole; constituent

cat, āte, fäther; pen, ēvil; if, kīte; nō, ôr, fōōd, book; boil, house; up, turn; chief, shell; thick, *the*; zh, treasure; ŋ, sing; ə for *a* in *about*; ′ as in *able* (ā′b'l)

Preread

Preview the following selection by reading the title, the headings, and the subheadings. Answer the following questions without looking back at the reading.

1. What is the subject?

   _____

2. What is the main idea?

   _____

   _____

3. Think about what you know about career planning, what you don't know, and what you might find out from reading the selection. Make up three questions.

   a. _____

b. _____

c. _____

Read

Read the selection without underlining.

Write your starting time here: _____

◆ *Choosing an Occupation or a Career*

Gerald Corey and Marianne Schneider Corey

What do you expect from work? What factors do you stress in selecting a career or an occupation? In working with college students, we find that many of you haven't thought seriously about why you are choosing a given vocation. For some, parental pressure or encouragement is the major reason for being in college. Others have idealized views of what it would be like to be a lawyer, an engineer, or a doctor. Many college students haven't looked at what they value the most and whether these values can be attained in their chosen vocation. John Holland's theory of career decision making is based on the assumption that career choices are an expression of personality. Holland believes that the choice of an occupation reflects the person's motivation, knowledge, personality, and ability. Occupations represent a way of life. Dave's personal story illustrates this search for a satisfying career. Dave chose college without knowing what he wanted. Eventually he found a direction by pursuing what interested him.

> *I went to college right out of high school even though I wasn't sure that college was for me. I went because I thought I needed a college degree to get a good job and to succeed.*
>
> *My first year was a bit rough because of the new surroundings. In my classes I felt like a number, and it didn't seem to matter if I attended classes or not. College provided a wide range of freedom. I was the one who was responsible to show up for class. It was hard for me to handle this freedom. I found it easier to go off with my friends. Needless to say, my grades took a nose dive. I was placed on academic disqualification. As a result, I decided to go to a community college. But my pattern of not taking school seriously remained the same.*
>
> *Although I wanted to eventually finish college, I knew that university life was not right for me at this time. I decided to move out of my parents' home and worked full time. Although I was working, I managed to take a few night*

classes at a community college. I knew that if I left college completely it would be harder to ever return.

Eventually I accepted a job with a promotional marketing firm. It was a fun job sampling different consumer goods targeted toward people participating in various sporting events (10K races, tournaments, bike races). I was given more responsible assignments, and I really enjoyed what I was doing. I asked myself: "How could I apply what I enjoyed doing and make it a career?" This question led me to doing research on the sports entertainment field to discover a career path.

My research convinced me of the importance of returning to college full time. Now I was focused and determined to receive my degree and to pursue a career in the sports entertainment industry. Knowing what I wanted as a career made selecting a major relatively easy. I majored in business with a marketing emphasis and did extremely well. My journey took me from academic disqualification to graduating with honors.

After graduation I accepted a job from the same marketing firm where I had worked earlier, only this time it was a higher level job that included travel. After many interviews I accepted a job with a professional baseball team. After working there for more than two years, I was offered a job with Disney Sports Enterprises (for the Mighty Ducks Hockey Team) in the sales and marketing department, where I am currently employed. I sell advertising, sponsorships, and various ticket packages. My work involves implementing much of what I learned in my major. This position is ideal because it allows me to do what I enjoy and use what I learned in college.

Following my interests has led to an exciting career. I look forward to getting up and going to work, which is both fun and challenging. I am able to combine my sports hobbies with my profession. This work is personally rewarding, and I feel energized and motivated on the job. My work doesn't seem like "work." To me, this is one of the keys to a meaningful life.

The Disadvantages of Choosing an Occupation Too Soon

So much emphasis is placed on what you will do "for a living" that you may feel compelled to choose an occupation or a career before you are really ready to do so. In our society, we are pressured from an early age to grow up and encouraged to identify with some occupation. Children are often asked: "What are you going to be when you grow up?" Embedded in this question is the implication that we're not grown up until we've decided to *be* something. Our society expects young people to identify their values, choose a vocation and a lifestyle, and then settle down. The implication is that once young people make the "right decision," they should be set for life. Yet deciding on a career is not that simple.

One of the disadvantages of focusing on a particular occupation too soon is that students' interest patterns are often not sufficiently reliable or stable in high school or sometimes even in the college years to predict job success and satisfaction. Furthermore, the typical student does not have enough self-knowledge or knowledge of educational offerings and vocational opportunities to make realistic decisions. The pressure to make premature vocational decisions often results in choosing an occupation in which one does not have the interests and abilities required for success. At the other extreme, however, are those who engage in delay, defensive avoidance, and procrastination. An individual on this end of the scale drifts endlessly and aimlessly, and life may be pretty well over when he or she asks, "Where am I going?" It is clear that either extreme is dangerous. We need to be cautious in resisting pressures from the outside to decide too quickly on a life's vocation, yet we also need to be alert to the tendencies within ourselves to expect that what we want will come to us easily.

Factors in Vocational Decision Making

Career development researchers have found that most people go through a series of stages when choosing an occupation or, more typically, several occupations to pursue. As with life span stages, different factors emerge or become influential at different times throughout this process. Factors that have been shown to be important in the occupational decision-making process include: self-concept; motivation and achievement; attitudes about occupations; abilities, interests; values; temperament and personality styles; socioeconomic level; parental influence; ethnic identity; gender; and physical, mental, emotional, and social handicaps. In choosing your vocation (or evaluating the choices you've made previously), consider which factors really mean the most to you. Let's take a closer look at how some of these factors may influence your vocational choice, keeping in mind that vocational choice is a process, not an event.

Self-Concept

People with a poor self-concept are not likely to envision themselves in a meaningful or important job. They are likely to keep their aspirations low, and thus their achievements will probably be low. They may select and remain in a job they do not enjoy or derive satisfaction from because they are convinced this is all they are worthy of. Choosing a vocation can be thought of as a public declaration of the kind of person we see ourselves as being. Casey and Vanceburg capture the notion that how we view ourselves has a great deal to do with how others perceive and treat us: "Our self-perception determines how we present ourselves. The posture

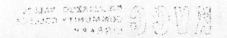

we've assumed invites others' praise, interest, or criticism. What others think of us accurately reflects our personal self-assessment, a message we've conveyed directly or subtly."

Motivation and Achievement

Setting goals is at the core of the process of deciding on a vocation. If you have goals but do not have the energy and persistence to pursue them, your goals will not be met. Your need to achieve along with your achievements to date are related to your motivation to translate goals into action plans. In thinking about your career choices, identify those areas where your drive is the greatest. Also, reflect on specific achievements. What have you accomplished that you feel particularly proud of? What are you doing now that moves you in the direction of achieving what is important to you? What are some of the things you dream about doing in the future? Thinking about your goals, needs, motivations, and achievements is a good way to get a clearer focus on your career direction.

Attitudes about Occupations

We develop our attitudes toward the status of occupations by learning from the people in our environment. Typical first graders are not aware of the differential status of occupations, yet in a few years these children begin to rank occupations in a manner similar to that of adults. As students advance to higher grades, they reject more and more occupations as unacceptable. Unfortunately, they rule out some of the very jobs from which they may have to choose if they are to find employment as adults. It is difficult for people to feel positive about themselves if they have to accept an occupation they perceive as low in status.

Abilities

Ability or aptitude has received a great deal of attention in the career decision-making process, and it is probably used more often than any other factor to evaluate potential for success. *Ability* refers to your competence in an activity; *aptitude* is your ability to learn. Both general and specific abilities should be considered in making career choices, but scholastic aptitude or IQ—a general ability typically considered to consist of both verbal and numerical aptitudes—is particularly significant because it largely determines who will be able to obtain the level of education required for entrance into higher-status occupations. You can measure and compare your abilities with the skills required for various professions and academic areas of interest to you.

Interests

Your interests reflect your experiences or ideas pertaining to work-related activities that you like or dislike. Interest measurement has become increasingly popular and is used extensively in career planning. Vocational planning should give primary consideration to interests. First, determine your areas of vocational interest. Next, identify occupations in your interest areas. Then, determine which occupations correspond to your abilities.

Occupational interest surveys can be used to compare your interests with those of others who have found job satisfaction in a given area. Researchers have shown that a significant relationship exists between interests and abilities. Abilities and interests are two integral components of career decision making, and understanding how these factors are related is essential. But remember that interest alone does not necessarily mean that you have the ability to succeed in a particular occupation.

Several interest inventories are available to help you assess your vocational interests. If you were going to select just one instrument, we recommend Holland's Self-Directed Search (SDS) Interest Inventory, which is probably the most widely used interest inventory. Other interest and personality inventories you may want to consider taking are the Vocational Preference Inventory, the Strong Interest Inventory, the Kuder Occupational Interest Inventory, and the Myers-Briggs Type Indicator. This last instrument assesses types of human personality. For further information about such inventories, contact the counseling center at your college.

Values

Your values indicate who you are as a person, and they influence what you want from life. It is important to assess, identify, and clarify your values so you will be able to match them with your career choices. An inventory of your values can reveal the pattern behind aspects of life that you prize and will also enable you to see how your values have emerged, taken shape, and changed over time.

Your *work values* pertain to what you hope to accomplish through your role in an occupation. Work values are an important aspect of your total value system, and knowing those things that bring meaning to your life is crucial if you hope to find a career that has personal value for you. A few examples of work values include: helping others, influencing people, finding meaning, prestige, status, competition, friendships, creativity, stability, recognition, adventure, physical challenge, change and variety, opportunity for travel, moral fulfillment, and independence. Because

specific work values are often related to particular occupations, they can
be the basis of a good match between you and a position.

2100 words

Write your ending time here:_____

Subtract your starting time: _____

Total time:_____

    Check the Rate Chart on p. 462 to find out how many words per minute
you have read, and then record your score on the Reading Efficiency Progress
Chart on p. 464.

Analyze What You Read—Create a Study Guide

Objective Questions

Go back to the reading and underline what you think might be on a test.
Make marginal self-test notes to remember what you have underlined. If you
prefer, you may write each self-test note on a flash card and paraphrase the
underlining on the back.

Essay/Application Questions

Predict Essay Questions: What is the most likely topic for an essay question
for this reading selection?

_____

Graphic Organizer: Fill in the following chart. For each topic on the left,
write the information that should be memorized for that topic in the space on
the right. The left column should be similar to your marginal notes, and the
right column should be similar to your underlining.

John Holland's theory	
Disadvantages of choosing too soon or too late	

continued

12 factors in vocational decision making	
Self-concept	
Motivation and achievement	
Attitudes and occupations	
Abilities	
Interests	
3 steps in vocational planning	
Interest inventories	
Values	
Work values	
Examples	

For explanation see p. 150

Skill Development: Summarizing

Use the underlining and marginal notes and the graphic organizer to summarize this reading selection. Use a separate piece of paper.

Remember What's Important

Use the marginal notes or the flash cards and the graphic organizer for self-testing. Keep testing or have someone test you until you know the material. Test yourself as needed on the Vocabulary Preview words.

Make Use of What You Read

When you are ready, complete the Comprehension Check on p. 399 and the Vocabulary Check on p. 400. Do them from memory, without looking back at the reading selection or the study guide.

Evaluate Your Active Critical Thinking Skills

After your tests have been graded, record your scores on the Progress Chart, p. 456, and answer the questions on the Evaluation Checklist on p. 457.

17   Causes of Infection: Pathogens

Vocabulary Preview

microorganism (mī′krō ôr′gən iz′əm): any microscopic or ultramicroscopic animal or vegetable organism; esp., any of the bacteria, protozoans, viruses, etc.

respiratory (res′pər ə tôr′ē): having to do with respiration (breathing)

toxin (täks′in): any of various poisonous substances produced by microorganisms and causing certain diseases

prostration (pras trā′shən): utter mental or physical exhaustion

recurrent (ri kʉr′ənt): appearing or occurring again or periodically

cat, āte, fäther; pen, ēvil; if, kīte; nō, ôr, fōōd, book; boil, house; up, tʉrn; chief, shell; thick, *the*; zh, treasure; ŋ, sing; ə for *a* in *about*; ′ as in *able* (ā′b′l)

Preread

Preview the following selection by reading the title, the headings, the boldface and italic print, and the illustration. Answer the first two questions without looking back at the reading.

1. What is the subject?

_____

2. What is the main idea?

_____

3. What is the main idea of the illustration?

_____

4. Think about what you know about the causes of infection, what you don't know, and what you might find out from reading this selection. Make up three questions.

  a. _____

  b. _____

  c. _____

Read

Read the selection without underlining.

Write your starting time here: _____

◆ *Causes of Infection: Pathogens*

Brian K. Williams and Sharon M. Knight

Many of the microorganisms that surround us are beneficial. An example is the bacteria in our intestines, which help in digestion. Here, however, we consider the types of microorganisms that are harmful—namely, pathogens. There are six kinds of pathogens, ranging in size from smallest to largest: *viruses, bacteria, rickettsia, fungi, protozoa,* and *parasitic worms.* (See Figure 1.)

Viruses: The Smallest and Toughest

Viruses may be the smallest of the pathogens, being visible only under an electron microscope. However, they are also the toughest to fight. The reason is that it is difficult to find drugs that will kill a virus without also killing the cell it has taken over. In addition, viruses withstand heat, formaldehyde, and radiation.

A virus is such a primitive form of life that it cannot exist on its own. Indeed, a virus is simply a protein structure containing the nucleic acids DNA or RNA. To survive and reproduce, it must attach itself to a cell and inject its own DNA or RNA. This tricks the cell's reproductive functions into producing new viruses. These new viruses expand the cell until it bursts. The viruses are then set free to seek other cells to take over.

Common characteristics of viruses that are important to know are the following:

- *Viruses are common:* There are many viruses—200 for the common cold alone. This makes them the most prevalent form of contagious disease. **Contagious** means a disease is "catching"—it is easily transmitted from one person (carrier) to another. Viruses include the common cold, influenza (flu), mononucleosis (mono), hepatitis, mumps, chicken pox, measles, rubella, polio, and **HIV,** the human immunodeficiency virus that causes AIDS.

- *Viruses vary in seriousness:* Some viruses cause relatively mild, short-lived illnesses. An example is the 24-hour flu that produces gastrointestinal upset. Other viruses have far more serious consequences. These include mononucleosis, hepatitis, polio, or AIDS. The key is which cells the viruses attack. For example, cold viruses attack respiratory cells, which can be replaced. However, the polio virus attacks nerve cells, which cannot be replaced, resulting in paralysis.

Viruses: Smallest pathogens. *Typical diseases:* Colds, influenza, herpes, rubella, mononucleosis, hepatitis, mumps, chicken pox, HIV.

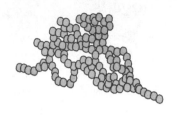

Bacteria: One-celled pathogens. *Typical diseases:* Strep throat, tetanus, bacterial pneumonia, Lyme disease, tuberculosis, scarlet fever, gonorrhea.

Fungi: Plant-like pathogens. *Typical diseases:* Athlete's foot, candidiasis ringworm.

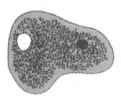

Protozoa: Simplest animal form. *Typical diseases:* amoebic dysentery, giardia, malaria.

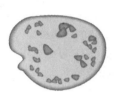

Rickettsia: Virus-like microbes. *Typical diseases:* Typhus fever, Rocky Mountain spotted fever.

Parasitic worms: Many-celled. *Typical diseases:* Pinworm, elephantiasis.

Figure 1　**Pathogens**
Examples of each of the six types of pathogens are shown.

- *Viruses are transmitted in different ways:* Some highly contagious viruses are transmitted in the air. When cold sufferers sneeze or cough, they spray extremely fine droplets of virus-bearing mucus and saliva into the environment. Hepatitis A is transmitted by water contaminated by sewage or by another fecal-oral route, as when infected food handlers don't wash their hands. HIV is transmitted by means of infected body fluids through anal, vaginal, or oral sex with an infected partner. It can also be transmitted through sharing drug needles with a person who has the virus, or by an infected pregnant woman to her fetus.

- *Viruses have varying incubation periods:* An **incubation period** is the time lapse between exposure to an organism and the development of symptoms. Cold viruses have short incubation periods, taking perhaps only 24 hours and lasting only 4–5 days. The flu, on the other hand, may develop after 4 days and last about 2 weeks. AIDS may not appear for 10–11 years after infection by HIV and may last 2 or more years.

■ *Drug treatment for viruses is limited:* Viruses are hard to reproduce in laboratories. This makes antiviral drug development difficult. Drugs may block viral reproduction for some viruses. For other viruses, drugs may control symptoms but not cure the problem.

A natural protection against some viruses is **interferon,** a protein substance produced by our bodies. It helps protect healthy cells in their battle with invaders.

Unfortunately, in recent years some old viruses (such as polio) have been causing what seem to be "new" diseases. What seem to be "new" viruses (such as influenza A and B) are also causing old diseases. New viruses and diseases emerge because of several factors. Urbanization and travel help disease travel faster and further afield. Agriculture exposes humans to animal-borne diseases. Organ transplants and blood transfusions can spread undetectable viruses.

Bacteria: The Most Plentiful

Next larger in size to viruses are **bacteria.** These single-celled organisms are visible through a standard microscope. They are the most plentiful of the pathogens. Unlike viruses, many bacteria do not enter cells but thrive on and around the cells. Some bacteria are actually helpful, such as those (*Escherichia coli*) in the digestive tract. However, when people are ill, these bacteria can become harmful. About 100 of the several thousand species of bacteria actually cause disease in people.

The characteristics of bacteria include the following:

■ *Bacteria cause a variety of diseases:* Three types of bacteria are spirilla, cocci, and bacilli. Among the types of bacterial infections they cause are strep infections (such as strep throat), staph infections, pneumonia, tuberculosis, scarlet fever, and gonorrhea.

■ *Bacteria are transmitted in various ways:* Some bacteria are transmitted through consumption of contaminated water or food. A type of bacteria called chlamydia is largely transmitted by sexual intercourse.

■ *Bacteria can harm the body in several ways:* Many bacteria release **toxins,** or poisonous substances. These can lead to diseases such as tetanus, diphtheria, or even that unpleasant traveler's diarrhea sometimes called "Montezuma's revenge."

Within the body, some bacteria work locally, killing cells near the source of infection. The infection then spreads to other tissue, producing boils, abscesses, and soreness. Other bacteria spread via the bloodstream, causing fever or attacking organs. Some bacteria simply grow until they obstruct vital organs, as in pneumonia.

- *Antibiotics may fight specific bacteria:* **Antibiotics** are bacteria-killing drugs in pill, cream, liquid, or injectable form. One of the most well known antibiotics is **penicillin,** a substance produced from a fungus. (Other antibiotics you may recognize are such drugs as erythromycin, tetracycline, streptomycin, gentamicin, and the cephalosporins.)

  Specific antibiotics work on specific bacteria. No antibiotic, therefore, can be used to treat all bacterial infections. Nor are antibiotics appropriate for treating viral infections. In addition, antibiotics have to be taken properly in order to be effective.

- *Some bacteria are drug-resistant:* Because of inappropriate use and overuse of antibiotics, some antibiotic-resistant strains of bacteria have developed. In addition, some strains of bacteria—for instance, some forms of tuberculosis—are transforming themselves into "superbugs." These bacteria are highly resistant or even invulnerable to some or all antibiotics.

Rickettsia

Rickettsia resemble bacteria but are more complex than viruses. They are disease-causing microorganisms that grow inside living cells. These organisms are generally transmitted by insects such as mites, ticks, and fleas. Rickettsia may cause rashes and fever, such as **typhoid fever (typhus),** a disease characterized by high, disabling fever. Infected ticks transmit **Rocky Mountain spotted fever,** a disease marked by chills, fever, prostration, and pain in muscles and joints.

Fungi: Yeasts, Molds, and the Like

Fungi are single-celled organisms (like yeasts) or multicelled organisms (like molds). Some cause diseases on the skin, mucous membranes, and lungs. The itching, burning, and scaling disorders of the feet and of the scrotal skin known as **athlete's foot** and **jock itch** are caused by a fungus that thrives in moist environments, such as locker-room shower floors. Another kind of fungal disorder is **candidiasis,** a yeast infection of the vagina. Treatment is with antifungal medications.

Protozoa: The Smallest Animals

The smallest animals in existence are **protozoa,** single-celled organisms responsible for many tropical diseases. One example is **malaria,** the severe, recurrent disease borne by mosquitoes. It remains one of the most serious and widespread tropical diseases, killing up to 2 million people a year. **African sleeping sickness** is a recurring disease whose chief characteristic is weariness and listlessness. **Amoebic dysentery** is an infection of the intestines.

If you spend time hiking or camping in North America, you need to be particularly careful about drinking unpurified water—even that from mountain streams. It may produce a protozoan infection called **giardia,** characterized by diarrhea, abdominal cramps, and fatigue.

Parasitic Worms

Parasitic worms may be microscopic in size or may range up to 10 feet long. Intestinal parasites, such as the tapeworm or pinworm, cause anal itching in children. They may be contracted by eating undercooked beef or pork. Some of these parasites are more a problem in developing countries than in North America. However, pinworm remains a common problem among school-aged children.

1600 words

Write your ending time here:_____

Subtract your starting time: _____

Total time: _____

Check the Rate Chart on p. 462 to find out how many words per minute you have read, and then record your score on the Reading Efficiency Progress Chart on p. 464.

Analyze What You Read—Create a Study Guide

Objective Questions

Go back to the reading and underline what you think might be on a test. Make marginal self-test notes to remember what you have underlined. If you prefer, you may write each self-test note on a flash card and paraphrase the underlining on the back.

Essay/Application Questions

Predict Essay Questions: What is the most likely topic for an essay question for this reading?

_____

Make Graphic Organizers: Fill in the blanks in the following chart. If the answer is not given in the reading, write "not given."

	Pathogens					
	Virus	Bacteria	Rickettsia	Fungi	Protozoa	Worms
Description						
Typical diseases						
Method of transmission						
Treatment						

Skill Development: Summarizing

For explanation see p. 150

Use the underlining and marginal notes and the chart to write a summary of this reading selection on a separate piece of paper.

Remember What's Important

Use the marginal notes or flash cards and the graphic organizer for self-testing. Keep testing or have someone test you until you know the material. Test yourself as needed on the Vocabulary Preview words.

Make Use of What You Read

When you are ready, complete the Comprehension Check on p. 403 and the Vocabulary Check on p. 404. Do them from memory, without looking back at the reading or the study guide.

Evaluate Your Active Critical Thinking Skills

After your tests have been graded, record your scores on the Progress Chart, p. 456, and answer the questions on the Evaluation Checklist on p. 457.

18   Family Violence

Vocabulary Preview

perpetrator (pur′pə trāt′ər): one who does or performs (something evil, criminal, or offensive)

dysfunctional (dis fuŋk′shən əl): of or characterized by abnormal or impaired psychosocial functioning [a *dysfunctional* family, *dysfunctional* behavior]

interaction (in′tər ak′shən): action on each other; reciprocal action or effect

traumatic (trô mat′ik; also trə-, trä-, trou-): *Psychiatry* having a painful emotional effect; shocking; often producing a lasting psychic effect

substantiate (səb stan′shē āt′): to show to be true or real by giving evidence; prove; confirm

accessible (ak ses′ə bəl, ək-): that can be got; obtainable

innuendo (in′yōō en′dō′): an indirect remark, gesture, or reference, usually implying something derogatory; insinuation

implicit (im plis′it): suggested or to be understood though not plainly expressed; implied: distinguished from EXPLICIT

ambiguous (am big′yōō əs): not clear; indefinite; uncertain; vague

callousness (kal′əs nes): lack of pity, mercy, etc.; lack of feeling

cat, āte, fäther; pen, ēvil; if, kīte; nō, ôr, fōōd, book; boil, house; up, turn; chief, shell; thick, *the*; zh, treasure; ŋ, sing; ə for *a* in *about*; ′ as in *able* (ā′b′l)

Preread

Preview the following selection by reading the title, the headings, the illustrations, and the last paragraph. Answer the first two questions without looking back at the reading.

1. What is the subject?

_____

2. What is the main idea?

_____

_____

3. Look at Figure 2.

   a. What is the subject?

   _____

b. What is the main idea?

_____

4. What is the subject of Table 1?

_____

5. Think about violence among family and acquaintances. Think about what you know, what you don't know, and what you might find out from reading the selection. Make up three questions.

a. _____

b. _____

c. _____

_____

STEP 2

Read

Read the selection without underlining.

Write your starting time here: _____

◆ *Family Violence*

Guy R. Lefrançois

Those who specialize in gloom have been warning us for some time that violence is rapidly becoming a way of life in contemporary societies. And perhaps they are correct. The U.S. Bureau of the Census (1994) data indicate that the percentage of households touched by crime was lower in 1992 than in 1981 (22.6 percent compared with 30 percent). However, rates for many violent crimes have increased (Figure 1). In particular, sexual violence seems to have increased dramatically in recent decades (Figure 2).

It might be tempting to assume that violence typically involves strangers and that surrounding ourselves with friends and family will therefore protect us. That, sadly, does not appear to be the case. Indeed, more than 25 percent of all assaults and homicides that are reported to police involve members of the same family. Forty-two percent of all crime victims know the perpetrator. Most of us think of rape as committed by disturbed strangers in dark parking lots. However, more than half of all rapes are committed by acquaintances or relatives—or "dates." One-third of all female murder victims are killed by boyfriends or husbands. As

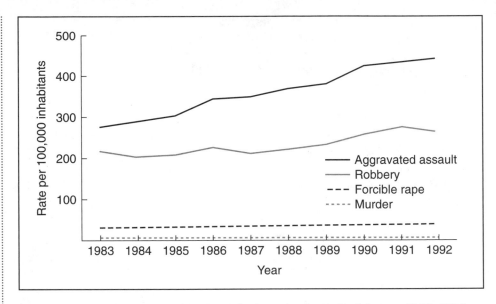

Figure 1   Increases in rates of selected crimes in the United States, 1983–1992. (Based on U.S. Bureau of the Census, 1994, p. 198.)

Gelles puts it, "We have discovered that violence between family members, rather than being a minor pattern of behavior, or a behavior that is rare and dysfunctional, is a patterned and normal aspect of interaction between family members." In a national survey, Resnik, Kilpatrick, and Dansky found that more than a third of American women had been exposed to some traumatic event (such as sexual assault or homicide) involving themselves or some close friend at some time in their lives.

Violence in the family takes a variety of forms. The majority of parents admit to using physical force to punish children. It is even more dramatically apparent in instances of child abuse. In 1992, almost 2.9 million children were involved in reported instances of abuse and neglect. Of these, more than 990,000 were substantiated by authorities.

Family violence is present, as well, in episodes of aggression among siblings. Violence among siblings seems to be common among young children, although it diminishes rapidly with age. In a sample of 2,143 families, Straus found that 74 percent of all 3- to 4-year-old children who had siblings occasionally resorted to some form of aggression in their interactions. Thirty-six percent of those ages 15 to 17 behaved in similar fashion.

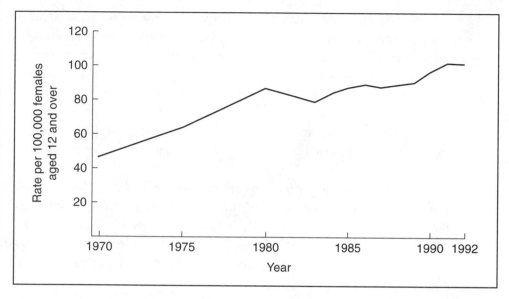

Figure 2   **Rate of forcible rape, 1970–1992. Rate per 100,000 females aged 12 and over.**   (Based on U.S. Bureau of the Census, 1994, p. 198.)

Interspousal Violence

Violence in the family is also apparent in instances of wife and husband beating. Verbal aggression almost always accompanies physical violence. In Straus and Gelles's investigation of American families, 3.8 percent of all husbands admitted to activities that the authors define as wife beating. These activities include kicking, biting, hitting with the fist or some other object, threatening with a knife or a gun, or actually using a knife or a gun. And an amazing 4.6 percent of all wives admitted to similar activities with respect to their husbands. However, Straus cautions that wife beating tends to be hidden and secretive more often than is husband beating. Wives are, in fact, far more often victims than are husbands.

The picture presented by surveys such as these is probably only a partial sketch, given the privacy of the family. Its affairs are not easily accessible to social science or to law enforcement agencies. In addition, our attitudes concerning the right of parents to punish their children physically, the normality of siblings fighting, and even the right of a husband to beat his wife tend to hide the prevalence and seriousness of violence in the family.

Why do some husbands beat their wives? There is no simple answer. Some, probably a minority, might be classified as suffering from a psychological disorder. In one study involving 100 battered wives, 25 percent of the husbands had received psychiatric help in the past. And, according to the wives, many more were in need of such help. Many of these husbands came to their marriages with a history of violence. Many had been physically abused and beaten as children. And compared with the general population, more of them were chronically unemployed and poorly educated.

Other factors that contribute to violence in the family include high incidence of violence in society, cultural attitudes that accept violence as a legitimate reaction in certain situations, and our predominantly sexist attitudes toward the roles of husband and wife in contemporary marriage. These and other contributing factors are summarized in Figure 3.

Sexual Assault and Acquaintance Rape

One form of violence that is not restricted to the family, but that occurs there as well, is sexual assault. Sexual assault can range from sexual innuendo and unwanted suggestions to forcible rape. It is an increasingly common problem with a range of sometimes extremely negative consequences.

Rape is ordinarily defined as forcible sexual intercourse with someone *other* than a spouse. In 1992, 100.5 out of every 100,000 American women over the age of 12 were subjected to attempted or actual forcible rape—a total of more than 109,000 incidents. This represents an increase of more than 180 percent since 1970, when the rate per 100,000 women was 46.3.

Note that the legal definition of rape specifically excludes the wife as victim. In this definition is an implicit acceptance of a husband's right to use physical force on his wife. It also explains the reluctance of law enforcement agencies to charge husbands with assault when wives are victims. English common law maintains that a man is still king in his castle, however humble that castle might be.

In many jurisdictions, then, it is legally impossible for a man to rape his wife—although he might well be guilty of sexual violence variously labeled "sexual aggression," "sexual coercion," or "sexual victimization." It is not legally impossible for a friend, a date, or an acquaintance to rape his partner. In fact, such behaviors are shockingly common, and are often termed *courtship violence, date rape,* or *acquaintance rape.*

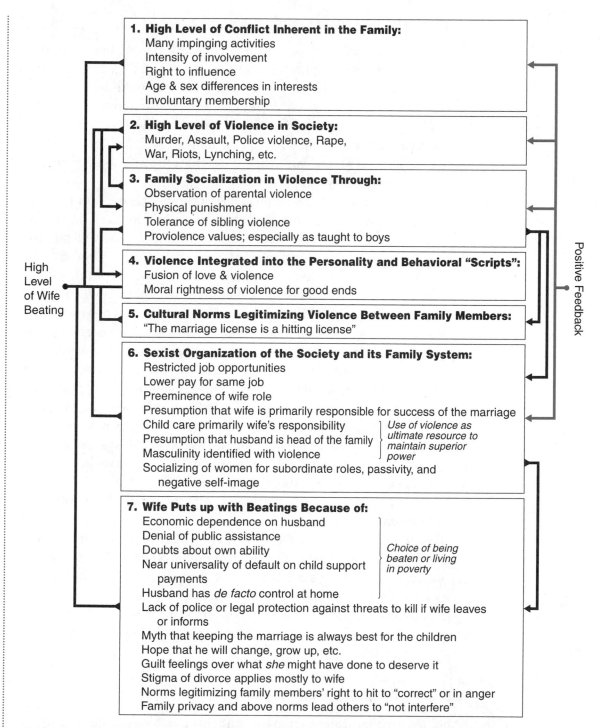

Figure 3   Some of the factors accounting for the high incidence of wife beating (solid lines) and positive feedback loops maintaining the system (colored lines). (From Straus, 1980a. Used by permission of the University of Minnesota Press.)

Acquaintance Rape on Campus

Ward and associates speak of four different kinds of rape that occur on college and university campuses (and elsewhere, too, of course): (1) the *stranger* incident in which the perpetrator attacks an unknown victim, (2) the *party* incident in which victim and perpetrator know each other from a single social function during or after which the assault occurs, (3) the *acquaintance* incident in which the man and woman know each other casually, and (4) the *date* incident in which the man and woman have an ongoing relationship.

Prevalence of sexual assault on college campuses is difficult to ascertain, as it is elsewhere. There are problems of definition, as well as problems having to do with underreporting. Koss found that only 58 percent of rape victims reported the incident to anyone at all. A mere 5 percent went to the police. Many women are uncertain or ambiguous about the seriousness of the incident and many think that little or nothing can be done.

In one survey of 531 college women, Finley found that one out of every six women had experienced some sort of sexual assault the preceding year. Other reports indicate that about one-third of college women experience unwanted sexual contact in any given year. The Ward and associates survey involved 524 women and 337 men on a college campus. Thirty-four percent of the women in this group had experienced unwanted sexual contact (kissing, fondling, or touching in a sexual way). Twenty percent had been subjected to attempted sexual intercourse. Ten percent had experienced completed sexual intercourse. The majority of these episodes occurred with an acquaintance at a party. About three-quarters involved alcohol use by the male and one-half involved alcohol use by the female. In almost half the cases of unwanted intercourse, no one was told later (see Table 1).

It is perhaps striking that, in this sample, men's recollections of sexual incidents were dramatically different from the women's. Only 9 percent of the men recalled having sexual contact with an unwilling woman. Another 9 percent claimed they had attempted intercourse with an unwilling partner (women reported 34 and 20 percent, respectively). A mere 3 percent of men admitted they had actually completed intercourse (women reported 10 percent).

Attitudes Toward Sexual Violence

Other research indicates that many students don't view date rape as a particularly serious problem. In one survey of 172 college men and women, only about half thought date rape was a problem; and very few

Table 1
Characteristics of "Most Serious" Unwanted Sexual Incidents

	Type of Experience		
	Contact (N = 176)	Attempted Intercourse (N = 102)	Intercourse (N = 50)
Location			
Dorm	32%	41%	50%
Fraternity	28	10	8
Apartment	29	43	36
Other	11	6	6
Occasion			
Date	9%	8%	14%
Party	68	65	57
Other	24	27	29
Alcohol Use			
Male use	80%	77%	76%
Female use	57	54	65
Relationship			
Stranger	18%	9%	12%
Acquaintance/friend	66	57	47
Boyfriend	14	30	33
Other	2	5	8
Male Tactics			
Just did it	77%	62%	46%
Verbal	15	28	33
Force	8	10	21
Female Response*			
Too frightened	6%	62%	46%
Said no	76	91	70
Cried	5	9	22
Struggled/fought	17	16	28
Other protests	17	7	12
What Resulted*			
Physical injury	0%	3%	10%
Psychological injury	18	30	51
Required counseling	2	2	8
Who Was Told*			
No one	23%	30%	41%
Roommate	41	38	25
Close friend	59	54	41
Counselor	<1	<1	4

*Percentages do not add to 100 because of multiple responses.

Source: From Ward, S. K., Chapman, K., Cohn, E., White, S., & Williams, K. (1991). Acquaintance rape and the college social scene. *Family Relations* 40, 65–71. Copyright 1991 by the National Council on Family Relations. Reprinted by permission.

believed it was a *major* problem. Even among college students, males are more likely than females to assign responsibility for date rape to the victim. They think that the woman probably wanted to have sex, and that she should have foreseen the man's actions. In this sense, sexual assault is a form of violence that reflects an attitude of male dominance and female passivity, and an implicit assumption of the male's rights to sexual satisfaction under certain circumstances. That these attitudes are slowly changing is reflected in what is termed *rape shield law,* which prohibits that the victim's sexual history or apparently promiscuous behaviors be used against her.

Many campuses organize and support workshops designed to increase student awareness of sexual violence, as well as to reduce male callousness toward date rape and to debunk the myths that still surround sexual aggression. These often result in significant attitude changes among males. Interestingly, male students who live in coeducational residences and fraternities typically have less traditional views of gender and are less accepting of rape myths.

1600 words

Write your ending time here:_____

Subtract your starting time: _____

Total time: _____

Check the Rate Chart on p. 462 to find out how many words per minute you have read, and then record your score on the Reading Efficiency Progress Chart on p. 464.

Analyze What You Read—Create a Study Guide

Objective Questions

Go back to the reading and underline what you think might be on a test. Make marginal self-test notes to remember what you have underlined. If you prefer, you may write each self-test note on a flash card and paraphrase the underlining on the back.

Essay/Application Questions

Predict Essay Questions: What are the three most likely topics for essay questions?

1. _____

2. _____

3. _____

Make Graphic Organizers: Following is an outline of the reading. On each blank line, write the missing statistic or other data. The first one has been done for you as an example.

Family Violence

I. Violence in the family

   A. Percent of assaults and homicides involving family or acquaintances
   25% involve family; 42% know the perpetrator
   _____

   B. Percent of rapes by acquaintances or relatives

   _____

   C. Percent of female murder victims killed by boyfriends or husbands

   _____

   D. Gelles' statement

   _____

   E. Resnik, Kilpatrick, and Dansky survey

   _____

   _____

   F. Number of parents who punish children physically

   _____

   G. Amount of child abuse and neglect

   _____

   _____

   H. Amount of sibling violence

   _____

II. Interspousal violence

   A. Amount of wife beating admitted by husbands

   _____

   B. Amount of husband beating admitted by wives

   _____

   _____

C. Accuracy of data

_____

D. Attitudes

_____

E. Reasons for wife beating

_____

_____

F. Other factors that contribute to family violence

_____

_____

III. Sexual assault and acquaintance rape
   A. Types of sexual assault

   _____

   _____

   B. Definition of rape

   _____

   C. Frequency of attempted or actual forcible rape

   _____

   _____

   _____

   D. English common law

   _____

   _____

   E. Marital rape

   _____

   _____

   F. Four kinds of acquaintance rape

   _____

   G. Prevalence of sexual assault on college campuses uncertain because of

   _____

   _____

   _____

H. Finley's survey

_____

_____

I. Ward and associates survey

_____

_____

_____

_____

_____

_____

_____

J. Men's recollections

_____

_____

_____

_____

K. Attitudes toward date rape

_____

_____

_____

L. Attitude change

_____

For explanation see p. 150

Skill Development: Summarizing

Use the underlining and marginal notes and/or the outline to summarize this reading selection on a separate piece of paper.

Remember What's Important

STEP 4

Use the marginal notes or the flash cards and the graphic organizer for self-testing. Keep testing or have someone test you until you know the material. Test yourself as needed on the Vocabulary Preview words.

Make Use of What You Read

When you are ready, complete the Comprehension Check on p. 405 and the Vocabulary Check on p. 407. Do them from memory, without looking back at the reading selection or the study guide.

Evaluate Your Active Critical Thinking Skills

After your tests have been graded, record your scores on the Progress Chart, p. 456, and answer the questions on the Evaluation Checklist on p. 457.

19 Why We Sleep

Vocabulary Preview

restoration (res'tə rā'shən): a bringing back to health or strength

ordeal (ôr dēl'): difficult, painful, or trying experience

unscrupulous (un skroō'pyə ləs): unprincipled; not honorable

superimpose (soō'pər im pōz'): to put on top of something else

circadian (sʉr ka'dē ən): having to do with the rhythms associated with the 24-hour cycles of the earth's rotation, such as rhythms of sleeping and waking

cat, āte, fäther; pen, ēvil; if, kīte; nō, ôr, foōd, book; boil, house; up, tʉrn; chief, shell; thick, *the*; zh, treasure; ŋ, sing; ə for *a* in *about*; ' as in *able* (ā'b'l)

Preread

Preview the following selection by reading the title, the headings, and the illustrations. Answer the following questions without looking back at the reading.

1. What is the subject?

   _____

2. What is the main idea?

   _____

3. Look at Figure 1.

   a. What is the subject?

   _____

   b. What is the main idea?

   _____

   _____

4. Look at Figure 2.

   a. What is the subject?

   _____

   b. What is the main idea?

   _____

5. Think about what you know about why we sleep, what you don't know, and what you might find out from reading the selection. Make up three questions.

a. _____

b. _____

c. _____

STEP 2

Read

Read the selection without underlining.

Write your starting time here: _____

◆ *Why We Sleep*

James W. Kalat

We would not have been born with a mechanism that forces us to sleep for 8 hours or so out of every 24 unless sleep did us some good. But what good does it do? Scientists have proposed two theories.

The Repair and Restoration Theory of Why We Sleep

According to the **repair and restoration theory,** the purpose of sleep is to enable the body to recover from the exertions of the day. During sleep the body increases its rate of cell division and the rate at which it produces new proteins. It also digests food. There is no doubt that these and perhaps other restorative processes do occur during sleep. However, nearly all of the same processes also take place when we are awake but sitting quietly. Evidently we do not need sleep in order to rest the muscles or any other tissues, other than perhaps the brain. We have several other reasons to doubt that sleeping is like resting to catch your breath after extensive exercise.

First, if sleep were simply a means of recovering from the exertions of the day, it would resemble the rest periods we have after bouts of activity. But people need only a little more sleep after a day of extreme physical or mental activity than after a day of inactivity.

Second, some people get by with much less than the "normal" 7½ to 8 hours of sleep a day. An extreme case was a 70-year-old woman who claimed that she slept only about 1 hour a night. Researchers who observed her over a number of days confirmed her claim; some nights she did not sleep at all. Nevertheless, she remained healthy.

Third, some people have intentionally gone without sleep for a week or more, suffering less severely than we might have expected. In 1965 a San Diego high-school student, Randy Gardner, stayed awake for 264 hours and 12 minutes—11 days—in a project for a high-school science fair. Gardner suffered no serious psychological consequences. On the last night of his ordeal he played about a hundred arcade games against sleep researcher William Dement and won every game. Just before the end of the 264 hours he held a television press conference and handled himself well. After sleeping 14 hours and 40 minutes, he awoke refreshed and apparently fully recovered.

You may have heard that unscrupulous people have used sleep deprivation as a means of brainwashing or torturing prisoners. Why would sleep deprivation produce so many more drastic effects on prisoners than it did on, say, Randy Gardner? Two reasons: First, Gardner may have been better able to tolerate sleep deprivation than most other people. Quite likely, many other people have tried to deprive themselves of sleep, but we never heard about them because they gave up after two or three days. Second, Gardner knew he was in control of the situation. If he became unbearably miserable, he could simply quit and go to sleep. Tortured prisoners do not have that option; if they stay awake night after night, they do so because of constant prodding, not because of their own decision. For the same reason, rats that have been forced to go without sleep for several days suffer severe health problems that human volunteers seldom experience after similar periods of sleep deprivation.

If you go without any sleep some night—as most college students do at one time or another—you probably will grow very sleepy by about 4:00 or 5:00 A.M. But if you are still awake at 7:00 or 8:00 A.M., you will feel less sleepy than you did before. For the rest of the day you may feel a little peculiar, but you probably will stay awake and keep reasonably alert. That night, however, you will feel very sleepy indeed. Apparently, the need to sleep is tied to particular time periods.

In one study, volunteers went without sleep for 3 nights; an experimenter periodically took their temperature and measured their performance on logical reasoning tasks. Both temperature and logical reasoning declined during the first night and then increased almost to their normal level the next morning. During the second and third nights, temperature and logical reasoning decreased more than they had the first night, but again they improved the following morning (Figure 1). Thus, sleep

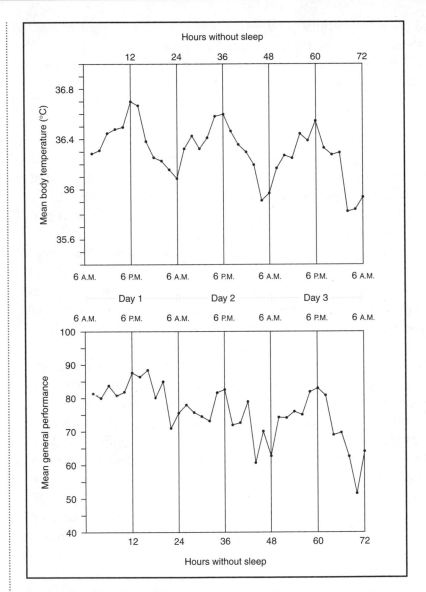

Figure 1   Cumulative effects of 3 nights without sleep.
Both body temperature and logical reasoning decrease each night and increase the next morning. They also deteriorate from one day to the next. Medical interns have to fight this loss of efficiency when they stay on duty for extended periods. (From Babkoff, Caspy, Mikulincer, & Sing, 1991.)

deprivation produces a pattern of progressive deterioration that is superimposed on the normal circadian cycle of rising and falling body temperature and reasoning ability.

In short, sleepiness apparently depends partly on how long one has gone without sleep and partly on the time of day (that is, where one is within the circadian rhythm). Evidently, sleep contributes to repair and restoration of the body, even if that is not its only reason for existence.

The Evolutionary Theory of Why We Sleep

Sleep may be a way of conserving energy. If we built a solar-powered robot to explore the planet Mars, we probably would program it to shut down almost all its activities at night in order to conserve fuel and in order to avoid walking into rocks that it could not see.

According to the **evolutionary theory of sleep,** evolution equipped us with a regular pattern of sleeping and waking for the same reason. The theory does not deny that sleep provides some important restorative functions. It merely says that evolution has programmed us to perform those functions at a time when activity would be inefficient and possibly dangerous.

Note, however, that sleep protects us only from the sort of trouble we might walk into; it does not protect us from trouble that comes looking for us! So we sleep well when we are in a familiar, safe place; but we sleep lightly, if at all, when we fear that burglars will break into the room or that bears will nose into the tent.

The evolutionary theory accounts well for differences in sleep among species. Why do cats, for instance, sleep so much, whereas horses and sheep sleep so little? Surely cats do not need five times as much repair and restoration as horses do. But cats can afford to have long periods of inactivity because they spend little time eating and are unlikely to be attacked while they sleep. Horses and sheep must spend almost all their waking hours eating, because their diet is very low in calories (Figure 2). Moreover, they cannot afford to sleep too long or too soundly, because their survival depends on their ability to run away from attackers. (Woody Allen once said, "The lion and the calf shall lie down together, but the calf won't get much sleep.")

Which of the two theories of sleep is correct? Both are, to a large degree. Supporters of the repair and restoration theory concede that the timing and even amount of sleep depend on when the animal is least efficient at finding food and defending itself. Supporters of the evolutionary theory concede that during a time that evolution has set aside for an animal to conserve energy, the animal takes that opportunity to perform repair and restoration functions.

1200 words

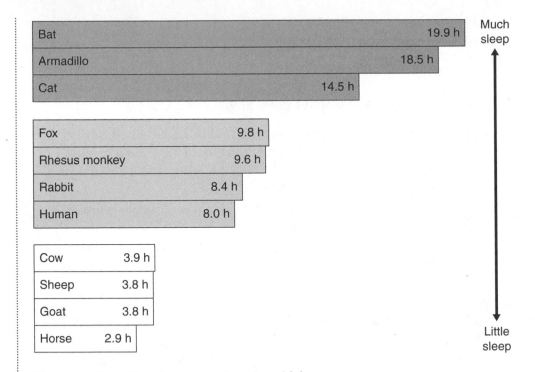

Figure 2 **Sleep time for mammals varies widely.**
Animals that are rarely attacked sleep a lot; those in danger of attack sleep only a few hours. Diet also relates to sleep. (Based on data from Zepelin & Rechtschaffen, 1974.)

Write your ending time here:_____

Subtract your starting time: _____

Total time: _____

Check the Rate Chart on p. 462 to find out how many words per minute you have read, and then record your score on the Reading Efficiency Progress Chart on p. 464.

Analyze What You Read—Create a Study Guide

Objective Questions

Go back to the reading and underline what you think might be on a test. Make marginal self-test notes to remember what you have underlined. If you prefer, you may write each self-test note on a flash card and paraphrase the underlining on the back.

Essay/Application Questions

Predict Essay Questions: What is the most likely topic for an essay question?

_____

Make Graphic Organizers: Fill in the spaces in the chart.

Why We Sleep

Theory	Evidence For	Evidence Against
Repair and restoration	1. 2.	1. 2. 3. 4.
Evolutionary	1. 2. 3.	

For explanation
see p. 150

Skill Development: Summarizing

Use the underlining and marginal notes and/or the chart to summarize this reading selection on a separate piece of paper.

Remember What's Important

Use the marginal notes or the flash cards and the graphic organizer for self-testing. Keep testing or have someone test you until you know the material. Test yourself as needed on the Vocabulary Preview words.

Make Use of What You Read

When you are ready, complete the Comprehension Check on p. 409 and the Vocabulary Check on p. 410. Do them from memory, without looking back at the reading selection or the study guide.

Evaluate Your Active Critical Thinking Skills

After your tests have been graded, record your scores on the Progress Chart, p. 456, and answer the questions on the Evaluation Checklist on p. 457.

20   Ethics and the Consumer

Vocabulary Preview

aphorism (afʹə rizʹəm): a short, pointed sentence expressing a wise or clever observation or a general truth; maxim; adage

scenario (sə nerʹē ōʹ; also, -närʹ-): an outline for any scene or expected series of events, real or imagined

trivial (trivʹē əl): unimportant; insignificant; trifling

statute (stachʹo͞ot): a law passed by a legislative body and set forth in a formal document

entity (enʹtə tē): a thing that has definite, individual existence outside or within the mind; anything real in itself

boon (bo͞on): welcome benefit; blessing

alleging (ə lejʹiŋ): asserting positively, or declaring; affirming; esp., asserting without proof

abstract (ab straktʹ): thought of as not being real or actual

reservations (rezʹər vāʹshənz): limiting conditions or qualifications; unspoken or expressed; doubts

constraint (kən strāntʹ): something that holds back action; restriction

cat, āte, fäther; pen, ēvil; if, kīte; nō, ôr, fo͞od, book; boil, house; up, turn; chief, shell; thick, _the_; zh, treasure; ŋ, sing; ə for _a_ in _about_; ʹ as in _able_ (āʹbʹl)

Preread

Preview the following selection by reading the title, the headings, and the last paragraph. Answer the following questions without looking back at the reading.

1. What is the subject?

_____

2. What is the main idea?

_____

3. Take a moment to think about consumer ethics. Think about what you know, what you don't know, and what you might find out from reading the selection. Make up three questions.

   a. _____

b. _____

c. _____

STEP 2

Read

Read the selection without underlining.

Write your starting time here: _____

◆ *Ethics and the Consumer*

Roger LeRoy Miller and Alan D. Stafford

When Americans make consumer decisions, they usually consider more than the price and quality of products offered for sale. Other factors that may influence their choices include where and how the items were produced, if they were made by union labor, and whether they were made in an environmentally responsible way. For example, you might choose not to shop at a store you believe discriminates against women or ethnic minorities. Many people are willing to pay higher prices for products manufactured or offered for sale in what they believe are socially responsible ways.

In a similar way consumers often make choices that reflect values they have set for their personal behavior. How often have you seen a store clerk make a mistake that would have caused you to pay less than the actual price for what you were buying? Did you tell the clerk that he or she had made a mistake, or did you take advantage of the situation to pay a lower price? If you broke a dish by accident in a china store would you feel responsible to pay for it? If you were harmed by a defective product you had purchased, would you sue for an amount of money that was greater than the value of your loss? Although some people do these things, many American consumers choose to behave in what they regard as a socially/morally responsible way.

All consumers have duties and responsibilities that can be summarized in one sentence: The consumer has a duty to act honestly and ethically when purchasing products and services. An age-old aphorism holds that "what goes around comes around." In the context of consumer dealings, this means that if enough consumers act dishonestly, prices of consumer products and services will rise, harming all other consumers.

What Is Ethical Behavior?

Ethical behavior essentially means acting in accordance with one's moral and ethical convictions as to what is right and what is wrong. Many commonly held ethical convictions are written into our laws. But ethical behavior sometimes requires us to do more than just comply with laws in order to avoid the penalty of breaking them. In some circumstances, one can break the law and be fairly certain no one will ever find out about it.

Imagine, for example, that you purchased a number of items from your local Wal-Mart and discovered when you got home that the cashier had failed to charge you for a $16 CD you had chosen. What is your obligation? Obviously, the CD does not legally belong to you—you have not paid for it. But why should you have to take the time and trouble to return to the store to pay for the item? After all, it wasn't your fault that the cashier did not ring up the purchase price of the item. What would your decision be? Would it make a difference if the item had a much higher or a much smaller price?

Consider another possible situation where you know something is wrong before you actually get a product home. Suppose you regularly buy a particular brand of spaghetti sauce that you know costs $2.19 per jar. One day while shopping at a convenience store (that does not use a barcode scanner to determine product prices at the checkout) you see several jars that have been mispriced at $1.19. What would you do? Would you try to buy all the jars at the lower price, only one or two of them, or would you tell the clerk that a mistake had been made? This time you cannot rationalize your decision by saying "I didn't know." But then it isn't your fault a mistake was made. What do you believe the ethical consumer choice would be?

It's Not Always Easy

These examples illustrate that it's not always easy to do the "right thing"—or even to know what the right thing to do is in a given set of circumstances. You could be pretty certain that in the case of the CD no one would ever know you had obtained the product without paying for it. Wal-Mart officials surely wouldn't report you to the police or come knocking at your door. They have no idea where their merchandise goes to. The case of the mispriced spaghetti sauce is only a little different. If anyone asked you about the price, you could simply say you didn't know what the price should have been. In cases like these, there is a temptation to take the "gift" offered to you by fate. In addition to having more money left over to buy other products, your sterling reputation in the community as an ethical person would not be marred in the slightest, because no one else would ever know what you had done. But you would. And this is what ethics is all about. At the heart of ethical decision making is determining whether you personally feel that a given action is right or wrong, and acting accordingly. After all, you're the one who has to live with your conscience.

Somebody Has to Pay

When trying to determine the rightness or wrongness of a given action, it is helpful to consider the consequences of each alternative. Keep in mind that if you don't pay for benefits you receive, someone else will have to. As economists are prone to emphasize, there is no such thing as a "free lunch." In other words, somebody, somewhere, has to pay for all that is produced and consumed. And that somebody is another consumer—or, rather, other consumers. This is because sellers who absorb these added costs will pass them on eventually to all purchasers in the form of higher prices.

Examples of Unethical Consumer Behavior

While most consumers act responsibly in their purchase transactions, they are obviously not saints any more than businesspersons are. And examples are plentiful of consumers who give in to the temptation to evade the letter of the law in order to get "something for nothing." Consider, for example, the following scenario: Jeannie orders by mail a new Nikon camera from Flash Electronics, a discount house in a distant city. The camera arrives by mail, and Jeannie immediately uses it to take photographs to be included in the book she is writing. A few days later, she drops the camera and breaks the casing. She decides to "pass the buck" to the seller and returns the camera to Flash Electronics, claiming that the camera was broken when it arrived and demanding a replacement. Jeannie, who eventually receives the replacement camera, has just saved herself the cost of repairing the broken camera—at the expense of the discount firm, of course, or the manufacturer. But she suffers few pangs of conscience about her dishonesty. After all, she reasons, Flash Electronics and Nikon are huge and profitable businesses. Whereas the repair bill would be but a drop in the bucket for Flash Electronics or Nikon, it would represent Jeannie's entire food budget for a week.

What Jeannie overlooks in her reasoning is the long-run consequences of her behavior. In the short run, yes, the discount house or the manufacturer will pay for the repairs. But, ultimately, who pays? Other consumers, like Jeannie, who buy cameras or other products from the discount house and Nikon and who have to pay more because of Jeannie's fraud. But Jeannie might still rationalize that the cost of the camera repair—when spread out over thousands of consumers—would represent no real burden to each individual consumer, which is true. But, if all—or even a substantial number of—consumers acted similarly to Jeannie, what then?

It takes little effort to imagine dozens of other ways in which consumers have behaved dishonestly or unethically to gain a personal benefit at the expense or inconvenience of others. We look here at just a few variations of this theme.

So Sue Me

Most consumers periodically receive in the mail invitations to subscribe to certain magazines, or to "sign here" and receive a product to try out for 30 days, and so on. A typical offer is to sign up for membership in a book club. All you have to do is sign and send a card to receive, say, four books for which you will be billed $1 at some future date. Of course, having signed up for membership in the club, you will be obligated to purchase a given number of books per year—or at least notify the club each month if you don't want a particular book or books. You receive the four books and, after a few months, have received several more. You haven't had time to read the books, don't really want them, and don't really want to be a member of the club. But you're busy and fail to do anything about it. Eventually, the book club begins to send stern demands for payment— you owe them $69. You are a struggling student, short of money, and you ignore the bill. It certainly does not take priority in your budget. If they want to sue you for collection, fine. You are not worried about it because you know that the amount is too trivial to justify any legal action against you by the book club. Eventually, to your relief, they stop sending you any bills at all—your account has been written off as a "bad debt"—along with hundreds of others. And you have acquired six "free" books.

Me First, Please

Many consumers have been inconvenienced by delays and other travel complications because of overbooked airline flights. They could not board their designated fight—for which they had reservations—because the plane was full. Airlines overbook flights because they can predict, based on past flight records, that a certain number of passengers will cancel or change their reservations at the last minute or simply not show. Some passengers pay higher rates for the privilege of changing flights at the last minute, if necessary. Other passengers cancel their planned trips owing to unforeseen circumstances that arise. But part of airline overbooking is due to consumers who make multiple reservations. Although airlines, by requiring advance ticketing, have curbed the problems caused by multiple reservations somewhat, it is still estimated that between one-third and one-half of overbooking is done because of multiple reservations made by consumers.

More "Me First"

Toni buys an expensive new dress for a special party she has been invited to attend. She wears the dress to the party, receives many compliments on it, but decides it was really far too expensive a purchase. She returns it to the store for a refund. The sales clerk does not inspect the dress closely and fails to notice the ginger ale stains on the front. Toni gets her refund. The result? Either the next purchaser gets a slightly soiled dress instead of the brand-new garment she paid for, or the store must discount the price of the dress heavily to sell it if the stain is discovered.

Make the Manufacturer Pay

In the past two decades American courts and consumer-protection statutes have increasingly sought to protect the "little person" against the powerful corporate entity or business firm. This has been a boon to consumers who are injured by faulty products they have purchased. It allows them to sue sellers and manufacturers for compensation, in the form of money damages, for injuries caused by carelessness in product design or production. But now and then a consumer will take advantage of these laws and of the court system to seek damages from the product manufacturer or retailer. Assume, for example, that John, a minibike enthusiast, purchases minibikes for his two sons, ages 9 and 11. In the instruction manual, and clearly indicated in large letters on the bikes themselves, are instructions not to use the bikes on city streets and always to wear a helmet while riding them. Nonetheless, John allows his sons to ride on the city streets without helmets. One day, while racing with another friend on a minibike, the oldest son, Chad, carelessly runs three stop signs and then enters a fourth intersection while looking backward toward his friend. Chad is hit by a truck and injured. John sues the manufacturer of the minibike for damages, claiming that the minibike is a dangerous product and should not have been placed on the market.

The Nuisance Suit

Sellers are also often faced with so-called nuisance lawsuits. A typical one might involve the following series of events: Jerry, in a daze about his latest girlfriend, walks through a hardware store, carelessly trips over a stepladder being displayed very close to a wall (and definitely not a hazard), falls, and falsely claims that he injured his back. Alleging that the owner was negligent by having the stepladder displayed as it was, he sues the owner for damages. Similarly, Jane sues the owner of a national chain store for $10,000, alleging that a can of paint displayed on a shelf in the owner's store fell on her toe and injured it. And on and on. Such suits are often settled by the store owners out of court, because it would cost them more to defend themselves in court than to settle. Even though most store owners carry liability insurance, out of which such claims are paid, the insurance is not free to the store—and the premiums will rise (and they have risen dramatically in recent years) as more claims have to be paid by insurance firms.

Ethics in an Impersonal Marketplace

In the increasingly impersonal and mechanized marketplace of today it is much easier to lose sight of our responsibilities toward others than it once was. This is because in today's consumer world, the "others" are usually abstract entities and not people we know personally. In the past, when stores were smaller and most transactions were conducted face to face, consumers were more motivated to act honestly and ethically because they also faced the consequences of their actions directly. Imagine, for example, that Jeannie in the camera example had lived in 1900 instead of the 1990s. After breaking her camera, she returned it to her local camera store, claiming that it was already broken when she purchased it from the seller. Very likely, the seller would remember the transaction, would know that the camera had been in good condition, and would know that Jeannie was acting dishonestly—regardless of whether he could prove it. Jeannie might be deprived of—or at least face a reduced quality in—the services of that store, and her reputation in the community could be affected. Because of these possible negative consequences, it might not even occur to Jeannie to defraud the seller. Moreover, if she knew the merchant quite well, she might have some strong ethical reservations about requiring the merchant to pay for the broken casing for which she alone was responsible.

Now let's return to the present and to a much different marketplace. When Jeannie returned the camera to the discount house, she knew that she was being dishonest, but she would not lose sleep at night over the "victim" of her fraud—who was not a real person but an X quantity of "others." Moreover, and perhaps most significantly, Jeannie was quite sure that she would never be "caught." No one would ever know of her dishonesty, and she would face no negative consequences. The worst that could happen is that the discount store would refuse to repair or replace her camera. In short, Jeannie felt little incentive to be ethical.

Because there are fewer *external* constraints to guide us toward ethical consumer behavior, an understanding of one's responsibilities in the marketplace is even more important today than it was in the past. Huge chain store operations and computerized networks are increasingly hiding the identities—and the behavior—of individual buyers and sellers in the marketplace. And if we are slightly dishonest or violate our own ethical standards occasionally, who will know?

2700 words

Write your ending time here:_____

Subtract your starting time: _____

Total time: _____

Check the Rate Chart on p. 462 to find out how many words per minute you have read, and then record your score on the Reading Efficiency Progress Chart on p. 464.

Analyze What You Read—Create a Study Guide

STEP 3

Objective Questions

Go back to the reading and underline what you think might be on a test. Make marginal self-test notes to remember what you have underlined. If you prefer, you may write each self-test note on a flash card and paraphrase the underlining on the back.

Essay/Application Questions

Predict Essay Questions: There is only one likely topic for an essay. Write it here:

_____

Make Graphic Organizers: Fill in the blanks.

Ethics and the Consumer

I. Consumer responsibility:

_____

_____

II. Consequences of unethical consumer behavior:

_____

III. Definition of ethical behavior:

_____

_____

_____

IV. Examples of unethical consumer behavior:

_____

_____

_____

_____

V. Ethics in an impersonal marketplace:

_____

_____

_____

For explanation
see p. 150

Skill Development: Summarizing

Use the underlining and marginal notes and/or the graphic organizer to summarize this reading selection on a separate piece of paper.

Remember What's Important

Use the marginal notes or the flash cards and the graphic organizer for self-testing. Keep testing or have someone test you until you know the material. Test yourself as needed on the Vocabulary Preview words.

Make Use of What You Read

When you are ready, complete the Comprehension Check on p. 411 and the Vocabulary Check on p. 412. Do them from memory, without looking back at the reading selection or the study guide.

Evaluate Your Active Critical Thinking Skills

After your tests have been graded, record your scores on the Progress Chart, p. 456, and answer the questions on the Evaluation Checklist on p. 457.

UNIT IV

Critical Reading
with the ACT Method

Critical reading means evaluating what an author is saying. Is it true or false? Does it explain what it claims to explain? Does it work? As a college student, you will have to make judgments about what you hear and what you read. Yet many students coming out of high school haven't been taught to do much more than memorize.

In this unit you will read persuasive nonfiction. Authors will try to convince you of their theses or points of view. Persuasion is seen all the time in fields such as advertising and politics. However, you will see persuasion in textbooks, too. Here are some examples of issues that call for persuasive writing:

Which theory best explains why we sleep?

Should immigration policies be changed?

When did the universe begin?

You will see persuasive writing in textbooks, in technical or professional writing, and in popular magazines and newspapers. Persuasion can work by fair means or foul. It can use fallacious reasoning and manipulation just as easily as logic and fairness. To be an informed voter or consumer, and a successful student, you must be able to read persuasive writing critically.

In Unit IV you will practice critical reading using five pairs of articles on controversial subjects: smoking, sports competition, crime, affirmative action, and euthanasia. The readings in each pair take opposing viewpoints. We believe that the goal of critical reading and thinking is to come as close as possible to the truth. The best way of figuring out the truth on any subject is to become familiar with the arguments supporting as many points of view as possible. Everyone is entitled to an opinion on any subject, but it is wrong to hold an opinion because you are ignorant of the arguments on the other side.

You should analyze arguments with an open mind, allowing yourself to be influenced. You should even be open to opinions that appear highly unconventional, because history has shown that majority approval often shifts. For example, at one time "loyal" Americans supported the Vietnam War, but later those who opposed the war were considered morally correct.

If you can develop an open mind, you will earn higher grades and be more successful in life. You will have better friendships and family relations because you will consider the other person's point of view. You will make better consumer and investment decisions because you will investigate for yourself instead of believing what you are told. You will be a better citizen because you will learn about the issues rather than following the party line. You will have the sense of confidence that comes from taking charge of your life. Finally, an active critical thinker is rarely either bored *or* boring.

Critical Thinking Using the ACT Method

Critical thinking means (1) identifying the subject, (2) identifying the author's thesis (opinion or point of view), (3) pinpointing the arguments supporting the thesis, (4) identifying the details used to support the arguments, and (5) evaluating the supporting details.

Preread

Before you begin reading, examine your opinions about both sides of the issue. Review the difficult vocabulary that precedes each reading, so that unfamiliar words will not interfere with your comprehension. Then quickly skim the reading to get an understanding of the subject and the author's thesis. Compare your opinions about the subject with the author's. Think about how open you are to what you are about to read.

Read

Read the selection without underlining or making notes. Try to understand the author's arguments and support.

Analyze What You Read

Go back to the reading and identify the arguments and their support. Support can consist of testimonials from convincing people, logical reasons, statistical or historical facts, or examples. You might want to ask the following questions when evaluating supporting details:

1. *Testimony:* If the author uses testimonials, are his or her sources really experts on the subject? Are they objective or biased? Did the author select the experts who were most qualified or merely those who would support his or her thesis?

2. *Reasons:* If the support consists of reasons, are they logical or is the author using faulty reasoning?

3. *Facts:* If the author uses facts, are they provable or unprovable? Have some facts been included and others omitted in order to support the thesis? You have heard about lying with statistics, but even with good intentions, facts are open to interpretation. Sometimes the author's opinions are disguised as facts.

4. *Examples:* If the author uses examples, are there enough of them? Are they representative enough to support the generalizations the author wants to make?

Loaded Language

Authors can also use loaded language to influence their readers' thinking. For example, supporters of a politician might refer to him or her as a diplomat, strategist, or tactician. Opponents might refer to the same politician as a bureaucrat, influence peddler, power broker—or even a Machiavelli. These loaded words can subtly influence our thinking. Another example of the tremendous importance of words occurred when feminists succeeded in changing sexist language such as *policeman, fireman, mailman,* and *chairman* to *police officer, firefighter, letter carrier,* and *chairperson.*

Guide for Analysis—Graphic Organizers

As part of this step, you will underline and make notes in the margin to highlight the arguments and supporting details. Then you will make graphic organizers as you did in Units II and III. This means putting the important ideas in visual form so that you can easily understand and remember them. The types of graphic organizers are those you are already familiar with: outlines, idea maps, charts, time lines, diagrams, tables, and graphs.

Remember What's Important

Review your underlining, marginal notes, and graphic organizers until you feel confident that you understand and remember the information.

Make Use of What You Read

In college, your instructor will usually guide your use of the information you have prepared: class discussion, a writing assignment, an oral presentation, or a test. In this book we have prepared a Comprehension Check and a Vocabulary Check for each reading. Remember that the answers to essay questions should follow the graphic organizers as in Units II and III. At the end of each pair of readings, we provide questions for writing and discussion that you can use to evaluate your understanding of the issue.

Evaluate Your Active Critical Thinking Skills

When you receive feedback about your performance in the form of a grade, critique, or other type of evaluation, use the information to build on your strengths and to build up your weaknesses. Use the Evaluation Checklist on p. 457.

ISSUE 1

"Three Strikes" Laws

"Three strikes" is a term that refers to laws that give life sentences to criminals convicted of three felonies. The two readings in this section take opposing points of view.

Self-Questioning

It is important to be aware of your own beliefs and biases when you read. Answering the following questions will help you clarify your views. Write the number from the rating scale that best expresses your opinion. You will take the same survey to reevaluate your views after you have completed Readings 21 and 22.

Rating Scale

1. No

2. Perhaps not

3. No opinion

4. Perhaps

5. Yes

Rate each question from 1 to 5.

_____ 1. Will tougher treatment of criminals reduce crime?

_____ 2. Is it worthwhile to try to reform people convicted of serious crimes?

_____ 3. Can the country afford to keep more people in prison?

_____ 4. Should judges have the power to decide on sentencing?

_____ 5. Are "three strikes" laws a good idea?

21 How Many Prisons Must We Build to Feel Secure?

Vocabulary Preview

rousing (rou′zing): exciting, stirring

initiative (i nish′ə tiv): the right of citizens to introduce a matter for legislation directly to the voters

ironically (ī rän′ik lē): showing a contrast between what might be expected and what actually occurs

incarcerate (in kar′sə rāt′): to imprison

concede (kən sēd′): to acknowledge, often reluctantly, as being true

abduct (ab dukt′): to carry off by force; to kidnap

assailant (ə sāl′ənt): attacker

reaffirm (rē ə fʉrm′): restate; uphold

clemency (klem′ən sē): leniency; mercy

deter (di tʉr′): to prevent or discourage from acting

cat, āte, fäther; pcn, ēvil; if, kīte; nō, ôr, fōod, book; boil, house; up, tʉrn; chief, shell; thick, *the*; zh, treasure; ŋ, sing; ə for *a* in *about*; ′ as in *able* (ā′b′l)

Preread

Preview the following selection by reading the title, the headings, and the first sentence of each paragraph. Answer the questions without looking back at the reading.

1. What is the subject?

_____

2. What is the thesis (the main point the author is trying to make)?

_____

3. Now take a moment to compare your beliefs about three strikes with the author's. On a scale of 1 (no way) to 5 (definitely), how open is your mind to the author's thesis?

_____

Read

Read the selection without underlining. Just try to understand the author's arguments.

Write your starting time here: _____

◆ *How Many Prisons Must We Build to Feel Secure?*

Jonathan Simon

President Clinton received roars of approval when he rousingly endorsed the "Three Strikes, You're Out" anti-crime proposal during his [1994] State of the Union Address. But now the idea of locking criminals up for life after their third serious felony is being attacked by critics as good politics but bad policy—as a catchy slogan with an expensive price tag that does little to protect people's security and covers too many crimes that aren't serious.

We heard those same concerns voiced in Washington state. But on Election Day [1993], nearly 77 percent of the voters launched the national movement for "three strikes" by approving Initiative 593 to put felons permanently behind bars after their third serious conviction. And ironically, while "three strikes" is under fire in the nation's capital, some opponents of the 1993 initiative now support the new law.

"Sentencing Law Isn't Striking Out" reads the lead editorial in the February 10, [1994], *Spokesman-Review* from [House Speaker] Tom Foley's hometown of Spokane. "We grudgingly admit the new law appears to be working," said the paper, which encouraged a "no" vote on 593. "We felt, and still do," the paper wrote, "that it will add greatly to the increasing cost of incarceration. We also worried that too many small-fry would be caught in the three-strikes net. We didn't want to see relatively harmless felons taking up prison space at age 60, 70 or 80."

"Maybe we've done too much hand wringing," the *Spokesman-Review* conceded, and pointed out that the new law was catching the two kinds of criminals it targeted: "high-profile predators who rape or kill repeatedly; and offenders who terrorize the community with chronic strings of lesser but still serious crimes, such as robbery."

Targeting Career Criminals

Precisely. At present eight criminals are facing the prospect of "striking out" here in Washington state. Three are sex criminals, all of whom have attempted murder (one successfully). Another is a four-time armed robber. The other four are career criminals. One, Larry Fisher, was described in the *New York Times* as a two-time felon. In fact, he has sixteen prior criminal convictions—six felonies, ten misdemeanors and numerous probation violations. Another has five felonies and nine misdemeanors. A third has four previous felonies and fifteen misdemeanors, and the fourth has had fifteen convictions in eight years, five of them felonies. That's sixty-four convictions among four street criminals. Essentially, whenever these fellows weren't in the joint they were out ripping off people's homes and businesses. Our new law locks the revolving door on their careers.

But in the nation's capital, a rehashed version of Washington state's election debate has resulted in a weak White House version of "three strikes" that would not cover six of our eight criminals, including two of the three violent rapists. Philip Heymann, the former number-two official with the Department of Justice, contends that some of the crimes weren't serious enough to be covered by "three strikes," such as second degree robbery, which he characterized as knocking someone down to steal a purse.

That's theory. Here's reality. The first criminal to face the "Three Strikes, You're Out" charge in our state is Cecil Emile Davis. His first strike was second degree robbery back in 1986. But Mr. Davis didn't knock down a lady while snatching her purse. He robbed a convenience store and beat both the clerk and a customer so severely that the judge noted at sentencing his "deliberate cruelty to the victims." So how long did Davis spend behind bars for that attack? Two years. Often, criminals are not charged with a crime or given a sentence that matches the severity of their actual offense, a reality not addressed by the Clinton version of "three strikes."

Davis is charged with abducting a young woman, repeatedly raping her, stabbing her in the throat and throwing her down the recessed stairwell of a church. She managed to survive and has identified Davis as her assailant. If convicted, Davis will "strike out" and be gone for life. Had he committed that crime on government soil, the Clinton bill would not have applied to him.

Other Benefits

As for the costs of incarceration, only 3 percent to 4 percent of most state budgets is spent on corrections, and several studies show that it's much cheaper to lock up a common criminal than allow him to roam free. However, if the governor is convinced that an aging third striker is too old to do harm any longer, our "three strikes" law reaffirms his power to grant pardons or clemency.

Three other benefits to our law should give pause to even its most liberal critics. First, although statistics haven't yet been tabulated, police officers report that the new law is already deterring criminal activity. Second, the tough new penalties are forcing some criminals to seek treatment and counseling they previously refused. Third, the new law is unquestionably driving criminals out of Washington state. In Seattle alone, since "three strikes" passed, seventeen registered sex offenders have moved out of state because their next offense would be their last. That may be good news for people here, but it will only be good for America if lawmakers across the country, including Congress, make the climate for crime as chilly in their states as it now is in Washington state.

900 words

Write your ending time here:_____

Subtract your starting time: _____

Total time: _____

Check the Rate Chart on p. 462 to find out how many words per minute you have read, and then record your score on the Reading Efficiency Progress Chart on p. 465.

Analyze What You Read

Identify the Thesis and Arguments

A. In the margin of the reading, write *thesis* next to the place where the author presents his point of view.

B. We believe the author presents eight major arguments:

1. The law is catching the types of criminals it targeted.

2. The federal law is too lenient.

3. Clinton's version does not address the problem that criminals are often not charged with a crime or given a sentence that matches the severity of the offense.

4. It's cheaper to lock up a common criminal than to allow him to roam free.

5. There is a way out for third strikers too old to cause harm.

6. Washington state's law seems to be deterring crime.

7. The law is forcing some criminals to seek treatment and counseling.

8. The new law is driving criminals out of state.

C. Go back to the reading and find each argument. Write *Arg. 1, Arg. 2,* etc., in the margin next to where each argument appears.

Identify Supporting Details

Following are details that support each argument. They are in random order and they have been paraphrased, so the words are not exactly the same as in the reading. However, the meaning is the same.

A. Go back to the reading and underline each supporting detail.

B. In the blank before each detail, write the number of the argument that the detail is supporting. For example, Detail a is supporting Argument 2, which says that the federal law is too lenient.

_____ a. It would not cover six of Washington state's eight criminals.

_____ b. Seventeen Seattle sex offenders moved out of state.

_____ c. Emile Davis

_____ d. The eight criminals facing "striking out"

_____ e. No support is given

_____ f. Several studies

_____ g. Governor can grant pardons or clemency

_____ h. Police reports

C. Write the most common type of support: facts, examples, testimony, or reasons.

Evaluate Supporting Details

Valid and Invalid Inferences: A valid inference is based on something the author implied. In part a, mark *V* before each valid inference and *I* before each one that is invalid. If you mark *V,* you should be able to point to the place in the reading where it is implied. In part b, indicate the extent to which you agree or disagree with each statement according to the following scale:

1 = disagree   2 = no opinion   3 = agree

_____ 1a. People convicted of second-degree robbery are actually violent criminals.

_____ 1b.

_____ 2a. If left up to judges, sentences would be too lenient.

_____ 2b.

_____ 3a. The Washington law is mostly catching drug offenders.

_____ 3b.

_____ 4a. The author is concerned about the law catching criminals who really don't deserve life imprisonment.

_____ 4b.

_____ 5a. The law contains a process by which a "third striker" can obtain early release for good behavior or other circumstances that indicate he/she is no longer a threat to society.

_____ 5b.

_____ 6a. Some criminals have a good chance to be rehabilitated.

_____ 6b.

_____ 7a. Criminals who are likely to keep committing serious crimes will move to states without "three strikes" laws.

_____ 7b.

_____ 8a. Liberals generally favor "three strikes" laws.

_____ 8b.

Make Graphic Organizers

Fill in the idea map on the next page. Write the thesis in the circle, the arguments in the rectangles, and the supporting details in the ovals.

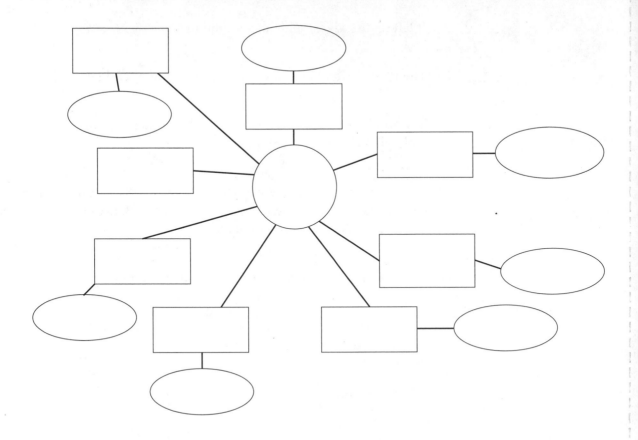

Remember What's Important

STEP 4

Review your marginal notes identifying the thesis and the major arguments. Review the underlining that identifies the supporting details. Review the idea map. Test yourself until you are sure that you will remember the material. Use flash cards to memorize the Vocabulary Preview words you don't know.

Make Use of What You Read

STEP 5

When you are ready, complete the Comprehension Check on p. 415 and the Vocabulary Check on p. 417. Do not look back at the reading or the idea map. Remember that essays must follow the graphic organizer.

Evaluate Your Active Critical Thinking Skills

STEP 6

After your tests have been graded, record your scores on the Progress Chart, p. 456, and answer the questions on the Evaluation Checklist on p. 457.

22   A Case for Discretion

Vocabulary Preview

discretion (di skresh′ən): freedom of action or judgment

misdemeanor (mis′di mēn′ər): a legal offense less serious than a felony

sporadic (spə rad′ik): occurring at irregular intervals

culpability (kul′pə bil′ə tē): guilt

mitigate (mit′ə gāt): to make or become less

mete (mēt): to distribute; allot

unsavory (un sā′və rē): morally offensive

relapse (rē′laps): a falling back to a former state; especially after an improvement

restitution (res′ti too′shən): making good for loss or damage

compassion (kəm pash′ən): sorrow for the sufferings of another, accompanied by an urge to help; deep sympathy; pity

cat, āte, fäther; pen, ēvil; if, kīte; nō, ôr, fōōd, book; boil, house; up, turn; chief, shell; thick, *th*e; zh, treasure; ŋ, sing; ə for *a* in *about*; ′ as in *able* (ā′b′l)

Preread

Preview the following selection by reading the title and the first sentence of each paragraph. Answer the questions without looking back at the reading.

1. What is the subject?

_____

2. What is the thesis?

_____

_____

3. Compare your beliefs about mandatory minimum sentences with the author's. On a scale of 1 (no way) to 5 (definitely), how open is your mind to the author's thesis?

_____

Read

Read the selection without underlining. Just try to understand the author's arguments.

Write your starting time here: _____

◆ *A Case for Discretion*

Michael Brennan

I stood before federal district court judge Kimberly Frankel. The date was May 28, 1995; the place, Portland, Ore. I had just pleaded guilty to five shoplifting charges and one felony count of cocaine possession.

In a similar case in San Diego, Steven White, 32, faced a mandatory sentence of 25 years to life for shoplifting a $130 VCR. He decided instead that a bullet through the brain was the less painful way to go. The suicide note he left offered apologies to his parents for the heartbreak he caused them, but suggested that spending that much time in prison was too high a price to pay for a misdemeanor. The sentence White faced is a result of one of the many federal and state "mandatory minimum" sentencing acts that have been enacted by Congress and various state legislatures since 1986. White's case fell under California's so-called "three strikes you're out" law.

Like me, White had a sporadic history of heroin addiction and non-violent criminal offenses. His first two strikes—burglary convictions—dated to 1983. His "third strike"—the shoplifting charge, which occurred in 1994—was elevated to a felony by being classed as "petty theft with a prior conviction of theft." Two judges pleaded with prosecutors not to seek the 25-to-life sentence that the recently enacted law called for. They refused.

Many groups oppose mandatory minimum sentences, including the National Association of Veteran Police Officers, the U.S. Sentencing Committee, the American Bar Association and Families Against Mandatory Minimums. Supreme Court Chief Justice William Rehnquist calls mandatory minimums "a good example of the law of unintended consequences."

There are currently 1.2 million people incarcerated in federal and state prisons in this country. The majority of them are up on drug-related crimes, and many are there as a result of mandatory minimum sentences. The average cost of housing a federal prisoner is $20,804 annually. It is ultimately the taxpayer who foots this enormous bill. Furthermore, the hodgepodge of state and federal mandatory drug sentences sometimes leads to violent offenders—Florida's rapists, robbers and murderers, for example—being released early to make room for nonviolent, first-time drug offenders serving lengthy, mandatory-minimum sentences.

Ironically, I came close to being classed as a violent offender. On one of my shoplifting sprees I struggled with a Fred Meyer's department-store security guard as I tried to escape her grasp. If she had described my desperate struggle as resistance and my shoplifting partner's presence as a threat, I could have been charged with robbery 2, which now carried a mandatory five-year sentence under Oregon's Measure 11. But the issue is only partially whether the punishment fits the crime. There are a number of federal prisoners doing life without parole for marijuana sales, for example, while rapists are routinely paroled after only four years.

The more central question, however, is this: is it the American way to remove all discretion from judges and invest prosecutors with an extraordinary degree of power? Are there no circumstances—youth, a previously clean record or varying levels of culpability among codefendants—that might mitigate the degree of punishment that must be meted out? Not under any of the mandatory minimum sentences.

In my case, by the time I appeared before Judge Frankel I had behind me a 15-year on-again, off-again history of heroin addiction that resulted in numerous petty theft convictions, three felony heroin-possession convictions and four stints in county jails.

Judge Frankel was free to weigh this unsavory history against what I had accomplished in the four drug-free years prior to my recent relapse. After my release from jail in 1989 I went from a homeless ex-offender to a working writer. I also initiated and managed a self-help work project in Boston that successfully employed 19 individuals who were dealing with homelessness, AIDS, addiction and mental illness.

The judge, using the discretionary powers that have been an integral part of the American judicial system for 200 years, sentenced me to 30 days in jail, 90 days of work-release, $700 in restitution fees and two years' probation. The work-release program allowed me to pay society back through community-work programs, maintain family connections, earn money at outside work to pay a substantial portion of my incarceration costs and to save funds for post-release living expenses.

Contrast my experience with that of Stephanie Lomax, a former Portland, Ore., resident whose family shared her story with me. Lomax and two codefendants were convicted in Nebraska on conspiracy charges involving crack cocaine. White House drug czar Lee Brown recently stated that crack-cocaine mandatory sentences primarily affect African-Americans, thus adding a racial bias to federal drug laws. He calls crack-cocaine mandatory sentences "bad law" based on "bad information."

Lomax, a 25-year-old pregnant black mother and first-time offender with no previous criminal history, continues to maintain her innocence. She was sentenced to life without parole. This means, literally, that she will die in the same prison system where she gave birth to the child she can no longer hold.

Americans are understandably frightened and frustrated by the impact of drugs and crime on society. One can only hope that our fears have not also destroyed our sense of compassion and justice, and that we can still respond to Stephanie Lomax (and untold thousands like her).

"Does anyone care about what is going on in the system today?" she writes from her cell at the Pleasanton federal prison in California. "I am poor. I have no assets and I'm very much in need of help. Can you help me and my family?"

900 words

Write your ending time here:_____

Subtract your starting time: _____

Total time: _____

Check the Rate Chart on p. 462 to find out how many words per minute you have read, and then record your score on the Reading Efficiency Progress Chart on p. 465.

Analyze What You Read

Identify the Thesis and Arguments

A. In the margin of the reading, write *thesis* next to the place where the author presents his point of view.

B. We believe the author presents seven major arguments:

1. Many knowledgeable people oppose mandatory minimum sentences.

2. Most of the 1.2 million people in federal and state prisons are there for drug-related crimes, and many are there because of mandatory minimum sentences.

3. The cost of incarcerating so many people, the majority of whom are up on drug-related crimes often as a result of mandatory minimum sentences, is too high.

4. The hodgepodge of state and federal mandatory drug sentences sometimes leads to violent offenders being released to make room for

nonviolent, first-time drug offenders serving lengthy, mandatory minimum sentences.

5. Punishments often don't fit the crime.

6. Some criminals can make valuable contributions to society.

7. Crack-cocaine mandatory minimum sentences primarily affect African-Americans, adding a racial bias to federal drug laws.

C. Go back to the reading and find each argument. Write *Arg. 1, Arg. 2,* etc. in the margin next to where each argument appears.

Identify Supporting Details

Following are details that support each argument, listed in random order.

A. Go back to the reading and underline each supporting detail.

B. In the blank before each detail, write the number of the argument that the detail is supporting.

C. Beneath each detail write the type of support: facts, examples, testimony, or reasons.

_____ a. White House drug czar Lee Brown

Type: _____

_____ b. National Association of Veteran Police Officers, U.S. Sentencing Committee, American Bar Association, Families Against Mandatory Minimums, Supreme Court Chief Justice William Rehnquist

Type: _____

_____ c. Florida's rapists, robbers, and murderers

Type: _____

_____ d. There are currently 1.2 million people incarcerated in federal and state prisons; the average cost of housing a federal prisoner is $20,804 annually.

Type: _____

_____ e. Steven White; Stephanie Lomax

Type: _____

_____ f. There are currently 1.2 million state and federal prisoners.

Type: _____

_____ g. Author Michael Brennan

Type: _____

Evaluate the Supporting Details

Valid and Invalid Inferences: If the author implied the statement in the reading, mark *V* in the blank before part a of each question. If not, mark *I*. In part b, indicate your agreement or disagreement using the following scale:

1 = disagree   2 = no opinion   3 = agree

_____ 1a. Mandatory minimum sentences make the judicial system more fair.

_____ 1b.

_____ 2a. Stephen White's judges would not have voluntarily imposed the sentence that the prosecutors insisted on.

_____ 2b.

_____ 3a. People with three convictions are career criminals.

_____ 3b.

_____ 4a. Many sentences are a matter of chance or luck.

_____ 4b.

_____ 5a. Judge Frankel made a poor decision.

_____ 5b.

_____ 6a. Selling drugs is as serious and harmful as rape.

_____ 6b.

_____ 7a. The United States has a bad drug policy.

_____ 7b.

Make Graphic Organizers

Fill in the following idea map the same way you did for Reading 21.

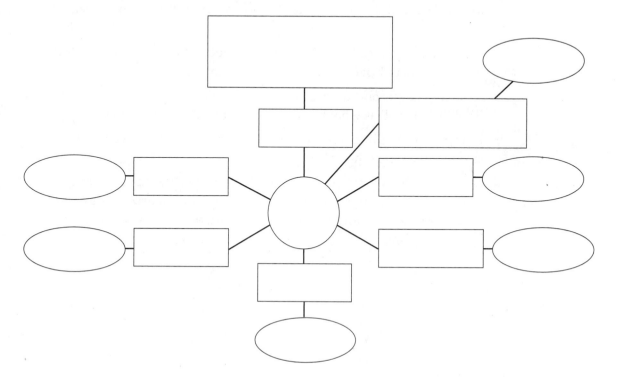

Remember What's Important

Review your marginal notes identifying the thesis and the major arguments. Review the underlining that identifies the supporting details. Review the idea map. Test yourself until you are sure that you will remember the material. Memorize unfamiliar Vocabulary Preview words.

Make Use of What You Read

When you are ready, complete the Comprehension Check on p. 419 and the Vocabulary Check on p. 421. Do not look back at the reading or the idea map.

Evaluate Your Active Critical Thinking Skills

After your tests have been graded, record your scores on the Progress Chart, p. 456, and answer the questions on the Evaluation Checklist on p. 457.

Comparing Views on "Three Strikes"

Use the following activities to evaluate your understanding of the issue of "three strikes" laws. Write your answers on a separate sheet of paper.

1. Summarize each reading. First, write the author's thesis in your own words. Then, in brief form, write each argument and its major support.

2. Evaluate the support for each reading. Consider what each author is implying as well as what he is stating. Is it true? Is it reasonable?

3. Compare the readings. Do you believe that one author's arguments are stronger than the other's? Why?

4. Go back to the self-questioning survey on p. 247. Would you change any of your responses after reading the selections? Summarize your opinion on the issue, noting any ways in which your opinion has been affected by your reading.

ISSUE 2

Competition in Sports and Games

The two readings take opposing views on the value of competitive sports.

Self-Questioning

It is important to be aware of your own beliefs and biases when you read. Answering the following questions will help you clarify your views. Write the number from the rating scale that best expresses your opinion. You will take the same survey to reevaluate your views after you have completed Readings 23 and 24.

Rating Scale

1. No

2. Perhaps not

3. No opinion

4. Perhaps

5. Yes

Rate each question from 1 to 5.

_____ 1. Is participating in sports good for people?

_____ 2. Are competitive sports harmful to people who are not good at sports?

_____ 3. Are competitive games of chance such as "musical chairs" harmful?

_____ 4. Can we have the benefits of sports without the competition?

_____ 5. Are intellectual competitions such as spelling bees harmful to people who lose?

23   No-Win Situations

Vocabulary Preview

counterproductive (koun'tər prə duk'tiv): bringing about effects or results that are contrary to those intended

benign (bi nīn'): harmless

inherent (in hir'ənt): existing in someone or something as a natural and inseparable quality

malicious (mə lish'əs): spiteful; intentionally mischievous or harmful

camaraderie (käm'ə räd'ər ē; kam'-): loyalty and warm, friendly feeling among comrades, comradeship

gloat (glōt): to express malicious pleasure or self-satisfaction

epithet (ep'ə thet'): a descriptive name or title, especially negative

detest (di test'): to dislike intensely; hate

conducive (kən doo'siv): that contributes; tending or leading (to)

aberration (ab'ər ā'shən): a deviation from the normal or the typical

cat, āte, fäther; pen, ēvil; if, kīte; nō, ôr, fōōd, book; boil, house; up, turn; chief, shell; thick, _the_; zh, treasure; ŋ, sing; ə for _a_ in _about_; ' as in _able_ (ā'b'l)

Preread

Preview the following selection by reading the title and the first sentence of each paragraph. Answer the following questions without looking back at the reading.

1. What is the subject?

   _____

2. What is the author's thesis?

   _____

3. Compare your beliefs with the author's. On a scale of 1 (no way) to 5 (definitely), how open is your mind to the author's thesis?

   _____

Read

Read the selection without underlining. Just try to understand the author's arguments.

Write your starting time here: _____

◆ *No-Win Situations*

Alfie Kohn

I learned my first game at a birthday party. You remember it: X players scramble for X-minus-one chairs each time the music stops. In every round a child is eliminated until at the end only one is left triumphantly seated while everyone else is standing on the sidelines, excluded from play, unhappy . . . losers.

This is how we learn to have a good time in America.

Several years ago I wrote a book called *No Contest*, which, based on the findings of several hundred studies, argued that competition undermines self-esteem, poisons relationships and holds us back from doing our best. I was mostly interested in the win/lose arrangement that defines our workplaces and classrooms, but I found myself nagged by the following question: If competition is so destructive and counterproductive during the week, why do we take for granted that it suddenly becomes benign and even desirable on the weekend?

This is a particularly unsettling line of inquiry for athletes or parents. Most of us, after all, assume that competitive sports teach all sorts of useful lessons and, indeed, that games by definition must produce a winner and a loser. But I've come to believe that recreation at its best does not require people to try to triumph over others. Quite to the contrary.

Terry Orlick, a sports psychologist at the University of Ottawa, took a look at musical chairs and proposed that we keep the basic format of removing chairs but change the goal; the point becomes to fit everyone on a diminishing number of seats. At the end, a group of giggling children tries to figure out how to squish onto a single chair. Everybody plays to the end; everybody has a good time.

Orlick and others have devised or collected hundreds of such games for children and adults alike. The underlying theory is simple: All games involve achieving a goal despite the presence of an obstacle, but nowhere is it written that the obstacle has to be someone else. The idea can be for each person on the field to make a specified contribution to the goal, or for all the players to reach a certain score, or for everyone to work with her partners against a time limit.

Note the significance of an "opponent" becoming a "partner." The entire dynamic of the game shifts, and one's attitude toward the other players changes with it. Even the friendliest game of tennis can't help but be affected by the game's inherent structure, which demands that each person try to hit the ball where the other can't get to it. You may not be a malicious person, but to play tennis means that you try to make the other person fail.

I've become convinced that not a single one of the advantages attributed to sports actually requires competition. Running, climbing, biking, swimming, aerobics—all offer a fine workout without any need to try to outdo someone else. Some people point to the camaraderie that results from teamwork, but that's precisely the benefit of cooperative activity, whose very essence is that *everyone* on the field is working together for a common goal. By contrast, the distinguishing feature of team competition is that a given player works with and is encouraged to feel warmly toward only half of those present. Worse, a we-versus-they dynamic is set up, which George Orwell once called "war minus the shooting."

The dependence on sports to provide a sense of accomplishment or to test one's wits is similarly misplaced. One can aim instead at an objective standard (How far did I throw? How many miles did we cover?) or attempt to do better than last week. Such individual and group striving—like cooperative games—provides satisfaction and challenge without competition.

If large numbers of people insist that we can't do without win/lose activities, the first question to ask is whether they've ever tested the alternative. When Orlick taught a group of children noncompetitive games, two-thirds of the boys and all of the girls preferred them to the kind that require opponents. If our culture's idea of fun requires beating someone else, it may just be because we don't know any other way.

It may also be because we overlook the psychological costs of competition. Most people lose in most competitive encounters, and it's obvious why that causes self-doubt. But even winning doesn't build character: It just lets us gloat temporarily. Studies have shown that feelings of self-worth become dependent on external sources of evaluation as a result of competition; your value is defined by what you've done and who you've beaten. The whole affair soon becomes a vicious circle: The more you compete, the more you *need* to compete to feel good about yourself. It's like drinking salt water when you're thirsty. This process is bad enough for us; it's a disaster for our children.

While this is going on, competition is having an equally toxic effect on our relationships. By definition, not everyone can win a contest. That means that each child inevitably comes to regard others as obstacles to his or her own success. Competition leads children to envy winners, to dismiss losers (there's no nastier epithet in our language than "Loser!"), and to be suspicious of just about everyone. Competition makes it difficult to regard others as potential friends or collaborators; even if you're not my rival today, you could be tomorrow.

This is not to say that competitors will always detest one another. But trying to outdo someone is not conducive to trust—indeed it would be irrational to trust a person who gains from your failure. At best, competition leads one to look at others through narrowed eyes; at worst, it invites outright aggression.

But no matter how many bad feelings erupt during competition, we have a marvelous talent for blaming the individuals rather than focusing on the structure of the game itself, a structure that makes my success depend on your failure. Cheating may just represent the logical conclusion of this arrangement rather than an aberration. And sportsmanship is nothing more than an artificial way to try to limit the damage of competition. If we weren't set against each other on the court or the track, we wouldn't need to keep urging people to be good sports; they might well be working *with* each other in the first place.

As radical or surprising as it may sound, the problem isn't just that we compete the wrong way or that we push winning on our children too early. The problem is competition itself. What we need to be teaching our daughters and sons is that it's possible to have a good time—a better time—without turning the playing field into a battlefield.

1200 words

Write your ending time here:_____

Subtract your starting time: _____

Total time: _____

Check the Rate Chart on p. 462 to find out how many words per minute you have read, and then record your score on the Reading Efficiency Progress Chart on p. 465.

Analyze What You Read

Identify the Thesis, Arguments, and Supporting Details

A. In the margin of the reading, write *thesis* next to the place where the author presents his point of view.

B. For each of the seven arguments in the reading, we have provided supporting details. Fill in the missing argument; if the argument is not clearly stated in the reading, use your own words.

C. Next, write in the type of supporting details (facts, examples, reasons, testimony.)

Argument 1: _____

_____

    Detail: Findings of several hundred studies about the workplace and classroom

    Type: _____

Argument 2: _____

_____

    Detail: They offer a workout and camaraderie.

    Type: _____

Argument 3: _____

_____

    Detail: How far did I throw? How many miles did we cover?

    Type: _____

Argument 4: _____

_____

    Detail: Orlick found that two-thirds of the boys and all the girls preferred noncompetitive games.

    Type: _____

Argument 5: _____

_____

    Detail: Losing causes self-doubt; winning causes gloating; self-worth becomes dependent on external evaluation.

    Type: _____

Argument 6: _____

_____

    Detail: View others as obstacles; envy winners; dismiss losers; be suspicious; learn aggression

    Type: _____

Argument 7: _____

_____

    Detail: Cheating and poor sportsmanship

    Type: _____

D. Go back to the reading selection. Write *Arg. 1, Arg. 2,* etc., in the margin of the reading next to the place where each argument appears.

E. Underline the supporting details for each argument.

Evaluate Supporting Details

Fact versus Opinion: Sometimes authors present their opinions as if they were facts. For the purposes of this exercise, a fact is something that can be proved or disproved. An opinion cannot be proved or disproved. Write *F* in the space before each statement of fact; write *O* if the statement is someone's opinion.

_____ 1. "I learned my first game at a birthday party."

_____ 2. "Several years ago I wrote a book called *No Contest. . . .*"

_____ 3. "This is a particularly unsettling line of inquiry for athletes or parents."

_____ 4. "Orlick and others have devised or collected hundreds of such games for children and adults alike."

_____ 5. "The underlying theory is simple. . . ."

_____ 6. "The dependence on sports to provide a sense of accomplishment or to test one's wits is similarly misplaced."

_____ 7. "When Orlick taught a group of children noncompetitive games, two-thirds of the boys and all of the girls preferred them to the kind that require opponents."

_____ 8. "There's no nastier epithet in our language than 'Loser!'"

_____ 9. "And sportsmanship is nothing more than an artificial way to try to limit the damage of competition."

_____ 10. "The problem is competition itself."

Evaluating Research

Alfie Kohn's book *No Contest,* based on the findings of several hundred studies, concluded that competition undermines self-esteem, poisons relationships, and holds us back from doing our best. Whether or not these conclusions are justified depends on the validity of the research. Below are a few questions that should be answered before we can judge the value of any research.

1. Is the sample representative of the people about whom we want to draw conclusions? In this case, are the people in the studies similar to the whole population of the United States in terms of age, background, and types of competitive activities?

2. Is the sample large enough to draw the conclusions? In this case, is it big enough to predict the effects of competition on people all across the United States?

3. How were the people assigned to groups? For example, were they able to choose the type of competition? If not, could this have been a source of bias?

4. Was the method of measurement adequate? In this case, how could they measure the intensity of the competition, the self-esteem before and after, and the effect of competition in relationships and achievements?

5. Are the results significant? For example, were the differences in self-esteem, relationships, and achievement big enough to warrant the conclusion that competition makes a difference?

A. The following study measures the effect of competition on self-esteem. Two groups of Little League boys were selected. Team 1 had a coach who worked very hard to make the team win. He scheduled a great deal of difficult practice, praised and rewarded the boys who did well and ignored the boys who did not, and kept close track of batting averages and scores. Team 2's coach was more relaxed about practicing, stressed teamwork, and rewarded the entire team for playing, whether they won or lost. After one season, both groups of boys were given a questionnaire that rated their self-esteem in terms of how lovable, how good, how attractive, how intelligent, and how competent they considered themselves. There was a slight difference in that the average boy's score from team 1 was higher. Rate the study on the following scale.

	Yes	No	Can't tell

1. Is the sample representative?

2. Is the sample big enough?

3. How were people assigned to groups?

4. Was the measurement adequate?

5. Are the results significant?

B. The following study measures the effects of competitive games on physical aggression in preschoolers. Wadsworth Nursery School, which has ten locations throughout Toronto, did a pilot project using all 1,000 of its pupils. The children, who were between 2 and 4 years old, were randomly assigned to one of two groups within their home school for twenty minutes each day. Physical aggression, defined as hitting, pinching, biting, and pushing, was measured for each group, and no significant differences were found. Group A then played competitive games that had clear winners and losers. Group B played games that were participatory and cooperative, without winners and losers. After one month, incidents of physical aggression were again counted. It was found that Group A had twice as many incidents as Group B. Rate the study on the following scale:

	Yes	No	Can't tell
1. Is the sample representative?			
2. Is the sample big enough?			
3. How were people assigned to groups?			
4. Was the measurement adequate?			
5. Are the results significant?			

Make Graphic Organizers

Draw an idea map. Use a circle for the thesis, rectangles for the arguments, and ovals for the support.

Remember What's Important

Review your marginal notes identifying the thesis and the arguments. Review the underlining that identifies the supporting details. Review the idea map. Test yourself until you are sure that you will remember the material. Test yourself on any unfamiliar Vocabulary Preview words.

Make Use of What You Read

When you are ready, complete the Comprehension Check on p. 423 and the Vocabulary Check on p. 425. Do not look back at the reading or the idea map.

Evaluate Your Active Critical Thinking Skills

After your tests have been graded, record your scores on the Progress Chart, p. 456, and answer the questions on the Evaluation Checklist on p. 457.

24 Who Wins? Who Cares?

Vocabulary Preview

ritualistic (rich'oo wəl is'tik): automatic; prescribed as in a ceremony or custom

rapport (ra pôr'): sympathetic relationship; harmony

classically (klas'ik lē): traditionally

tantamount (tant'tə mount'): equal [to] in value or effect

connote (kə nōt'): to suggest or convey

eschew (es choo'): to shun; avoid

polarize (pō'lə rīz'): to separate into opposed or antagonistic groups

steroid (stir'oid): any of a group of compounds that include the sex hormones, cortisone, and bile acids

myriad (mir'ē əd): very many

seductive (si duk'tiv): tempting

ascribe (ə skrīb'): to refer to a supposed cause or source

devastating (dev'ə stāt'ŋ): destroying completely

cliché (klē shā'): an overused expression

intuit (in too'it, -tyoo'-): to know or understand by instinct, without conscious thought

divisive (də vi'siv): causing disagreement or dissension

cat, āte, fäther; pen, ēvil; if, kīte; nō, ôr, food, book; boil, house; up, turn; chief, shell; thick, _the_; zh, treasure; ŋ, sing; ə for _a_ in _about_; ' as in _able_ (ā'b'l)

Preread

Preview the following selection by reading the title and the first sentence of each paragraph. Answer the following questions without looking back at the reading.

1. What is the subject?

   _____

2. What is the author's thesis?

   _____

3. Compare your beliefs with the author's. On a scale of 1 (no way) to 5 (definitely), how open is your mind to the author's thesis?

   _____

Read

Read the selection without underlining. Just try to understand the author's arguments.

Write your starting time here: _____

◆ *Who Wins? Who Cares?*

Mariah Burton Nelson

Competition can damage self-esteem, create anxiety and lead to cheating and hurt feelings. But so can romantic love. No one suggests we do away with love; rather, we must perfect our understanding of what love means.

So too with competition. "To compete" is derived from the Latin *competere*, meaning "to seek together." Women seem to understand this. Maybe it's because we sat on the sidelines for so long, watching. Maybe it's because we were raised to be kind and nurturing. I'm not sure why it is. But I've noticed that it's not women who greet each other with a ritualistic, "Who won?"; not women who memorize scores and statistics; not women who pride themselves on "killer instincts." Passionate though we are, women don't take competition that seriously. Or rather, we take competition seriously, but we don't take winning and losing seriously. We've always been more interested in playing.

In fact, since the early part of this century, women have devised ways to make sport specifically inclusive and cooperative. Physical educators of the 1920s taught sportswomanship as well as sport skills, emphasizing health, vigor, high moral conduct, participation, respect for other players and friendship. So intent were these women on dodging the pitfalls of men's sports that many shied away from competition altogether.

Nowadays, many women compete wholeheartedly. But we don't buy into the "Super Bull" mentality that the game is everything. Like Martina Navratilova and Chris Evert, former "rivals" whose rapport has come to symbolize a classically female approach to competition, many women find ways to remain close while also reaching for victory. We understand that trying to win is not tantamount to trying to belittle; that winning is not wonderful if the process of play isn't challenging, fair or fun; and that losing, though at times disappointing, does not connote failure. For women, if sports are power plays, they're not about power over (power as dominance) but power to (power as competence). Sports are not about domination and defeat but caring and cooperation.

"The playing of a game has to do with your feelings, your emotions, how you care about the people you're involved with," says University of Iowa basketball coach C. Vivian Stringer.

Pam Shriver has said of Steffi Graf, "I hope in the next couple of years that I get to be friends with her because it's just easier. It's more fun. I don't think it affects the competitive side of things."

Friendship has been a major theme of my sporting life as well, along with physical competence, achievement and joy. Though I've competed in seven sports from the high school to the professional level, I have few memories of victories or losses. I don't think winning taught me to be a gracious winner. I don't think losing readied me for more serious losses in life. Rather, my nearly 30 years of competition have taught me how to *play*, with empathy, humor and honesty. If another player challenges me to row harder, swim faster or make more clever moves toward the basket, the games take on a special thrill. But the final score is nearly irrelevant. Chris Evert once said the joy of winning "lasts about an hour."

I'm choosy about whom I compete with, and how. I don't participate in games in which "losers" are no longer allowed to play. Monopoly, poker, musical chairs, and single-elimination tournaments are a few examples. If playing is the point, then exclusion never makes sense. I also eschew competitions that pit women against men; they only serve to antagonize and polarize. I no longer injure myself in the name of victory. Nor, as a coach, will I allow players to get that carried away.

Some women, scarred by childhood exclusion, shamed by early "defeats," or sickened by abuses such as cheating and steroid use, still avoid competition. They're right to be wary. Although these things are more visible in men's sports, female athletes and coaches can also succumb to the "winning is the only thing" myth, committing myriad ethical and personal offenses, from recruiting violations to bulimia, in the name of victory.

But once one understands the spirit of the game, it's not a matter of *believing* that winning and losing aren't important, it's a matter of noticing that they're not. Women seem to notice. Most women can play soccer, golf, or run competitively and enjoy themselves, regardless of outcome. They can play on a "losing" team but leave the court with little or no sense of loss. They can win without feeling superior.

I think it's the responsibility of these women—and the men who remain unblinded by the seductive glow of victory—to share this vision with young players. Children, it seems to me, naturally enjoy comparing their skills: "How far can you throw the ball? Farther than I can? How did you do it? Will you show me?" It's only when adults ascribe undue importance to victory that losing becomes devastating and children get hurt.

Adults must show children that what matters is how one plays the game. It's important that we not just parrot that cliché, but demonstrate our commitment to fair, participatory competition by paying equal attention to skilled and unskilled children; by allowing all children to participate fully in games, regardless of the score; and by caring more about process than results. This way, children can fully comprehend what they seem to intuit: that competition can be a way to get to know other people, to be challenged, and to have fun in a close and caring environment. To seek together.

Some of my best friends are the women and men who share a court or pool or field with me. Together we take risks, make mistakes, laugh, push ourselves and revel in the grace and beauty of sports. Who wins? Who cares? We're playing *with*, not *against* each other, using each other's accomplishments to inspire.

At its best, competition is not divisive but unifying, not hateful but loving. Like other expressions of love, it should not be avoided simply because it has been misunderstood.

1000 words

Write your ending time here:_____

Subtract your starting time: _____

Total time: _____

Check the Rate Chart on p. 462 to find out how many words per minute you have read, and then record your score on the Reading Efficiency Progress Chart on p. 465.

Analyze What You Read

Identify the Thesis, Arguments, and Supporting Details

A. In the margin of the reading, write *thesis* next to the place where the author presents her point of view.

B. For each of the five arguments in the reading, we have provided supporting details. Fill in the missing argument; if the argument is not clearly stated in the reading, use your own words.

C. Next, write in the type of supporting detail (facts, examples, reasons, testimony).

Argument 1:_____

_____

Detail: . . . it's not women who greet each other with a ritualistic "Who won?"; not women who memorize scores and statistics; not women who pride themselves on "killer instincts."

Type: _____

Argument 2: _____

_____

Detail: Physical educators of the 1920s taught sportswomanship as well as sport skills. . . .

Type: _____

Argument 3: _____

Detail: Martina Navratilova and Chris Evert

Type: _____

Argument 4: _____

Detail: . . . games in which "losers" are no longer allowed to play . . . competitions that pit women against men . . . I no longer injure myself in the name of victory . . . Nor . . . will I allow players to get that carried away.

Type: _____

Argument 5: _____

_____

Detail: . . . demonstrate our commitment to fair, participatory competition by paying equal attention to skilled and unskilled children; by allowing all children to participate fully in games, regardless of the score; and by caring more about process than results.

Type: _____

D. Write *Arg. 1, Arg. 2,* etc. in the margin of the reading next to the place where each argument appears.

E. Underline the supporting details for each argument.

Evaluate Supporting Details

Fact versus Opinion: Sometimes authors present their opinions as if they were facts. We have defined a fact as something that can be proved or disproved. An opinion cannot be proved or disproved. Write *F* in the space before each statement of fact; write *O* if the statement is an opinion.

_____ 1. "Competition can damage self-esteem, create anxiety and lead to cheating and hurt feelings."

_____ 2. "We must perfect our understanding of what love means."

_____ 3. "'To compete' is derived from the Latin *competere*, meaning 'to seek together.'"

_____ 4. "Maybe it's because we sat on the sidelines for so long, watching."

_____ 5. "Passionate though we are, women don't take competition that seriously."

_____ 6. "Physical educators of the 1920s taught sportswomanship as well as sport skills, emphasizing health, vigor, high moral conduct, participation, respect for other players and friendship."

_____ 7. "But we don't buy into the 'Super Bull' mentality that the game is everything."

_____ 8. "For women, if sports are power plays, they're not about power over (power as dominance) but power to (power as competence)."

_____ 9. "I don't participate in games in which 'losers' are no longer allowed to play."

_____ 10. "I also eschew competitions that pit women against men. . . ."

Evaluating Research: Author Mariah Burton Nelson believes that women engage in a healthier type of competition than men do. Go back to the five questions for evaluating research, which were presented on pp. 269–270. Using the questions as a guide, design a research study to measure whether competition differs in women and in men. You want to be able to draw conclusions to apply to the general population of the United States.

1. How can you make sure your sample is representative?

_____

_____

2. How big a sample do you need?

_____

_____

3. Into what subgroups will you divide your people?

_____

_____

_____

_____

4. How will you decide which people go into which group?

_____

_____

5. How will you measure the differences between your groups concerning your topic?

_____

_____

6. How will you decide whether the results are significant?

_____

_____

_____

_____

Make Graphic Organizers

Draw an idea map. Use a circle for the thesis, rectangles for the arguments, and ovals for the support.

Remember What's Important

Review your marginal notes identifying the thesis and the arguments. Review the underlining that identifies the supporting details. Review the idea map. Test yourself until you can remember the material. Test yourself as needed on the Vocabulary Preview words.

Make Use of What You Read

When you are ready, complete the Comprehension Check on p. 427 and the Vocabulary Check on p. 429. Do not look back at the reading or the idea map.

Evaluate Your Active Critical Thinking Skills

After your tests have been graded, record your scores on the Progress Chart, p. 456, and answer the questions on the Evaluation Checklist on p. 457.

Comparing Views on Competition in Sports and Games

Use the following activities to evaluate your understanding of the issue of competition in sports and games. Write your answers on a separate sheet of paper.

1. Summarize each reading. Be sure to include the thesis, the arguments, and their major support.

2. Evaluate the support for each reading. Consider what the author is implying as well as what he or she is saying. Is it true? Is it reasonable?

3. Compare the readings. Do you believe that one author's arguments are stronger than the other's? Why?

4. Go back to the self-questioning survey on p. 263. Would you change any of your responses after reading the selections? Summarize your opinion on the issue, noting any ways in which your opinion has been affected by your reading.

ISSUE 3

Smoking

The two selections take opposing views on the settlement between tobacco companies and the states.

Self-Questioning

It is important to be aware of your own beliefs and biases when you read. Answering the following questions will help you clarify your views. Write the number from the rating scale that best expresses your opinion. You will take the same survey to reevaluate your views after you have completed Readings 25 and 26.

Rating Scale

1. No

2. Perhaps not

3. No opinion

4. Perhaps

5. Yes

Rate each question from 1 to 5

_____ 1. Is tobacco advertising a major cause of teen smoking?

_____ 2. Does smoking have huge social costs, such as health care, paid for by nonsmokers?

_____ 3. Does the $200 billion settlement really punish tobacco companies?

_____ 4. Are the anti-smoking lawyers, politicians, and public-health advocates morally superior to the tobacco industry?

_____ 5. Are tobacco companies more responsible for smoking than individual smokers are?

25   The Amazing Smoke Screen

Vocabulary Preview

closure (klō′zhər): a finish; end; conclusion

parody (par′ə dē): a poor or weak imitation

impose (im pōz′): to place or set (a burden, tax, fine, etc. *on* or *upon*) as by authority

contention (kən ten′shən): a statement or point that one argues for as true or valid

bolster (bōl′stər): to prop up; support, strengthen, or reinforce

advocate (ad′və kit): a person who speaks or writes in support of something [an *advocate* of lower taxes]

hypocrisy (hi päk′rə sē): a pretending to be what one is not, or to feel what one does not feel; esp., a pretense of virtue, piety, etc.

gratification (grat′ə fi kā′shən): cause for satisfaction

disheartening (dis härt′n iŋ, dis′-): depriving of courage or enthusiasm; discouraging; depressing; daunting

mandate (man′dāt): to require, as by law

divert (də vʉrt′, dī-): to turn (a person or thing) aside from a course, direction, etc. into another; deflect

dubious (dōō′bē əs, dyōō′-): doubtful; questionable

compensate (käm′pən sāt′): to make equivalent or suitable return to; recompense; pay [to *compensate* an owner for land taken by a city]

sanctify (saŋk′tə fī′): to make holy; specif., *a*) to set apart as holy; consecrate *b*) to make free from sin; purify

enshrine (en shrīn′, in-): to hold as sacred; cherish [*enshrined* in memory]

arbitrator (är′bə trāt′ər): a person selected to judge a dispute; arbiter, esp. one, as in collective bargaining negotiations, named with the consent of both sides

rebate (ri bāt′): to give back (part of an amount paid) or make a deduction from (a bill)

covet (kuv′it): to desire strongly (esp., something that another person has); long for with envy

gullible (gul′ə bəl): easily cheated or tricked; credulous

pliant (plī′ənt): adaptable or compliant

cat, āte, fäther; pen, ēvil; if, kīte; nō, ôr, fōōd, book; boil, house; up, tʉrn; chief, shell; thick, *the*; zh, treasure; ŋ, sing; ə for *a* in *about*; ′ as in *able* (ā′b'l)

Preread

STEP 1

Preview the following reading selection by reading the title and the first sentence of each paragraph. Answer the questions without looking back at the reading.

1. What is the subject?

_____

2. What is the thesis?

_____

_____

3. Now take a moment to compare your beliefs about the anti-smoking crusade with the author's. On a scale of 1 (no way) to 5 (definitely), how open is your mind to the author's thesis?

_____

Read

STEP 2

Read the selection without underlining. Just try to understand the author's arguments.

Write your starting time here: _____

◆ *The Amazing Smoke Screen*

By Robert J. Samuelson

We may have closure—at least temporarily—to the anti-smoking crusade of the 1990s. The agreement between state attorneys general and the tobacco companies for the industry to pay the states roughly $200 billion over 25 years may quiet the controversy. If so, this will be the agreement's main benefit, because otherwise it is a parody of good government policy. It imposes a steep tax on a heavily poor part of the population; it offers only modest health benefits, and it deepens popular confusion about the public consequences of smoking.

Let's concede the small possible health gains. The agreement will raise cigarette prices; tobacco analyst Martin Feldman of Salomon Smith Barney figures that retail prices will go from an average $2.07 a pack now to $2.90 in the year 2000. Higher prices might reduce the number of smokers by a few percentage points of the population. However, it seems unlikely that the restrictions on advertising (banning billboards and promotional giveaways) will lower teen smoking. In the 1990s, the country has been awash in anti-smoking news stories and TV programs that are worth billions of dollars in counter-advertising. Meanwhile, some surveys show teen smoking has risen. This seems to confirm the industry's contention that advertising mainly determines which brands people smoke, not whether they smoke.

Let's also note that the agreement aids the tobacco industry. By reducing the threat of lawsuits, it bolsters companies' stock prices. Still, the great myth of this struggle is that, just because cigarettes are unhealthy and the tobacco industry is often dishonest, the people on the other side must be morally superior. In truth, they—meaning plaintiffs' lawyers, politicians and public-health advocates—also frequently pursue their goals with a single-minded dishonesty and hypocrisy. And their motives are often selfish: personal enrichment (the lawyers); power and popularity (the politicians); and ego gratification (the public-health advocates). Little wonder the results are disheartening. Almost everyone has long known that smoking is dangerous, as a review of surveys by Julia Saad for the Roper Center for Public Opinion Research at the University of Connecticut reveals: in 1954, 70 percent of the public thought smoking "harmful" and 42 percent thought it "one of the causes of lung cancer"; by 1990, these responses were 96 percent and 94 percent. Most Americans also think that smokers decide for themselves whether to smoke. A 1997 poll asked who is "more responsible for . . . smoking-related illnesses," smokers or tobacco companies. By 76 percent to 17 percent, respondents said smokers. The debate's central issue ought to be: how much is society entitled to penalize smokers for their decisions, because—in society's view—the decisions are unhealthy? Should present smokers be punished (via higher taxes) to deter future smokers? Should Congress order the Food and Drug Administration to mandate safer, and maybe less satisfying, cigarettes? These hard questions pit Americans' belief in personal freedom against the desire to protect public health. Precisely because the questions are hard, anti-smoking advocates diverted the debate to three other ideas, all dubious.

First, smokers aren't responsible for their behavior. As teens, they're seduced by industry ads; then they can't stop because smoking is addictive.

Second, smoking creates huge social costs—mainly higher health spending—that nonsmokers pay through higher taxes.

Finally, the tobacco industry should be punished and forced to compensate nonsmokers for smoking's social costs.

Well. Even if smoking is addictive, people can—often with much pain and hard work—break addictions. There are now more ex-smokers than smokers. As for higher government costs, studies have shown that—because smokers die earlier than nonsmokers—they create savings through lower lifetime health and pension costs. The states' anti-tobacco suits alleged that smokers raised states' health costs under the Medicaid program. This, too, is unproven; the industry's analysis disputed it.

But suppose smokers lack free will and raise government's costs. Still, the industry could not pay those costs directly without going bankrupt. The money always has had to come from smokers through higher cigarette prices—the equivalent of a tax increase. Anti-smoking advocates rarely discuss this, because the implications are devastating. Smokers have low incomes. Only 20 percent of cigarette taxes are paid by those with incomes over $50,000; 34 percent are paid by those with incomes under $20,000 and 19 percent by those with incomes between $20,000 and $30,000. More-over, smokers already pay steep federal and state cigarette taxes (now averaging about 58 cents a pack) that more than cover any possible public costs they create.

As a result, the anti-smoking crusade becomes a reverse Robin Hood arrangement: it sanctifies soak-the-poor taxes and robs the poor to pay the rich. The attorneys general's agreement now enshrines this. The rich, of course, are the private lawyers who represent the states in their tobacco suits. The agreement allows up to $500 million in annual fees for perhaps a few hundred and at most a few thousand lawyers. For how long? Arbitrators will decide; these payments come atop fees to be paid in four existing state settlements that will almost certainly total billions. The ciga-rette dispute has evolved into a welfare program that may create some instant billionaires and many multimillionaires.

Because none of this can be defended, it is camouflaged. For self-interested reasons, the anti-smoking advocates never openly described public choices. Beyond taxing smokers to cut smoking, politicians want to keep the taxes—and not to rebate them. Public-health advocates covet extra money for pet programs; and lawyers crave their fees. All this has involved an adept manipulation of courts and legislatures. A gullible public—aided by a pliant press—embraced the anti-smoking hysteria. Because the campaign succeeded, it will inspire assaults against other industries. We can't tell the target (whether alcohol, or autos or fatty foods) or the tactics. But it's just a matter of time.

1000 words

Write your ending time here:_____

Subtract your starting time: _____

Total time: _____

Check the Rate Chart on p. 462 to find out how many words per minute you have read, and then record your score on the Reading Efficiency Progress Chart on p. 465.

Analyze What You Read

STEP 3

Identify the Thesis, Arguments, and Supporting Details

A. In the margin of the reading, write *thesis* next to the place where the author presents his point of view.

B. Following are the 14 major arguments used by the author. In the blanks, fill in the supporting details. Note that the details are not always located near the arguments they support. You may have to look throughout the reading selection. Some support is implied; you will have to infer it.

1. The settlement imposes a steep tax on a heavily poor part of the population.

   _____

   _____

   _____

2. The settlement offers only modest health benefits.

   _____

   _____

   _____

3. It deepens popular confusion about the public consequences of smoking. (The support is stated indirectly; put it in your own words.)

   _____

   _____

   _____

4. The agreement aids the tobacco industry.

   _____

   _____

5. The anti-tobacco leaders are dishonestly and hypocritically pursuing selfish goals.

   _____

   _____

6. Everyone knows smoking is dangerous.

   _____

   _____

7. Most Americans think that smokers decide for themselves whether to smoke.

   _____

8. Because the real issues of conflict between Americans' belief in personal freedom and the desire to protect public health are hard to resolve, anti-smoking advocates diverted the debate into three dubious ideas.

   _____

   _____

   _____

   _____

9. The tobacco industry cannot pay the costs directly.

   _____

   _____

10. Smokers have low incomes.

    _____

    _____

    _____

    _____

11. Smokers already pay federal and state cigarette taxes that more than cover any costs they create.

    _____

12. The cigarette dispute has evolved into a welfare program that may create some instant billionaires and many multimillionaires.

    _____

    _____

    _____

    _____

13. Courts and legislatures have been manipulated; the public is gullible and the press is pliant.

    _____

14. Because the campaign succeeded, it will inspire assaults against other industries. (The support is implied. Put it in your own words.)

_____

_____

_____

_____

C. Go back to the reading selection and find each argument. Write *Arg. 1,* *Arg. 2,* etc. in the margin next to where each argument appears.

D. Underline the supporting details.

E. Write the most common type of support: facts, examples, testimony, or reasons.

Evaluate Supporting Details

Fact versus Opinion: For this exercise, a fact is something that can be proved or disproved. An opinion cannot be proved or disproved. Write *F* in the space before each statement of fact; write *O* before each statement of opinion.

_____ 1. ". . . it is a parody of good government."

_____ 2. ". . . Martin Feldman of Salomon Smith Barney figures the retail prices will go from an average $2.07 a pack now to $2.90 in the year 2000."

_____ 3. ". . . some surveys show teen smoking has risen."

_____ 4. "Little wonder the results are disheartening."

_____ 5. ". . . the Roper Center for Public Opinion Research at the University of Connecticut reveals: in 1954, 70 percent of the public thought smoking 'harmful'. . . ."

_____ 6. "The debate's central issue ought to be: how much is society entitled to penalize smokers for their decisions. . . ."

_____ 7. ". . . anti-smoking advocates diverted the debate to three other ideas, all dubious."

_____ 8. ". . . the tobacco industry should be punished and forced to compensate nonsmokers for smoking's social costs."

_____ 9. "There are now more ex-smokers than smokers."

_____ 10. ". . . smokers already pay steep federal and state cigarette taxes (now averaging about 58 cents a pack). . . ."

Loaded Language: In his discussion of the anti-smoking campaign, the author uses the following words: crusade, hypocrisy, sanctifies, enshrine, covet, hysteria. Think about what these words imply. Write one or two sentences that summarize the main idea the author is trying to imply by this choice of words.

_____

_____

_____

Make Graphic Organizers

Fill in the following chart. Write the thesis on top, list the 14 arguments on the left, and the support for each argument on the right.

Thesis:	
Arguments	**Supporting Details**
1.	
2.	
3.	
4.	
5.	

continued

Arguments	Supporting Details
6.	
7.	
8.	
9.	
10.	
11.	
12.	
13.	
14.	

Remember What's Important

Review your marginal notes identifying the thesis and the major arguments. Review the underlining that identifies the supporting details. Review the graphic organizer. Test yourself until you are sure you will remember the material. Test yourself as needed on the Vocabulary Preview words.

Make Use of What You Read

When you are ready, complete the Comprehension Check on p. 431 and the Vocabulary Check on p. 432. Do not look back at the reading or the graphic organizer. Remember that essays must follow the graphic organizer.

Evaluate Your Active Critical Thinking Skills

After your tests have been graded, record your scores on the Progress Chart, p. 456, and answer the questions on the Evaluation Checklist on p. 457.

26   Remarks on the Tobacco Settlement

Vocabulary Preview

milestone (mīl′stōn′): a significant or important event in history, in the career of a person, etc.

momentum (mō men′təm): strength or force that keeps growing or moving

partisanship (pärt′ə zən ship, -sən): party politics

comprehensive (käm′prē hen′siv): dealing with all or many of the relevant details; including much; inclusive [a *comprehensive* survey]

jurisdiction (joor′is dik′shən): authority or power

cat, āte, fäther; pen, ēvil; if, kīte; nō, ôr, foōd, book; boil, house; up, turn; chief, shell; thick, *the*; zh, treasure; ŋ, sing; ə for *a* in *about*; ′ as in *able* (ā′b′l)

Preread

Preview the following reading selection by reading the title and the first sentence of each paragraph. Answer the questions without looking back at the reading.

1. What is the subject?

   _____

2. What is the thesis?

   _____

   _____

3. Now take a moment to compare your beliefs about the tobacco settlement with the author's. On a scale of 1 (no way) to 5 (definitely), how open is your mind to the author's thesis?

   _____

Read

Read the selection without underlining. Just try to understand the author's arguments.

Write your starting time here: _____

◆ *Remarks on the Tobacco Settlement*

Bill Clinton (transcript of speech)

Thank you very much. To Attorney General Gregoire and all the others who are here, and the attorneys general of North Carolina and California, who are not here but who are part of this initial group, I want to congratulate you. Bruce Reed, who spoke first and is my Domestic Policy Adviser, and I, and the rest of us have been at this for quite a long time, and we are very pleased by your success . . .

Now, let me join the others in once again saying that today is a milestone in the long struggle to protect our children from tobacco. This settlement between the State attorneys general and the tobacco companies is clearly an important step in the right direction for our country. It reflects the first time tobacco companies will be held financially accountable for the damage their product does to our Nation's health.

Again, let me thank Attorney General Gregoire, the others who are here, and those who are not. And I believe there were four States who previously signed individual settlements with the tobacco companies. All of them deserve the thanks of the country.

With this very large settlement which every other State has the opportunity to join, we are moving forward. But we have a lot more to do, for only the National Government can take the full range of steps needed to protect our children fully from the dangers of tobacco. So it is still up to Congress to act, to rise to its responsibility to pass national tobacco legislation.

Our administration began this effort nearly 4 years ago, with the strong leadership of Vice President Gore and the then-Commissioner of the Food and Drug Administration. The FDA then put in place a strong crackdown on tobacco advertising aimed at teenagers, the broadest and most significant effort to date to protect our children from the dangers of tobacco.

It has been challenged, as all of you know, in court by tobacco companies from the beginning. Today I want to report that the Solicitor General will ask the Supreme Court to resolve this matter. But let us be clear: When it comes to protecting our children from tobacco, ultimately, it is up to Congress to finish the job.

The past Congress began with strong momentum toward action, only to see national tobacco legislation derailed by partisanship and special pleading. In the new Congress, I am determined that all of us will choose progress over partisanship. I think that's what the voters were saying to us on election day.

Comprehensive national tobacco legislation must include many things, but especially it must clarify the jurisdiction of the FDA. And because of the cost inherent in this settlement and any further action by Congress, it should also include appropriate protections for tobacco farmers, as I have said from the beginning. It should be, it must be, one of the top priorities for the new Congress. I will work hard to see that it becomes law.

We should always remember what the real stakes are. Let me say them one more time: Every day we fail to act, more than 3,000 children start to smoke, even though it is illegal to sell them cigarettes. More than 1,000 will die earlier than they would have as a result. Our children continue to be targeted by multimillion-dollar marketing campaigns designed to recruit what the industry has called in its confidential documents "replacement smokers." With strong legislation, working with what the attorneys general have already done, we can save a million lives in the first 5 years.

Our duty to our children, therefore, is clear. We should give them the future they deserve. We can do it.

This is a good day for our country, and I thank all of you who have helped to bring it about.

Thank you very much.

NOTE: The President spoke at 4:12 p.m. in the Roosevelt Room at the White House. In his remarks, he referred to State attorneys general Christine Gregoire of Washington, Daniel Lungren of California, and Mike Easley of North Carolina.

700 words

Write your ending time here:_____

Subtract your starting time: _____

Total time: _____

Check the Rate Chart on p. 462 to find out how many words per minute you have read, and then record your score on the Reading Efficiency Progress Chart on p. 465.

Analyze What You Read

Identify the Thesis and Arguments

A. In the margin of the reading, write *thesis* next to the place the author presents his point of view.

B. Following are the five major arguments used by the author. In the blanks, fill in the supporting details. If no supporting details are given, write "none."

1. The Clinton administration began the effort nearly 4 years ago.

_____

_____

_____

2. The Supreme Court needs to resolve this matter.

_____

_____

3. The goal of passing tobacco legislation should come before partisanship.

_____

_____

4. Tobacco legislation must clarify the jurisdiction of the FDA, and it must protect tobacco farmers. (The support is not stated; try to infer what it must be.)

_____

_____

_____

_____

5. This legislation could save a million lives in the first 5 years.

_____

_____

C. Go back to the reading selection and find each argument. Write _Arg. 1, Arg. 2,_ etc. in the margin next to where each argument appears.

D. Underline the supporting details.

E. Write the most common type of support: facts, examples, testimony, or reasons.

_____

Evaluate Supporting Details

Fact versus Opinion: For this exercise, a fact is something that can be proved or disproved. An opinion cannot be proved or disproved. Write _F_ in the space before each statement of fact; write _O_ before each statement of opinion.

_____ 1. "... today is a milestone in the long struggle to protect our children from tobacco."

_____ 2. "... there were four states who previously signed individual settlements...."

_____ 3. "All of them deserve the thanks of the country."

_____ 4. "... only the National Government can take the full range of steps needed to protect our children fully from the dangers of tobacco."

_____ 5. "Our administration began this effort nearly 4 years ago...."

_____ 6. "It should be, it must be, one of the top priorities for the new Congress."

_____ 7. "... it is illegal to sell them cigarettes."

_____ 8. "... we can save a million lives in the first 4 years."

_____ 9. "Our duty to our children, therefore, is clear."

_____ 10. "This a good day for our country...."

Make Graphic Organizers

Draw an idea map. Use a circle for the thesis, rectangles for the arguments, and ovals for the support.

Remember What's Important

Review your marginal notes identifying the thesis and the major arguments. Review the underlining that identifies the supporting details. Review the graphic organizer. Test yourself until you are sure you will remember the material. Test yourself as needed on the Vocabulary Preview words.

Make Use of What You Read

When you are ready, complete the Comprehension Check on p. 435 and the Vocabulary Check on p. 437. Do not look back at the reading or the graphic organizer. Remember that essays must follow the graphic organizer.

Evaluate Your Active Critical Thinking Skills

After your tests have been graded, record your scores on the Progress Chart, p. 456, and answer the questions on the Evaluation Checklist on p. 457.

Comparing Views on Smoking

Use the following activities to evaluate your understanding of the issue. Write your answers on a separate sheet of paper.

1. Summarize each reading. First, write the author's thesis in your own words. Then, in brief form, write each argument and its major support.

2. Evaluate the support for each reading. Is it true? Is it reasonable?

3. Compare the readings. Do you believe that one author's arguments are stronger than the other's? Why?

4. Go back to the self-questioning survey on p. 281. Would you change any of your responses after reading the selections? Summarize your opinion on the issue, noting any ways in which your opinion has been affected by your reading.

ISSUE 4

Euthanasia

The two readings take opposing views on euthanasia (mercy killing).

Self-Questioning

To help you become aware of your own beliefs and biases about euthanasia, answer the following questions. Write the number from the rating scale that best expresses your opinion. You will reevaluate your views after you have completed Readings 27 and 28.

Rating Scale

1. No
2. Perhaps not
3. No opinion
4. Perhaps
5. Yes

Rate each question from 1 to 5.

_____ 1. Does a human being have the right to take his or her own life?

_____ 2. Do we have the right to kill for political reasons (in war)?

_____ 3. Do we have the right to kill criminals (capital punishment)?

_____ 4. Do we have the right to abort a fetus?

_____ 5. Do we have the right to help another person die if he or she is suffering terribly with no hope of recovery?

_____ 6. Would you "pull the plug" on a relative who was never going to regain consciousness?

_____ 7. If your parent left a "living will" asking to die if there were no hope of recovery, would you follow his or her wishes?

27 | **Acting to End a Life Is Sometimes Justified**

Vocabulary Preview

intercede (in′tər sēd′): to make an appeal on behalf of another

welter (wel′tər): confusion; turmoil

salient (sāl′yənt): outstanding; striking

euthanasia (yo͞o′thə nā′zhə): act of causing a painless death so as to end suffering

elicit (i lis′it): to draw forth; to evoke (a response)

qualified (kwôl′i fīd): modified, limited

refrain (ri frān′): to hold back; keep oneself (from doing something). *Example:* Please *refrain* from talking in class.

intercurrent (in′tər kʉr′ənt): occurring during another disease

gradation (grā dā′shən): a stage or step

compos mentis (käm′pəs men′tis): of sound mind; sane

squeamishness (skwēm′ish nəs): ease with which one becomes nauseated or shocked

humanitarian (hyo͞o man′ə ter′ē ən): person devoted to promoting the welfare of humanity, especially through the elimination of pain and suffering

arbiter (är′bə tər): judge

theological (thē′ə läj′i k′l): having to do with the study of God or religion

glibly (glib′lē): smoothly (spoken), often too smoothly to be convincing

cat, āte, fäther; pen, ēvil; if, kīte; nō, ôr, fo͞od, book; boil, house; up, tʉrn; chief, shell; thick, *the*; zh, treasure; ŋ, sing; ə for *a* in *about*; ′ as in *able* (ā′b′l)

Preread

STEP 1

Preview the following selection by reading the title and the first sentence of each paragraph. Answer the following questions without looking back at the reading.

1. What is the subject?

_____

2. What is the author's thesis?

_____

3. Compare your beliefs with the author's. On a scale of 1 (no way) to 5 (definitely), how open is your mind to the author's thesis?

_____

Read

Read the selection without underlining. Just try to understand the author's arguments.

Write your starting time here: _____

◆ *Acting to End a Life Is Sometimes Justified*

Christiaan Barnard

Whether life ends with a bang or a whimper, the end is a private moment. No one can share the last fears or hopes at the bedside, and no one can intercede in a confrontation that concerns only the dying and the approach of death.

Certainly, the concept of "death with dignity" has become an increasing focus of debate, not the least because of medical progress that has brought about demographic changes and a major increase in the number of retired and aged persons. The issue has generated a welter of legislation, much of which confuses rather than clarifies a salient question in euthanasia: Who will pull the plug?

Possibly one of the more useful outlines of the problem was put forward by Dr. Joseph Fletcher, a professor of medical ethics at the University of Virginia, in a paper given at a 1974 Euthanasia Conference in New York City. He listed eight levels of attitude and opinion on the human initiatives that can be exercised in the case of a patient dying of an incurable disease, as follows:

1. An absolute refusal to elicit any human initiative in the death or the dying. Life must always be considered as the ultimate human value.

2. A qualified refusal, in that the doctor can refrain from employing extraordinary means of preserving life but would nevertheless do whatever possible by ordinary means to keep life going.

3. Declining to start treatment in a patient who has an incurable disease and is suffering from a curable intercurrent illness (for example, the terminally ill cancer patient with pneumonia). The doctor refuses to

initiate treatment for the lung infection that can be cured and in this way may actually hasten death.

4. Stoppage of treatment, with consent, where it is the patient's wish not to be treated any further.

5. Stoppage of treatment, without consent, when the attending physician feels that further treatment can only prolong suffering.

6. Leaving the patient with an overdose of narcotic or sedative, thus assisting the dying person to take his own life.

7. Prior permission is given by the patient to the doctor to administer an injection, under certain circumstances, from which the patient will not recover.

8. Without consent, and on his own authority, the doctor ends the patient's life with an overdose of drugs.

It is clear that the second, third, fourth and fifth situations are gradations of passive euthanasia. In none of these does the doctor take the initiative in ending the patient's life. The sixth, seventh and eighth describe grades of active participation.

There is thus a distinct difference between passive—or indirect—euthanasia, where death is induced by suspension of treatment, and the so-called active or direct euthanasia, where death is brought about by a definite act.

In general, the layman's view of euthanasia is one of "mercy killing," or active intervention to end life, with little or no concept of the possibility of a passive form.

I make no excuses and ask no forgiveness for admitting that I have practiced passive euthanasia for many years. In fact, I gave instructions to the doctor attending my own mother in her last illness that she should receive no antibiotics nor be tube fed. At that stage, she was in her 98th year, suffering from her third stroke and unconscious with pneumonia.

I have never practiced active euthanasia, a deed that in my country is regarded as murder and could merit the death penalty. But I do believe that in the clinical practice of medicine, active euthanasia has a definite place. I also believe that we should not be afraid to discuss its place in the scheme of things and to explore the possibilities in this approach to the terminally ill.

I cannot accept the simple statement that a doctor does not have the right to take life; furthermore, I believe the greatest difficulty is to define life. I myself have defined it as joy in living. Given the absence of this quality, without hope of restitution, the request of the suffering person—if conscious and compos mentis—and the satisfaction of other criteria such as good faith on the part of those caring for the person and the completion of legal requirements, there is no ethical reason why active medical euthanasia may not be administered.

Indeed, I have always wondered at the kind of person who would mercifully end the life of a suffering animal, yet would hesitate to extend the same privilege to a fellow human being. It may be that in all of us there lurks a sense of guilt—and what more guilt-making burden can we assume than that of responsibility for another's death?

The error, perhaps, is one of category—that of regarding squeamishness as mercy.

As a scientist and a humanitarian, I find society's attitude toward the different ways of causing the death of an individual both hypocritical and illogical. Consider that, for as long as man has inhabited the earth, he has accepted with few reservations the right to kill and be killed on the battlefield, even when this leads to not only his own but multiple deaths.

I have talked to legal, ethical and medical authorities in many parts of the world on the need for active euthanasia, the problems that would confront the doctor in such situations and the safeguards required. Again and again the same questions came up:

Who will decide when a life is to be terminated and how can mistakes be avoided?

Would doctors perhaps misuse the right to take life by getting rid of the people they do not like?

Would the medical profession not lose a lot of the trust that is placed in it if doctors were given the right to take a life?

Does a doctor have the right to play God?

Must God be the final arbiter on the taking of life?

If it is feared that a doctor is playing God when he terminates a life, it can just as readily be argued that he is playing the same role when he prolongs the life of a terminally-ill patient. And surely, when the terminally-ill person develops an intercurrent infection that will cause death if not treated, are we not also interfering with God's will by instituting treatment and preventing the patient from dying of the infection?

Generally, these same questions can be raised about war, capital punishment and abortion. I maintain that if doctors are given the right to practice active euthanasia, and all the necessary safeguards are developed, then most of these objections would fall away.

And at the risk of finding myself out on a theological limb, I say that if it is playing God to reduce human suffering, then I do not believe that the God of mercy and compassion would mind if we mere mortals play God under such circumstances. When we glibly bracket talk of terminating life with mention of the Deity, what in fact do we know of God's interpretation of life?

1150 words

Write your ending time here:_____

Subtract your starting time: _____

Total time: _____

Check the Rate Chart on p. 462 to find out how many words per minute you have read, and then record your score on the Reading Efficiency Progress Chart on p. 465.

Analyze What You Read

STEP 3

Identify the Thesis, Arguments, and Supporting Details

A. In the margin of the reading, write *thesis* next to the place where the author presents his point of view.

B. For each supporting detail, fill in the argument. Some of the arguments are not stated directly; you will have to infer and paraphrase.

C. Then fill in the type of supporting detail (facts, examples, reasons, testimony).

Argument 1:_____

_____

Detail: Eight gradations

Type: _____

Argument 2:_____

Detail: Joy in life

Type: _____

Argument 3:_____

_____

Detail: We are willing to end the life of a suffering animal but not of a suffering human.

Type: _____

Argument 4: _____

_____

   Detail: People don't mind killing other people in wars.

   Type: _____

Argument 5: _____

_____

   Detail: Treating intercurrent infections.

   Type: _____

Argument 6: _____

   Details: War, capital punishment, and abortion

   Type: _____

Argument 7: _____

   Details: God may have mercy and compassion; we don't know His will.

   Type: _____

D. Write *Arg. 1, Arg. 2,* etc., in the margin of the reading next to the place where each argument appears.

E. Underline the supporting details for each argument.

Evaluate Supporting Details

Fact versus Opinion: Write *F* in the space before each statement of fact; write *O* if the statement is someone's opinion.

_____ 1. "I gave instructions to the doctor attending my own mother in her last illness that she should receive no antibiotics nor be tube fed."

_____ 2. "He [Fletcher] listed eight levels of attitude and opinion on the human initiatives that can be exercised in the case of a patient dying of an incurable disease. . . ."

_____ 3. "In the clinical practice of medicine, active euthanasia has a definite place."

_____ 4. "I have never practiced active euthanasia, a deed that in my country is regarded as murder and could merit the death penalty."

_____ 5. "There is no ethical reason why active medical euthanasia may not be administered."

_____ 6. "I find society's attitude toward the different ways of causing the death of an individual both hypocritical and illogical."

_____ 7. "I have talked to legal, ethical and medical authorities in many parts of the world on the need for active euthanasia. . . ."

_____ 8. "If doctors are given the right to practice active euthanasia, and all the necessary safeguards are developed, then most of the objections would fall away."

_____ 9. The God of mercy and compassion wouldn't mind if we reduced human suffering through euthanasia.

_____ 10. In passive euthanasia the doctor does not take the initiative in ending the patient's life.

Author's Credibility—Background and Reputation: When judging the credibility of a speaker or writer it is valuable to know the background of the person. Here are some facts about Dr. Christiaan Barnard, whose opinions are key to the discussion of euthanasia in Reading 27.*

Use this scale to rate each fact on whether it increases or decreases credibility.

Greatly increases	Increases	Neither increases nor decreases	Decreases	Greatly decreases
1	2	3	4	5

_____ 1. Christiaan Barnard was born in 1923 and was raised in Cape Town, South Africa.

_____ 2. He conducted the first successful human heart transplant operation in medical history in December 1967.

_____ 3. Louis Washkansky, the first transplant recipient, died eighteen days after the transplant.

_____ 4. He teaches surgery at University of Cape Town Medical School and directs surgical research at the school's Groote Schuur Hospital.

_____ 5. His father was a Dutch Reformed minister.

_____ 6. Barnard and his three brothers grew up in conditions bordering on poverty.

_____ 7. He received his MD degree in 1953.

*The information on Christiaan Barnard is excerpted from _Current Biography Yearbook, 1968._ (New York: The H. W. Wilson Company, 1969), pp. 45–48.

_____ 8. He did all his early research on animals.

_____ 9. He came to the United States and studied at the University of Minnesota Medical School under the renowned surgeon Dr. Owen H. Wangensteen.

_____ 10. At first he supported himself by mowing lawns, washing cars, and doing other odd jobs.

_____ 11. He was able to complete all the work for a Ph.D. degree within two years.

_____ 12. In 1960 he attracted international attention in scientific circles by transplanting a second head onto a dog.

_____ 13. In the early 1970s, he retired from surgery because of severe arthritis in his hands.

_____ 14. He has two daughters.

_____ 15. His temper can be short and sharp.

Make Graphic Organizers

Draw an idea map. Use a circle for the thesis, rectangles for the arguments, and ovals for the support.

Remember What's Important

Review your marginal notes identifying the thesis and the arguments. Review the underlining that identifies the supporting details. Review the idea map. Test yourself until you can remember the material. Test yourself as needed on the Vocabulary Preview words.

Make Use of What You Read

When you are ready, complete the Comprehension Check on p. 439 and the Vocabulary Check on p. 441. Do not look back at the reading or the idea map.

Evaluate Your Active Critical Thinking Skills

After your tests have been graded, record your scores on the Progress Chart, p. 456, and answer the questions on the Evaluation Checklist on p. 457.

28   In Crisis, She Rejected Plea to Expedite Dying

Vocabulary Preview

expedite (ek′spə dīt′): to speed up or make easy

stimulus (stim′yə ləs): something that causes action; incentive

inexplicable (in eks′pli kə bəl): cannot be explained or understood

obliged (ə blījd′): compelled by moral, legal, or physical force

affirmative (ə fur′mə tiv): positive; confirming

objets d'art (äb′zhā där′): small objects of artistic value

salutary (sal′yo͞o ter′ē): beneficial; healthful

recoiling (ri koil′iŋ): drawing back, as in fear

predecease (prē′dē sēs′): to die before (someone else)

commonweal (käm′ən wēl): public good; general welfare

cat, āte, fäther; pen, ēvil; if, kīte; nō, ôr, fo͞od, book; boil, house; up, turn; chief, shell; thick, *the*; zh, treasure; ŋ, sing; ə for *a* in *about*; ′ as in *able* (ā′b'l)

Preread

Preview the following selection by reading the title and the first sentence of each paragraph. Answer the following questions without looking back at the reading.

1. What is the subject?

   _____

2. What is the thesis?

   _____

   _____

3. Compare your beliefs with Elisabeth Kübler-Ross's. On a scale of 1 (no way) to 5 (definitely), how open is your mind to her thesis?

   _____

Read

Read the selection without underlining. Just try to understand the author's arguments.

Write your starting time here: _____

◆ *In Crisis, She Rejected Plea to Expedite Dying*

Derek Gill

In the early summer of 1967, Elisabeth and Manny Ross moved for the fifth time. They now felt comfortably settled in Chicago and, assuming they would be living and working there for the foreseeable future, they bought a home a few blocks away from the house they had been renting.

Elisabeth and Manny had decided to postpone their annual summer vacation and instead take a holiday at Christmas in order, as they had just explained to their 7-year-old son, Kenneth, to give him and his little sister, Barbara, "a real Swiss Christmas" with sleigh bells and festivals.

Suddenly, and apparently without stimulus or prompting, Elisabeth felt a deep and inexplicable concern about her mother's wellbeing. She turned to Manny and told him she had to fly to Switzerland immediately—tomorrow, if they could get plane reservations. She admitted that her impulsive decision sounded crazy, but there was some very important reason—a purpose she did not yet understand—why she should be with her mother as quickly as possible. A week later, she and the two children arrived in Zurich. There they boarded the train for Zermatt, where Mrs. Kübler and other members of Elisabeth's family were staying.

Zermatt was the ideal place for a restful vacation and for what Elisabeth called "a time for old-fashioned happiness." Mrs. Kübler looked in the pink of health and had, on the day the Ross family arrived, been on an eight-mile hike with Elisabeth's older brother, Ernst, and her fraternal triplet, Eva (her identical triplet, Erika, could not be there).

On the last evening at the resort where they were all staying, when the sun was setting over the peaks, Mrs. Kübler sat with Elisabeth on the balcony of her bedroom where Kenneth and Barbara, exhausted after the day's outing, were fast asleep.

Mother and daughter sat through a long silence and watched shadows move like ragged fingers across the green valleys far below. Then Mrs. Kübler turned to face Elisabeth and said, "I want your solemn promise that you'll do something for me. I want you to promise that, when I become incapable, when I become a human vegetable, you'll help me to die." She spoke with an uncharacteristic urgency.

Elisabeth was taken aback, both by the appeal and by its timing. She reacted not as an expert on dying, not as a teacher who instructed others to be alert for symbolic language, but as a shocked daughter. She replied too quickly, "What nonsense is this! A woman who is in her 70s and who can hike miles every day in the mountains is sure to die very suddenly. Mother, you're the last person to become a human vegetable."

Mrs. Kübler continued to speak as if she had not heard her. She again asked for a promise that, when she became incapable of caring for herself, Elisabeth would help her to die.

Elisabeth looked at her mother with astonishment and again protested that the question was purely hypothetical. In any case, she said firmly, she was totally opposed to mercy killing, if that was what her mother was talking about. In her opinion, no physician had the right to give a patient an overdose to relieve suffering. She could not promise her mother—or, for that matter, anyone else—to expedite dying. In the unlikely event that her mother did in fact become physically incapable, all that she could promise was that she would help her to live until she died.

Mrs. Kübler began to cry softly. It was only the second time in her life that Elisabeth had seen her mother shed tears.

Mrs. Kübler rose from her chair and went inside. For a while, Elisabeth sat alone and thought about her mother's request, her own response to it and her attitude toward euthanasia. It was tempting to avoid the issue. She remembered some lines of Erich Fromm, the psychiatrist-philosopher: "There is no such thing as medical ethics. There are only universal human ethics applied to specific human situations."

There were times, she was obliged to admit, when it was wrong to keep someone alive—but such a time would occur when a patient was clearly beyond medical help, when organs were kept functioning only with machines. So long as there was a meaningful life, so long as a patient could express and receive feelings, it had to be wrong to "play God" and decide arbitrarily whether a patient should live or die. Surely, though, it was not to answer this hypothetical question that she had changed the family's vacation plans and come to Switzerland.

Next day, when Mrs. Kübler accompanied Elisabeth and the children to the train station, both women were tense and uncomfortable. However, when the train came in, Elisabeth turned to her mother, hugged her and said, "All I can promise you is that I will do for you what I do for all my patients. I promise I will do my best to help you live until you die."

Mrs. Kübler appeared to understand now what Elisabeth was saying. She nodded, wiped her eyes, smiled and said, "Thank you."

Those were the last words Elisabeth heard her mother speak. Hardly had the family arrived back in Chicago when a cable came from Eva. It read, "Mother has had a massive stroke."

Three days later Elisabeth was back in Switzerland.

At the hospital Elisabeth found her mother unable to speak, unable to move anything except her eyelids and, very feebly, her left hand. It was obvious, however, from the expression in her eyes, that Mrs. Kübler understood what was said to her.

They devised a method of communicating. Her mother would use her eyelids and her slightly mobile left hand to indicate affirmative or negative answers to questions put to her. One blink of the eyelids or one squeeze of the hand would signify an affirmative and two blinks or two squeezes would mean a negative response.

Using this form of communication, Mrs. Kübler made it very clear that she did not want to remain in the hospital. Elisabeth confronted her mother with the impossibility of her returning home, where she would require round-the-clock nursing attention. It was Eva who came up with the solution.

She knew of an infirmary, more a rest home than a hospital, in Riehen, a few miles outside of Basel. Set in spacious well-tended grounds, it was run by a dedicated group of Protestant nuns.

Immediately after taking her mother to the infirmary, Elisabeth spent a couple of painful days quite alone at the Klosbachstrasse apartment. She sorted clothes, furniture and objets d'art; she took down pictures and curtains and labeled everything for subsequent distribution according to her mother's expressed wishes.

Elisabeth now believes that in closing down the family home in Zurich, she was given a new and important understanding about life and death. Life, she now sees, is a series of losses, and every loss is a "little death." In the hour or so before she finally left the home on Klosbachstrasse she had gone through the five identifiable stages of dying: denial, anger, bargaining, depression and acceptance.

Each "little death"—and this was one of hers—was a salutary and perhaps essential preparation for death itself. But every ending was also a new beginning.

Another lesson, long and difficult, now focused on the infirmary at Riehen. Mrs. Kübler, paralyzed and unable to speak, held on to life—not just for the few weeks that Elisabeth and her sisters had anticipated, not for months, but for four years. She had clearly foreseen the manner of her dying and, recoiling at the prospect, had pleaded with Elisabeth for mercy killing.

For Elisabeth, the issue of euthanasia was no longer a hypothetical one, no longer an intellectual debating point, but a question of the heart and conscience. There were times when she was ready to change her views, moments when she wondered agonizingly whether she should have given her mother the promise she had asked for; but these doubts stalked her only when she was far away from Switzerland.

For when she was with her mother, her conviction remained that neither she nor anyone else had the right to take the life of someone who could still express and receive feelings. Mrs. Kübler was not a human vegetable. She needed no machines to keep her heart beating or her lungs breathing.

Today, Elisabeth Kübler-Ross sees her prime task as helping people to live a full life without being burdened by their "negativities," helping people to take care of "unfinished business" before they die.

She claims that the evidence of patients who have had near-death encounters with spiritual guides and relatives who have predeceased them supports her belief that physical existence—with all its pain, stress, struggle and challenge—is, in effect, "a learning experience and a growth period" for an ongoing journey.

She is convinced that the only thing of value that man carries with him through the "transition" is the record of how much he contributed to the commonweal—"how much he cared and how much he loved."

1400 words

Write your ending time here:_____

Subtract your starting time: _____

Total time: _____

Check the Rate Chart on p. 462 to find out how many words per minute you have read, and then record your score on the Reading Efficiency Progress Chart on p. 465.

Analyze What You Read

STEP 3

Identify the Thesis, the Argument, and the Supporting Detail

This reading has only one argument and one piece of support. Fill in the blanks below.

Thesis: _____

_____

Argument: _____

_____

Supporting detail: _____

Type of support (facts, examples, testimony, reasons): _____

A. In the margin of the reading, write *thesis* next to the place where the point of view is presented.

B. Write *Arg.* next to where the argument is presented.

C. Underline the supporting detail.

Evaluate Supporting Details

Fact versus Opinion: Write *F* in the space before each statement of fact; write *O* if the statement is someone's opinion.

_____ 1. "There were times . . . when it was wrong to keep someone alive. . . ."

_____ 2. "Three days later Elisabeth was back in Switzerland."

_____ 3. "Each 'little death' . . . was a salutary and perhaps essential preparation for death itself."

_____ 4. "They devised a method of communicating."

_____ 5. "Physical existence . . . is . . . 'a learning experience and a growth period' for an ongoing journey."

_____ 6. "The only thing of value that man carries with him through the 'transition' is the record of how much he contributed to the commonweal. . . ."

_____ 7. "She needed no machines to keep her heart beating or her lungs breathing."

_____ 8. "She had clearly foreseen the manner of her dying. . . ."

_____ 9. "So long as there was a meaningful life, so long as a patient could express and receive feelings, it had to be wrong to 'play God' and decide arbitrarily whether a patient should live or die."

_____ 10. "Those were the last words Elisabeth heard her mother speak."

Author's Credibility—Background and Reputation: When judging the credibility of a speaker or writer it is valuable to know the background of the person. Here are some facts about Dr. Elisabeth Kübler-Ross, whose opinions are key to the discussion of euthanasia in Reading 28.*

---

*The information on Elisabeth Kübler-Ross is excerpted from *Current Biography Yearbook, 1980.* (New York: The H. W. Wilson Company, 1981), pp. 191–194.

Use this scale to rate each fact on whether it increases or decreases credibility.

Greatly increases	Increases	Neither increases nor decreases	Decreases	Greatly decreases
1	2	3	4	5

_____ 1. Elisabeth Kübler-Ross was born on July 8, 1926, in Zurich, Switzerland.

_____ 2. She weighed barely two pounds at birth.

_____ 3. During her own critical illness from pneumonia at the age of five, Elisabeth Kübler was taken to a children's hospital and kept in isolation for weeks.

_____ 4. Before going to medical school she worked as a cook, a mason, and a roofer.

_____ 5. She is a psychiatrist.

_____ 6. She is known for her pioneering work in counseling terminally ill patients.

_____ 7. She was the first doctor to describe the stages a terminally ill patient goes through: denial, anger, bargaining, depression, acceptance.

_____ 8. Her books have brought generous praise from medical colleagues and laypeople and earned her a reputation as a scientist of courage and compassion.

_____ 9. Her later research has been directed toward verifying the existence of life after death.

_____ 10. She has said, "I know for a fact that there is life after death."

_____ 11. In recent years she has met with growing skepticism from the medical community.

_____ 12. She obtained her MD degree in 1957.

_____ 13. She became an assistant professor of psychiatry at the University of Chicago Medical School.

_____ 14. In 1973, she became the medical director of Family Services and Mental Health Center of South Cook County, Chicago Heights.

_____ 15. She has a son, Kenneth Lawrence, and a daughter, Barbara Lee.

Make Graphic Organizers

Draw an idea map. Use a circle for the thesis, a rectangle for the argument, and an oval for the supporting detail.

Remember What's Important

Review your marginal notes identifying the thesis and the argument. Review the underlining that identifies the supporting detail. Review the idea map. Test yourself until you can remember the material. Test yourself as needed on the Vocabulary Preview words.

Make Use of What You Read

When you are ready, complete the Comprehension Check on p. 443 and the Vocabulary Check on p. 445. Do not look back at the reading or the idea map.

Evaluate Your Active Critical Thinking Skills

After your tests have been graded, record your scores on the Progress Chart, p. 456, and answer the questions on the Evaluation Checklist on p. 457.

Comparing Views on Euthanasia

Use the following activities to evaluate your understanding of the issue. Write your answers on a separate sheet of paper.

1. Summarize each reading, including the thesis, the arguments, and the major supporting details.

2. Evaluate the support for each reading. Are the examples good ones, are the reasons logical, are the facts provable, does loaded language degrade the message?

3. Compare the readings. Do you believe that one author's arguments are stronger than the other's? Why?

4. Go back to the self-questioning survey on p. 298. Would you change any of your responses after reading the selections? Summarize your opinion on the issue, noting any ways in which your opinion has been affected by your reading.

ISSUE 5

Affirmative Action

The two readings take opposing views on affirmative action.

Self-Questioning

To help you become aware of your own beliefs and biases about affirmative action, answer the following questions. Write the number from the rating scale that best expresses your opinion. You will reevaluate your views after you have completed Readings 29 and 30.

Rating Scale

1. No

2. Perhaps not

3. No opinion

4. Perhaps

5. Yes

Rate each question from 1 to 5.

_____ 1. Is the reason that women and minorities are underrepresented in the work force that they are not as qualified or competent as white males?

_____ 2. If affirmative action were removed, would most companies go back to hiring mostly white males?

_____ 3. Do you believe that we have achieved the goal of equal opportunity for everyone?

_____ 4. Do we need affirmative action now?

_____ 5. Is "reverse discrimination" against white males a serious problem?

29   The Dream, the Stars and Dr. King

Vocabulary Preview

affirmative action (ə fʉrmʹə tiv akʹshən): a policy or program for correcting the effects of discrimination in the employment or education of members of certain groups, such as women and minorities

commemorate (kə memʹə rātʹ): to honor the memory of

suppress (se presʹ): to keep from appearing or being known

legacy (legʹə sē): something handed down, as from an ancestor

squander (skwanʹdər): to spend or use wastefully or extravagantly

pander (panʹdər): to help satisfy the immoral or vicious ambitions, vices, or desires of another

intractable (in trakʹtə bəl): hard to manage or change

eradicate (ē radʹi kātʹ): to wipe out; remove

seminal (semʹə nəl): of essential importance

apartheid (ə pärʹtīdʹ): strict racial segregation and economic and political discrimination

cat, āte, fäther; pen, ēvil; if, kīte; nō, ôr, fo͞od, book; boil, house; up, tʉrn; chief, shell; thick, *the*; zh, treasure; ŋ, sing; ə for *a* in *about*; ʹ as in *able* (āʹb'l)

Preread

Preview the following selection by reading the title and the first sentence of each paragraph. Answer the following questions without looking back at the reading.

1. What is the subject?

_____

2. What is the thesis?

_____

_____

3. Compare your beliefs with Jesse Jackson's. On a scale of 1 (no way) to 5 (definitely), how open is your mind to his thesis?

_____

Read

Read the selection without underlining. Just try to understand the author's arguments.

Write your starting time here: _____

◆ *The Dream, the Stars and Dr. King*

Jesse Jackson

Last week in Memphis, we commemorated the death of Dr. Martin Luther King. He was struck down 27 years ago—not a dreamer, but a man of action. We have come a long way since then, in part as a fruit of his labors.

In less than 30 years, as schools opened and ceilings lifted, a large African American middle class has been created. High school graduation rates, even intelligence test results, grow closer between whites and blacks with each passing year.

The civil-rights movement that Dr. King led also helped women lift the shackles on their opportunity. The same laws that guarantee equal opportunity for African Americans apply to women, to other minorities, to the disabled. Our society benefits as fewer of its people have their genius suppressed or their talents wasted.

We have come a long way—but we have far to go. Commission after commission, report after report, show that systematic discrimination still mars our country.

African Americans have more difficulty obtaining business loans, buying homes, getting hired. Schools and housing patterns are still largely separate and unequal. Women still face glass ceilings in corporate offices. Ninety-seven percent of the corporate CEOs of the Fortune 500 are white men. That does not result from talent being concentrated among males with pale skin.

Today, Dr. King's legacy—the commitment to take affirmative actions to open doors and opportunity—is under political assault. Dr. King worked against terrible odds in a hopeful time. America was experiencing two decades of remarkable economic growth and prosperity. It was assumed, as the Kerner Commission made clear, that the "growth dividend" would enable us to reduce poverty and open opportunity relatively painlessly. But the war on poverty was never fought; instead, the dividend and the growth were squandered in the jungles of Vietnam.

Three decades later, the country is more prosperous but the times are less hopeful. Real wages for working people have been declining for 20 years. People are scared for good reason, as layoffs rise to record levels even in the midst of a recovery.

In this context, political predators flourish, feeding on old hates, pandering to old fears. What else could explain the remarkably dishonest assault on affirmative-action programs that seek to remedy intractable patterns of discrimination?

House Speaker Newt Gingrich, a history professor, sets the tone by simply eradicating history. The *Washington Post* reported: "Gingrich dismissed the argument that the beneficiaries of affirmative action, commonly African Americans, have been subjected to discrimination over a period of centuries. 'That is true of virtually every American,' Gingrich said, noting that the Irish were discriminated against by the English, for example."

As Roger Wilkins writes in a seminal essay in the *Nation* magazine, this is breathtakingly dishonest for a history professor. Blacks have been on the North American continent for nearly 375 years. For 245 of those, the country practiced slavery. For another 100 or so, segregation—legal apartheid—was enforced throughout the South and much of the North, often policed by home-grown terrorists. We've had only 30 years of something else, largely the legacy of the struggle led by Dr. King.

The media plays up the "guilt" African Americans supposedly suffer about affirmative action. I can tell you this. Dr. King felt no guilt when special laws gave us the right to vote. He felt no guilt about laws requiring that African Americans have the opportunity to go to schools, to enter universities, to compete for jobs and contracts. This supposed guilt is at best a luxurious anxiety of those who now have the opportunity to succeed or fail.

If Dr. King were alive today, he would be 66, younger than Sen. Bob Dole (R-Kan.) who suggests that discrimination ended "before we were born." Unlike Dole, Dr. King would be working to bring people together, not drive them apart.

Modern-day conservatives haven't a clue about what to do with an economy that is generating greater inequality and reducing the security and living standards of more and more Americans. So they seek to distract and divide.

Now, as the Republican "contract with America" fizzles into an ad campaign, Dole reaffirmed his abandonment of affirmative action. Sen. Phil Gramm (R-Tex.) called for more cuts from the poor.

As we head into this coyote time, we would do well to remember Dr. King's legacy. No matter how desperate things were, no matter how grave the crisis, no matter how many times his dreams were shattered, Dr. King refused to grow bitter. Men and women, he taught, "have the capacity to do right as well as wrong, and [our] history is a path upward, not downward. It's only when it is truly dark that you can see the stars."

800 words

Write your ending time here:_____

Subtract your starting time: _____

Total time: _____

Check the Rate Chart on p. 462 to find out how many words per minute you have read, and then record your score on the Reading Efficiency Progress Chart on p. 465.

Analyze What You Read

STEP 3

Identify the Thesis, the Arguments, and Supporting Details

A. In the margin of the reading, write *thesis* next to the place where the author presents his point of view.

B. Following are eight arguments. Fill in the supporting details and the type of supporting details for each one.

1. We have come a long way in less than 30 years.

   Support: _____

   _____

   _____

   Type: _____

2. Society benefits from affirmative action.

   Support: _____

   _____

   Type: _____

3. Systematic discrimination still mars our country.

   Support: _____

   _____

   _____

_____

_____

Type: _____

4. Affirmative action is under political assault.

Support: _____

_____

Type: _____

5. Opponents of affirmative action are dishonest.

Support: _____

Type: _____

6. African American guilt is not an important issue.

Support: _____

_____

Type: _____

7. Bob Dole is using dishonesty to drive people apart.

Support: _____

_____

Type: _____

8. We should not grow bitter.

Support: _____

_____

Type: _____

C. Write *Arg. 1, Arg. 2,* etc. in the margin of the article next to the place where each argument appears.

D. Underline the supporting details for each argument.

Evaluate Supporting Details

Provable versus Unprovable: If the statement can be proved (or disproved), write *P.* If it is unprovable, write *U.*

_____   1. A large African American middle class has been created.

_____   2. Dr. King's civil-rights work has also helped women, other minorities, and the disabled.

_____ 3. African Americans have more difficulty obtaining business loans.

_____ 4. Women still face glass ceilings.

_____ 5. 97% of corporate CEOs of Fortune 500 companies are white men.

_____ 6. Newt Gingrich knows he isn't telling the truth.

_____ 7. An expansion of opportunities for African Americans began about 30 years ago.

_____ 8. Bob Dole is intentionally trying to divide people along racial lines.

_____ 9. Modern-day conservatives don't know what to do to solve the problem of reduced security and living standards.

_____ 10. Times will get better.

Loaded Language: Write the implied meaning of the underlined words in the following statements:

a. "... also helped women lift the shackles on their opportunity."

Implication: _____

_____

b. "... political predators flourish ..."

Implication: _____

c. "As we head into this coyote time ..."

Implication: _____

_____

_____

Valid and Invalid Inferences: A valid inference is based on something the author implied. Mark *V* before each valid inference and *I* before each one that is invalid. If you write *V*, also write the sentence in which it was implied.

_____ 1. Without affirmative action, white males would be preferred for jobs.

Sentence: _____

_____

_____ 2. The percent of African Americans living in poverty has reduced since the civil-rights movement.

Sentence: _____

_____

_____ 3. School segregation still exists.

Sentence: _____

_____

_____ 4. African Americans have had the same problems with discrimi-
              nation that other groups of immigrants have had.

Sentence: _____

_____

_____ 5. Intelligence tests accurately measure intelligence.

Sentence: _____

_____

_____ 6. Dr. King's civil-rights work has helped all Americans.

Sentence: _____

_____

_____ 7. Newt Gingrich minimizes the effects of slavery on African
              Americans.

Sentence: _____

_____

_____ 8. Reverse discrimination is a serious problem.

Sentence: _____

_____

_____ 9. Republicans are purposely raising false issues.

Sentence: _____

_____

_____ 10. Democrats have a better political platform than Republicans.

Sentence: _____

_____

Make Graphic Organizers

Draw an idea map. Use a circle for the thesis, rectangles for the arguments, and ovals for the major support.

Remember What's Important

Review your marginal notes that identify the thesis and the arguments. Review the underlining that identifies the supporting details. Review the idea map. Test yourself until you remember the material. Test yourself as needed on the Vocabulary Preview words.

Make Use of What You Read

When you are ready, take the Comprehension Check on p. 447 and the Vocabulary Check on p. 448. Do not look back at the reading or the idea map.

Evaluate Your Active Critical Thinking Skills

After your tests have been graded, record your scores on the Progress Chart, p. 456, and answer the questions on the Evaluation Checklist on p. 457.

30 Spiral of Silence

Vocabulary Preview

appease (ə pēz′): to quiet, esp. by giving in to the demands of others

subverted (sub vʉr′tid): undermined

Orwellian (ôr wel′ē ən): like the works of George Orwell, who wrote *1984,* a novel about a totalitarian society

prima facie evidence (prī′mə fā′shē): evidence adequate to establish a fact or presumption of fact unless refuted

craven (krā′vən): very cowardly

litigation (lit′i gā′shən): lawsuit

diffuse (di fyōōz′): spread out

acquiesce (ak wē es′): to agree or consent quietly without protest, but without enthusiasm

latent (lāt′′nt): hidden and undeveloped

judicious (jōō dish′əs): showing sound judgment; wise and careful

fanatical (fə nāt′ik′l): unreasonably enthusiastic

ideological (ī′dē ə läj′i kəl): based on the ideas or opinions or way of thinking of an individual, class, or group

intimidating (in tim′ə dāt′iŋ): causing fear or timidity

defection (de fek′shən): abandonment of loyalty

stifle (stī′fəl): to keep or hold back; suppress

cat, āte, fäther; pen, ēvil; if, kīte; nō, ôr, fōōd, book; boil, house; up, tʉrn; chief, shell; thick, *the*; zh, treasure; ŋ, sing; ə for *a* in *about*; ′ as in *able* (ā′b′l)

Preread

STEP 1

Preview the following article by reading the title and the first sentence of each paragraph. Answer the following questions without looking back at the reading.

1. What is the subject?

_____

2. What is the thesis?

_____

3. Compare your beliefs with the author's. On a scale of 1 (no way) to 5 (definitely), how open is your mind to his thesis?

_____

Read

Read the article without underlining. Just try to understand the author's arguments.

Write your starting time here: _____

◆ *Spiral of Silence*

Peter Brimelow

"I have already given two cousins to the war, and I stand prepared to sacrifice my wife's brother rather than the rebellion be not crushed."

Humorist Artemus Ward's joke during the Civil War applies today, says Claremont McKenna College sociologist Frederick R. Lynch to the American political elite's attempt to appease minority and feminist groups by imposing "affirmative action" quotas against white, often younger and blue-collar males.

Government-imposed quotas were explicitly banned in the 1964 Civil Rights Act. Nevertheless they immediately spread through the economy. For most of that time, they received eerily little media and even less academic attention. Of some 1,300 papers given at a recent American Sociological Association conference on Race and Ethnic Relations, the topic attracted only one.

The result: the situation summarized in the title of Lynch's new paperback, *Invisible Victims: White Males and the Crisis of Affirmative Action*. The ideal of merit hiring has been subverted by politicized hiring, with white men unable to defend themselves against open discrimination. But quotas bring other problems, including conflict among the "protected classes" they benefit, and growing racial polarization, particularly as the articulate middle class begins to suffer.

Lynch just laughs at the suggestion, recently made by a columnist in a business weekly, that affirmative action, while a regulatory burden, is not massive in scale.

"Race-norming [adjusting test scores to produce racially proportionate results] alone affected millions of people," he says. "Many state and local governments did it with their GATBS [General Aptitude Test Batteries, taken by job seekers and supplied to potential employers]. And private testing agencies did it to protect their clients against lawsuits—they called it "EEO-proofing." (The federal Equal Employment Opportunity Commission muscles business into quotas.)

But Lynch is not surprised at the blunder. "There's incredible denial," he says. He cites California Democratic representative Don Edwards, a mouthpiece of the civil rights establishment, claiming on the *New York Times* Op Ed page that quotas did not exist—within weeks of three Supreme Court decisions about them. And, using similar Orwellian doublethink, supporters insisted that the 1991 Civil Rights Act did not impose quotas, although its key point was to override the Supreme Court and make work force racial imbalance prima facie evidence of employer discrimination.

Corporate America's craven terror of litigation and political punishment makes research into quotas extremely difficult. "We're not letting you anywhere near our program," a Kmart executive told Lynch recently.

It's understandable—in a way. Sears, Roebuck & Co. spent 15 years and perhaps as much as $20 million to defeat an EEOC discrimination suit. Sears prevailed largely because it was able to show it had a voluntary quota program. Corporations cling to such programs as a defense in court, even if it means putting up with some unqualified or incompetent workers. They hate white male employees moaning about quotas—and, above all, suing to expose reverse discrimination's legal inconsistencies.

The white male victims of affirmative action are diffused through the population and hard to track down. After finding and interviewing a sample, Lynch has identified several reasons for their helplessness.

"Affirmative action has been an administrative revolution imposed by judges and bureaucrats," he says. It is not easily opposed, particularly because much of it is implemented informally and orally. Recently, the secrecy has in part been a response to the increasingly unstable legal situation as the influence of the Reagan-Bush judicial appointments is felt. But Lynch says some affirmative action personnel openly tell him they intend to get around any law.

A few of Lynch's male victims were political liberals who felt obliged to rationalize their fate. But most acquiesced with varying degrees of anger; some changed jobs. Usually totally isolated, these men felt that no one would help them.

They were right. The older generation of white male managers has compromised, Lynch argues, because they think quotas will fall only on the younger, baby-boom generation. And the EEOC discourages white male discrimination complaints about corporations with approved, i.e., anti-white male, affirmative action plans. Litigation, for the tiny group that tried it, proved expensive, exhausting, chancy and immensely time-consuming—one case remains unsettled after more than six years.

A further factor in this male paralysis: the peculiar male psychology itself. These victims seem really to have believed that real men don't cry. A considerable number did not even mention their disappointment to friends, relatives or fellow workers.

Their wives almost always felt no such inhibitions. "My wife is mad as hell; she's angrier than I am," said a victim. Some wives absolutely insisted on being interviewed for Lynch's study. One woman made a telling point: Discrimination against white males injures not only the men themselves but their wives and families. "This 'hidden' or latent conflict generated by affirmative action between career women versus homemaker wives has gone virtually unnoticed in the affirmative action literature," Lynch notes judiciously.

"Karl Marx insisted that for any sort of class consciousness to arise, there must be communication of a common sense of oppression," Lynch writes. "With the mass media and the social sciences rarely recognizing the phenomenon, much less portraying it sympathetically, white males have been easily and silently victimized one by one."

Lynch's survey of the media indicates that quotas have been basically ignored. Thus he was unable to find one TV show portraying a white male being damaged by affirmative action.

Partly the media were able to ignore the issue because neither conservatives nor liberals raised it. For example, the likelihood that Robert Bork would find quotas unconstitutional spurred the civil rights establishment's fanatical resistance to his Supreme Court nomination. But White House lobbyists said nothing.

Partly, however, the media's motive is ideological. From J. Anthony Lukas' bestseller about busing, *Common Ground*, Lynch quotes a *Boston Globe* reporter: "If they [the Boston Irish] don't like integration, we'll shove it down their throats."

All of which, Lynch argues, has induced a classic "spiral of silence," whereby people assume their doubts are not shared and suppress them, thus mutually intimidating each other. But in fact opinion polls show quotas are overwhelmingly unpopular, even with the "protected classes" themselves. And when the Democratic Party asked pollster Stanley Greenberg to investigate blue-collar defection in the 1984 presidential election, quotas emerged as the crucial factor. The party promptly tried to stifle Greenberg's report.

Lynch is now researching his next book on "diversity management"— the use of quotas, with no pretense that they are remedial or temporary, for the current beneficiaries of affirmative action and the ongoing wave of nonwhite immigrants. This is the new frontier for affirmative action professionals. However, Lynch reports that they receive his research on white males with much interest.

"They're worried about 'The White Male Problem,' white males resisting their work," he says. "They just can't understand it."

1150 words

Write your ending time here:_____

Subtract your starting time: _____

Total time: _____

Check the Rate Chart on p. 462 to find out how many words per minute you have read, and then record your score on the Reading Efficiency Progress Chart on p. 465.

Analyze What You Read

STEP 3

Identify the Thesis, Arguments, and Supporting Details

A. In the margin of the reading write *thesis* next to the place where the author presents his point of view.

B. In the following exercise, arguments are in the left column and supporting details are in the right column. Go back to the article and find which details support which arguments. Write the letter of the detail in the blank before the argument it supports. There may be more than one piece of support for some arguments. Other arguments may not have any support. In that case, write *none* in the blank.

Arguments	Details
_____ 1. Affirmative action quotas are an attempt by the political elite to appease minority and feminist groups.	a. The media's motive is partly ideological. b. Affirmative action personnel just can't understand the white male's problem.

_____ 2. Affirmative action imposes quotas against white males.

_____ 3. Government-imposed quotas are illegal.

_____ 4. Quotas have received eerily little media or academic attention.

_____ 5. Affirmative action has subverted the ideal of merit hiring.

_____ 6. Quotas cause conflict among "protected classes."

_____ 7. Quotas cause racial polarization.

_____ 8. Affirmative action is massive in scale.

_____ 9. There is denial.

_____ 10. Using workforce racial imbalance as prima facie evidence of employer discrimination is a way of imposing quotas.

_____ 11. Research into quotas is difficult.

_____ 12. To avoid litigation, employers cling to voluntary quotas.

_____ 13. Voluntary quotas mean putting up with some unqualified or incompetent workers.

_____ 14. White male victims of affirmative action are helpless.

c. "We're not letting you anywhere near our program" a Kmart executive told Lynch recently.

d. Quotas were explicitly banned in the 1964 Civil Rights Act.

e. Don Edwards claimed that quotas did not exist.

f. Race-norming affected millions.

g. Supporters insisted that the 1991 Civil Rights Act did not impose quotas.

h. Affirmative action is not easily opposed because much of it is informal and oral.

i. Stanley Greenberg's research

j. Politically liberal victims feel obliged to rationalize their fate.

k. Opinion polls

l. Male psychology that real men don't cry

m. Most felt that no one would help.

n. Of some 1,300 papers given at a recent American Sociological Association conference, there was only one on reverse discrimination.

o. Corporate America is afraid of lawsuits and political punishment.

p. Older white male managers think quotas will only fall on younger workers.

q. Lynch was unable to find one TV show portraying a white male being damaged by affirmative action.

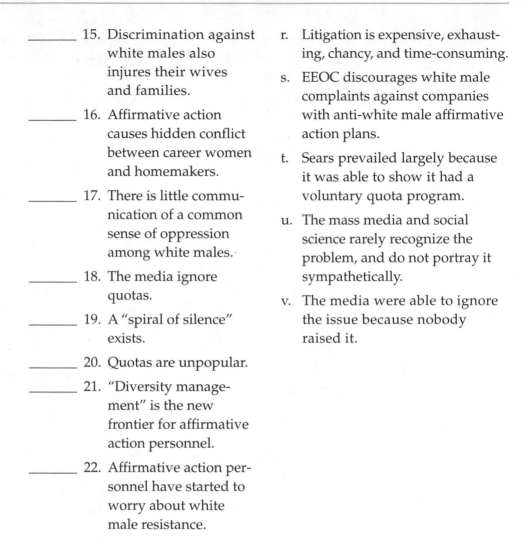

_____ 15. Discrimination against white males also injures their wives and families.

_____ 16. Affirmative action causes hidden conflict between career women and homemakers.

_____ 17. There is little communication of a common sense of oppression among white males.

_____ 18. The media ignore quotas.

_____ 19. A "spiral of silence" exists.

_____ 20. Quotas are unpopular.

_____ 21. "Diversity management" is the new frontier for affirmative action personnel.

_____ 22. Affirmative action personnel have started to worry about white male resistance.

r. Litigation is expensive, exhausting, chancy, and time-consuming.

s. EEOC discourages white male complaints against companies with anti-white male affirmative action plans.

t. Sears prevailed largely because it was able to show it had a voluntary quota program.

u. The mass media and social science rarely recognize the problem, and do not portray it sympathetically.

v. The media were able to ignore the issue because nobody raised it.

C. Go back to the reading selection and write the number of each argument (*Arg. 1–Arg. 22*) in the margin next to where it appears.

D. Underline the supporting details.

Evaluating Supporting Details

Type of Supporting Details: Go back to the 22 supporting details listed above. For each one, identify how it is used to support the argument (facts, testimony, examples, reasons) and fill in the blanks on p. 333.

a. _____   l. _____

b. _____   m. _____

c. _____   n. _____

d. _____   o. _____

e. _____   p. _____

f. _____   q. _____

g. _____   r. _____

h. _____   s. _____

i. _____   t. _____

j. _____   u. _____

k. _____   v. _____

Provable versus Unprovable: If the statement can be proved or disproved, write *P.* If it cannot be proved or disproved, write *U.*

_____ 1. The 1964 Civil Rights Act explicitly banned quotas.

_____ 2. The ideal of merit hiring has been subverted by politicized hiring.

_____ 3. White men are unable to defend themselves against discrimination.

_____ 4. Affirmative action increases racial polarization.

_____ 5. There's incredible denial.

_____ 6. The 1991 Civil Rights Act imposes quotas.

_____ 7. Clinging to voluntary quota programs means putting up with some unqualified or incompetent workers.

_____ 8. The EEOC discourages white male discrimination complaints about corporations with approved, i.e., anti-white male, affirmative action plans.

_____ 9. Affirmative action causes a conflict between career women and homemaker wives.

_____ 10. He was unable to find even one TV show portraying a white male being damaged by affirmative action.

Loaded Language: Write the implied meaning of the underlined words in the following statements.

1. . . . they received <u>eerily</u> little media attention . . .

   Implication: _____

   _____

2. . . . California Democratic representative Don Edwards, a <u>mouthpiece</u> of the civil rights establishment . . .

   Implication: _____

   _____

3. . . . using . . . <u>Orwellian doublethink</u>, supporters insisted that the 1991 Civil Rights Act did not impose quotas . . .

   Implication: _____

4. Corporate America's <u>craven terror</u> of litigation . . .

   Implication: _____

5. . . . corporations with approved, i.e., <u>anti-white male</u>, affirmative action plans. . . .

   Implication: _____

   _____

6. . . . the civil rights establishment's <u>fanatical resistance</u> to his Supreme Court nomination. . . .

   Implication: _____

7. The federal Equal Employment Opportunity Commission <u>muscles</u> business into quotas. . . .

   Implication: _____

Valid and Invalid Inferences: A valid inference is based on something the author implied. Mark *V* before each valid inference and *I* before each one that is invalid. If you write *V*, also write the sentence in which it was implied.

_____ 1. Hiring on the basis of merit would produce a higher proportion of white males than we have now.

Sentence: _____

_____

_____

_____ 2. White males are more frequently married to homemakers than to career women.

Sentence: _____

_____

_____

_____ 3. Affirmative action always involves quotas.

Sentence: _____

_____

_____

_____ 4. The only reason employers have voluntary affirmative action programs is fear of litigation.

Sentence: _____

_____

_____ 5. Affirmative action often requires employers to hire less qualified or competent employees.

Sentence: _____

_____

_____

_____ 6. The reason for underrepresentation of women and minorities is that they are not as qualified or competent as are white males.

Sentence: _____

_____

_____ 7. Companies have affirmative action programs because of cowardice.

Sentence: _____

_____

_____ 8. If white males united, they could get rid of affirmative action.

Sentence: _____

_____

_____

Make Graphic Organizers

Because there are 22 arguments, use a separate piece of paper large enough to make an idea map showing all of them. Show the thesis, the arguments, and the major supporting details.

Remember What's Important

Review your marginal notes, underlining, and idea map. Test yourself until you can remember the material. Test yourself as needed on the Vocabulary Preview words.

Make Use of What You Read

When you are ready, take the Comprehension Check on p. 451 and the Vocabulary Check on p. 452. Do not look back at the reading or the idea map.

Evaluate Your Active Critical Thinking

After your tests have been graded, record your scores on the Progress Chart, p. 456, and answer the questions on the Evaluation Checklist on p. 457.

Comparing Views on Affirmative Action

Use the following activities to evaluate your understanding of the issue. Write your answers on a separate sheet of paper.

1. Summarize each reading, including the thesis, the arguments, and the major supporting details.

2. Evaluate the support for each reading. Are the examples good ones, are the reasons logical, are the facts provable, does loaded language degrade the message?

3. Compare the readings. Do you believe that one author's arguments are stronger than the other's? Why?

4. Go back to the self-questioning survey on p. 317. Would you change any of your responses after reading the selections? Summarize your opinion on the issue, noting any ways in which your opinion has been affected by your reading.

Additional Resources

Tests: Comprehension and Vocabulary Checks   339

1 How to Improve Your Vocabulary

Comprehension Check

Multiple Choice

Circle the letter before the best answer to each of the following questions.

1. English

   a. is not based on any other language.

   b. is at least 2,000 years old.

   c. has more words than any other language.

   d. cannot differentiate shades of meaning like most European languages.

2. The first thing you should do when you see an unfamiliar word is to

   a. look up the meaning in the dictionary.

   b. look for the roots.

   c. look for the prefixes.

   d. try to figure out the word's meaning from its context.

3. Randall says you become a word detective when

   a. the word has more than one meaning.

   b. you can look up the meaning in the dictionary.

   c. you begin to trace a word's origin.

   d. you use the word's context to find the meaning.

4. There are

   a. more than 100 major prefixes.

   b. about 100,000 words in the English language.

   c. about half a million words in the average adult's vocabulary.

   d. fewer than 100 major prefixes.

5. We can infer that Randall was asked to write this article because he

   a. is an actor.

   b. is recognized as an expert in word usage.

   c. was a college professor.

   d. is a college graduate.

6. Word memory is improved by

   a. learning the roots.

   b. remembering the context in which the word was used.

   c. using the words in speaking and writing.

   d. all of the above.

7. According to the article,

   a. dictionaries have existed since before Shakespeare's time.

   b. you can learn new words without using the dictionary.

   c. the most important part of using the dictionary is learning the pronunciations of words.

   d. Aristophanes spoke English.

8. The author feels that

   a. people with large vocabularies are more successful in life.

   b. guessing the meaning of an unknown word is a bad habit.

   c. the average adult who speaks English knows most of the words in the language.

   d. the best way to build vocabulary is to read the dictionary.

Short Answer

9. Why does Randall say that learning the root is the most important part of going to the dictionary?

   _____

   _____

   _____

10. What is the main idea of the prefix chart Randall uses in making his fourth point in the reading?

   _____

   _____

   _____

Essay

Describe the five ways to improve vocabulary.

_____

_____

_____

_____

_____

_____

_____

_____

_____

_____

Vocabulary Check

Write the best word from the following list in the blank in each sentence below.

addicting   differentiate   context   extensive   heritage

origin   emancipating   corroborated   literal   elated

1. The base of the Great Pyramid in Egypt could hold ten football fields because it is so _____.

2. The _____ of the word assassin came from the drug hashish, which one extreme religious group in Persia always smoked before terrorizing and killing its victims.

3. For years, criminals have escaped conviction for crimes they have committed because other people have falsely _____ their alibis.

4. Until recently, it was not realized that Valium, the most widely prescribed drug in the United States, was psychologically and sometimes physically

   _____.

5. The _____ of a sentence will tell you which meaning a person is using when he or she says "That's baloney."

6. Abraham Lincoln is credited with _____ the slaves in 1863, but actually he freed the slaves only in those states that had left the Union and over which he had no control.

7. Nose prints, not paw prints, are used by breeders and trainers to _____ prize dogs because, like human fingerprints, nose prints are all different.

8. Before writing *Roots,* Alex Haley spent years researching his African _____ .

9. People are usually _____ when they receive a promotion or pay raise at work.

10. The _____ meanings of the individual words do not help define an expression such as "Drop in any time."

2 | How Almost Anyone Can Become a Millionaire: Simple Rules for Attaining Future Wealth

Comprehension Check

True–False

Mark T or F.

_____ 1. If you know how much money you want to have at a certain age you can figure out how much you have to save each year in order to achieve your goal.

_____ 2. The reason the author recommends staying in school is that an investment in education has a high rate of return.

_____ 3. The author implies that a man who wants to become wealthy should marry a beautiful woman who dresses well, gets regular beauty care, and has a personal trainer.

_____ 4. The author implies that a woman who wants to become wealthy should marry a man who has a small house in a modest neighborhood, a cheap car, and a regular investment program.

Multiple Choice

Circle the letter before the best answer to each of the following questions.

5. The author implies that the best investment is

   a. stocks and bonds.

   b. gold and precious stones.

   c. real estate.

   d. owning a business.

6. The author implies that the easiest way to become wealthy is to

   a. start your own business like Sam Walton or Bill Gates.

   b. start a regular investment program early in life.

   c. marry a rich person.

   d. speculate in stocks or real estate.

7. The author implies that marriage helps you become rich only if

a. you stay married.

b. both partners bring in money.

c. both are willing to live modestly.

d. all of the above are true.

8. A compounded rate of return means that

a. you can spend the income from the money, but you must leave the principal intact.

b. you have to add to the investment every year.

c. you must leave both principal and income invested.

d. your money should be in an interest-bearing bank account.

9. The author implies that

a. in order to become rich you have to know a lot about investments.

b. it's better to work and save early than to spend time in college.

c. starting a savings program in middle age is soon enough.

d. young people who spend their earnings on expensive cars and clothes will probably never become rich.

10. The rate of return that the author thinks is reasonable based on the 50-year stock market average is

a. 5%

b. 10%

c. 15%

d. 20%

Essay

According to the author, what should you do if you want to become wealthy?

_____

_____

_____

_____

_____

_____

_____

_____

_____

_____

Vocabulary Check

A. Write the best word from the following list in the blank in each sentence below.

attain   **virtual**   **subsistence**   **fritter**   **forgo**

avail   **frugal**   **cite**   **plethora**   **rationally**

1. The heavy rains in Malibu caused mudslides that brought traffic to a _____ standstill.

2. Americans are bombarded by a _____ of advertisers who tempt us to spend money unnecessarily.

3. In some less-developed parts of the world, the people will survive by _____ farming.

4. Since we are stuck in the same elevator, I'd like to _____ myself of this opportunity to ask for a favor.

5. Time is too valuable to _____ away watching TV sitcoms.

6. If you want to lose weight, you should _____ sugar and white flour.

7. The millionaire cartoon character Scrooge MacDuck was Scottish because Scots have a reputation for being _____.

8. In term papers, students must _____ sources in footnotes or risk being accused of cheating.

9. Acting _____ means behaving in ways that will help you achieve your goals.

10. When you have a big project to do, it is important to set some goals you can _____ quickly, so that you don't get discouraged.

B. Write the best word from the following list in the blank in each sentence below.

substantial   compound interest   frivolous   incentive   diligence

amassed   derisive   perseverance   retort   validated

11. Sometimes new clothes are a good investment; at other times they are a _____ waste of money.

12. Grades are an external _____ for studying; curiosity and the love of learning are internal ones.

13. Getting a college degree requires a _____ investment of time and money.

14. _____ is the theme of the saying, "If at first you don't succeed, try, try again."

15. It's always easier to think up a witty _____ when it's too late to use it.

16. The author believes that most wealthy people acquired their fortunes by _____ rather than by genius.

17. Some of Einstein's theories were so far ahead of their time that they are just now being _____.

18. The most creative ideas often seem so odd that they are greeted by _____ laughter from more conventional thinkers.

19. If you save $1 a week starting at age 20 at a rate of 11% _____, you will have a quarter of a million dollars when you reach 65.

20. Bill Gates has _____ the largest personal fortune in the world.

3   The Many Miracles of Mark Hicks

Comprehension Check

Multiple Choice

Circle the letter before the best answer to each of the following questions.

1. John Joseph was

    a. another art instructor.

    b. Mark's attendant.

    c. a cinema student at UCLA.

    d. the person who presented the Academy Award.

2. Mark had injured himself

    a. in an auto accident.

    b. by falling from a tree.

    c. during an art class.

    d. while making a film.

3. At first, the art teacher thought that Mark

    a. should take the class to improve his drawings.

    b. did not like him very much.

    c. couldn't draw very well.

    d. would not be able to pass the class.

4. The person who wrote the story for the movie was

    a. the art instructor.

    b. Mark.

    c. John Joseph, a cinema student.

    d. nobody; there was no real story or plot.

5. You can infer from the article that

    a. an Academy Award can be won by an amateur.

    b. Mark did not know many people.

    c. Mark became rich as an artist.

    d. Mark's parents blamed themselves for the accident.

6. You can infer from the article that Mark

    a. was a good filmmaker.

    b. was an angry young man.

    c. felt good about himself.

    d. was a person who gave up easily.

7. The gallery director probably

    a. could tell that Mark was handicapped by the drawings.

    b. would not have let Mark show his paintings if he had known that Mark was handicapped.

    c. was surprised to find out that Mark was handicapped.

    d. took the paintings because he felt sorry for Mark.

8. The film about Mark

    a. was sad for the people who made it.

    b. cost Mark his life.

    c. was much more expensive than the art teacher thought it would be.

    d. looked amateurish.

Short Answer

9. The author says, "True, I was his teacher, but in a larger sense, he was mine." What did the art teacher learn from Mark?

    _____

    _____

10. What message did the art teacher hope was communicated to film students by winning the Academy Award for *Gravity Is My Enemy*?

    _____

    _____

Essay

Explain the story, "The Many Miracles of Mark Hicks," as if you were telling it to someone who had not heard it before.

    _____

    _____

    _____

_____

_____

_____

_____

_____

_____

_____

_____

_____

_____

_____

Vocabulary Check

Write the best word from the following list in the blank in each sentence below.

portfolios   quadriplegics   intrigued   severed   disarming

impassioned   documentary   excruciating   transposed

lithographic   wry   aspirating   prestigious   integrity   banter

1. It is now possible to sew a _____ finger back on.

2. Dancers sometimes have to go on stage even when they have _____ pain in their legs.

3. _____ smoke can make people cough.

4. A Nobel Prize is one of the most _____ awards that a person can win.

5. Instead of just presenting the facts, lawyers often make _____ speeches that play on the jury's emotions.

6. A police officer's testimony used to be unquestioned, but today people doubt the _____ of the police.

7. The invitation to attend a wrestling match _____ me, and I decided to go.

8. "Gravity is my enemy" was a _____ observation made by Mark Hicks.

9. There is a lot of good-natured _____ at a class reunion.

10. The musician _____ the song into an easier key for him to sing.

11. Actors carry _____ of pictures to show producers the various types of characters they can portray.

12. The doctor's _____ manner put her patient at ease.

13. _____ have great difficulty doing the simple tasks we take for granted.

14. A great deal of research should be done before making a _____ film.

15. After a certain number of prints, _____ plates are destroyed so that no unauthorized prints can be made.

4   Superstitions: Just Whistling in the Dark

Comprehension Check

Multiple Choice

Circle the letter before the best answer to each of the following questions.

1. The author thinks people who believe in superstitions are
   a. abnormal.
   b. logical.
   c. a bit silly.
   d. correct.

2. From the reading we can infer that superstitions
   a. are no longer believed.
   b. have been believed in every period of time.
   c. are religious in origin.
   d. are dangerous.

3. A triskaidekaphobiac
   a. stays home on Friday the thirteenth.
   b. believes the number thirteen has religious importance.
   c. thinks the number thirteen is lucky.
   d. thinks numbers determine our fate.

4. If you break a mirror, you are supposed to
   a. stay indoors that day.
   b. bury the pieces.
   c. throw the pieces into a river, ocean, or lake.
   d. throw a piece over your shoulder.

5. Whistling is a superstition that started with
   a. sailors.
   b. soldiers.
   c. artists.
   d. chefs.

6. The author implies that

    a. superstitions are based on scientific fact.

    b. superstitious people do silly things.

    c. educated people are not superstitious.

    d. superstitions have no place in modern society.

Matching

Match the background to the superstition; write the letter from the second column in the space in the first column.

_____ 7. The unlucky number 13   a. The Holy Trinity

_____ 8. Meeting a black cat   b. Right is right and left is wrong

_____ 9. Walking under ladders   c. Witches and Satan

_____ 10. Getting out of bed on   d. The Last Supper
               the wrong side

Essay

Discuss the backgrounds of at least five superstitions.

_____

_____

_____

_____

_____

_____

_____

_____

_____

_____

_____

_____

_____

_____

_____

_____

_____

_____

_____

_____

Vocabulary Check

Write the best word from the following list in the blank in each sentence below.

irrational   philosopher   Norse   wrath   rationalize

incorruptibility   consternation   episodes   distort   aversion

1. Some people have such a strong _____ to cabbage that even the smell of it cooking makes them sick.

2. Thursday was named after the _____ god Thor, the god of thunder.

3. Most _____ of television programs are recorded on video-tape for later broadcast rather than presented live.

4. During the Middle Ages, beliefs about witchcraft were so _____ that cows, insects, and birds were convicted of being witches and put to death.

5. You must make someone very angry to incur his or her _____.

6. Mirrors in carnival fun houses are shaped to _____ people's reflections.

7. Scandals such as Nixon's Watergate, Reagan's Iran-Contra, and Clinton's Monicagate have shaken our faith in the _____ of our political leaders.

8. People _____ continuing to smoke by pointing to healthy elderly people who have smoked all of their lives.

9. Eighteenth-century patients at St. Bartholomew's Hospital must have felt
_____ at being asked to pay their funeral expenses when
they were admitted.

10. Socrates, probably the best known Greek _____ , never
wrote down his own teachings; we know what he said because a student,
Plato, took notes.

5   Saved

Comprehension Check

Multiple Choice

Circle the letter before the best answer to each of the following questions.

1. Malcolm X read to

    a. gain status and power.

    b. become wealthy.

    c. become a great speaker.

    d. help black people.

2. Malcolm X completed

    a. high school.

    b. college.

    c. eighth grade.

    d. junior college.

3. An aardvark is

    a. a termite.

    b. an African bird.

    c. a burrowing mammal.

    d. an armadillo.

4. Malcolm X read in semi-darkness because

    a. he didn't pay his electric bill.

    b. the prison guards were cruel.

    c. there was no window in his room.

    d. he read after "lights out."

5. Malcolm X began reading books after

    a. completing high school.

    b. improving his vocabulary.

    c. getting out of prison.

    d. finishing second grade.

6. Malcolm X copied the dictionary because

   a. he didn't know a better method of vocabulary improvement.

   b. there are no better methods of vocabulary improvement.

   c. he didn't have any other books.

   d. he was bored.

7. Malcolm X's story shows that

   a. illiterate people are stupid.

   b. illiterate people are articulate.

   c. prison helps people reform.

   d. illiterate people can learn.

8. The administration at Norfolk Prison Colony

   a. encouraged prisoners to improve themselves.

   b. forced prisoners to work constantly.

   c. kept prisoners isolated.

   d. allowed prisoners to read whenever they wished.

Short Answer

What conclusion can you draw from this article . . .

  9. about the possibility of rehabilitating prisoners?

   _____

10. about the effects of reading on one's life?

   _____

   _____

Essay

Explain the story "Saved" as if you were telling it to someone who had not heard it before.

_____

_____

_____

_____

_____

_____

_____

_____

_____

_____

_____

_____

_____

_____

_____

Vocabulary Check

A. Write the best word from the following list in the blank in each sentence below.

dormant   alma maters   convey   feigned   afflicting

confer   emulate   articulate   immense   vistas

1. Many politicians are so _____ that their speaking ability alone gets them elected to office.

2. Because of the different shades of meaning of words, it is sometimes difficult to _____ to others exactly what we mean.

3. Susan had always admired her successful uncle, and when she grew up she tried to _____ him.

4. The _____ portions served at the restaurant were impossible to eat.

5. He _____ illness to avoid work.

6. The invention of the printing press opened new _____ for the common person.

7. The seed, planted in the fall, lay _____ until the spring rains.

8. Many universities _____ more than 2,000 degrees a year.

9. The most common disease, _____ over 53 percent of the people in the United States, is tooth decay.

10. Until recently, most top business executives claimed Ivy League colleges as _____ .

B. Write the best word from the following list in the blank in each sentence below.

engrossing   inevitable   riffling   rehabilitation   hustlers

isolation   functional   motivation   circulation   devours

11. People who favor the death penalty usually don't believe in the _____ of criminals.

12. Two-dollar bills are no longer in general _____ .

13. My daughter loves fairy tales so much that she _____ the Disney videos of Snow White, Cinderella, and Sleeping Beauty.

14. Con artists are _____ who take advantage of people.

15. Success in school depends on _____ as well as on ability.

16. You can get a general idea of a book by _____ through its pages.

17. Death and taxes are said to be the only two things that are _____ .

18. In order to be _____ in society, you need to know basic mathematics.

19. For those who like them, crossword puzzles are _____ .

20. Solitary confinement is considered a severe punishment because people suffer from _____ .

6 How to Strengthen Your Memory Power

Comprehension Check

Multiple Choice

Circle the letter before the best answer to each of the following questions.

1. The type of person who remembers best is
   a. brilliant.
   b. well organized.
   c. very young.
   d. a student.

2. A major reason for forgetting is
   a. low intelligence.
   b. drinking.
   c. amnesia.
   d. failure to pay attention.

3. Scientists believe that memory is
   a. electronic, like a computer.
   b. chemical.
   c. physical, like a mark or groove.
   d. all of the above.

4. Short-term memory usually lasts
   a. a few hours.
   b. almost forever.
   c. less than 20 seconds.
   d. about 20 minutes.

5. From the story about Albert Einstein, you can infer that he didn't have a
   good memory for
   a. everyday things.
   b. anything.
   c. numbers.
   d. physics.

6. The author implies that the best way to remember a lecture is to

   a. try to copy down everything that's said.

   b. use a tape recorder.

   c. use drugs that aid memory.

   d. repeat the key concepts over and over.

7. The author implies that a good way to remember material for tests is to

   a. organize it in categories.

   b. make visual and verbal associations.

   c. repeat the facts you don't remember over and over.

   d. do all of the above.

8. Memory experts

   a. are still learning about memory.

   b. believe that the principles of memory are based on cosmological physics.

   c. believe that long-term memories fade within a few days and cannot be retrieved.

   d. have finally identified all the chemicals involved in the memory process.

Short Answer

9. Make up a list of at least three items. Then use the "link" method to memorize it. Write the list on the left and the links on the right.

   Item   **Mental picture**

   a. _____

   b. _____

   c. _____

10. Give an example of something you can remember by making a physical change in your environment. Explain how the change will work as a cue.

_____

_____

_____

Essay

Explain what the reading says about remembering and forgetting.

_____

_____

_____

_____

_____

_____

_____

_____

_____

_____

_____

_____

_____

_____

_____

_____

_____

_____

_____

_____

_____

_____

_____

_____

_____

_____

Vocabulary Check

Write the best word from the following list in the blank in each sentence below.

cosmology   retrieval   retention   distinctive   heredity

neuropsychologist   associative   perception   physiological   senility

1. Scientists are experimenting with new "antiaging" substances such as Ginko Biloba to prevent _____ .

2. The _____ markings on certain animals serve as a form of camouflage in their natural habitats.

3. If you were hearing the voices of invisible beings, you might go to a _____ .

4. _____ determines the color of our eyes.

5. No one has yet found a _____ cause for mental illness, although it has long been suspected that it is not completely psychological.

6. The _____ of game by some breeds of hunting dogs almost seems to be an inborn ability.

7. Musicians become skilled at the _____ of small differences in sound that most of us can't hear.

8. The eye's _____ of visual images enables us to see a motion picture as a flowing unit rather than as a series of separate pictures.

9. The principle of _____ memory involves relating new information to what is already known.

10. Einstein's theory on the _____ of the spatial universe is that it curves back on itself and is, therefore, infinite.

7 | Don't Tell Jaime Escalante Minorities Can't Meet (High) Standards!

Comprehension Check

Multiple Choice

Circle the letter before the best answer to each of the following questions.

1. Jaime Escalante emigrated from
   a. East Los Angeles.
   b. Mexico.
   c. Bolivia.
   d. Ecuador.

2. He taught
   a. English.
   b. mathematics.
   c. both English and mathematics.
   d. only advanced calculus classes.

3. Escalante
   a. could not get any job but teaching.
   b. secured a teaching job as soon as he arrived in Los Angeles.
   c. finally got a teaching job after waiting 15 years.
   d. had to take his teaching credentials again.

4. The students
   a. took an SAT test and failed.
   b. took an advanced calculus test but cheated.
   c. took an advanced calculus test and passed.
   d. never got to take the test because they were Hispanic.

5. An additional 150 students signed up for Escalante's high-level math courses because
   a. he walked around campus with a sign-up list.
   b. their parents insisted.
   c. they were required to do so.
   d. the other students had been so successful.

6. Escalante's students were able to succeed because

    a. he made them more intelligent.

    b. he recognized their abilities and motivated them.

    c. he restructured the classes so they were no longer difficult.

    d. they took easier versions of the Advanced Placement exams.

7. Because of their success in the math courses,

    a. the students got great jobs.

    b. all Escalante's students went to college.

    c. the students increased their belief in themselves.

    d. many of his students became student teachers.

8. From the article we can infer that Escalante

    a. has a Ph.D. in child psychology.

    b. is a good lecturer.

    c. has children of his own.

    d. hates the American school system.

Short Answer

9. How did Jaime Escalante give his students *ganas?*

_____

_____

10. Why do you think Escalante has his students and their parents sign a learning contract?

_____

_____

_____

Essay

Explain the story "Don't Tell Jaime Escalante Minorities Can't Meet (High) Standards!" as if you were telling it to someone who had not heard it before.

_____

_____

_____

_____

_____

_____

_____

_____

_____

_____

_____

_____

_____

_____

_____

_____

_____

_____

Vocabulary Check

Write the best word from the following list in the blank in each sentence below.

barrio   Hispanic   rigorous   demographic   morale

aspirations   turmoil   cosmetology   culminates   skeptical

proficiency   feat   idiosyncratic   sequence   podium

1. Military boot camp includes a very _____ physical training program.

2. The teacher was _____ about whether or not Susan's dog had really eaten her homework.

3. Driver's education courses are designed to build driving

   _____.

4. A weird _____ of events led the star of *Amistad* from a life on the streets to a life of fame as a movie star.

5. People's _____ are often based on what they think they deserve; someone who doesn't think much of himself will not try for a challenging career.

6. Famous _____ artists include Goya and Velázquez from Spain, and Rivera and Orozco from Mexico.

7. Working for bonuses and other prizes helps to increase employees' _____ .

8. Rolling over and over while balancing a ball on the nose would be quite a _____ for a human, but it's not too hard for a seal.

9. The Middle East is usually in _____ , with conflicts involving Israel, Palestine, and Iraq.

10. A great baseball team's season _____ in playing in the World Series.

11. Students who learn _____ make people more beautiful than they were before.

12. Many _____ habits become irritating to others.

13. When a speaker wants to add emphasis, he might pound on the _____ he's standing behind.

14. There's often a strong sense of community among Mexican American families living in the _____ .

15. The amount of money given to a state by the federal government is often determined by _____ studies.

8 9 Obstacles to Creativity—and How You Can Remove Them

Comprehension Check

True–False

Mark T or F.

_____ 1. The author believes that some people are born more creative than others.

_____ 2. No group can reliably produce valuable, profitable concepts unless they generate ideas in the hundreds.

_____ 3. The author suggests setting a strict time limit for solving a problem and sticking to it.

_____ 4. Revisiting the same ideas and assumptions over and over is a waste of time.

_____ 5. Visual thinking can include drawing a picture of the problem you're working on.

Multiple Choice

Circle the letter before the best answer to each of the following questions.

6. The author refers to his list of obstacles as "Creativity for Dummies" because

   a. only stupid people make these mistakes.

   b. the most common errors should be obvious to everyone

   c. smart people are already aware of the list.

   d. people who haven't gone to business school rarely learn about these errors.

7. The typical staff meeting is uncreative because

   a. there is no clear agenda.

   b. the atmosphere is too informal.

   c. the leader fails to ask for creative ideas.

   d. there is a lack of focus.

8. The author recommends
    a. keeping an idea journal.
    b. recording ideas on an audio recorder.
    c. leaving ideas on your own voice mail or e-mail.
    d. doing any or all of the above.

9. There are strong social mechanisms in most organizations against
    a. revisiting ideas and assumptions.
    b. expressing creative ideas.
    c. asking questions.
    d. thinking in new ways.

10. Thomas Edison said, "Genius is 1% inspiration and 99% perspiration." By this he meant that
    a. 1% of all people are creative geniuses.
    b. people have to do a lot of work to get a creative idea.
    c. 99% of ideas are not very creative.
    d. all of the above are true.

Essay

List the nine obstacles to creativity and explain what each one means. Use a separate piece of paper.

Vocabulary Check

A. Write the best word from the following list in the blank in each sentence below.

novel   **jettison**   **impulsive**   **blatant**   **viable**

debris   **scrutinize**   **status quo**   **analogy**   **realm**

1. Many TV ads make a _____ appeal to sexuality by showing actors in revealing clothing and poses.

2. Hyperactive children typically exhibit _____ behavior.

3. If you don't have an assignment, you should think up a more _____ excuse than saying the dog ate it.

4. Having an income of $1 million a year is beyond the _____ of most people's expectations.

5. People are called packrats when they are unable to _____ things they don't need.

6. The way to brainstorm is to write down all ideas before considering which ones might be _____.

7. Traditionally, political groups who want to preserve the _____ are called conservatives, those who want change are called liberals, and those who want to go back to an earlier time are called reactionaries.

8. When you put a new roof on your house, the contract should state that the roofing contractor must clear away all the _____.

9. You can make an _____ between bees in a hive and workers in a factory.

10. If you have a lot of itemized deductions, you should be prepared for the IRS to _____ your tax return.

B. Write the best word from the following list in the blank in each sentence below.

compiles   relentlessly   phenomenon   opportune   formalize

innovation   syndrome   superficial   tangible   facilitate

11. It's a good idea to wait for an _____ moment, when your boss is in a good mood, to ask for a raise.

12. Having your own desk with good lighting in a quiet environment will _____ studying.

13. The flu _____ includes runny or stuffy nose, aches and pains, and stomach upset.

14. To qualify for a patent, an invention must be an _____.

15. People hope that their careers will offer _____ rewards such as money as well as inner satisfaction.

16. Let's _____ our agreement by drawing up a contract.

17. The saying, "Beauty is only skin deep" means that a person's character is more important than _____ qualities.

18. "Old Faithful," a geyser in Yellowstone National Park, is a natural _____ , erupting approximately every 66 minutes.

19. The Bureau of the Census _____ population data that are used by social scientists and government planners.

20. Many people today oppose the sport of fox hunting, in which the fox is _____ pursued by hounds and finally killed.

9 Improving Test-Taking Strategies

Comprehension Check

True–False

Mark T or F.

_____ 1. Students shouldn't go back and change their answers.

_____ 2. Your essay answers will be better if you write using a graphic organizer.

_____ 3. You should look over a test as a first step so that you can make time allocations.

_____ 4. On a multiple-choice question, you should eliminate incorrect options first.

_____ 5. The author implies that, unless there is a penalty for guessing, you should not leave any questions unanswered.

Multiple Choice

Circle the letter before the best answer to each of the following questions.

6. One tip that objective and essay tests have in common is
   a. use technical vocabulary.
   b. eliminate implausible options.
   c. organize your answers.
   d. budget your time.

7. You can infer that
   a. very few things are always true or always false.
   b. your first hunch on a test is your best hunch.
   c. you should be on the lookout for "trick" questions.
   d. all of the above are true.

8. You can infer that
   a. testwise people still have to study.
   b. testwiseness can be learned.
   c. students who are testwise get better grades than those who are not.
   d. all of the above are true.

Short Answer

9. Give a definition of testwiseness.

_____

_____

10. How should you allocate your time during a test?

_____

_____

Essay

1. List some tips for taking multiple-choice tests.
2. List some tips for taking essay tests.

_____

_____

_____

_____

_____

_____

_____

_____

_____

_____

_____

_____

_____

_____

_____

_____

_____

_____

Vocabulary Check

Write the best word from the following list in the blank in each sentence below.

format   cognitive   adage   empirical   explicit

implausible   generalization   vigilant   assertions   concise

1. "A penny saved is a penny earned" is an _____.

2. "Asians are good in math" is a _____ that is only sometimes true.

3. Instructors appreciate written work that is _____, so they don't have to spend time wading through meaningless or repetitious words in order to find the point.

4. If you want people to be able to follow your directions, you should be very _____; leave nothing open to interpretation.

5. The traditional _____ of a newspaper article is the "inverted pyramid"; the most important information is at the top, and the details are underneath.

6. Jurors have to weigh the evidence that points to guilt against the defendant's _____ of innocence.

7. Some people find it _____ that anyone other than O. J. Simpson had a motive to kill his ex-wife.

8. Being a good parent has _____ as well as emotional aspects; while you have to love your kids, you also have to know something about child rearing.

9. "Neighborhood watch" programs require that neighbors be _____ and report anything that looks suspicious.

10. We have only _____ evidence about some medicines; we know they work for some ailments, but we don't know why.

10 Conflict and Communication: Learning How to Disagree

Comprehension Check

Matching

Match the following statements with the type of conflict by writing the letter preceding the best answer in the blank.

_____ 1. Let's take time to explore our similarities and differences to see if we can solve the problem to the satisfaction of both of us.

_____ 2. Conflict is such a hassle. I'd as soon let the other person have his or her way just to keep the peace.

_____ 3. I hate conflict. If I can find a way to avoid it, I will.

_____ 4. I'm willing to negotiate to see if the other person and I can meet halfway.

_____ 5. You can't just let people walk over you. You've got to establish your point of view.

a. avoidance

b. accommodation

c. domination

d. compromise

e. integration

Multiple Choice

Circle the letter before the best answer to each of the following questions.

6. Acting out your feelings while denying them is called

   a. disparagement.

   b. alienation.

   c. passive aggression.

   d. good communication.

7. The author implies that compared with bad relationships, good relationships have

   a. less conflict.

   b. more love.

   c. better communication.

   d. more ability to compromise.

8. The author implies that the best way to bring about good communication is to be

   a. unselfish.

   b. willing to compromise.

   c. totally honest.

   d. logical.

9. The author implies that

   a. people's communication styles change depending on who they are dealing with.

   b. these communication styles are appropriate to use at home but not at work.

   c. male dominance/female submission will lead to poor relationships.

   d. people should use different styles of conflict resolution with children.

10. The author implies that

    a. most people use poor communication.

    b. communication styles can be changed.

    c. people pass their communication styles on to their children.

    d. men have less effective communication styles than women.

Essay

Describe the five styles of dealing with conflict and the author's opinion of each one.

_____

_____

_____

_____

_____

_____

_____

_____

_____

_____

_____

_____

_____

_____

_____

_____

_____

_____

Vocabulary Check

A. Write the best word from the following list in the blank in each sentence
    below.

confrontation   accommodation   martyrdom   preceding   integration

disparaging   suppress   chronic   divergent   defensive

1. Resolving conflict by _____ requires openness for mutual
    problem solving, disagreement with the ideas instead of the person, and
    emphasis on similarities rather than differences.

2. Some experts say that _____ television viewing is harmful
    to the mental and social development of children.

3. Most of the time it's wise to avoid a _____ when you
    disagree with an instructor.

4. Creativity requires _____ thinking.

5. It's difficult for most of us to accept criticism without becoming

    _____.

6. "People pleasers" typically deal with conflict by using _____.

7. People who try to win by domination often use aggressive, bullying
    tactics such as _____ those who disagree with them.

8. _____ for a noble cause is admired, but people who suffer
    needlessly are not respected.

9. If you _____ your feelings, you are likely to develop resentment.

10. Because some animals show unusual, restless behavior _____ earthquakes, it is believed that they are picking up signals that humans cannot sense.

B.   Write the best word from the following list in the blank in each sentence below.

stance   passive aggression   attributes   alienating   empathy

subtle   responsive   diplomacy   invariably   inhibited

11. The contenders for the heavyweight championship had a certain _____ for each other because they understood how much sacrifice and pain had gone into their training.

12. When the coffee shop raised its prices, the owners found they were _____ their regular customers.

13. A boxer's _____ includes fists up, feet in a stable position, and knees slightly bent.

14. One reason for social drinking is that alcohol makes us less _____, so that socializing is easier.

15. If you want an expensive gift, a _____ approach may be better than asking for it directly.

16. An example of _____ would be cheerfully agreeing to do the dishes when asked, and then "accidentally" breaking them.

17. The position of ambassador required _____.

18. Honesty and integrity are _____ that many politicians seem to lack.

19. Good listeners are _____ to what is said.

20. It seems that when you are in the middle of something important the phone will _____ ring.

11 | The Stages of Death and Loss

Comprehension Check

True–False

Mark T or F.

_____ 1. Many people who are dying will show anger toward family, friends, and others who do not deserve it.

_____ 2. It's a good sign if a dying person believes he or she will get well.

_____ 3. Understanding the process of dying helps us cope with our own fear and denial.

_____ 4. The author implies that our own fears of death may cause us to be dishonest with a dying relative.

_____ 5. The author implies that people who believe in God and Heaven do not need to go through all five stages when they die.

Multiple Choice

Circle the letter before the best answer to each of the following questions.

6. The best way to help a person who is dying is to

   a. deny or minimize the seriousness of his or her condition

   b. talk only about pleasant topics.

   c. be available when the person wants to talk about death.

   d. keep a cheerful attitude no matter what you are really feeling.

7. The reason that physicians should tell dying patients the truth is

   a. so the patient can make final plans and preparations.

   b. so that family and friends can be honest with the patient and with each other.

   c. so the patient and his loved ones can come to terms with their loss.

   d. all of the above.

8. If the parent of a small child were dying, Kübler-Ross would probably recommend
   a. encouraging the child to talk about her feelings and ask as many questions as possible.
   b. protecting the child by telling her as little as possible.
   c. hiding the family's feelings of sadness and fear.
   d. telling the child more than she can handle.

9. The author implies that
   a. the role of religion is unimportant in death and dying.
   b. doctors should not artificially prolong life.
   c. doctors should judge how much truth a patient can handle.
   d. increased openness about the subject of death is good.

10. People who are dying need to
   a. talk about their death.
   b. take care of their unfinished business.
   c. resolve their feelings about dying.
   d. do all of the above.

Essay

Describe the stages of dying and what can be done to assist the dying person in each stage.

_____

_____

_____

_____

_____

_____

_____

_____

_____

_____

_____

_____

_____

_____

Vocabulary Check

A. Write the best word from the following list in the blank in each sentence below.

psychologists   taboo   seminar   universal   resolution

delineated   essence   remission   deplete   serenity

1. Dreaming is _____; laboratory tests have shown that those who claim to have no dreams, simply forget them more easily than others.

2. Cancer is almost never considered "cured"; instead we say it is "in _____."

3. According to _____, most people's short term memory is between five and nine items or digits; this is why phone numbers are seven digits long.

4. The _____ of Darwin's theory of evolution is that all species of plants and animals developed from earlier forms by inheriting slight variations down through the generations, and that natural selection determines which forms will survive.

5. We hope we can come to a _____ of our childhood fears and resentments of our parents after we grow up.

6. Gasoline engines _____ our supply of fossil fuel and contribute to global warming.

7. Scientists have _____ three stages of prenatal development: the germinal stage (conception to 2 weeks), the embryonic stage (2 weeks to 2 months), and the fetal stage (2 months to birth).

8. Tonight I will attend a _____ on seventeenth century French literature.

9. People who meditate believe that it increases their mental

_____ .

10. The Victorians considered sex a _____ topic for polite
society.

B. Write the best word from the following list in the blank in each sentence
below.

**psychiatrists   sociologists   devoid   impending   compartmentalized
displace   subjected   chemotherapy   contemporary   dehumanizing**

11. Astronauts in training are _____ to zero gravity and
other conditions they will experience in space.

12. Because _____ are physicians, they can prescribe drugs.

13. Most prisoners on death row try to prevent or at least delay their
_____ executions.

14. Sigmund Freud, the father of psychoanalysis, _____ the
personality into three structures: the id, the ego, and the superego.

15. People often _____ the anger they cannot express at
work onto their families.

16. _____ study human society.

17. Robots are taking over many of the more repetitive, dangerous, and
_____ jobs that were created during the Industrial
Revolution.

18. It is hard to find classes in _____ nightclub dancing
because the styles change so often that instructors can't keep up.

19. A successful con artist has to be _____ of compassion
for his or her victims.

20. _____ brought about more humane treatment of the
mentally ill, who can now be managed by drugs instead of straight
jackets.

<table>
<tr><td>**12**</td><td></td></tr>
</table>

Intellectual Health: Critical Thinking and the Art of Living

Comprehension Check

Multiple Choice

Circle the letter before the best answer to each question below.

1. The danger of uncritical thinking is that

   a. it will prevent us from accurately perceiving the world around us.

   b. we will not be able to make good decisions.

   c. we will pay attention to what we want to believe and overlook the rest.

   d. all of the above are true.

2. If the following were an argument, which statement would be the conclusion?

   a. All living things die.

   b. Plants are alive.

   c. Animals are alive.

   d. Plants and animals die.

True–False

Mark T or F.

_____ 3. The preceding argument (question 2) is an example of inductive reasoning.

_____ 4. Fallacies are a type of deductive reasoning.

Matching

Identify the following types of fallacies by writing the name of the fallacy in the blank after each sentence.

   Jumping to Conclusions
   Irrelevant Reason or False Cause
   Irrelevant Attack on a Person or an Opponent
   Appeal to Authority
   Questionable Statistics
   Slippery Slope

5. People who buy organic foods are "health nuts."

_____

6. This pollution is terrible. See how everyone is coughing?

_____

7. More school children are losing their ability to distinguish right from wrong. Just look at the vandalism that occurred at Middletown Elementary School.

_____

8. There are more bugs in the United States than anywhere else in the world.

_____

9. Some religions oppose killing insects because they believe it's a step on the way to killing people.

_____

10. Jean Kelley, who plays Dr. Janet Jones on *The Guiding Gift*, says that Aspergrim relieves headaches five times faster than any other aspirin or nonaspirin product.

_____

Essay

Define and give examples of at least six of the nine fallacies listed in the reading selection. Use a separate piece of paper.

Vocabulary Check

A. Write the best word from the following list in the blank in each sentence below.

prevailed   faculties   alleviate   absurdity   subconscious

deductive   premise   exposition   non sequitur   causal

1. According to the "use it or lose it" philosophy, doing crossword puzzles and playing chess is better for the mental _____ than watching TV sitcoms.

2. It's an _____ to think you can become a rocket scientist after studying in college for only one year.

3. The Surgeon General has found a _____ relationship between smoking and lung cancer.

4. Doctors are often reluctant to prescribe enough drugs to _____ the patient's pain because of fear of drug addiction.

5. According to Freudian psychology, a lot of behavior doesn't seem to make sense because the motivation is _____.

6. In Homer's epic poem the *Iliad*, the Greeks _____ over the Trojans after hiding soldiers inside a gigantic wooden horse.

7. The statement that "That young woman is too good looking to be a good airplane pilot" is an example of a _____.

8. _____ reasoning tells us that humans cannot live more than around 120 years.

9. The conclusion that students who failed the test didn't study is based on the _____ that the test covered the assigned reading.

10. If you describe an event you have observed, you are using _____ rather than argument.

B. Write the best word from the following list in the blank in each sentence below.

pornography   prospective   unprecedented   debunkers   paranormal
conversely   inductive   anecdote   logician   fallacy

11. A _____ is an expert in the science of correct reasoning.

12. In the film *Carrie*, the title character has the _____ ability to move objects using only her mind.

13. A _____ once widely believed was that warts were caused by contact with toads.

14. There is always an argument about how far laws can go to protect against _____ without abridging freedom of speech.

15. Global warming is expected to melt part of the polar ice and cause _____ flooding in coastal areas.

16. A good way to capture the audience's attention at the beginning of a speech is to tell a joke or an interesting _____.

17. Before getting married, most people want to introduce the _____ bride or groom to their families.

18. We use _____ reasoning when we try to prevent heart attacks by lowering our fat intake and increasing cardiovascular exercise.

19. People's childhood feelings about their parent of the opposite sex can influence who they are attracted to as adults, or _____, who they find unattractive.

20. Magicians are great _____ of those who claim psychic powers because they know all the tricks.

13   Shared Characteristics of Life

Comprehension Check

Multiple Choice

Circle the letter before the best answer to each question below.

1. Living and nonliving things both have
   a. molecules.
   b. cells.
   c. tissues.
   d. organs.

2. Only living things have
   a. molecules.
   b. atoms.
   c. particles.
   d. DNA.

3. A population is a group of
   a. cells.
   b. molecules.
   c. organs.
   d. organisms.

4. Living things can be categorized as
   a. molecules or mutations.
   b. metabolic or homeostatic.
   c. populations, communities, or biosystems.
   d. producers, consumers, or decomposers.

5. A group of lions, zebras, and rhinos living in the African plains comprises
   a. a population.
   b. a community.
   c. an ecosystem.
   d. a biosphere.

6. The advantage of mutation is that it

  a. weeds out the weaker organisms.

  b. is a creative energy.

  c. may lead to better adaptations.

  d. prevents defective organisms from reproducing.

7. Animals that require a great deal of energy to live must have a high rate of

  a. homeostasis.

  b. metabolism.

  c. reproduction.

  d. all of the above.

8. Photosynthesis is accomplished mainly by

  a. atoms.

  b. cells.

  c. plants.

  d. animals.

Fill-ins

Fill in the following blanks.

9. A _____ is an organized unit that can survive and reproduce

10. on its own, given _____ instructions and sources of energy and raw materials.

Essays

1. What are the characteristics that are shared by all living things?

2. List the levels of organization in nature.

_____

_____

_____

_____

_____

_____   _____

_____   _____

_____   _____

_____   _____

_____   _____

_____   _____

Vocabulary Check

Write the best word from the following list in the blank in each sentence below.

emerged   convergence   initially   secretion   hormone

tolerable   drastic   sabotage   predators   variant

1. Using animals in laboratory experiments is not _____ to animal rights activists.

2. Like many people, actor Tom Cruise has ear lobes that are attached to the side of his head and do not flap back and forth, because of _____ genetic information.

3. Estrogen is a female _____.

4. Most scientists agree that human life _____ first in Africa.

5. The word _____ came from French factory workers' practice of breaking machinery by throwing their wooden shoes (*sabots*) into it during labor disputes.

6. Life on Earth was _____ confined to the sea.

7. An example of _____ in biology is a shark's fin, a penguin's flipper (originally a wing), and a porpoise's flipper (originally a front leg); they started out quite differently but came together both in form and in function.

8. Lions and tigers are _____.

9. The _____ of perspiration is the function of our body's sweat glands.

10. Some countries have used such _____ punishments as cutting off a person's hand for stealing.

14 Interpersonal Attraction: Liking and Loving

Comprehension Check

True–False

Mark T or F.

_____ 1. Using ingratiation is a good way to get people to like you.

_____ 2. Opposites attract.

_____ 3. Most people believe that "Beauty is only skin deep."

_____ 4. The similarity effect is caused by either the attraction of like to like or the repulsion between like and unlike, or both.

Multiple Choice

Circle the letter before the best answer to each question below.

5. The matching hypothesis says that we prefer others who

   a. are similar to us in personality.

   b. live or work near us.

   c. like us.

   d. are about as attractive as we are.

6. Similarity is associated with

   a. greater marital happiness.

   b. adolescent friendships.

   c. adult friendships.

   d. all of the above.

7. The repulsion hypothesis says that people dislike those who

   a. are less attractive.

   b. are different.

   c. don't like us.

   d. don't live or work near us.

8. You can infer from the reciprocity effect that

   a. friendly, caring people get more love.

   b. people who are "hard to get" get more love.

   c. high achievers get more love.

   d. beautiful people get more love.

Short Answer

9. What are some gender differences in the tactics people use to pursue romantic relationships?

_____

_____

10. What is the difference between showing that you like someone and using ingratiation as a strategy?

_____

_____

_____

Essay

Discuss the key factors in interpersonal attraction. Use a separate piece of paper.

Vocabulary Check

A. Write the best word from the following list in the blank in each sentence below.

dynamics   social psychologist   proximity   reciprocity

spatial   arbitrary   evolve   idealized

1. When you work in close _____ to a good-looking person of the opposite sex, an attraction is likely to develop.

2. A _____ might study how people react to peer pressure.

3. "You scratch my back and I'll scratch yours" is an example of

_____.

4. The choice of a career should be made carefully; it should not be based on something _____ such as having a brother-in-law who knows somebody in the business.

5. Species, including humans, either _____ or they die.

6. During the 1940s, singer-actress Judy Garland was the _____ image of the wholesome girl, so she could never play a villain or a sex symbol in a movie.

7. Psychologists try to explain the personality _____ that cause deviant behavior such as child abuse and spousal abuse.

8. Architects and decorators often use models to illustrate the _____ relationships between design elements.

B. Write the best word from the following list in the blank in each sentence below.

hypothesis   illicit   self-concept   status
ethnicity   repulsion   disdain

9. Most people react to slugs with _____.

10. People's levels of ambition are related to their _____; they tend to get the kinds of jobs they think they deserve.

11. The ultimate solution to racism will probably be intermarriage, so everyone's _____ will be mixed.

12. Marijuana and cocaine are _____ drugs.

13. Scientists cannot presume that something is true; they must test each _____ to find out how often and under what circumstances it works.

14. After the politician was convicted of taking bribes, the voters looked on him with _____.

15. The _____ of women and minorities has been improving in recent years.

15   Safer Sex

Comprehension Check

True–False

Mark T or F.

_____   1. Most viral STDs can be cured.

_____   2. The author implies that if a married person "cheats," he or she should stop having sex with the spouse (and all others) for six months and then take an HIV test.

_____   3. Information about breakage rates for different brands of condoms is available from the Consumers Union.

_____   4. A person's social class and educational level are good guidelines for safer sex.

_____   5. In many states, you can call the health department to find out the names of people who have tested positive for HIV.

Multiple Choice

Circle the letter before the best answer to each of the following questions.

6. The author implies that

   a. if you are too embarrassed to ask the right questions, you should not have sex.

   b. nobody should have sex unless they are monogamous.

   c. most high-risk people practice safer sex.

   d. a negative blood test for HIV proves that a person is not infected.

7. Which of the following is *not* recommended for safer sex?

   a. using condoms made of natural skin

   b. using nonoxynol-9 as a lubricant

   c. buying condoms of the correct size

   d. storing condoms in a cool, dry place

8. The fact that 12 out of 100 women become pregnant during their first year of using condoms implies that

   a. condoms offer better protection against STDs than against pregnancy.

   b. you might as well use nothing at all.

   c. condoms do not offer very good protection against STDs.

   d. most people do not use condoms correctly.

9. In FDA tests, what percent of the time did condom breakage occur?

   a. 2–11

   b. 12–21

   c. 22–31

   d. 32–41

10. Which of the following sexual practices is safest?

   a. intercourse with a latex condom and nonoxynol-9

   b. oral sex with a non-menstruating woman using a dental dam

   c. French kissing with a lot of saliva

   d. mutual masturbation without contacting bodily fluids

Essay

What strategies should you use to protect yourself from sexually transmitted diseases?

_____

_____

_____

_____

_____

_____

_____

_____

_____

_____

_____

_____

_____

_____

_____

Vocabulary Check

A. Write the best word from the following list in the blank in each sentence below.

promiscuous   antibodies   hypothetical   presumably

mandatory   stringent   cohabit   breach

1. Attendance in some classes is _____; you will be dropped after a certain number of absences.

2. A _____ question always refers to something that hasn't happened yet.

3. Because Social Security benefits can be reduced when couples marry, some elderly couples prefer to _____.

4. Many people assume that women who wear scanty clothing are

    _____.

5. Failing to keep promises will cause a _____ of trust in a relationship.

6. A vaccination is the injection of organisms into the body for the purpose of building _____ against a particular disease.

7. Most companies are _____ in business to make money.

8. Elite colleges usually have _____ standards for admission.

B. Write the best word from the following list in the blank in each sentence below.

casualties   respondents   divulge   anonymous

enhance   vulnerability   euphemism

9. The police will accept _____ tips to help them solve crimes.

10. Usually additional education will _____ one's standard of living.

11. People who take polls or surveys usually try to get the broadest possible cross-section of _____.

12. Saying that people have "passed away" is a _____ for saying they have died.

13. Nobody knows the exact number of _____ during the sinking of the *Titanic* because the number of passengers was unknown; estimates range between 1490 and 1517.

14. A good diet, exercise, and plenty of rest will decrease our _____ to colds and flu.

15. Because of age bias, job applicants are not required to _____ their age.

16   Choosing an Occupation or a Career

Comprehension Check

Multiple Choice

Circle the letter before the best answer to each of the following questions.

1. The first thing to consider in career planning is your

   a. values.

   b. abilities.

   c. interests.

   d. motivation.

2. The author believes that choosing a career is

   a. an event that should take place as early as possible.

   b. an ongoing process that takes time.

   c. something that should be done while in college.

   d. the goal of any good college program.

3. The author would probably

   a. prefer students to get career guidance in high school.

   b. not believe in tests as an aid in career planning.

   c. like to see more guidance counselors hired in colleges.

   d. encourage students to make a decision and stick to it.

4. The author implies that

   a. most career counselors do a poor job of helping students choose an occupation.

   b. adults should not pressure students to choose a career in high school.

   c. students change majors too many times in college.

   d. all of the above are true.

Short Answer

List 6 of the factors the author mentions as important in vocational decision making.

5. _____

6. _____

7. _____

8. _____

9. _____

10. _____

Essay

Discuss the factors that should be considered in choosing a career. Use a separate piece of paper.

Vocabulary Check

Write the best word from the following list in the blank in each sentence below.

implement   compelled   implications   procrastination   envision

differential   aptitude   competence   integral   components

1. It's sad when a child who loves to sing lacks the _____ for it.

2. Some writers have the ability to _____ fantastic scenes, while others can write only about what they have experienced.

3. Taking tests is an _____ part of student life.

4. People who have a problem with _____ follow the motto, "Don't do today what you can put off until tomorrow."

5. Politicians often slur each other by making _____ rather than direct statements, so they can deny that they said it.

6. Chinese men were _____ to wear their hair in a pigtail as a sign of humiliation after being conquered by the Manchus in 1644; however, after the Manchus were defeated in 1912, the pigtail had become so popular that Chinese men didn't want to give it up.

7. Coca-Cola was so named because one of its original _____ was coca, the source of cocaine.

8. When you apply for a driver's license, you will be tested to determine your _____ to operate a motor vehicle.

9. Because men and women often have _____ training in how to get what they want, by college age most people will view the same behavior as more aggressive coming from a woman than coming from a man.

10. Businesses have been forced to _____ policies to prevent sexual harassment.

17 Causes of Infection: Pathogens

Comprehension Check

Matching

Write the letter before the pathogen in the space before each disease.

_____ 1. AIDS   a. rickettsia

_____ 2. tuberculosis   b. bacteria

_____ 3. athlete's foot   c. virus

_____ 4. pinworm   d. fungus

_____ 5. typhoid fever   e. protozoa

_____ 6. amoebic dysentery f. parasitic worm

Short Answer

7. Describe the variations in incubation periods for viral diseases.

_____

_____

8. Which pathogen is the most common cause of contagious diseases?

_____

9. What are the problems concerning drug treatments for viral diseases?

_____

_____

_____

10. What are some problems in the treatment of bacterial diseases?

_____

_____

_____

Essay

Describe each pathogen and give at least one method of transmission for each one. Use a separate piece of paper.

Vocabulary Check

Write the best word from the following list in the blank in each sentence below.

microorganisms   respiratory   toxins   prostration   recurrent

1. Symptoms of heat _____ include dizziness, nausea, low body temperature, and clammy skin.

2. Many people have a _____ nightmare in which they have signed up for a class and then forgotten all about it until just before the final exam.

3. Asthma causes such _____ symptoms as wheezing, coughing, and difficulty in breathing.

4. People cannot catch colds at the North Pole in winter; the temperature is so low that none of the standard disease-causing _____ can survive.

5. Molds, fungi, and bacteria can be desirable, producing cheese, yogurt, and wine. Others release _____: for example, salmonella causes food poisoning, and botulism is deadly.

18 Family Violence

Comprehension Check

True–False

Mark T or F.

_____ 1. Sexual violence has decreased in recent decades.

_____ 2. In some jurisdictions it is legally impossible for a husband to rape his wife.

_____ 3. Research indicates that most college students consider date rape a major problem on campus.

_____ 4. The rape shield law protects the perpetrator when the victim has a long history of sexual activity.

Multiple Choice

Circle the letter before the best answer to each question below.

5. Children should be taught how to deal with abusive behavior from
   a. strangers.
   b. friends of the family.
   c. relatives.
   d. all of the above.

6. The author implies that wife beating is most common among the
   a. rich.
   b. poor.
   c. middle class.
   d. foreign born.

7. The author implies that family violence is considered
   a. abnormal and unacceptable to society.
   b. normal and acceptable to many Americans.
   c. acceptable to social scientists in some forms but not others.
   d. more acceptable than it once was.

8. Which forms of family violence do Americans tend to accept as normal?

   a. physical punishment of children

   b. siblings fighting

   c. wife beating

   d. all of the above

9. The causes of wife beating include

   a. psychological disorders.

   b. history of violence.

   c. unemployment and poor education.

   d. all of the above.

10. Factors that contribute to violence in the family include

   a. high incidence of violence in society.

   b. cultural attitudes that accept violence in certain situations.

   c. sexist attitudes toward the roles of husband and wife.

   d. all of the above.

Essay

Describe the types and the frequency of violent crimes against family members, friends, and acquaintances as they were described in the reading selection.

_____

_____

_____

_____

_____

_____

_____

_____

_____

_____

_____

_____

_____

_____

_____

_____

_____

_____

_____

_____

_____

_____

_____

_____

_____

_____

_____

_____

_____

Vocabulary Check

Write the best word from the following list in the blank in each sentence below.

perpetrator   dysfunctional   interaction   traumatic   substantiate

accessible   innuendo   implicit   ambiguous   callousness

1. Psychologists refer to families that include such behaviors as child abuse, alcoholism, and neglect as _____.

2. In good friendships there is an _____ understanding that you can call upon the friend when you are in need.

3. The kinds of off-color jokes told in most offices rely more on _____ than on obscenity.

4. Hiding your valuables or keeping them in a safe makes them less _____ to burglars.

5. John Dillinger was the _____ of so many criminal acts during the 1920s that the FBI declared him Public Enemy Number 1.

6. Being in a serious car accident is a very _____ experience.

7. There is an _____ between the food you eat and the drugs you take; for example, most drugs, especially antibiotics, should be taken on an empty stomach. However, other drugs, especially the pain relievers, should be taken with meals.

8. If you are accused of a crime, but you were somewhere else when it was committed, you hope someone can _____ your alibi.

9. Genghis Khan cultivated _____ in his army; after each victory every soldier had to murder as many as 50 civilians and collect their ears in sacks as proof.

10. Sometimes politicians are _____ on purpose, so they can avoid taking a clear stand.

19   Why We Sleep

Comprehension Check

True–False

Mark T or F.

_____ 1. Sleepiness depends partly on how long you have gone without sleep and partly on the time of day.

_____ 2. If a person stays up all night, he or she is usually very sleepy around 4 A.M., but less sleepy around 7 A.M.

_____ 3. You can infer from the reading that scientists don't really know why we sleep.

_____ 4. It seems that both theories of sleep are correct.

_____ 5. Logical reasoning is usually better at night than in the morning.

Multiple Choice

Circle the letter before the best answer to each question below.

6. The repair and restoration theory of why we sleep does not explain
   a. why resting without sleeping is enough to restore the muscles and other tissues.
   b. why the amount of sleep needed is not much different after a day of extreme activity than after a day of inactivity.
   c. why some people sleep less than others do.
   d. all of the above.

7. According to the reading, human beings
   a. cannot stay awake more than 24 hours.
   b. can go for at least 11 days without sleep.
   c. suffer physical damage if they go more than a week without sleep.
   d. become brainwashed after several days without sleep.

8. You can infer from the reading that the main reason some people can tolerate sleep deprivation better than others is that
   a. people differ in the amount of sleep they need.
   b. people differ in their evolutionary levels.
   c. some people work harder than others.
   d. all of the above are true.

Short Answer

9. Give an example of an animal that sleeps a lot and explain why, according to evolutionary theory.

_____

_____

_____

10. Give an example of an animal that sleeps very little and explain why, according to evolutionary theory.

_____

_____

Essay

Explain both theories of why we sleep, and give the evidence supporting each one. Use a separate piece of paper.

Vocabulary Check

Write the best word from the following list in the blank in each sentence below.

restoration   ordeal   unscrupulous   superimpose   circadian

1. Jet lag is caused by disrupting the _____ cycle.

2. The word "_____" originally referred to a trial in which the accused person was exposed to physical dangers such as being thrown into deep water with weights attached to his body. If he was innocent, he was supposed to be protected by God; if he died, he was guilty.

3. Doctors usually take credit for cures that are really a result of the body's own processes of _____.

4. If you _____ yellow cellophane over blue cellophane and look through them both, you see green.

5. If you are selling your house it is considered _____, and in some states illegal, to conceal any known defects from the buyer.

20   Ethics and the Consumer

Comprehension Check

True–False

Mark T or F.

_____ 1. The author believes consumers should act ethically because dishonest behavior causes prices to rise and hurt other consumers.

_____ 2. The author would consider it unethical for consumers to band together to boycott companies whose policies they disagree with.

_____ 3. The author implies that consumers are less ethical than businesses are.

_____ 4. The author implies that it's all right to behave unethically toward a business that is unethical.

_____ 5. The author implies that most people's moral convictions about right and wrong are less ethical than they were 20 years ago.

Multiple Choice

Circle the letter before the best answer to each question below.

6. The author implies that it's easiest to cheat when

   a. you are unlikely to get caught.

   b. you don't personally know the merchant you are cheating.

   c. no one is likely to find out you cheated.

   d. all of the above are true.

7. Which of the following would the author consider unethical?

   a. participating in a class-action suit when you had only a small amount of damages

   b. refusing to buy products that were made by non-union labor

   c. reporting a salesclerk for poor service

   d. making a dinner reservation and not showing up

8. Which of the following would most people find easiest to cheat without pangs of conscience?

   a. the phone company

   b. a charity

   c. a neighborhood restaurant

   d. a local grocery store

9. The power of the consumer to drive prices up can be used for good as well as bad. Which of the following is an example of using consumer power ethically?

   a. paying more for foods grown without pesticides

   b. refusing to buy cosmetics that were tested on animals

   c. preferring to buy the products of companies that have minorities in top management positions

   d. all of the above

10. An example of unethical consumer behavior *not* mentioned in the reading selection is

   a. keeping items that were accidentally not paid for.

   b. filing nuisance lawsuits.

   c. returning items after damaging them.

   d. shoplifting.

Essay

Discuss the ethical responsibilities of consumers in today's marketplace. Use a separate piece of paper.

Vocabulary Check

Write the best word from the following list in the blank in each sentence below.

aphorism   scenario   trivial   statute   entity

boon   alleged   abstract   reservations   constraints

1. The word "_____" came from the Latin "tri" (three) and "via" (road); apparently ancient Romans liked to stand around and chitchat near the intersections of roads.

2. "You can't judge a book by its cover" is an _____.

3. The Pledge of Allegiance contains _____ ideas such as liberty and justice, which children find difficult to understand.

4. The invention of the copy machine was a _____ for secretaries, who no longer had to struggle with carbon paper.

5. In a typical college acquaintance rape _____, the man and woman are at a party and consuming alcohol.

6. Because a corporation is a legal _____, it may enter into contracts, buy and sell property, etc. as if it were a person.

7. A _____ in Kentucky requires every citizen to take a bath once a year.

8. The church, the family, and the law all put _____ on our behavior.

9. It is normal to have a few mental _____ about big decisions such as buying or selling a house.

10. The defendant _____ that he was temporarily insane when he committed the crime.

How Many Prisons Must We Build to Feel Secure?

21

Comprehension Check

True–False

Mark T or F.

_____ 1. The Washington state "three strikes" law is stronger than the federal government's version.

_____ 2. The reading discusses the problems with the Washington state law.

_____ 3. The Washington state law gives the same penalty to "third strikers" whether they are robbers or murderers.

_____ 4. The state version and the federal version cover the same crimes.

Multiple Choice

Circle the letter before the best answer to each question below.

5. The author implies that

   a. as crime in Washington decreases, crime in neighboring states will increase.

   b. judges have the ability to decide when to apply the three strikes law.

   c. the three strikes law will not increase the number of prisoners.

   d. all of the above are true.

6. The author implies that

   a. many small-time crooks are caught by the three strikes law.

   b. the cost of imprisoning the three strikes offenders is too high.

   c. the Washington state law is catching the right criminals.

   d. new prisons will have to be built to accommodate the three strikes offenders.

7. The author implies that

    a. the law excludes sex offenders.

    b. only the governor can pardon those who have "struck out."

    c. before the three strikes law many sentences were too severe, and many were too lenient.

    d. the three strikes law discriminates racially.

Short Answer

What are three types of offenses the author mentions being targeted by the Washington law?

  8. _____

  9. _____

10. _____

Essay

Why does the author think the United States should opt for a tough three strikes law like Washington state's?

_____

_____

_____

_____

_____

_____

_____

_____

_____

_____

_____

_____

_____

_____

Vocabulary Check

Write the best word from the following list in the blank in each sentence below.

rousing   initiative   ironically   incarceration   concede

abducted   assailants   reaffirm   clemency   deters

1. Supporters of the death penalty say that it _____ people from committing capital crimes.

2. _____, seizing imported drugs at the borders increases domestic production because it drives the prices up.

3. The returning war hero received a _____ welcome in her hometown.

4. It is usually people with wealthy relatives who are _____ for ransom.

5. With "three strikes" laws, judges will no longer be able to show _____ to offenders who can be rehabilitated.

6. An _____ often gets on the ballot as a result of a petition signed by a sufficient percentage of the voters.

7. When the results of an election are in, the loser is expected to publicly _____.

8. Because they fear revenge, crime victims are sometimes unwilling to identify their _____.

9. _____ of criminals serves several purposes in addition to protecting society: conservatives see it as a means of punishment, and liberals see it as an opportunity for rehabilitation.

10. Some married couples have a second wedding later in life to _____ their vows.

22 A Case for Discretion

Comprehension Check

True–False

Mark T or F.

_____ 1. Those opposing mandatory minimum sentences such as "three strikes" are groups known to have a liberal bias.

_____ 2. The author implies that the penalties for nonviolent drug offenses are unreasonable.

_____ 3. The author implies that allowing judges to use their judgment in sentencing is good for society as well as for the defendants.

_____ 4. A solution that would have prevented Steven White's suicide would have been to limit "three strikes" to violent offenders.

_____ 5. The author implies that we have laws that unfairly penalize African-Americans.

Multiple Choice

Circle the letter before the best answer to each question below.

6. The example of Steven White's suicide supports the argument that

  a. "three strikes" punishments often don't fit the crime.

  b. violent criminals are often released to make room for nonviolent drug offenders.

  c. suicide costs the taxpayers less than incarceration.

  d. many groups oppose mandatory minimum sentencing.

7. The author implies that

  a. many criminals can be rehabilitated.

  b. rehabilitation is cheaper than incarceration.

  c. judges make better decisions than prosecutors.

  d. all of the above are true.

8. The sentence that the author received from Judge Frankel allowed him to

   a. repay the victims of his crime.

   b. repay society with money and community service.

   c. be supervised by a probation officer.

   d. do all of the above.

Short Answer

9. What points is the author making by using the example of Stephanie Lomax?

   _____

   _____

10. What point is the author making by using the example of his own recent trial?

    _____

    _____

Essay

Why is the author opposed to mandatory minimum sentences?

_____

_____

_____

_____

_____

_____

_____

_____

_____

_____

_____

Vocabulary Check

Write the best word from the following list in the blank in each sentence below.

discretion   misdemeanor   sporadic   culpability   mitigate

mete   unsavory   relapse   compassion   restitution

1. The good fairy in *Sleeping Beauty* was able to _____ the bad fairy's curse by changing it so that the princess would fall asleep instead of dying.

2. One can never make _____ for a murder.

3. After the flu, you should take care of yourself so you don't have a _____.

4. People in positions of authority over children, such as parents and teachers, _____ out rewards and punishments as a way of teaching them how to behave.

5. Most obese people make _____ attempts at dieting, which usually fail.

6. The purpose of a trial is to determine the _____ of the defendant.

7. You should stay away from back alleys that are inhabited by _____ characters.

8. The saying "_____ is the better part of valor" means that you should use judgment about when to show bravery.

9. In California and many other states, possession of a small amount of marijuana is a _____.

10. Several religions teach that human shortcomings should be treated with _____ rather than anger.

23 No-Win Situations

Comprehension Check

Multiple Choice

Circle the letter before the best answer to each of the following questions.

1. The writer of the selection wrote a book called
   a. *The Competitive Edge.*
   b. *No Context.*
   c. *No Contest.*
   d. *Don't Compete.*

2. The author believes competition
   a. undermines self-esteem.
   b. poisons relationships.
   c. holds us back from doing our best.
   d. does all of the above.

3. The author talks about Terry Orlick, who is a
   a. famous author.
   b. sports psychologist.
   c. professional athlete.
   d. physical education teacher.

4. When Orlick taught a group of children noncompetitive games
   a. two-thirds of the girls liked them.
   b. two-thirds of all the children liked them.
   c. two-thirds of the boys liked them.
   d. none of the children enjoyed them.

5. From the reading we can infer that the author
   a. believes he is a "loser."
   b. is a coach of a sports team.
   c. believes physical activity is important.
   d. feels that periodic competition such as on the weekend is acceptable.

6. If the author were a member of a school board he would

   a. favor programs that would encourage women to participate in sports.

   b. eliminate all physical education.

   c. favor less competitive physical education programs.

   d. hire only female coaches for team sports.

7. Which activity would the author be most likely to participate in?

   a. volleyball

   b. recreational swimming

   c. tennis

   d. touch football

8. We can infer from the reading that the author would

   a. rather play football than monopoly.

   b. enjoy working in sales.

   c. favor schools that don't have grades.

   d. enjoy being a professional athlete.

Short Answer

9. Give an example of a cooperative activity that offers a physical workout (you may make it up).

   _____

10. Give an example of a cooperative activity that allows us to test our accomplishment (you may make it up).

   _____

Essay

How and why does the author think that we ought to change the types of sports and games that most children participate in?

_____

_____

_____

_____

_____

_____

_____

_____

_____

_____

_____

_____

_____

_____

_____

_____

_____

_____

Vocabulary Check

Write the best word from the following list in the blank in each sentence below.

counterproductive   benign   inherent   malicious   camaraderie

gloat   epithets   detest   conducive   aberration

1. Because children often _____ spinach, parents are wise to let them watch Popeye eat his spinach in the cartoon.

2. The comment was meant to be _____, but it actually hurt the feelings of several people.

3. It can be _____ to stay up all night to work on a paper, because you make more mistakes when you are tired.

4. Some studies have shown that listening to classical music is more _____ to studying than listening to rap music.

5. Children can be very _____ in teasing other children because they have trouble imagining themselves in the other person's place.

6. It is considered poor sportsmanship to _____ after winning a game.

7. Using rude _____ when talking to another person can lead to a fight.

8. The _____ among the co-workers grew stronger after they formed a bowling team.

9. There is an _____ assumption that a clergyman is honest.

10. Having six toes on one foot is an _____.

24   Who Wins? Who Cares?

Comprehension Check

Multiple Choice

Circle the letter before the best answer to each question below.

1. The author calls the highly competitive mentality

    a. the "Superbowl" mentality.

    b. the "Who Wins, Who Cares" mentality.

    c. the "Ends Justify the Means" mentality.

    d. the "Super Bull" mentality.

2. The author says that

    a. losing does not mean you have failed.

    b. women would rather die than lose.

    c. trying to win is trying to upset the other person.

    d. women don't like to compete.

3. The author doesn't like

    a. losing to anyone when competing.

    b. games that require quick thinking.

    c. games that are not competitive.

    d. games in which "losers" are no longer allowed to play.

4. The author says she

    a. hates losing.

    b. has fond memories of every time she won a game.

    c. has few memories of victories or losses.

    d. thinks losing games as a child prepared her for more serious losses in life.

5. From the reading you can infer that women

    a. are becoming more like men as they enter the job market.

    b. are superior athletes compared to men.

    c. are not raised to enjoy athletic sports.

    d. are better "sports" than men when they lose.

6. From the reading you can infer that most women

    a. would make good coaches of professional sports teams because they would emphasize playing for fun.

    b. would not be respected by male athletes because they are not as talented.

    c. would tend not to make good coaches of professional sports teams because they wouldn't play to win at all costs.

    d. have more difficulty than men trying to make friends with a competitor.

7. From the reading you can infer that

    a. women are inferior athletes.

    b. women should be allowed to play in all professional sports.

    c. if you understand the meaning of competition, winning will not be so important.

    d. women are going to become more like men as time goes on.

8. Who would probably believe in the proverb "It's not whether you win or lose, it's how you play the game"?

    a. gamblers

    b. women

    c. coaches for varsity sports teams

    d. men

Short Answer

Name some bad effects of the "winning is the only thing" myth.

9. _____

10. _____

Essay

Why does the author say that competition can be good?

_____

_____

_____

_____

_____

_____

_____

_____

_____

_____

_____

_____

_____

_____

_____

_____

_____

_____

Vocabulary Check

A. Write the best word from the following list in the blank in each sentence below.

rapport   **classically**   **tantamount**   **connotes**

eschewed   **seductive**   **ascribed**   **devastating**

1. The student _____ her good grades to studying hard every night.

2. Failing a class can be a _____ experience.

3. To an overeater, a well-stocked refrigerator is very _____.

4. Couples in a good relationship develop a _____ that is the envy of their friends.

5. Passing a friend without saying "hello" is _____ to an insult.

6. The word *mother,* besides meaning a female parent, _____ feelings of warmth and caring.

7. The alley cat _____ all areas he knew were inhabited by dogs.

8. Jumping in puddles on a rainy day is a _____ childlike behavior.

B. Write the best word from the following list in the blank in each sentence below.

polarize   steroid   myriad   cliché
ritualistic   intuit   divisive

9. A _____ is an overused expression.

10. Successful poker players _____ how good a hand their opponents have.

11. Taking sides on an issue can often _____ a community.

12. A _____ of animals can be found in any large zoo.

13. _____ statements can bring disagreement to an otherwise agreeable discussion.

14. Athletes can be disqualified from some competition if illegal _____ use is detected.

15. A handshake is a _____ greeting in many countries.

25 The Amazing Smoke Screen

Comprehension Check

True–False

Mark T or F.

_____ 1. In saying that there are now more ex-smokers than smokers, the author implies that nicotine addiction can be broken.

_____ 2. The author believes that smoking causes higher public health costs.

_____ 3. The author suspects that tobacco advertising mainly determines which brands people smoke, not whether they smoke.

_____ 4. Most Americans believe that tobacco companies are more responsible for smoking-related illnesses than smokers are.

Multiple Choice

Circle the letter before the best answer to each question below.

5. According to the author, the main advantage of the agreement between the state attorneys general and the tobacco companies is that it

   a. limits cigarette advertising to teens.

   b. makes the tobacco companies pay more of the public health costs of smoking.

   c. will reduce smoking.

   d. provides closure to the anti-smoking crusade.

6. The author implies that which of the following groups are participating in camouflaging the truth about the anti-smoking campaign?

   a. politicians

   b. lawyers

   c. public-health advocates

   d. all of the above

7. The effect of the $200 billion payment by tobacco companies is

    a. to hurt the tobacco industry by lowering stock prices.

    b. to aid the tobacco industry by raising stock prices.

    c. to neither hurt nor help the tobacco industry.

    d. impossible to determine.

8. Which of the following statements is *false*?

    a. Government taxes smokers.

    b. Tobacco companies pass their costs on to smokers.

    c. Most smokers have low incomes.

    d. Most Americans do not understand the dangers of smoking.

Short Answer

Fill in the blanks.

9. What is the "reverse Robin Hood arrangement"?

    _____

    _____

10. What does the author mean by "a gullible public aided by a pliant press"?

    _____

    _____

Essay

Explain what the author means by "the amazing smoke screen." Give the author's major arguments. Use a separate piece of paper.

Vocabulary Check

A. Write the best word from the following list in the blank in each sentence below.

closure   **parody**   **imposed**   **contention**   **bolster**

advocates   **hypocrisy**   **gratification**   **disheartening**   **mandate**

1. Heavy penalties are _____ for drunk driving.

2. Bragging is an attempt to _____ one's self-esteem.

3. It is _____ to go to a fabulous buffet when you are on a diet.

4. The newly rich sometimes buy expensive but tasteless houses, furniture, and clothing in a _____ of the upper classes.

5. One of the reasons that apologies are needed is that they help achieve _____ to a conflict.

6. "Three strikes" laws _____ life imprisonment for repeat offenders.

7. Saving money means postponing the immediate _____ of spending money in order to provide for the future.

8. _____ of the death penalty argue that executions reduce the chance that other people will commit capital crimes.

9. It is _____ when a politician who supports family values divorces his wife to marry a younger, prettier woman.

10. It was the president's _____ that the other party was responsible for crime, poverty, and the drug problem.

B.   Write the best word from the following list in the blank in each sentence below.

diverting   dubious   compensate   sanctified   enshrined
arbitrator   rebates   covet   gullible   pliant

11. The memory of Elvis Presley is _____ in Graceland, his former home.

12. People who get their feelings of self-worth from their financial status usually _____ expensive cars and jewelry.

13. Teenagers who make up stories about why they stayed out too late hope their parents are _____.

14. Research shows that very few people who send in the paperwork for _____ actually receive any money.

15. The old-fashioned idea of marriage is that husbands should dominate and wives should be _____.

16. An _____ can help you resolve a dispute without going to court.

17. American culture in the 1950s _____ Mom, the flag, and apple pie.

18. Fad diets have _____ value in long-term weight loss.

19. Graft can mean _____ public money to a public official's personal use.

20. If the government takes your land to build a highway, they have to _____ you for the value of what they took.

26   Remarks on the Tobacco Settlement

Comprehension Check

True–False

Mark T or F.

_____ 1. President Clinton believes that the group who should lead the struggle against tobacco is Congress.

_____ 2. "Replacement smokers" means new smokers replacing those who quit or died.

_____ 3. President Clinton outlines the specific steps that Congress should take to protect children from tobacco.

_____ 4. President Clinton blames the Republicans for the lack of progress on tobacco legislation.

Multiple Choice

Circle the letter before the best answer to each question below.

5. President Clinton considers the 1998 tobacco settlement to be

   a. a smoke screen.

   b. a milestone in an ongoing struggle.

   c. the end of a long journey.

   d. a drop in the bucket.

6. The main obstacle to national tobacco legislation is

   a. the tobacco lobby.

   b. tobacco farmers.

   c. political partisanship.

   d. the Supreme Court.

7. Approximately how many children start to smoke each day?

   a. 300

   b. 3,000

   c. 30,000

   d. 300,000

8. The group mostly responsible for the 1998 tobacco settlement was

    a. state attorneys general.

    b. the FDA.

    c. Congress.

    d. the Supreme Court.

Short Answer

Fill in the blanks.

9. What is the thesis of President Clinton's speech?

_____

_____

_____

10. What did the Clinton administration contribute to the anti-tobacco struggle?

_____

_____

_____

_____

Essay

What does President Clinton say about the past, present, and future of the anti-tobacco campaign?

_____

_____

_____

_____

_____

_____

_____

_____

_____

_____

_____

_____

_____

_____

Vocabulary Check

Write the best word from the following list in the blank in each sentence below.

milestone   momentum   partisanship   comprehensive   jurisdiction

1. The Nineteenth Amendment to the Constitution, passed in 1920, was an important _____ in the struggle for civil rights; it gave all women in the United States the right to vote.

2. _____ insurance covers a number of risks in the same policy.

3. In physics, _____ refers to the amount of motion in an object, which is the product of the size and speed.

4. The Federal Aviation Administration (FAA) has _____ over air traffic.

5. _____ goes too far when the good of the party is placed before the good of the nation.

27 ▪ Acting to End a Life Is Sometimes Justified

Comprehension Check

Multiple Choice

Circle the letter before the best answer to each question below.

1. An example of passive euthanasia is

   a. giving the patient an overdose of drugs.

   b. giving the patient an injection that will kill him or her.

   c. leaving an overdose of drugs with the patient, in case the patient wants to kill himself or herself.

   d. stopping treatment of the patient.

2. Barnard defines life as

   a. having a heartbeat.

   b. having brainwaves.

   c. breathing.

   d. having joy in living.

3. Barnard states that euthanasia has become an increasing focus of debate because

   a. more doctors are quietly practicing it.

   b. it has caused a large number of malpractice suits.

   c. there have been medical breakthroughs that can prolong life artificially.

   d. many doctors have been arrested for practicing it.

4. To those who believe that God is against euthanasia, Barnard says that

   a. a merciful God would approve of it.

   b. prolonging life artificially is also playing God.

   c. we do not know how God interprets life.

   d. all of the above are true.

5. Barnard seems to believe that doctors

   a. cannot prolong life.

   b. never practice euthanasia now.

   c. should accept some responsibility for their patients' lives.

   d. should prolong life, hoping for new medical breakthroughs for the terminally ill.

6. Barnard suggests that people who are against euthanasia are really

   a. ethical.

   b. cowardly.

   c. vicious.

   d. brave.

7. After reading the selection, one might conclude that Barnard

   a. has practiced active euthanasia without admitting it.

   b. would not practice passive euthanasia even if it were legal.

   c. wouldn't practice active euthanasia in any situation.

   d. would practice active euthanasia if it were legal.

8. Barnard feels that the public

   a. is naive about euthanasia.

   b. believes in active euthanasia.

   c. is convinced that active euthanasia occurs constantly.

   d. should sign statements telling their doctors not to administer life-prolonging treatment in terminal cases.

Short Answer

What are the two main types of euthanasia discussed in the reading?

9. _____

10. _____

Essay

Why does the author support active euthanasia?

_____

_____

_____

_____

_____

_____

_____

_____

_____

_____

_____

_____

_____

_____

_____

_____

Vocabulary Check

A. Write the best word from the following list in the blank in each sentence below.

salient   euthanasia   elicit   refrained

compos mentis   arbiter   theological   glib

1. Veterinarians have been practicing _____ on people's pets for many years.

2. The most _____ feature of the blue whale is its enormous length, which can equal three Greyhound buses.

3. Discussions about sex, politics, and religion can be relied on to _____ strong feelings.

4. A plea of insanity will not stand up if the court has ruled the accused

_____ .

5. A baseball umpire is the _____ in close decisions during

a game.

6. Becoming a clergyman takes many years of _____ study.

7. I _____ from eating the whole box of cookies because I was

on a diet.

8. Used-car salespeople often appear _____ in TV

commercials.

B. Write the best word from the following list in the blank in each sentence
below.

intercede   welter   qualified   intercurrent

gradations   squeamishness   humanitarians

9. Examples of famous _____ are Albert Schweitzer, Mother

Teresa, Mahatma Gandhi, and Martin Luther King, Jr.

10. Parents often give their _____ consent when teenagers start

dating. They have to know where they are, whom they are with, and

when they will be home.

11. An example of an _____ infection is when a terminal cancer

patient dies of pneumonia.

12. The intensities of most colors come in many _____ , from

very pale to very dark.

13. _____ is not a good quality in a doctor or nurse.

14. People who _____ when a husband and wife are arguing

often lose the friendship of both.

15. The _____ of outdated laws still on the books includes one

that makes it illegal to hunt camels in Arizona.

28   In Crisis, She Rejected Plea to Expedite Dying

Comprehension Check

Multiple Choice

Circle the letter before the best answer to each question below.

1. Kübler-Ross went to Switzerland in early summer because

    a. her mother had sent a telegram saying she was ill.

    b. her mother hadn't seen her grandchildren in years.

    c. it was a planned vacation.

    d. she was concerned about her mother.

2. When Kübler-Ross arrived in Switzerland, she found that her mother was

    a. dying.

    b. dead.

    c. in fine health.

    d. depressed.

3. Closing down the family home made Kübler-Ross

    a. reconsider her mother's request.

    b. deny that her mother was dying.

    c. afraid of death.

    d. understand life and death better.

4. After Mrs. Kübler had her stroke, she could

    a. use sign language with her hands.

    b. talk with great difficulty.

    c. not communicate at all.

    d. blink her eyes and barely use her left hand.

5. The reading implies that Kübler-Ross

    a. is skeptical of extrasensory perception.

    b. believes in extrasensory perception.

    c. went to a psychic about her mother.

    d. saw a ghost.

6. Mrs. Kübler's relationship with Elisabeth seemed

    a. impersonal and cold.

    b. warm and close.

    c. not so warm as with her other daughters.

    d. abnormal for a mother and daughter.

7. The last time Kübler-Ross saw her mother before her mother's stroke she thought

    a. they were arguing.

    b. they parted on good terms.

    c. her mother was becoming senile.

    d. her mother was in poor health.

8. If Kübler-Ross were to develop an illness similar to her mother's, she would probably

    a. request euthanasia.

    b. change her mind about euthanasia.

    c. see her illness as a valuable experience.

    d. go to Switzerland, where euthanasia is legal.

Short Answer

Elisabeth Kübler-Ross believed that people should be kept alive as long as two criteria were met. They are:

9. _____

10. _____

Essay

Why does Kübler-Ross take the position she takes on euthanasia?

_____

_____

_____

_____

_____

_____

_____

_____

_____

_____

_____

Vocabulary Check

Write the best word from the following list in the blank in each sentence below.

expedite   stimulus   inexplicable   obliged   affirmative

objets d'art   salutary   recoiling   predecease   commonweal

1. Before you give an _____ answer to a request for a loan, be sure you clarify when it will be repaid.

2. When somebody does you a favor, you may feel _____ to them.

3. To _____ solving criminal cases, the police look for eyewitnesses.

4. Priceless _____ are found in museums around the world.

5. The increase in crime is a problem affecting the _____.

6. Your will should have additional beneficiaries in case your children _____ you.

7. People start thinking about the supernatural when _____ events occur.

8. A proper diet is _____.

9. _____ when someone startles you is a natural defense mechanism.

10. Babies show a startle response to a _____ of loud noise.

29   The Dream, the Stars and Dr. King

Comprehension Check

True–False

Mark T or F.

_____ 1. Affirmative action has been a failure.

_____ 2. According to the author, conservatives have a plan to solve the country's economic problems.

_____ 3. The author implies that liberals know how to solve the country's economic problems.

_____ 4. Conservatives seek to distract and divide Americans.

Multiple Choice

Circle the letter before the best answer to each question below.

5. The war on poverty was never fought because

   a. conservatives opposed it.

   b. we spent the money on the war in Vietnam.

   c. the amount of poverty was just too great.

   d. Dr. King was killed.

6. The American economy is

   a. increasing the gap between rich and poor.

   b. making people feel less secure.

   c. reducing the living standards of more and more Americans.

   d. doing all of the above.

7. Compared to the 1960s, the country is

   a. poorer.

   b. more optimistic.

   c. more racist.

   d. less hopeful.

8. According to the author, Newt Gingrich and Bob Dole are

   a. ignorant of history.

   b. lying about history.

   c. addressing important economic issues.

   d. trying to unite the country.

Short Answer

9. What does Jesse Jackson mean when he says that "political predators flourish, feeding on old hates, pandering to old fears"?

   _____

   _____

10. What are the historical facts about opportunities for African Americans in the United States?

   _____

   _____

   _____

Essay

Why does Jesse Jackson think about affirmative action programs and about the current attack on them? Use a separate piece of paper.

Vocabulary Check

Write the best word from the following list in the blank in each sentence below.

affirmative action   commemorate   suppress   legacy   squandering

pander   intractable   eradicate   seminal   apartheid

1. The word _____ comes from a word that means "separate" in Afrikaans, a language of South Africa.

2. _____ programs included giving preference to equally qualified women and minorities in hiring, in college admission, and in awarding business contracts.

3. We now have a national holiday to _____ Dr. Martin Luther King.

4. Censorship of the press exists to _____ opinions or language the people in power don't like.

5. Nearly everyone wishes we could _____ poverty, ignorance, and suffering.

6. Charles Darwin was a _____ thinker in the field of evolution.

7. Allowances should be given to train children to manage their money instead of _____ it on candy and video games.

8. The antique clock was a _____ from my grandmother.

9. Opponents of gambling argue that state lotteries _____ to the fantasies of people too ignorant to understand the odds against winning, usually the poor.

10. Ethnic hatred has proven an _____ problem, leading to bloodshed in areas such as Ireland, Bosnia, and parts of Africa.

30 | Spiral of Silence

Comprehension Check

True–False

Mark T or F.

_____ 1. Lynch views white males as helpless victims of discrimination.

_____ 2. Lynch implies that racial imbalance in the workforce is not necessarily evidence of employer discrimination.

_____ 3. Lynch is opposed to "diversity management."

_____ 4. Lynch believes that affirmative action involves putting up with unqualified or incompetent workers.

Multiple Choice

Circle the letter before the best answer to each question below.

5. The reason most white males put up with affirmative action is that

   a. they feel that no one will help them.

   b. they don't have the resources to litigate.

   c. the EEOC discourages them.

   d. all of the above are true.

6. The reason white males lack a class consciousness is that

   a. the mass media ignores their problem.

   b. the social sciences ignore their problem.

   c. nobody is sympathetic to their problem.

   d. all of the above are true.

7. Most people who read Lynch's books are likely to be

   a. conservatives.

   b. liberals.

   c. social scientists.

   d. in the media.

TESTS

8. Lynch believes that affirmative action requires

   a. quotas.

   b. reverse discrimination.

   c. race-norming.

   d. all of the above.

Short Answer

9. What does Lynch mean by a "spiral of silence"?

   _____

   _____

10. What is meant by the following statement: "A further factor in this male paralysis: the peculiar male psychology itself."?

   _____

Essay

How does the author explain affirmative action and the white male response to it? Use a separate piece of paper.

Vocabulary Check

A. Write the best word from the following list in the blank in each sentence below.

appease   litigation   stifle   latent

judiciously   ideological   intimidating   defect

1. During the days of the Soviet Union, ballet dancers and other artists who went on tour would regularly _____ to the West.

2. "Henpecked husbands" in cartoons give in to _____ their nagging wives.

3. Parents must use punishment _____, or it will lose its effect.

4. Lawyers earn a living from _____.

5. Dictatorships usually take over newspaper and radio and TV stations so they can _____ any opposition.

6. Having a large, muscular person give you a hostile stare is very

_____.

7. Republicans and Democrats in Congress must overcome some of their _____ differences in order to do their jobs and pass legislation.

8. A child with a _____ talent in music should be encouraged to develop it.

B. Write the best word from the following list in the blank in each sentence below.

subverted   Orwellian   prima facie evidence   craven

diffused   fanatical   acquiesce

9. She was so _____ about her diet that she refused to take a bite of her own wedding cake.

10. The feathers all over the cat's face were _____ that he ate the bird.

11. If your child asks you to take over his paper route while he has the flu, you will probably _____ reluctantly.

12. The ideal of social justice has been _____ by people who will sell out for money.

13. Lying to avoid facing the consequences of your action is a

_____ response.

14. The toxic chemicals got into the groundwater and

_____ throughout the city.

15. The Soviet Union under Stalin was an _____ society in which individual rights were not important.

Progress Chart

Record your score in each column on the next page as a percent by dividing the number correct by the number of questions. The Comprehension Checks all have 10 questions, so you can use the 10-question column below. The Vocabulary Checks have either 5, 10, 15, or 20 questions, so the percentages are:

5 questions	10 questions	15 questions	20 questions
5/5 = 100%	10/10 = 100%	15/15 = 100%	20/20 = 100%
		14/15 = 93%	19/20 = 95%
	9/10 = 90%		18/20 = 90%
		13/15 = 87%	17/20 = 85%
4/5 = 80%	8/10 = 80%	12/15 = 80%	16/20 = 80%
		11/15 = 73%	15/20 = 75%
	7/10 = 70%		14/20 = 70%
		10/15 = 67%	13/20 = 65%
3/5 = 60%	6/10 = 60%	9/15 = 60%	12/20 = 60%
		8/15 = 53%	11/20 = 55%
	5/10 = 50%		10/20 = 50%
		7/15 = 47%	9/20 = 45%
2/5 = 40%	4/10 = 40%	6/15 = 40%	8/20 = 40%
		5/15 = 33%	7/20 = 35%
	3/10 = 30%		6/20 = 30%
		4/15 = 27%	5/20 = 25%
1/5 = 20%	2/10 = 20%	3/15 = 20%	4/20 = 20%
		2/15 = 13%	3/20 = 15%
	1/10 = 10%		2/20 = 10%
		1/15 = 7%	1/20 = 5%

PROGRESS CHART

Comprehension Checks	Vocabulary Checks
1.	1.
2.	2.
3.	3.
4.	4.
5.	5.
6.	6.
7.	7.
8.	8.
9.	9.
10.	10.
11.	11.
12.	12.
13.	13.
14.	14.
15.	15.
16.	16.
17.	17.
18.	18.
19.	19.
20.	20.
21.	21.
22.	22.
23.	23.
24.	24.
25.	25.
26.	26.
27.	27.
28.	28.
29.	29.
30.	30.

Evaluation Checklist

1. Score on Comprehension Check_____

2. Which section was your weakest: objective or essay?_____

   _____

3. Objective section:

   a. Do you understand why your wrong answers were wrong? _____

   b. Did your underlining and marginal notes cover the correct
      information? _____

   c. Did you review enough to remember the information? _____

   d. Other problem: _____

4. Essay/application:

   a. Do you understand why you got the score you did? _____

   b. Did your graphic organizer(s) cover the correct information? _____

   c. Did you review enough to remember the information? _____

   d. Other problem: _____

      _____

5. Test-taking skills:

   a. Did you use the time available to maximize your score?_____

   b. Did you follow the directions?_____

   c. Did you answer the easy questions first?_____

   d. If you changed any answers, did it improve your score? _____

   e. Did you leave anything blank? _____

   f. Other problem: _____

      _____

Reading Efficiency

Increasing Reading Flexibility

Because they have to read so much, efficient reading is crucial for college students. But if your response is to say "I read _____ words per minute," you do not understand a basic principle of efficient reading. Good readers are flexible; they adjust their reading speeds. They read a textbook more slowly than a newspaper. They read Shakespeare more slowly than *Newsweek*.

The most important thing to keep in mind is the purpose of your reading. If you are trying to read and memorize textbook material for a test, you read much more slowly than if you are relaxing with a detective story or looking through a newspaper.

Types of Reading

There are four basic types of reading: study reading, rapid reading, skimming, and scanning. Each type is suited to a particular type of reading material and reading purpose, and each should be practiced at different speeds.

Use **study reading** on difficult textbook or technical material when your purpose is thorough understanding and/or memorization. Study reading rates usually do not exceed 250 words per minute. (Study reading is discussed in Unit III.)

Rapid reading should be used when your purpose is to get a general idea of what you read and when the material is not extremely complicated. Types of materials suitable for rapid reading include newspapers, magazines, novels, and light nonfiction.

Skimming is quickly looking over a selection to get the general idea rather than reading every word. It is used (1) when surveying a chapter or

	Study Reading	Rapid Reading	Skimming	Scanning
Speed	Up to 250 wpm	250–800 wpm	Up to thousands of wpm	Up to thousands of wmp
Purpose	Thorough understanding and recall	Recreation, information, light reading	Survey, overview, review	Locating specific information
Types of Material	Textbooks, technical materials	Newspapers, magazines, novels	Any type	Any type

article, (2) when all you need is a general overview, and (3) when reviewing something you once read to refresh your memory. To give you an example of skimming, we have emphasized some words in the following article. Read the bold print only; then, without looking back, answer the questions that follow the article.

If you are seriously interested in a **car,** you should **haggle with the dealer** over the price. The sticker price on the window of a car is there because the law says it must be, but only a naive buyer accepts the sticker price as anything but a starting point for negotiations. Shop around, shop carefully, and **never pay the asking price.**

You can easily **learn the dealer's cost for a new car** (invoice price) by buying an inexpensive guide titled **Edmund's New Car Prices,** available at bookstores and newsstands. Total the dealer's cost including options, and then **offer $125 to $200 above** this cost. You should aim to settle for **no more than $200 to $500 over** the dealer's cost for an **American** car, **or $500 for a foreign** car.

A **good time to close** a deal is often **late Sunday night** (or the last night of the week the dealer is open) **or at the end of the month.** (Many dealerships offer bonuses to the person who has the best sales record at the end of the week or month.) It is good **to deal directly with the sales manager or assistant** manager, because this person is authorized to agree on a price.

When you have settled on the car you want and have agreed with the salesperson on a price, you should **have the dealer put the agreement in writing before** you make a **deposit.** The order form for this agreement should **include a statement of the precise car** being bought, the **accessories** agreed on (if any), the **sales tax, registration fee,** and the **value of the trade-in** (if any). In addition, an **officer of the firm must sign** the order form or it has no legal value. The salesperson's signature means nothing; you may find that when the time comes to close the deal, you have been low-balled (promised a better deal than you are actually able to get) or high-balled (offered more on your trade-in than you will actually get). A person might be both high-balled and low-balled during the course of the negotiations. Both practices are very common among car dealers.

1. What is the article about? _____

2. What is the main idea? _____

3. How much should you pay for a new foreign car? _____

4. Who should you try to deal with? _____

The answers are (1) buying a car; (2) you can get a better deal if you know what you're doing; (3) no more than $500 over the dealer's cost; (4) manager or assistant manager.

Scanning is locating specific information, such as a name, a place, or a date. For example, when you look up something in the dictionary or in the telephone book, you are scanning. You run your eyes over the page and read only the information surrounding what you are looking for. You may also use scanning in textbooks—for example, when you are looking for a particular name or date in a chapter.

Factors in the Reader

In addition to your purpose and the type of material you are reading, factors in yourself also affect the rate at which you read.

One cause of slow reading is a small vocabulary. If you encounter many unfamiliar words, your thought processes will be interrupted. This will interfere with both speed and comprehension.

Another factor that influences reading rate is your comprehension skills. The ability to quickly identify the author's organization (subject, main ideas, and support) is essential to grasping the overall picture that he or she is trying to get across.

Your speed and comprehension will also increase if you have some familiarity with the concepts you will be reading about. Your background knowledge also affects your level of interest and, therefore, your ability to concentrate.

Finally, the way you read affects your speed and comprehension. Phrase reading—grouping words into meaningful phrases—allows you to read faster. Poor readers read word by word.

Poor | readers | read | like | this.

Good readers | read like this.

One way of overcoming word-by-word reading is to practice drawing lines between thought units, as in the second example above. After you have drawn lines, you can practice reading by looking at each unit rather than each word. Phrase reading also reduces some other common bad reading habits, such as habitually looking back at what you have just read.

Rate Chart

To find your reading rate, first look in the left-hand column of the chart on page 462 to find the time it took you to read the article. Then look along that line until you come to the column headed by the number of words you read.

Where the two lines cross, you will find a number indicating how many words per minute you have read. For example, if you read 1200 words in five minutes, you have read 240 wpm.

To find your reading rate for timings that do not appear on the chart, first compute your time in seconds. (Multiply the number of minutes by 60 and add the number of remaining seconds.) Then divide the number of words read by your time in seconds. Multiply the result by 60 to get back to minutes and seconds.

Reading Efficiency Progress Chart

At the bottom of the chart on pages 463–465, enter the date, your reading rate (in words per minute), and your comprehension score for each article you read. Then construct a graph by putting a dot in the square closest to your reading rate for each article. Make the graph by connecting the dots.

Your goal is to show improvement in rate with no loss in comprehension. A score of 80 percent comprehension is considered adequate for most purposes. However, even if you stay at the same reading rate for all 30 articles, you are still showing improvement. This is because the articles get harder in each section of the book. Don't worry if you see some dips as well as increases in your reading rate. Articles vary in difficulty because of the content, the vocabulary, your familiarity with the subject matter, and your level of interest. More difficult material should be read more slowly. However, if your reading rate appears to be dropping, you should discuss the problem with your instructor.

Rate Chart

$$\text{WPM} = \frac{\text{Words read}}{\text{Time in minutes}} \quad \text{OR} \quad \frac{\text{Words read}}{\text{Time in seconds}} \times 60$$

Reading Time Min.	Sec.	600	700	800	900	1000	1150	1200	1400	1500	1600	1700	2100	2200	2500	2600	2700	3250	3700
0	40	900	1050	1200	1350	1500													
0	50	720	790	960	1084	1200	1380	1440											
1	00	600	700	800	900	1000	1150	1200	1400	1500									
1	10	514	600	685	769	855	983	1026	1200	1285	1371	1457	1800						
1	20	450	520	600	677	752	865	902	1050	1125	1200	1275	1575						
1	30	400	467	533	600	667	767	800	933	1000	1067	1133	1400	1467	1667				
1	40	360	420	480	539	599	689	719	840	900	960	1020	1260	1320	1500	1560			
1	50	327	372	436	492	546	628	656	764	818	872	927	1145	1200	1364	1418			
2	00	300	350	400	450	500	575	600	700	750	800	850	1050	1100	1250	1300	1350	1600	
2	10	276	337	369	415	461	530	553	646	692	738	785	969	1015	1154	1200	1246	1477	1708
2	20	257	300	342	386	429	494	515	600	643	685	729	900	942	1071	1114	1157	1371	1586
2	30	240	280	320	360	400	460	480	560	600	640	680	840	880	1000	1040	1080	1280	1480
2	40	225	262	300	337	375	431	449	525	562	600	637	788	825	938	975	1012	1200	1388
2	50	212	242	282	318	353	406	424	494	529	565	600	741	776	882	918	953	1129	1306
3	00	200	233	267	300	333	383	400	467	500	533	567	700	733	833	867	900	1067	1233
3	20	180	210	240	270	300	345	360	420	450	480	510	630	660	750	780	810	960	1110
3	40	163	200	218	245	272	313	327	382	409	436	463	573	600	682	709	736	873	1009
4	00	150	175	200	225	250	287	300	350	375	400	425	525	550	625	650	675	800	925
4	30	133	162	192	200	222	256	267	311	333	355	377	467	489	556	578	600	711	822
5	00	120	140	160	180	200	230	240	280	300	320	340	420	440	500	520	540	640	740
5	30	109	127	145	164	189	209	218	254	273	290	309	382	400	455	473	491	582	673
6	00	100	116	133	150	167	192	200	233	250	267	283	360	367	417	433	450	533	617
7	00			114	129	143	164	171	200	214	229	243	300	314	357	371	386	457	529
8	00			100	113	125	144	150	175	187	200	212	263	275	313	325	337	400	463
9	00				100	111	128	133	156	167	178	189	233	245	278	289	300	356	411
10	00					100	115	120	140	150	160	170	210	220	250	260	270	320	370
11	00						105	109	127	136	145	155	191	200	227	236	245	291	336
12	00							100	117	125	133	142	175	183	208	217	225	267	308
13	00								108	115	123	131	162	169	192	200	208	246	285
14	00								100	107	114	121	150	157	179	186	193	229	264
15	00									100	107	113	140	147	167	173	180	213	247
16	00										100	106	131	137	156	163	169	200	231

Reading Efficiency Progress Chart

WPM

WPM										
1,000										
950										
900										
850										
800										
775										
750										
725										
700										
675										
650										
625										
600										
575										
550										
525										
500										
475										
450										
425										
400										
375										
350										
325										
300										
275										
250										
225										
200										
175										
150										
125										
100										
Article	1	2	3	4	5	6	7	8	9	10
Rate (WPM)										
Comprehension										
Score										
Date										

READING EFFICIENCY

READING EFFICIENCY

Reading Efficiency Progress Chart

WPM

1,000										
950										
900										
850										
800										
775										
750										
725										
700										
675										
650										
625										
600										
575										
550										
525										
500										
475										
450										
425										
400										
375										
350										
325										
300										
275										
250										
225										
200										
175										
150										
125										
100										
Article	11	12	13	14	15	16	17	18	19	20
Rate (WPM)										
Comprehension										
Score										
Date										

Reading Efficiency Progress Chart

WPM										
1,000										
950										
900										
850										
800										
775										
750										
725										
700										
675										
650										
625										
600										
575										
550										
525										
500										
475										
450										
425										
400										
375										
350										
325										
300										
275										
250										
225										
200										
175										
150										
125										
100										
Article	21	22	23	24	25	26	27	28	29	30
Rate (WPM)										
Comprehension										
Score										
Date										

Word Parts

Most of the difficult words in English come from Latin, or from Greek through Latin. Following are 60 common prefixes and 150 common roots. You already know many of them, and learning the rest will greatly improve your vocabulary.

Here are some suggested ways to learn them:

As you look at each word part, read the meaning and the examples. Then try to think of another word that comes from the same word part. If you can think of another word, check it in a dictionary that gives the etymology of each word, to make sure that it does come from the same word part. Some pocket-size dictionaries save space by omitting the etymology. If your dictionary doesn't have etymologies, you can use a dictionary in a library. If you can't think of another word, try to find one by looking in the dictionary.

To memorize the word parts you don't already know, you can put them on flash cards. Put the word part on the front. Put the meaning and some examples on the back. Examples that you have made up yourself will be easier to memorize than ones that have come from our list or from the dictionary. Then test yourself until you have memorized the word part. The average person takes seven self-testing sessions to learn a new word part. Following is a sample flash card:

Front	Back
mem (men, mn, min)	mind, memory remind memorial demented remember memento reminisce mnemonic

60 Common Prefixes

Prefix	Meaning	Examples
a (an)	not	anonymous, atypical
ab (a)	away, from, down	absence, amoral
ad (ac, af, ag, an, ap, ar, as, at)	to	admit, accept, affect, aggravate, annex, appeal, arrange, assess, attract
ambi (amphi)	both	ambidextrous, amphibian
ante (ant)	before	antecedent, anterior

Prefix	Meaning	Examples
anti (ant)	against	antisocial, antonym
auto	self	autobiography, autocrat
bene	good	benediction, benefit
con (com, co, col, cor)	with, together	concurrent, communicate, cooperate, collate, correspond
contra	against	contradict, contraband
de	from, away, down	derail, descend
dia	through, across	diameter, diaphanous
dis (dif)	apart, not	discontinue, different
epi	on, over, among	epidermis, epidemic
eu (ev)	good	eulogy, evangelical
ex (extra, e, ec, ef)	out, former, beyond	exit, ex-wife, extraordinary, emit, eccentric, effect
hetero	different	heterogeneous, heterosexual
homo	same	homogenize, homosexual
hyper	over, beyond	hyperactive, hypersensitive
hypo	under	hypodermic, hypoallergenic
in (il, im, ir, en, em)	not, into, very	inaction, insight, invaluable, illogical, immobile, implicit, irregular, encompass, embrace
inter	between	interrupt, intercollegiate
intra (intro)	into, within	intramural, introduce
mal	bad, wrong, ill	malicious, malfunction
mega	big	megaphone, megalopolis
micro	small	micrometer, microbe
mis	wrong	misspell, misgivings
multi	many	multiply, multimillionaire
non (n)	not	nonprofit, neither
ob (oc, of, op, o)	against	obstruct, occasion, offend, oppose, omit
omni	all	omnivorous, omnipotent
pan	all	pan-African, panacea
para	alongside, beyond	paragraph, paraphrase
per	through, by, thorough	per annum, perspective
peri	around	perimeter, peripheral
poly	many	polygon, polyester
post	after	posterity, posterior
pre	before	preliminary, prevent
pro (pur)	before, forward, for	prospect, pursuit

WORD PARTS

Prefix	Meaning	Examples
re (retro)	again, back	reenter, retroactive
se	apart	secede, secret
sub (suc, suf, sup, sus)	under, below	submarine, succumb, suffer, suppress, suspect
super (sur)	above, beyond	superior, surpass
tele	distance	telegraph, telepathy
trans	across	transatlantic, transfer
ultra	beyond, extremely	ultrasonic, ultraviolet
un	not, reverse of an action	unwise, undo

Numbers

Prefix	Meaning	Examples
uni, mono	one	unison, unit, monotone
du (di), bi	two	duo, dioxide, biennial
tri	three	tripod, triple, trilogy
quarter (quadr), tetra	four	quartet, quadrangle, tetrahedron
quint, penta	five	quintuplet, pentagon
sex (hex)	six	sexagenarian, hexagon
sept (hept)	seven	September,* heptagon
oct	eight	octopus, October*
nov (non)	nine	November,* nonagenarian
dec	ten	decade, December*
hemi (semi, demi)	half, partial	hemisphere, semicircle, demigod
kilo, mil	thousand	kilowatt, milligram, mile
cent	hundred	century, bicentennial

*Note that prefixes for the months are based on their places in the Roman calendar.

150 Common Roots

Root	Meaning	Examples
act (agi)	drive, do	activate, agitate
aer (aero)	air	aerial, aerodynamics
al (alt)	other	alien, altruist
am (amat, amour)	love	amicable, amateur, paramour
anim	mind, soul	inanimate, animal
ann (enn)	year	annual, biennial
anthro (anthrop)	man, human	anthropology, misanthrope
aqu	water	aquatic, aqueduct
arch	chief, ruler	monarchy, anarchist

Root	Meaning	Examples
aster (astr)	star	asterisk, astronomy
aud (audit)	hear	audible, audition
biblio, bibl	book	bibliography, bible
bio	life	biology, biography
cad (cas, cid)	fall	cadence, cascade, coincidence
cap (cep, ceive)	hold, seize	capacity, reception, deceive
capit (cap, chap, chief)	head	capitulate, captain, chapter, chief
cav	hollow	cavity, cavern
cede (ceed, cess)	go	secede, succeed, process
chrom(e)	color	chromatic, monochrome
chron	time	chronicle, anachronism
cide (cis)	cut, kill	matricide, scissors
cir, cycl	round	circular, cyclone
cit (civ)	government	citizen, civil
claus (close, clus, clude)	shut	claustrophobia, foreclose, cluster, exclude
cline (clim)	slope	incline, climax
corp	body	corporate, corpulent
crat (cracy)	rule	democratic, aristocracy
cre (crease, cres)	grow	increment, increase, crescent
cred	believe	credible, credit
cult	develop	cultivate, acculturate
cur (cour)	run	recurrent, recourse
cur (sur)	care	manicure, curator, insure
dem	people	democratic, epidemic
dent (dont)	teeth	denture, orthodontist
derm	skin	dermatologist, hypodermic
dic (dict, dit)	say, speak	indicate, dictate, edit
doc (dox)	opinion, belief	doctrine, orthodox
duc	lead	conductive, aqueduct
dynam	power	dynamic, dynamo
ego	self	egotistical, egocentric
equa (equi)	equal	equanimity, equilibrium
fac (fec, fic)	make, do	facilitate, effect, fiction
fal (fals)	deceive	fallacy, falsify
fend (fens)	against, from	defendant, offensive
fer	carry	prefer, ferry
fic (fig)	form	fiction, figure
fid	faith	confidant, infidel

Root	Meaning	Examples
fin	limit	infinite, finish
fix	stationary	prefix, fixate
flect (flex)	bend	inflection, reflex
flu	flow	fluid, influential
fort (forc)	strong	fortress, reinforce
fract (frag)	break	fraction, fragment
fund (fuse, found)	pour or melt	refund, fusion, profound
gamy	marriage	bigamy, misogamy
gen (gin)	birth, origin, race	genetic, origin, genocide
geo	earth	geology, geography
grad (gress)	go, walk, step	graduate, progress
gram (graph)	write	telegram, graphics
grat (grac)	pleasing, thanks, favor	gratis, gracious
her (hes)	stick	inherent, adhesive
hydr (hydro)	water	dehydrate, hydroelectric
jac (ject)	throw	jacket, reject
jud (jus, jur)	right	judicial, justice, injure
jug (junc, just)	join	conjugate, juncture, adjust
kine (cine)	move	kinetic, cinema
labor	work	collaborate, laboratory
lect (leg)	gather, read, law	collect, legal
libr (liber)	book, free	library, liberal
lic	permit, allure	license, elicit
liter	letter	literate, literature
loc	place	location, allocate
log (logy)	word, speech, study of	logo, logic, geology
luc (lum, lus, lun, lux)	light	lucid, luminous, illustrate, lunar, luxury
magn (max)	great	magnify, maximum
man	hand	manual, emancipate
mania	madness	kleptomania, manic
mater (matr)	mother	alma mater, matriarch
mem (men, mn, min)	mind, memory	memo, mental, amnesia, remind
meter (metr)	measure	thermometer, metric
mis (mit)	send	emissary, emit
mob (mot, mov)	move	mobile, motivate, remote, remove
mort	die	mortal, mortuary
nat (nai, neo, nov)	new, born	prenatal, naive, neoclassic, novel
naut, nav	water	astronaut, navigate

Root	Meaning	Examples
nom, onym	name	nomenclature, synonym
ocle (ocul, opt)	eye	monocle, binocular, optical
pac (pact)	peace	pacify, pact
par (part)	equal, share	disparity, compartment
pass (path)	feel, disease	passion, antipathy, pathology
pater (patr)	father	paternal, patriotic
ped	child	pediatrician, pedagogy
ped (pod)	foot	pedal, podiatrist
pel (puls)	drive	compel, repulsive
pend (pens, pond)	hang, weight, pay	pending, expense, ponder
pet (peat)	seek, request	perpetual, repeat
phil	love	philanthropy, philologist
phobia	fear	claustrophobia, hydrophobia
phon	sound	phonograph, symphony
photo (phos)	light	photographic, phosphorus
pict (pig)	paint	depict, pigment
plac (plea)	please, calm	placate, implacable, please
plic (plex, ply)	bend, fold	implicate, perplex, reply
polis (polit)	city, citizen	metropolis, politician
port	carry	porter, opportune
pose (posit, pound)	put	dispose, deposit, impound
press (prim, print)	squeeze, press	pressure, reprimand, imprint
psych	mind, soul	psyche, parapsychology
punct (pung, point, pug)	prick	punctuate, pungent, appoint, pugnacious
quer (ques, quir, quis)	ask, seek	query, question, inquiry, inquisition
reg (rect, right)	straight, direct	irregular, erect, forthright
rog	ask, seek	derogatory, interrogate
rupt	break	interrupt, rupture
scope	see	telescope, microscope
scrib (script)	write	inscribe, manuscript
sens (sent)	feel, think	sensitive, sentiment
sequ (secut, suit)	follow	sequence, persecute, pursuit
sid (sed, sess)	sit	reside, sediment, session
sign	mark, signal	insignia, designate
sim (sym, syn, syl)	together, same	simulate, sympathy, synonym, syllable
sol	alone	solo, solitude
solv (solu)	loosen, explain	solvent, solution

Root	Meaning	Examples
son (sound)	sound	sonar, resound
spec (spect, spic, spis)	see, look	speculate, inspect, despicable, despise
spir	breathe	respiration, expire
stat (stan, sist, stit)	stand	static, stand, resist, constitute
struct	build	construct, structure
tact (tag, tang, ting)	touch	contact, contagious, tangible, tinge
temp	time, heat	contemporary, tempo, temperature
ten (tain, tin)	hold	contain, retention, pertinent
tend (ten)	stretch	tendon, extensive
ter (terr)	earth	interment, terrestrial
text	weave, construct	textile, texture
theo (the)	god	theology, atheist
therm	hot, warm	thermos, thermometer
thesis	put, place	synthesis, hypothesis
tom (tomy)	cut	atom, tonsillectomy
torq (tort)	twist, wind	torque, contort
tract	draw, pull	subtract, traction
urb	city	urbane, suburban
vac (void)	empty	vacuum, evacuate, void
val (valu)	worth, strength	ambivalent, evaluate
ven (vent)	come	intervene, adventure
verb	word	adverb, verbatim
vers (vert, verg)	turn	versus, avert, verge
vic (van, vinc)	conquer, change	vicarious, vanquish, invincible
vid (vis, view)	see	video, visual, review
vita (viv)	life	vital, vivacious
voc (vok)	call	vocal, revoke
volv (volu)	roll, will	revolve, voluntary

Credits

These pages constitute an extension of the copyright page.

Dictionary excerpts and pronunciation guides are used with permission from *Webster's New World Dictionary*, Second College Edition, copyright © 1980 by Simon & Schuster, Inc., and from *Webster's New World Dictionary*, Popular Library Paperback Edition, copyright © 1979 by William Collins Publishers, Inc.

Cover. Maurice de Vlaminck, "Olives". © 2000 Artists Rights Society (ARS), New York/ADAGP, Paris.

Page 1. Photodisc

Page 23. Photodisc

Page 27. "How to Improve Your Vocabulary" by Tony Randall. Reprinted by permission of International Paper Company, 1979.

Page 36. "How Almost Anyone Can Become a Millionaire: Simple Rules for Attaining Future Wealth" by Richard B. McKenzie & Dwight R. Lee. Reprinted with permission of the World Future Society. 7910 Woodmont Ave., Bethesda, MD 20814.

Page 50. "The Many Miracles of Mark Hicks" by Jan Stussy. Originally appeared in the *Reader's Digest*, July 1980. Copyright © 1980 by The Reader's Digest Association, Inc. Reprinted by permission.

Page 60. "Superstitions: Just Whistling in the Dark" by Don Boxmeyer. *Knight-Ridder Newspapers*, 1980. Reproduced by permission.

Page 69. "Saved" by Malcom X. From *The Autobiography of Malcom X* by Malcom X, with the assistance of Alex Haley. Copyright © 1964 by Alex Haley and Malcom X. Copyright © 1965 by Alex Haley and Betty Shabazz. Reprinted by permission of Random House.

Page 78. "How to Strengthen Your Memory Power" by Mary Russ. Reprinted by permission of *Family Weekly*, copyright 1981, 641 Lexington Avenue, New York, NY 10022.

Page 89. "Don't Tell Jamie Escalante Minorities Can't Meet (High) Standards!" by David Savage. From *Instructor*, Spring 1986 issue. Copyright © 1986 by Scholastic Inc. Reprinted by permission of Scholastic Inc.

Page 97. "Nine Obstacles to Creativity" by Alexander Hiam. Reprinted with permission of the World Future Society. 7910 Woodmont Ave., Bethesda, MD 20814.

Page 113 and 175. From *Psychology: Themes and Variation, 4th edition*, by W. Weiten. © 1998. Reprinted with permission of Wadsworth, a division of Thomson Learning. Fax 800-730-2215.

Page 125, 153, and 183. From *Healthy for Life: Wellness and the Art of Living, First Edition* by B. K. Williams and S. M. Knight. © 1994. Reprinted with permission of Wadsworth, a division of Thomson Learning. Fax 800-730-2215.

Page 135. Photodisc

Page 145 and 196. From *I Never Knew I Had a Choice, 6th edition*, by G. Corey and M. S. Corey. © 1997. Reprinted with permission of Wadsworth, a division of Thomson Learning. Fax 800-730-2215.

Page 164. From *Biology: Concepts and Applications (Hardcover Version), 3rd edition*, by C. Starr. © 1997. Reprinted with permission of Brooks/Cole, a division of Thomson Learning. Fax 800-730-2215.

Page 205. From *Healthy for Life: Wellness and the Art of Living*, by B. K. Williams and S. M. Knight. © 1994. Reprinted with permission of Brooks/Cole, a division of Thomson Learning. Fax 800-730-2215.

Page 213. From *Lifespan, 6ᵗʰ edition,* by G. R. Lefrançois. © 1999. Reprinted with permission of Wadsworth, a division of Thomson Learning. Fax 800-730-2215.

Page 219. From Ward, S. K., Chapman, K., Cohn, E., White, S., & Williams, K (1991). *Acquaintance rape and the college social scene. Family Relation 40,* 65–71. Copyright 1991 by the National Council on Family Relations. Reprinted by permission.

Page 226. From *Introduction to Psychology, 4ᵗʰ edition,* by J. W. Kalat. © 1996. Reprinted with permission of Wadsworth, a division of Thomson Learning. Fax 800-730-2215.

Page 228. From "Monotonic and Rhythmic Influences: A Challenge for Sleep Deprivation Research," by H. Babkoff, T. Caspy, M. Mikulincer, and H. C. Sing, 1991, *Psychological Bulletin, 109,* p. 411–428. Copyright © 1991 by the American Psychological Association. Reprinted with permission.

Page 234. From *Economic Issues for Consumers, 8ᵗʰ edition,* by R. L. Miller and A. D. Stafford. © 1997. Reprinted with permission of Wadsworth, a division of Thomson Learning. Fax 800-730-2215.

Page 243. Photodisc

Page 249. "How Many Prisons Must We Build to Feel Secure?" by Jonathan Simon. From *Los Angeles Times,* Jan. 17, 1994. Reprinted by permission of the author.

Page 256. "A Case for Discretion" by Michael Brennan. From *Newsweek,* 11/13/95. All rights reserved. Reprinted by permission.

Page 265. Copyright 1990 by Alfie Kohn. Reprinted from *Women's Sports & Fitness* (July/August 1990, pp. 56, 58) with the author's permission.

Page 274. Mariah B. Nelson. First appeared in *Women's Sports & Fitness,* July/August 1990, pp. 57, 59. Used by permission of the author.

Page 283. "The Amazing Smoke Screen" by Robert J. Samuelson. From *Newsweek,* 11/30/98. All rights reserved. Reprinted by permission.

Page 292. Remarks on Tobacco Settlement (transcript of speech) by Bill Clinton.

Page 299. "Acting to End a Life Is Sometimes Justified" by Christiaan Barnard. Reprinted with permission of Simon & Schuster, Inc. from *Good Life, Good Death* by Christiaan Barnard. Copyright © 1980 by Dr. Christiaan Barnard.

Page 308. "In Crisis She Rejected Plea to Expedite Dying" by Derek Gill. Excerpts from Chapter 27 from *Quest: The Life of Elisabeth Kübler-Ross* by Derek Gill. Copyright © 1980 by Derek Gill. Reprinted by permission of HarperCollins Publishers, Inc.

Page 318. "The Dream, the Stars and Dr. King," by Jesse Jackson. © 1995 The Los Angeles Times Syndicate. Reprinted by permission.

Page 327. "Spiral of Silence" by P. Brimelow. Reprinted by permission of *Forbes Magazine* © Forbes Inc., 1999.

Index